DIVE BOMBER!

The Stackpole Military History Series

THE AMERICAN CIVIL WAR

Cavalry Raids of the Civil War
Ghost, Thunderbolt, and Wizard
Pickett's Charge
Witness to Gettysburg

WORLD WAR II

Armor Battles of the Waffen-SS, 1943–45
Army of the West
Australian Commandos
The B-24 in China
Backwater War
The Battle of Sicily
Beyond the Beachhead
The Brandenburger Commandos
The Brigade
Bringing the Thunder
Coast Watching in World War II
Colossal Cracks
D-Day to Berlin
Dive Bomber!
Eagles of the Third Reich
Exit Rommel
Fist from the Sky
Flying American Combat Aircraft
  of World War II
Forging the Thunderbolt
Fortress France
The German Defeat in the East, 1944–45
German Order of Battle, Vol. 1
German Order of Battle, Vol. 2
German Order of Battle, Vol. 3
Germany's Panzer Arm in World War II
GI Ingenuity
Grenadiers
Infantry Aces
Iron Arm
Iron Knights
Kampfgruppe Peiper at the Battle
  of the Bulge
Luftwaffe Aces
Massacre at Tobruk

Messerschmitts over Sicily
Michael Wittmann, Vol. 1
Michael Wittmann, Vol. 2
Mountain Warriors
The Nazi Rocketeers
On the Canal
Packs On!
Panzer Aces
Panzer Aces II
The Panzer Legions
Panzers in Winter
The Path to Blitzkrieg
Retreat to the Reich
Rommel's Desert War
The Savage Sky
A Soldier in the Cockpit
Soviet Blitzkrieg
Stalin's Keys to Victory
Surviving Bataan and Beyond
T-34 in Action
Tigers in the Mud
The 12th SS, Vol. 1
The 12th SS, Vol. 2
The War against Rommel's Supply Lines

THE COLD WAR / VIETNAM

Flying American Combat Aircraft:
  The Cold War
Here There Are Tigers
Land with No Sun
Street without Joy

WARS OF THE MIDDLE EAST

Never-Ending Conflict

GENERAL MILITARY HISTORY

Carriers in Combat
Desert Battles

DIVE BOMBER!

How Low-Level Attacks Changed World War II in the Air

Peter C. Smith

STACKPOLE
BOOKS

Essex, Connecticut
Blue Ridge Summit, Pennsylvania

STACKPOLE BOOKS

An imprint of The Globe Pequot Publishing Group, Inc.

64 South Main Street

Essex, CT 06426

www.globepequot.com

Distributed by NATIONAL BOOK NETWORK

British Library Cataloguing in Publication Information available

Library of Congress Cataloging-in-Publication Data

ISBN 978-0-8117-7659-2 (pbk: alk. Paper)

♾™ The paper used in this publication meets the minimum requirements of American National Standard for Information Sciences—Permanence of Paper for Printed Library Materials, ANSI/NISO Z39.48-1992.

Contents

CHAPTER 1

Early Experiments

The Genesis and Practice of Low-Level Attack, 1910–18

In trying to trace the origins of dive bombing, one is immediately faced with a mass of conflicting evidence. Just as it is almost impossible to find anyone who agrees on the diving angle at which dive bombing begins, so no two historians agree on who invented this method of attacking surface targets. The majority of published sources conclude that the U.S. Marine Corps should be given the credit. My own research suggests that this widely held belief is false, and my case is set out in the following chapters.

No study of dive bombing can exclude the concept of low-level attack in general. The two are so intertwined, especially in the formative years, that a basic outline of low-level bombing is essential for a complete understanding of dive bombing. I do not, however, intend to look closely at ground-attack aircraft and methods, but only to record those initial operations and experiments from which dive bombing evolved. For those seeking further information on ground attack, there are several excellent books on the subject.

What angle of dive is required for true dive bombing? This is perhaps the most vexing question of all and that which provokes the most discord. The British Air Ministry produced three definitions, all of which were accepted by other nations at one stage or another. *Shallow glide bombing:* the bombs are released while the aircraft descends at an angle not greater than 20 degrees. *Steep glide bombing:* the bombs are released while the aircraft descends at an angle of between 20 and 60 degrees. *Dive bombing:* the bombs are released while the aircraft dives at an angle of between 60 and 90 degrees.

1

But to confine these studies to operations meeting only the third definition would exclude a number of significant developments. For example, perhaps the most famous dive bombing attack by a British force was the sinking of the German light cruiser *Königsberg*. Under the RAF's rules, we would have to ignore this watershed completely, since the Fleet Air Arm (FAA) Skuas that carried out this daring and successful assault approached at angles between 40 and 70 degrees. Again, can one ignore the operations by aircraft designed solely as dive bombers, but which were in fact carried out in the traditional ground-attack manner, as with the U.S. Marine Corps' SBD missions in the Philippines in 1945? Overlap is unavoidable. Hardly known as a dive bomber, the British Spitfire carried out important sorties in this role, diving at angles above the 60-degree mark. The prewar RAF tested the Fairey Battle and even the Handley Page Hampden at angles of 30 to 40 degrees to see how they would perform as dive bombers.

Who invented dive bombing? The most accurate answer is probably that of historian Lee M. Pearson, who said, "No one knows who first turned his plane nose down and dove nearly into the ground to hit a pinpoint target with bombs." There are still books that claim that the U.S. Navy invented dive bombing in the 1920s, but we can dismiss such assertions as parochial wishful thinking rather than history.

Although an earlier reference to the issue of a "dive bombing patent" on December 9, 1911, in Great Britain to Alexander von Willisch of Wilmersdorf was investigated, examination revealed it to be a red herring. More significant was the subsequent issue of Patent No. 15,871 on July 9, 1914, to Henri Coanda. This French engineer filed a patent for what was, in fact, an automatic bomb- or projectile-discharging tube designed particularly for air attacks on ground targets. Although clearly not specific to dive bombing, this so-called "complete means for discharging projectiles from aerial machines" is of great interest as a pioneering ground-attack system. It was probably far too heavy and cumbersome for application to aircraft of that period, but it was a far-sighted effort at a time when bombs were often dropped by hand.

A more primitive means of enabling the missile to reach its target from the sky was being practiced in the Mexican Civil War

(1913–15). An American aviator, Leonard W. Bonney, was scouting around Mexico City, Yucatan, and Tampico using a Moisant aircraft. But he by no means restricted himself to scouting and has one of the best claims to be the father of the dive bombing technique. He carried out bombing missions with spherical dynamite bombs designed by Mexican engineers. The explosive was fired by a pin, which exploded a rifle cartridge.

His usual method of attack was to fly at between 1,200 and 1,600 feet to avoid clouds. He thus learned the major lesson of aircraft vulnerability, for his machine was frequently shot up by rifle fire. He returned from one trip with eleven bullet holes in his aircraft and a severed spark plug wire. But it is the eyewitness descriptions of his bomb-dropping methods that are of the greatest interest, for they state quite clearly that Bonney dropped his bombs himself at the end of a dive, before he leveled out and that he employed no sighting or other device to assist in this.

Early in World War I, the French War Office reconnoitered the German airship hangars at Metz in preparation for their destruction. When the attacking aircraft arrived over the target, its engine failed at 8,000 feet. Some quick thinking followed, and according to a contemporary account, the pilot, not wishing to fall before executing his mission, volplaned—i.e., descended by glidiing without the engine—and while doing so, he dropped his bombs. Smoke from antiaircraft fire obscured the results, but it was believed at the time that the French pilot had hit his mark.

One of the most daring and successful of these early attacks was carried out by Flight Lieutenant R. L. G. Marix of the Royal Naval Air Service (RNAS) against the Zeppelin shed at Düsseldorf on October 8, 1914. Piloting a Sopwith Tabloid, one of the most advanced aircraft of the period, Marix took off from Antwerp armed with 20-pound bombs and arrived over the sheds in misty conditions. Once in position, he dived to an altitude of only 600 feet and released his Cooper bombs. Direct hits were scored, and the shed collapsed, with the flames rising to a height of 500 feet. Despite a barrage of defensive fire, Marix managed to withdraw safely from the target, although his aircraft was hit. This brilliant attack was later found to have resulted in the destruction of the new Zeppelin Z-IX, which had only just been completed and placed in the shed.

A contemporary assessment of the raid concluded that the results showed the advantages of Marix's approach and, therefore, that aircraft had to descend at a perilous attitude to achieve accuracy.

The same methods were used with similar success in an attack the following month, again by the Royal Naval Air Service. The aircraft used were Avro 504s belonging to a special unit formed at Manchester. Carrying four 20-pound Cooper bombs in improvised racks mounted under their lower mainplanes, the four aircraft flew 120 miles from Belfort to the Zeppelin sheds at Friedrichshafen, Lake Constance, on November 21. Although one aircraft had to turn back, the remaining three—piloted by Squadron Commander E. F. Briggs (873), Flight Lieutenant S. V. Sippe (874), and Flight Commander J. T. Babington (875)—continued to the target. After a low-level approach across the lake, at five miles from the target they climbed to 1,200 feet to deploy for the bombing run. Once in position, the three aircraft dived down to about 700 feet and released their bombs. One bomb failed to release, but all the others fell within an area of 700 yards around the works and sheds. Two fell on the sheds themselves, one greatly damaging a Zeppelin under construction; a gas works was also destroyed.

As early as December 1914, a writer in a British magazine was discussing the merits of diving attacks as a means of achieving accuracy, arguing that when gliding from a height, with the aircraft under power, the tangent to the trajectory and the axis of the machine would gradually become parallel and therefore accuracy of aim would be increased when flying low and at high speed. He concluded that for the best results, the bomb should be released at the end of a dive of 500 feet, right when the axis of the aircraft was pointing at the target.

That diving attacks were far from rare is illustrated by the following journalistic reports describing sorties of this kind:

French and British pilots did some very daring bomb dropping in the first year of the war. Arriving over their objectives, they dive to a height counted by a few hundreds of feet with engines full on, reaching almost incredible speeds as speeds were then regarded, and releasing their bombs at what they thought the crucial moment before making the best of their way out of the danger zone.

An English warplane hovered over Zeebrugge and, defying the concentrated fire, made a sudden dive to within 300 feet of the ground . . . the airman coolly dropped his bombs at short range on a submarine moored alongside the mole.

Despite the above examples, it was not dive bombing that developed as the principal aerial tactic of World War I, but rather strafing, low-level ground-support missions by fighters and light bombers. Although it was again the British who first developed this form of warfare and later perfected it with great effect, Germany, France, and later the U.S. all experimented with the method and made extensive and effective use of it during 1916–18.

Perhaps the first indication of this use was contained in a memo originated at Royal Flying Corps (RFC) headquarters in October 1914 and sent to Major Musgrave: "Several instances have occurred lately in which targets suitable for attack have been passed over without any action being taken. In future all aeroplanes carrying out reconnaissances will carry bombs and whenever suitable targets . . . present themselves they should be attacked by dropping bombs."

The momentum soon increased. A directive from the same source in February 1915 stated: "Accuracy to within fifty yards is essential. If it cannot be obtained from heights of 5,000 to 6,000 feet, the target must be attacked at low level—500 feet."

From the time of the Somme offensive (1916) onward, the mass use of fighters for strafing missions had become firmly established. The results were often spectacular, as with No. 43 Squadron during the Third Battle of the Scarpe on May 3, 1917.

One historian noted how, at the battles of Ypres and Cambrai in 1917, strafing had become a significant factor in the fighting. This was emphasized by the part the fighter-bombers played in breaking up the German offensive that began in March 1918, when the RFC's attacks often prevented the British retreat from becoming a rout.

Nor were the Germans slow in adopting such measures, and at Verdun in March 1916, their own scouts were employed in a similar

manner. Formed into special *Schlachtstaffeln*, the German scouts
were used en masse during the 1918 breakthrough. The Germans
also developed special aircraft with armor protection for low-level
attacks, an idea that the British copied after the war with the Salamander.

When the fledgling U.S. Air Corps arrived on the Western
Front, General Billy Mitchell was profoundly impressed by these
methods and formed strafing units, which made their debut at the
St. Mihiel salient in the summer of 1918.

Farther afield, the British gave striking demonstrations of the
potency of this form of attack against unprepared troops, and three
of the most notable incidents took place at the end of the war. The
Turkish troops trapped in the defile northeast of Nablus on September 21, 1918, were subjected to five hours of concentrated strafing, at the end of which they had become "a dispersed horde of
trembling individuals, hiding for their lives." The armies of Austro-
Hungary broke and fled after the battle of Vittorio Veneto, and a
similar retribution overtook them on October 29–30, 1918, when
their fleeing columns were caught on the Conegliano-Pordonone
road. Finally, again on September 21, 1918, the ill-fated Bulgarian
Army met the same fate in Macedonia's Kosturino Pass.

As effective as this form of attack proved to be, it was also
extremely expensive to the attacker in terms of men and machines.
Wing Commander Slessor made this very point between the wars
when explaining in a series of lectures just why the RAF was at that
time no longer interested in following such a policy in future wars.
He said that at Cambrai casualties in the British strafing squadrons
averaged about 30 percent per day, and similarly ghastly losses were
incurred during the low-flying attacks carried out during the
March retreat and the Amiens offensive of 1918. He cited the
example of No. 80 Squadron in 1918, which he said was almost
continuously in action from the beginning of the March retreat
until the armistice in November. Their average strength was twenty-
two officers, and during those final ten months of combat, no
fewer than 168 officers were struck off the strength from all causes,
an average of about 75 percent per month.

It is therefore obvious why the policy lost its appeal after the
war. Its fall from favor was accelerated by the embracing of Hugh

Trenchard's conception of future warfare, which the British general saw as being won by the heavy bomber unaided by armies or navies. This doctrine, the cornerstone of interwar RAF policy, saw little need for any kind of ground-attack capability. The dive bomber, although not strictly a ground attacker, suffered for the same reasons.

Nonetheless, the RFC and the infant RAF had done much to test the dive bombing concept in the latter stages of World War I, even if they subsequently turned away from it.

CHAPTER 2

Birth of the Dive Bomber

British Pioneering Work, 1915–18

The number of individuals claiming to have originated the dive bombing form of attack is probably exceeded only by the number of nations and air services claiming that honor. Some of the British pilots who flew on the Western Front have described in their memoirs how they used diving techniques for bombing attacks, and they have as good a case as anyone.

One of these was Lieutenant Duncan Grinnell-Milne, who was flying BE2cs with No. 16 Squadron from Lys in France in the early winter of 1915. The BE2c was to gain an unenviable distinction in the months ahead, when heavy losses earned it a reputation as the main course of "Fokker fodder" (a reference to German planes manufactured by the Fokker company). A single 70-horsepower Renault engine pulled this two-seat biplane through the air at a stately 72 miles per hour. Though these were still early days for bombers, the aircraft was fitted to carry two 112-pound or ten 20-pound bombs under the wings. Aiming these weapons was a hit-or-miss affair, and No. 16 Squadron was given the task of trying out a newly developed bomb sight in the hope of improving matters. Grinnell Milne took off on his bombing mission on November 27, 1915, after a mere two days' instruction on this "rather complicated apparatus." The target was known to be well defended by antiaircraft guns. The new sight demanded a straight and level run in, but on arriving over the target, he found a throng of aircraft jostling for position and being heavily fired on. Grinnell-Milne therefore decided to adopt his own method.

Putting his aircraft into a dive with the engine at half throttle, he lined up on the target, a rail junction. He dived from 10,000 feet to 2,000 feet and released the bombs, missing the target but hitting motor transport instead. He returned that afternoon, when the sky over the target proved to be less crowded. Nonetheless he attacked in the same way as before, this time pressing in much closer. The first bomb hit a building, and he circled the area before diving to drop the second. "I watched the bomb go down, diminishing rapidly to a pinpoint, then suddenly expanding again as it struck a building in the goods yard. A flash, bricks and dust, and lots of slow-spreading smoke . . . I flew home humming a tune."

The results of these attacks, in which the RFC dropped four tons of bombs on one small railway station in the course of its biggest raid yet, were in fact very disappointing. But the raid showed the advantages of dive bombing versus level bombing. Only if a specific target could be located and pinpointed were the results worth the effort, and the destruction of an ammunition dump, ship, or Zeppelin required a degree of accuracy which only dive bombing could provide.

BE2c aircraft of No. 13 Squadron lined up on their airfield in France. This improbable mount saw some of the first experimental dive bombing experiments in combat during World War I.

Another attack deserves mention. Lieutenant Arthur Gould Lee, flying with No. 46 Squadron from Izel-le-Hameau, west of Arras gave a graphic description of an attack he carried out on November 30. He had to attack one particular house in the village of Bourlon with four 20-pound Cooper bombs. The original plan called for four separate attacks dropping one bomb each time, but the flak proved too heavy for that to be attempted. Instead, Lee went into an attack down to 200 feet in a steep dive into the concentration of fire. His first attempt resulted in a near-miss by himself and his wingman, and Lee had to return for a second attempt alone.

This time his steep dive was carried down to 100 feet, and the remaining three bombs were released at this height. He made his escape at the suicidal height of 20 feet and, despite the opposition, escaped with but one bullet which shattered the handle of his throttle control, while another almost ignited his Verey pistol cartridges.

These then are typical examples of unofficial dive bombing attacks. But in my opinion the strongest claim is held by 2nd Lieutenant William Henry Brown, RFC, who staked his claim with No. 84 Squadron in France in March 1918. The attack is well-documented and was, significantly in the light of what was to come, directed against a ship target of sorts.

No. 84 was operating standard offensive patrols (OPs) with the SE5a fighter from Flez near St. Quentin. The SE5a was an unlikely contender at first sight for a dive bomber, but as one historian later recalled, it was a very versatile fighter, both strong and capable of being dived steeply.

Experiments were conducted early in March to ascertain the most accurate methods of utilizing this machine as a bomber, and Brown, being the smallest pilot in his unit, was the "volunteer." No bombsight was utilized and the target was a 100-foot circle. He used wooden bombs and found that with a diving attack he could hit the circle every time. On March 14, 1918, he was allocated a live target, four ammunition barges located on a canal near Bernot.

The mission was described as "Special Mission (Low Bombing Attack)" in No. 84 Squadron's combat reports, and his SE5a (No. 5384) was equipped with four Cooper bombs to perform the task.

Early morning mist delayed the sortie until midday, and it was still foggy when he finally got airborne. Nonetheless, only twenty minutes flying time sufficed to bring him to his target from his base. At Bois de Savy he climbed to 5,000 feet and soon reached Bernot and the barges. He made two dives and scored near-misses each time. The third attempt was different: "I dived straight for the barge." His bombs struck it amidships from a release height of 500 feet and it exploded very satisfactorily indeed. Within a week all his squadron had been similarly equipped and, added one magazine, "a new word was added to the vocabulary of aerial warfare . . . dive bombing."

The arguments about which pilot, squadron or nation invented dive bombing will undoubtedly continue into the future. But it can be claimed with complete confidence that it was the RAF (formed in April 1918 from a merger of the Royal Flying Corps and the Royal Naval Air Service) that carried out the first air tests of the new method under carefully controlled conditions, at the RAF Armament Experimental Station early in 1918. The RAF's subsequent vigorous opposition to the dive bomber tends to obscure the fact that it was Britain that first conducted controlled tests of the method. For example, one historian states clearly:

> Another interesting manifestation of the Camel was as the world's first dive bomber. The Camel had been so widely used for land attack that dive bombing seemed a logical development. Not many modifications were made to the Camel fighter which was tested in action. Some armor plating was added to protect the pilot from ground-fire. A mechanical airspeed indicator was fitted to the inter-plane struts to assist him in his attack.

But the Sopwith Camel was not the only aircraft to be used in the trials, which took place at Orfordness. Lieutenant Brown's exploit with his SE5a in March 1918 may or may not have been the first real combat dive bombing, but the type was actually used in dive bombing tests several significant weeks before his action.

The work was carried out by Section 6, under Captain C. E. Fairburn, with Major B. M. Jones as chief experimental officer. Five different pilots were employed on this series, one of them being

Oliver Stewart, who subsequently explained why the Sopwith fighter, with its reputation as a killer of inexperienced pilots, should have been chosen as a test-bed for such experiments: "The Camel set a new standard in powers of maneuver, and even today it probably remains the most highly maneuverable aeroplane that has ever been seen." Fine praise from a veteran pilot for a plane that almost killed him on the lonely Suffolk shoreline during these tests.

For the first tests the SE5a was employed. A small yellow flag was planted in the shingle as the target. A bomb rack was fitted under the left-hand wing of the aircraft and four dummy bombs were carried on each flight. The placing of the bomb load off-centre now appears strange, but it was done to avoid interference with the flying gear and this position was simplest. Further tests were carried out later to find out whether the SE5a could more usefully accommodate such a bomb load centrally under the fuselage.

Once in position over the target marker, the pilots were to dive their aircraft from about 1,500 feet at 110–130 miles per hour with the engine throttled back. The bomb was to be released at 800–1,000 feet. This seems quite high for the period and size of the bombs, but was no doubt determined by safety factors.

It was found that the pilots adopted the following method. After a few preliminary dives to get the feel of it, they would look along the left side of the engine cowling while diving at the target, the bomb being released when the target just passed out of sight under the cowling. This method was used generally after the first few attempts and worked quite well.

In all the tests the SE5a was dived upwind "very approximately." The trials were run in varying weather and, particularly, wind conditions, again to give an average result. The tests produced no startling results, though fully 26 percent of the bombs fell within 10 yards of the target. No sight of any kind was used, and it was found that, as expected, the pilots' shooting rapidly improved with practice.

According to the report, these tables gave a good indication of the amount of practice needed to become "moderately proficient" in this form of bombing. The final verdict was that the lower the release the more accurate the bombing with the SE5a.

Because the tests with the SE5a had been based on "eye shooting" only, it was suggested that the degree of accuracy, already impressive, would be much increased if the normal machine-gun sights were used in the dive to locate the target. Using the same target specified for the first tests, it was proposed that "if a bomb be released from a Camel dived at about 160 miles per hour when the Aldis gunsight bears on the target a good aim will be obtained." It was specified that bomb-release height should not be more than 1,000 feet. The 130-horsepower Clerget-engined Camel was the version used by all the pilots in these second tests.

TABLE 1: THE SE5a DIVE BOMBING TRIALS AT ORFORDNESS, 1918

Pilot	Date	Height at Start of Dive (ft)	Bomb Release Height (ft)	Speed (mph)	Wind Speed (mph)	Distance Off Target (ft)
1	Feb 27	1,500	500	120	10	108, 88, 104, 150, 33, 35, 44, 45, 52, 31, 45, 26, 17, 21, 20
1	Feb 28	1,500	300	120	20	28, 8, 6, 6, 19, 0*, 16, 11
1	Mar 21	1,500	300	120	10	14, 7, 13, 25, 2.5, 10, 7, 13
1	Mar 21	1,500	3/500	120	10	14, 9, 23, 7, 7, 10, 13, 13
1	Apr 25	1,000	1/200	130/40	15	8, 17, 20, 22, 15, 9, 12, 18, 8, 9
2	Feb 24	1,500	500	110/30	20	6, 22, 30, 33, 25, 12, 26
2	Feb 26	1,500	3/600	110/30	20	13, 14, 14, 14, 15, 22
3	Apr 2	1,500	5/600	110/30	10	31, 20.5, 4
3	Apr 6	1,500 400	500	110/30	9	49 16.5

TABLE 1: THE SE5a DIVE BOMBING TRIALS
AT ORFORDNESS, 1918 (*cont'd.*)

Pilot	Date	Height at Start of Dive (ft)	Bomb Release Height (ft)	Speed (mph)	Wind Speed (mph)	Distance Off Target (ft)
1	Feb 27	1,500	500	120	10	108, 88, 104, 150, 33, 35, 44, 45, 52, 31, 45, 26, 17, 21, 20
		200				30
		100				1.5
3	Apr 7	1,500	500	120	10	36
		500				8
		150				17.5
		150				5.5
4	Apr 22	1,500	500	120	10	55
		2,000	700	115/25		52
		1,800	700	115/25		50
5	Apr 23	800	300	105	10	44
		800	300	105	10	
		900	200	100		87
		600	200	100		10
		1,000	500	110		17.5
		1,000	500	100		21
		1,000	500	110		39
		1,000	500	120		6
5	Apr 26	1,000	200	120	12	21.5
		1,000	200	120		18
		1,000	100	100		2.5
		700	300	110		14
		800	250	115		32
		1,000	100	130		5.5
		1,000	100	130		5
		500	200	105	10	

* Direct hit on minute target from 300 feet on second day of tests.

TABLE 2: THE SOPWITH CAMEL DIVE BOMBER TRIALS
AT ORDFORDNESS, 1918

Pilot	Height at Start of Dive (ft)	Bomb Release Height (ft)	Speed (mph)	Wind Speed (mph)	Distance Off Target (ft)
1	1,800	400	160	17	70.5, 18
	1,500	200	140	20	143, 55, 91, 24, 21, 188
2	1,200	150/50	120	20	92, 13, 28, 33, 43, 10, 16, 32, 34, 7, 7, 11, 7, 17
3	2,000	1,000	140	9	328
	2,000	600			180
	2,000	500			175
	2,000	400			89
	2,000	400			140
	1,500	100			13

Bomb racks were fitted one under each wing of the Camel and carrying one twenty-pound bomb each for the trial. It was decided not to place the racks under the front fuselage lest the bombs foul the undercarriage bracing wires. Placing the racks under the fuse-lage farther aft would have upset the trim too much.

Three different pilots worked on these trials, dropping a total of twenty-eight bombs on the flag marker used for the SE5a tests. Once again, the pilots were chosen for their wide range of flying experience. The most experienced, Captain Stewart, had logged about 1,000 hours, his colleagues 600 and 250, respectively.

The Aldis sight was used exclusively in the first tests, by Cap-tain Stewart. On runs two, four, six, and eight, the Aldis was aimed well ahead of the target to compensate for the shortfall found to be common when using the sight thus.

On the second of these runs, after the bomb had been released at 400 feet, the Camel suffered engine failure, crashing into the shingle and rolling over. Stewart survived the impact, but was left upside down in his straps for more than two hours, jammed in the cockpit, with petrol dripping on him before the rescue party could reach him.

The most inexperienced pilot, No. 3, aimed at the target with the sight for every shot except for the last one, which proved to be the most accurate of all. This last bomb was dropped by eye in the manner of the SE5a tests.

Pilot No. 2, seeing that the bombs would always fall short of the target when aimed with the Aldis sight, deliberately aimed well over, gradually increasing the distance of the "aim-over" all the time. The difference in bombing accuracy was immediately apparent.

The three pilots reached the same conclusions:

1. Dive bombing with the Aldis sight was very unsafe as a result of the high speed called for at a low height while carrying bombs, "more especially if the air is at all bumpy." The use of the Aldis sight made the technique even more hazardous, preventing the pilot from getting a true impression of his closeness to the ground.
2. It was far easier to drop the bombs in a vertical dive with no sight at all. It could be put to limited use, not by looking through it, but by sighting along the top of it. This method indicated the target quite well if the aircraft was directed straight at the target.
3. At speeds of 120–130 miles per hour the sighted and unsighted methods were equally accurate, though the former required more practice. The sight was also found to require lower bomb-release heights and the safety factor was nowhere near as high.

They concluded that use of the Camel with the Aldis sight was "quite unsafe" for an average pilot and that the results expected would not be worth the expenditure in machines and trained pilots. Thus RAF opposition to dive bombing was to be deeply set early on. They also stated that there was no advantage to be gained from using the Aldis sight at slower speeds than those specified, except in improving line errors by the pilot looking along the sight when approaching the target.

These trials, although proving the greater accuracy of dive bombing, had the ultimate effect of turning the RAF against it. The service was convinced that use of the method in combat would lead to casualties for little return. In much the same way, wartime experience had turned the RAF against "strafing," as the Slessor lectures of the 1930s were to confirm.

By 1919, there was little RAF enthusiasm for any form of ground attack. Despite continued testing, and calls for specific aircraft to fulfill this role, dive bombing was relished least of all. This naturally affected army cooperation, and in the twenty years between the wars, the rift was to open into a chasm. One very distinguished general noted: "Between the wars the former cooperation between the army and the air force, close, intimate and effective in the Great War, ceased when the air force became a separate service."

This indifference to dive bombing was also to have a crippling effect on the Royal Navy. Control of all RN aircraft had passed to the RAF in 1918 and the allocation of funds to that part of the service meant that the Fleet Air Arm was very much a Cinderella in both aircraft and designs.

Strangely enough, despite his experience during the trials, Stewart himself remained a dive bombing enthusiast. Over the years he was to become the major critic of the RAF's neglect of the method, conducting a campaign that culminated in a series of pointed articles during 1942. He remained convinced that dive bombing was a valid and valuable method of attack at a time when the official line was very different.

CHAPTER 3

The Momentum Falters

Immediate Postwar Developments, 1919–22

We have seen how by the end of World War I the air forces of the major powers were using aircraft to support their armies, mainly by means of ground-attack operations. This was true of Britain, Germany, France, and the United States, though Britain was unique in studying dive bombing as such. But the end of a highly destructive war was followed by a strong reaction against all forms of warfare, armaments, and military experiments, leading to a heavy cutback in manpower, equipment, funds, and research.

This applied to those powers that were allowed the rest of peace. But other nations were not so fortunate: in particular, Poland and the Soviet Union fought a murderous war in 1919–20 before Polish independence was secured. As this was more or less a continuation of World War I in that troubled area of Central Europe, the lessons were similar to those learned elsewhere in 1918. Both nations soon recognized the value and the appalling dangers of ground-support operations.

Italy, influenced by the RAF's example at Vittorio Veneto in 1918, made similar advances and followed the same road. In Germany the ban on all armaments, especially aircraft, simply acted as a spur, and the re-creation of an effective air force was soon underway. Dominated, as the new force was, by ex-army flyers, it is not surprising that close support found high favor. Ironically, it was at this low point in German fortunes that the first tentative moves were made, in Sweden and the Soviet Union, towards the Stuka of a decade later, the means by which a resurgent Germany turned the tables on the victors of 1918 in a campaign of only a few weeks duration.

In America the situation was more complex. As in Britain, two strands of thought began to emerge: the naval, which favored dive bombing for accuracy, and the air force, which saw the heavy bomber as the decisive factor in any war. But this polarization did not take effect immediately, and it was the army air force that was to provide the spark, which rekindled the whole dive bomber fire.

Immediately after the war France led the world in the development of some dive bombing techniques for use against warships. But this proved a flash in the pan, and although the French Navy maintained an interest in this method of attack, it was so short of funds and had so many obsolete warships to replace that little could be done to follow through her early postwar advances.

Japan was in a similar state. Still nominally an ally of Britain, her growing designs on the Chinese mainland were rapidly drawing her into conflict with China and the Western powers. A British naval mission was, however, sent to Japan soon after the war to assist in the building up of Japanese naval air power, which was then almost nonexistent. This tuition was to come home to roost with a vengeance in the South China Sea twenty years later!

This is the background to the years 1919–22. Let us now examine in more depth each nation's problems and ideas in this period, to see how the seed began to germinate in some and was neglected in others.

During the grim campaigns fought in 1919–20 to defend the newly established state of Poland against a variety of opponents, the Polish air force, equipped with surplus aircraft from all over Europe, made a lasting impression on friend and foe alike with the effectiveness of its ground strafing. As a result, ground-attack aircraft predominated in the Polish air force from the mid-1920s onwards, culminating in the production of the purpose-built PZL P23 *Kara*. No interest was shown in the dive bomber until the mid-1930s.

The Red Army had been on the receiving end of most of Poland's strafing attacks and had suffered grievous infantry and cavalry casualties. As a result, the Soviet Union adopted this form of attack wholeheartedly in the late 1920s, developing the technique into the 1930s and largely perfecting air/ground coordination.

Out of this grew the famous *Shturmovik* units, but the USSR came even later than Poland to dive bombing design and no development took place before the late 1930s.

Japan's embryo army and navy air arms followed the general European trend. The first dive bombing experiments did not take place until the late 1920s, influenced by developments in the USA. Not until the early 1930s did detailed design and testing of dive bombers take place.

As early as 1917 the German air arm was using to great effect units specially trained in ground attack, the "battle flights." After the war all efforts were concentrated on evading the limitations of the Versailles Treaty, which prohibited Germany from maintaining any military arm. The signing of the Treaty of Rapallo with the Soviet Union in 1922 cleared the way for the first exhaustive tests of combat aircraft. Here again the first experiments were directed at development of the strafing role, Dutch-built Fokker D-XIIIs and Heinkel HD17s and HD21s being used as fighter-bombers when they failed to perform well as fighters. Work on true dive bombing was hardly possible at this stage in Germany, but it was soon to develop.

One of the three nations which were experimenting with dive bombing was Britain; research was continuous, but much curtailed by the strict economic measures adopted by successive governments. The continued wrangling between the Royal Navy, which wanted the dive bomber, and the RAF, which had little time for it, also caused constant delays. The RAF saw the strategic bomber as its ultimate goal and regarded army cooperation more as a reconnaissance than an attack function, using aircraft like the Audax and similar types. On the other hand, FAA fighter squadrons, under RAF control, but with mixed personnel, developed a form of light dive bombing with the biplane fighters of the period.

Britain's dive bombing units in the 1920s operated the Nieuport Nightjar (1922–24) and the Parnall Plover (1923–24), the former finally being sold to Japan and renamed the Sparrowhawk. By 1926 these types had been replaced by the Fairey Flycatcher, vehicle of the continued development of British dive bombing. Carrying four 20-pound bombs on underwing bomb racks, the Flycatcher was used to develop such tactics as the "converging" attack. By 1928 exercises in the Mediterranean had shown that the "natural" targets for light dive bombing attacks at sea were aircraft carriers and this continued to be the role of these units in the 1930s.

The earliest French experiments owe much to Lieutenant Pierre Henri-Clement La Burthe. He served in *Escadrille FSO* of the army based at Dunkirk and he put forward, as a means of obtaining accuracy, a diving attack placing the bombs plumb on the target, "like a hand." His ideas were taken up by Lieutenant Teste who modified them in a series of trials in 1920–21 with the ACI Squadron 1 based in the south of France at the St. Raphael School.

The most vulnerable part of a modern warship, even a battleship, was known to be the underwater hull; shockwaves from near misses, the "hammer-blow" of General Mitchell, were able to fracture the hull seriously in the right conditions. To achieve the near-miss effect required detonating these "undersea bombs." Teste carried out a series of trials using the modern battleship *Bretagne* as a live target. In the first attack, conducted by Teste flying an HD R39 aircraft, he dived from 5,250 feet on the port side of the vessel at an angle of thirty degrees then flew horizontally for 330 feet before releasing his bomb. The missile struck the sea about 100 feet from the target, which Teste put down to too long an approach. He began his second attack at an angle of 70 degrees and pressed down to 1,970 feet, but found that the steepness of his dive prevented him from operating his bomb-release. He tried a third time at an angle of 30 degrees again from a height of almost four miles. Unfortunately, when he tried to open up the throttle again, the engine would not respond and he finally crash-landed in the water close to the *Bretagne*, his aircraft capsizing and sinking. Teste himself was picked up unharmed by the destroyer *Potet*. Although he did not have time to work out completely the cause of the accident, the loss of his aircraft did not stop his enthusiasm for the method. He reported that such diving attacks were quite simple to achieve and that great accuracy could be achieved, especially against targets the size of 23,000-ton battleships. He wanted to continue the tests. The C-in-C, Mediterranean Squadron, Vice Admiral Salaun, agreed strongly, stating that the method used appeared interesting and that it could be improved upon.

Teste's experiments led to further and more exacting trials at St. Cloud by a commission studying bombing methods for use against targets at sea. The *Commission d'Etude Pratiques d'Aviation* carried out practical trials of three types of attack: "point-blank," low-altitude, and high-altitude. It is the first named—*attaque a bout portant*—which concerns our story.

It was described as follows: a fast aircraft armed with a delayed action bomb approached at high altitude before diving towards the bows of the target ship. On release of the bomb the aircraft escaped by flying at wave-top level across the ship's bow. The bomb was activated by the shock of striking the water and with a four-second-delay fuse exploded against the hull of the ship underwater.

Preliminary trials flown by nine different pilots gave very encouraging results, and the commission asked for material and funds for further work, saying that the method should be carefully studied. Although money was tight, the French Navy remained interested in this method. Pending development of an aircraft designed especially for the role, further tests were conducted with a variety of types, principally the Levasseur PL7, a single-engined biplane that first flew in 1920. The whole design was a leftover from World War I, with a maximum speed of only 90 miles per hour. These antiques kept on flying until the late 1930s, so starved of money was the French naval air arm.

It was the U.S. Army Air Force, rather than the Navy or Marines, that kept the dive bombing concept alive in the immediate postwar years. The U.S. had in turn been influenced by what it had learned of British methods during 1918. The American *Air Service Journal* of the period reveals the depth of this influence. Commenting on the lessons of World War I, it said: "There were in use by the British two methods of aiming bombs . . . one of which . . . was to dive directly at your target and release the bombs the instant you are pulling out of your dive. The bombs continue in the line of flight of your dive, which is aimed at the target."

In a discussion with Marine pilot "Rusty" Rowell in the early 1920s, Lieutenant (later Brigadier General) Tourtellot of the USAS made the following statements about dive bombing at this time, as recalled by Rowell some years later. Asked his opinion of where the dive bombing idea had originated, Tourtellot said that he had learned the method while flying with the British. In one of the later phases of World War I, when the British had gained air superiority, they had made frequent patrols over German lines without encountering the enemy. To avoid wasting fuel on such missions, two light bombs were attached to the fighters, to be dropped wherever they would do the most good. Tourtellot said that the British pilots found that they could dive on German staff cars and other objectives not protected by AA batteries, and attack by diving their aircraft to low altitudes and drop their bombs by guesswork. These ideas had been adopted by the American pilots working with the British.

Major Norbert Carolin, referring to the period when he was commanding officer of Air Service Troops at the Aberdeen Proving Ground in late 1919, recalled the following test in the September of that year. He was approached by 1st Lieutenant Lester B. Sweeley, Air Services Reserve, who asked permission to carry out a vertical bombing test. This was granted and the test was witnessed by Lieutenant Colonel R. R. Studler and Colonel Stribling.

Sweeley used a DH4B carrying a 300-pound bomb in a Mark XVI bomb rack. From between 4,000 and 5,000 feet Sweeley dived nearly vertically to within 1,000 feet of the ground before releasing his bomb. Although the bomb hit the landing gear and was knocked off its trajectory, it continued towards the target and exploded.

A more persuasive demonstration of dive bombing was described by "Rusty" Rowell after he had completed an advanced course of instruction at the army air force base at Kelly Field in May 1923. It was here that he first heard of the experiences of army flyers during the air border patrol of the Mexican frontier during 1919–21. The 3rd Attack Group, flying old de Havillands, had assembled a group of highly drilled pilots who had successfully flown over the desert terrain and in the high altitudes of the border country. When Rowell arrived at Kelly this organization had four squadrons equipped with DH4s under the command of Major Lewis H. Brereton (later Lieutenant General Brereton, commander First Allied Airborne Army, Europe), and was using typical dive bombing techniques of the period. Rowell describes these as follows.

A pilot-operated bomb release was fitted in the cockpit of the DH4Bs, a novel idea for a two-seater, and the American Type A-3 bomb rack developed just after the war. Each plane carried ten small bombs in racks on each wing, and despite the strains imposed on these old aircraft, by diving steeply and at modest speed, they operated with accuracy and no casualties from accidents whatsoever. The pilots selected a sighting point over the engine using any convenient projection for this purpose according to their eye height above their seat. Using their own judgment, they attacked in dives of between 60 and 70 degrees with "most impressive" accuracy. Not surprisingly Rowell was impressed by the scope this method gave for attacking similar moving targets, but at sea.

U.S. Marines had first been sent to Haiti in 1915 to restore order to that chaotic island under the U.S. Senate's interpretation of the Monroe Doctrine. The 4th Air Squadron of Marines, under Captain Harvey B. Mims, was stationed there from the end of March 1919, disembarking at Port-au-Prince. They were to remain there for fifteen years, operating against the rebel leaders of the

In the Virginia Capes bombing trials against old German warships in 1921, Lieutenant Tourtellot made low-level runs on the destroyer *G-102* in an ex-British SE-5 armed with 25-pound bombs. These attacks were later described by him as dive bombing attacks, but they were not strictly so. One of the planes can be seen just below the smoke of the sinking ship.

"Caco" group and the like. In 1919, one Marine pilot contributed his own method to the history of the dive bomber.

At this time the 4th Air Squadron was equipped with de Havilland DH4B-2Bs, which were not fitted with bomb sights. The inaccuracy of level bombing prompted Lieutenant L. H. Sanderson to develop his personal ideas of increasing precision by diving on to the target. A canvas mail sack strong enough to take the weight of a bomb was tied at one end to the fuselage and the bomb loaded into it. The sack was then closed by ties of the draw rope leaving it horizontal. The rear end was eventually tied to the rear cockpit so that it could be dropped open in flight.

On reaching his target the aircraft was put into a 45-degree dive down to 250 feet. At the judged moment the rear end of the sack was released and gravity carried the bomb down and out, just clearing the propeller. Despite the primitive method it worked quite well, and although subsequent claims that this constituted the true "invention" of dive bombing are silly in the extreme, it is worth recording these experiments in combat as one interesting sidelight on the development of the technique.

In a series of tests laid on by General Mitchell in an attempt to prove his concept of air power as the only defense needed by the U.S., a succession of captured German warships were sunk by bombers on July 13–21 and September 23–26, 1921, off Virginia Capes, among them the old battleship *Ostfriesland*. Although mainly high-level attacks and not dive bombing, one attack was made by "Turk" Tourtellot who subsequently claimed it did constitute real dive bombing. He flew a British SE-5 fighter aircraft with Cooper 25-pound bombs in a single rack under the fuselage with a bomb release in the cockpit identical to those used at Kelly. He dived on the *Ostfriesland* in an attempt to prove that by such methods fragmentation or gas bombs could be accurately delivered against exposed personnel aboard such warships. Although he was successful, he concluded that such an attack against a well-armed target would be too risky in real life. This is an argument we shall be hearing a great deal of later.

Thus the spark of dive bombing was kept aglow, albeit dimly, in the immediate postwar years by the Army and Marine Corps in America, the Fleet Air Arm in Britain, and the French Navy. Rowell himself was to take the story on to its next stage with a dramatic flourish. Before turning to that watershed, let us take a brief look at the U.S. Navy's opinion of dive bombing in 1924, as revealed by the following points from the Naval War College lecture, *Aviation*, for that year.

> Another use for fighting planes is ship strafing. The object to be gained is the reduction of morale of exposed personnel, such as those who might be in antiaircraft gun crews and unprotected tops. However, both material and personnel damage may also be done on the lighter surface craft. Bombing will probably be done at an altitude above 6,000 feet. To bomb accurately it is necessary for bombing planes to be making good a course directly over their target at the instant the bombs are released. Pattern bombing will usually be employed, rather than individual bombing.

Such thinking was commonplace the world over in 1924, but the U.S. Navy's experience over the next few years was to alter that picture in a most dramatic way.

CHAPTER 4

Re-forging the Weapon

The U.S. Marines and U.S. Navy Flyers Take Up the Running, 1925–29

The first flush of American postwar enthusiasm for the dive bombing techniques taken home from the European battlefields by U.S. Army Air Service flyers, died with Mitchell's change of heart under the all-pervading influence of Trenchard. Luckily, Marine Corps Major Rowell had not forgotten his lessons on the method at Kelly Field, and it was he, almost alone, who nursed the flickering flame. Breathing new life into the technique by gaining actual combat experience, he converted the Corps. The U.S. Navy also began to show interest once again, and by the end of the decade the dive bomber was poised to become the major air warfare development of the 1930s.

Although I cannot go along with the many historians who claim that the United States Marine Corps "invented" dive bombing, I would certainly agree that the Marines should receive most of the credit for keeping the techniques at the fore and for its remarkable renaissance in the late 1920s.

When Rowell's period of duty with the 1st Pursuit Group ended, he was assigned to the command of VO-1-M, which at that time, the late summer of 1924, was on its way to the mainland after the withdrawal of U.S. occupation forces from Santo Domingo. The squadron was the first Marine aviation unit to be established on the west coast. Based at Naval Air Station San Diego from August 1924, it was equipped with the old DH4B Liberty. Rowell immediately decided to train his squadron as a dive bomber unit, reasoning that the technique would prove highly effective in support of Marine ground troops.

"I wrote to Lieutenant Walter Peck," recorded Rowell, "and asked him for sample assemblies of the remote-control gun gear, and at the same time I made requisitions on BuAer [U.S. Bureau of Aeronautics] for the A-3 bomb racks which the Army was then using but which the Navy had not yet procured."

Although an old-stager like the DH4 might be thought a strange mount for dive bombing trials, the British could claim to have already used the type for this purpose during World War I. One British veteran wrote: "Even in an aircraft of the last war I remember finding myself actually below ground level, down inside a lock, on the termination of a dive-in attack. Because of the lack of airbrakes and the consequent mush in halting and diverting, the speed built up in the dive. That was in a DH4, a very lightly loaded aircraft by modern standards."

Rowell described how he personally trained his squadron in dive bombing methods, using miniature racks of the Navy type until the Type A-3 arrived. He recalled that at this time, the spring of 1925, many of the west coast cities were beginning to open their own airports and that there was a great demand for the air services to give flying displays at the opening ceremonies. This gave Rowell an opportunity to train his unit in the new art and to show off the technique to a far larger audience.

Their combined formation flying and dive bombing exhibitions with smoke bombs went down well and he gained the definite feeling that some naval air officers present were much taken by this form of attack and began to practice it themselves, at North Island base.

It may indeed have been like that, but it is also certain that the Navy ran the Marines very close in this period of experimentation. Another extremely valuable firsthand account of this time comes from Admiral F. D. Wagner, one of the pioneer Navy pilots. He stated that in 1925 Captain Joseph Mason Reeves took command of the Aircraft Battle Force on the west coast and in the summer of the following year had concentrated all Pacific Fleet aircraft at North Island, San Diego, for trials. He originated a large list known

The driving forces behind the U.S. Navy's dive bomber development in the 1920s: Rear Admiral Moffett (left) and Captain Reeves (right), aboard the USS *Langley* in 1925. Reeves developed the dive bomber concept, and Moffett showed what it could do in exercises.

as "Reeves' Thousand and One Questions" and Lieutenant F. W. Weed began collating their responses. "To dive down, drop a bomb on a ship and pull away before her guns could be manned became an objective, while a bomb sight accurate enough to make such an attack really effective was still a sort of will-o'-the-wisp," wrote one historian of this era.

Admiral Wagner recalled how dive bombing came to appear high on the list of experiments. Reporting to Captain Reeves in June 1926, when he was in command of VF-2 equipped with Curtiss F6C fighters, Wagner found that one of the questions being considered was how to repel a force trying to land on a beach.

Strafing seemed the obvious answer, and VF-2 was investigating a combination of low flying and machine-gun fire. But accuracy proved poor and losses from antiaircraft fire seemed likely to be high. Wagner found that

> The answer to the problem lay in approaching at high altitude [above 10,000 feet] to attain surprise and avoid antiaircraft fire, before diving at steep angles [70 degrees or more] to attain very high speed in the dive and to obtain the optimum of accuracy in hitting and in changing the emphasis from machine-guns to bombs.
>
> The squadron knew it had developed a very important form of attack that would be effective against the strongest of targets and one that *in no way resembled the old strafing conception of attack.* We also appreciated the fact that attacks must not all be made from the same direction and that the formation from which the attack started must be a flexible one so that entry into the dive could be made promptly after sighting a target. Accordingly, the Vee of echelon and the ABC formations were developed.

Full of enthusiasm at their "discovery," the squadrons carried out prolonged trials in the back country of San Diego that summer.

The young pilots, having satisfied themselves that they had perfected their art, were eager to give a demonstration in the hope of convincing others of the value of their new tactic. Accordingly, they persuaded Captain Reeves to take up position in the center of North Island and to act as the "target" for a simulated attack. This he agreed to do, and the spectacular results made a lasting impression on those there, including Felix Stump (later a vice admiral). So impressed was he that Reeves had no hesitation in giving his squadrons permission to use their tactic in front of a bigger audience, the U.S. Pacific Fleet.

This was done on October 22, 1926. The fleet had sailed from San Pedro for exercises at sea and VF-2 flew to Long Beach to join in. They arrived over the battleships at 12,000 feet undetected and began their dives at exactly the time the fleet had been told to expect an air attack. Screaming down in their dives the aircraft were not spotted until the final stages of their near vertical approach. They leveled off and, while the battleships were still sounding off "General Quarters," were landing back at their base.

At the same time, and independently of Reeves and his men, Rear Admiral A. C. Davis and Lieutenant George Cuddihy on the east coast had been working along similar lines. They reported dives against destroyer targets, flying aircraft equipped with gun cameras to record estimated hits. These trials were conducted by Lieutenant O. B. Hardison, and Lieutenant Commander Davis of the Bureau of Aeronautics set up improved bomb rack purchases and better equipment for the aircraft generally to take advantage of the technique. The dive bomber had re-emerged, and many old rules had to go overboard as a result. As Wagner recalled, prior to 1926 there had been no provision for dropping bombs from fighters, but that changed completely the following year. The F6C had proved to be well equipped in this respect. Wagner made two other points. First, the fighters that followed the F6C proved to be less sturdy, resulting in some fatal accidents when the aircraft disintegrated during dive bombing. Secondly, the film *Hell Divers*, made by VF-1 and VF-2, was made mandatory viewing for Japanese aviators. The British were equally impressed by it, especially *Flight* magazine and its contemporaries, according to Wagner.

Both Wagner's points were introduced to reinforce his claim that the U.S. Navy had invented the tactic of dive bombing in 1926. Although this is not so, there is no disputing that by the summer of that year the U.S. Navy had passed an historic milestone on the dive bomber road.

Turnbull and Lord record in their history how not all the members of the bureau shared Commander Davis's enthusiasm for the new concept. Some had reservations about the suitability of existing aircraft for dive bombing while others opposed the resulting diversion of fighters away from their primary defensive role. A series of tests was ordered in an attempt to settle the matter. These tests proved that dive bombing gave unprecedented results with regard to accuracy and converted many doubters. Dive bombing of unarmored warships like carriers or destroyers with gas, fragmentation, and demolition bombs up to 100 pounds was considered practicable as a result.

In the 1926 Bureau of Aeronautics tests, a Chance Vought seaplane, the UO, was used because it was the only airplane that could be fitted with small bombs. The success of VF-1 and VF-2 changed all that and bomb racks were soon fitted on VE-7s, Boeing FBs, and the Curtiss F6C. During the initial trials, the aircraft dived at 45 degrees from 1,000 to 400 feet. The length and steepness of the dive were based on the structural limitations of the aircraft, while the minimum altitude was set to keep bomb fragments from hitting the aircraft. When other aircraft were fitted for dive bombing, the length and angle of the dive were determined by the CO in the light of structural limitations.

This work led to a feeling that there was no need to develop a specialized dive bomber, since the fighters then available could do the job, and in March 1927 such a view was put from the fleet. But a more realistic approach came from the Taylor Board, which recommended, for the first time in the world, that such an aircraft should be built.

Tests were carried out at Hampton Roads, Virginia, in October 1927 by VF-SS commanded by Lieutenant Wallace M. Dillon. The target was a platform towed at twenty knots behind a destroyer. The results, confirmed with camera guns, again completely vindicated the dive bombing method and supported the previous year's findings.

There followed further investigations of the bomb-carrying potential and diving capabilities of other types of aircraft, even though the F4B-1 and O2U-2 were strong enough to carry a 500-pound bomb and dive with it. By December 1928 a large variety of aircraft had been equipped as bomb carriers by the U.S. Navy.

Also well under way was development of a generation of true dive bombers, as distinct from adaptations from other types. The Bureau of Aeronautics began the development, at the end of 1928, with the XF8C-2 for carrying a 500-pound bomb, and, even more significantly, the XT2N-1 for carrying a 1,000-bomb. The XF8C-2 was designed to show whether an aircraft especially designed for dive bombing would in fact be better at the job than a strengthened fighter.

TABLE 3: U.S. NAVY AIRCRAFT TYPES CAPABLE
OF CARRYING BOMBS, 1928

Aircraft Type	Size of Bombs	Number Carried
F4B-1	30	10
F4B-1	500	1
O2U-2	30	10
O2U-2	50	1
F6C-1/5	30	5
F7C-1	30	5
FB-1/5	30	5
F2B-1	30	5
F3B-1	30	5
OC-1/2	100	4
OD-1	100	4
OL-6/8	30	10

This transformation of tactics within such a brief period as demonstrated in the air and on the Bureau of Aeronautics drawing boards by the end of 1928, was matched with the formation of the first tentative theoretical doctrines about the uses and advantages of a dive bomber force in a modern fleet. In this the U.S. Navy undoubtedly established a substantial margin over the other leading powers of the day. By 1928, they were, in fact, very nearly a decade ahead of the British and Japanese Navies in this field.

This new-found doctrine can be found expounded in a lecture delivered at the time at the Naval War College by Lieutenant Commander B. G. Leighton, of which brief extracts will serve to show that the trend of thought had radically changed since the Bellinger paper of a few years before.

From the point of view of the defense of surface ships against air attack Leighton pointed out that hitherto considerable confidence was held in the ships' ability, especially battleships with their heavy antiaircraft batteries, to protect themselves against level bombing attacks. The steady and level approach which was vital to accuracy in this form of bombing could be accurately predicted by the ships' fire control and could be met by long-range antiaircraft fire and massed automatic weapons at closer ranges. But this did not apply to dive bombing:

> Many of you are familiar with the so-called "strafing" form of attack which is now being used by light fast planes in delivering machine-gun, or light bomb attacks against exposed positions on surface ships. In this form of attack the conventional fire control system breaks down, for the plane approaches on irregular courses with rapid and irregular changes in altitude throughout the approach; settling down to a straight flight path in a steep dive for considerably less than ten seconds before actually releasing the bomb. Bombs are released at an altitude of 1,500 feet or less. Target practice conducted against targets towed at a speed of twenty knots in the open sea, indicate an accuracy of about 30 percent hits on four destroyer target, in the neighborhood of 50 percent on light cruiser targets and approximately 60 percent on battleship targets.

As if this was not sufficient food for thought he also pointed out that this was combined with almost complete invulnerability to the attacking dive bomber.

> The speed of approach of the plane, due to her diving approach, is upwards of 200 miles per hour (or about 300 feet per second). This form of attack gives to the plane unrestricted freedom of movement throughout the approach and until it has reached the final point of release; it makes accurate prediction of future positions impossible; and, if conducted by several planes in concerted attack renders barrage fire completely ineffective.

Leighton then went on to preempt claims that light bomb loads, such as those carried by contemporary aircraft, could never be effective against anything other than superstructure and could not sink ships, only damage them. In the case of battleships with their powerful armored decks this point was still valid, and would remain so, but against all other types of warship it might well apply currently, but would no do so for very much longer. As the bomb loads were bound, on development, to increase in size, so would the lesser ships' vulnerability increase. In fact he told them that work was even then proceeding on just those lines:

> The diving form of attack is now being extended to use of heavier bombs up to 500-pound weight. We are now putting into the fleet a new type of two-seater machine to replace the old two-seat observation machines, which have been operating from battleship and cruiser catapults. These new machines are fitted to be operated as seaplanes from catapults or as straight land planes with arresting gear from the decks of carriers.

The potential of the dive bomber against ship targets was clear for all to see, although a decade of development lay ahead before it was able to prove itself. The equally high factor of the effect of the dive bomber on the morale of land forces, as expounded by Stewart in Britain at the same time, was also being graphically demonstrated in actual combat conditions by the U.S. Marine Corps, even as Leighton was giving his lecture.

CHAPTER 5

Emergence of the Helldivers

U.S. Marine Corps Combat in Nicaragua and Subsequent Developments, 1927–32

The Marines had been employed in their troubleshooting role in Nicaragua before in the 1920s, but in the middle of that decade, the forces of Moncada rose up against the rule of Diaz and to preserve the status quo, restore order, and stop the fighting from spreading, the U.S. Senate sent in the 5th Marines at the beginning of January 1927, and by May 11, they had been reinforced to brigade strength. Due to the terrain it soon became obvious that they would require air support and in February Rowell's unit, VO-1-M, suddenly received orders to proceed immediately to Nicaragua. Within forty-eight hours the unit, still equipped with the DHs fitted with the A-3 bomb racks, moved out and by February 25 according to Sherrod (or February 19 according to Rowell) had disembarked at Cortinto. Here they moved up by rail to Managua, hauling their six DHs on flat cars with wings detached.

At Managua they set up their base at the baseball park and were joined by two barnstorming pilots (Mason and Brooks) who were flying old Laird Swallows for the Nicaraguan Federal forces, discards from the Checkered Cab Company of San Francisco! The Marine airmen worked all night assembling this base and their aircraft and were ready to fly within forty-eight hours of landing. The ground forces were thin and the seven operational DHs finally assembled held the city on their own for a time until Brigadier General Feland arrived from Quantico.

There was complete anarchy in the land and the U.S. Marines held fourteen strongpoints at strategic sections along the vital linking railroad, interposing themselves between the two rival factions. Later they were reinforced by VO-4-M and these two units combined to form an aircraft squadron under Rowell's command, flying constant reconnaissance patrols over the two armies while Mr. Stimson negotiated an armistice. They had strict instructions to avoid involvement in battle and, although often shot at, did not fire back. With the signing of the armistice it seemed that their work was done and troop reductions began in June. But one of the rebel officers, Augusto Sandino, refused to accept the peace agreement as valid and took to the northern mountains to fight on, while the rest of the troops on both sides lay down their arms.

Sensing an opportunity, Sandino moved. On the evening of July 15, he launched an attack with several hundred men on the tiny outpost of Octoal, which was defended by thirty-seven Marines under Captain Hatfield, together with about four dozen of the new Nicaraguan guard commended by a Marine NCO, which were cut off from the rest across the town plaza. It was estimated that some 700–800 of Sandino's men attacked at three in the morning but were beaten off by dawn. However the town was completely cut off and besieged. The nearest friendly outpost was 125 miles away in direct line, but in terms of land travel by mule trains and bull carts it would take ten to fourteen days for the relieving force of sixty-five Marines under Major Floyd to reach them. The position seemed hopeless.

Rowell's unit soon made aerial contact, and two pilots of the squadron, now known as VO-7-M, discovered Hatfield's plight at 10:10 the next morning and reported back after a daring landing. Rowell had five DHs available for operations and these were immediately dispatched. They did not have their full outfit of bombs aboard due to the limitations of the improvised runway, which was only 400 yards long, and the need for each aircraft to carry 110 gallons of fuel for the round trip. Nonetheless they all got safely airborne. "Rusty" Rowell later described the attack in detail. All his pilots had been trained in dive bombing, and he determined to test it out. They made their approach at a height of 1,500 feet, being fired upon without effect as they formed their bombing column.

As the five DHs made the target zone, they made one complete circuit of the town to assess the situation and decided quickly where to deliver the attack to do the most good. A tropical storm was threatening and the attack was made as the rain started to fall. Rowell led, diving out of column at 1,500 feet and pulling out of his dive at 600 feet. The enemy had not been subjected to any serious form of bombing before and exposed themselves regardless. Their casualties were subsequently heavy, it being estimated that between forty to eighty of them were killed outright in this attack. Subsequent dives were made from 1,000 feet with pullout at 300 feet. The 17-pound fragmentation bombs were very effective, and the rebels broke and fled.

Back in the States, a second Taylor Board, established in April 1927, reached the conclusion that general-purpose aircraft were a waste of money, even if they looked cheaper in theory. Commander Newton White for example deplored such aircraft, condemning them as "an inefficient hybrid in which both types were ruined." Dive bomber, torpedo bomber, and fighter were the three recommended types to concentrate on. But during this early stage of experimentation, the splitting of the U.S. Navy dive bombers into "light" types, fighters that could dive bomb, and "heavy" types (dive bombers that could also scout) continued and was not halted until the end of the decade. In Britain this habit of building aircraft for more than one function was to have tragic results for the FAA, but the U.S. Navy was more fortunate in that it could control its own destiny with regard to aircraft.

Structural strength remained the chief problem for the designers, dive bombing setting up higher strains than normal on aircraft. The use by the Marines of the Curtiss Falcon (OC-1), which was a Navy-modified version of the Army plane with an air-cooled Pratt & Whitney R-1340 Wasp engine, indicated the need for greater strength and this was incorporated in the XF8C. Even so it was clear that the stress problem was still an unknown factor, for the first XF8C crashed on test flight. Curtiss therefore built a stronger, but heavier, model as a flying test-bed and from this resulted the F8C-4.

Martin had similar difficulties with their XTSM-1, for the initial test program of October 1929 resulted in badly damaged wings. Renewed testing in March 1930 under three different conditions again produced minor distortion of the wings. Even the first production model, BM-1, crashed on acceptance trials and it had to have yet further strengthening before entering service.

Further accidents were involved in the bomb dropping, with the bomb striking the parts of the aircraft on release, while their flight paths were identical during the vertical stage before pullout. In 1929 a string of such accidents, although not fatal, led to a re-appraisal after a small bomb hit the prop of an XF6C-4, and F6C-4 and F3B aircraft had their landing gear struck by their own missiles.

Although it could be proved on paper that in dive bombing the bomb would always hit the landing gear of the aircraft due to the relative trajectories of the two, it was already known that in fact this only happened rarely, so the problem was not hopeless. Further tests were conducted at the Naval Proving Grounds at Dahlgren, during which dive bombing took place and motion pictures were taken of the bomb leaving the aircraft at various angles. From this a maxi-

A view of a Martin BM-1 dive bomber taking off from the USS *Lexington* in 1934. The BM-1 was one of the first true dive bombers capable of carrying a bomb load effective against small warships.

mum safety angle was deduced but the human element involved in this form of attack was such that it was determined that the true angle of dive was miscalculated by pilots by as much as 15 to 30 degrees, and a foolproof automatic device was considered necessary to compensate for this human error.

The answer lay, for a single heavy bomb load, in a simple displacing gear arrangement incorporating a bomb-crutch which had two pivoted arms fixed to the fore end of the under-fuselage. On release this mechanism swung the bomb down and out away from the body of the aircraft, thus clearing both the prop arcs and the bulky undercarriage gear in one quick movement. This invention was the combined work of Lieutenant Commander A. C. Miles, Bureau of Aeronautics; Commander C. L. Schuyler; and Mr. George A. Chadwick, Bureau of Ordnance; and their invention cleared the way for the rapid development of the true dive bomber.

The bomb-crutch was tried at the Martin test plant in static tests and then flight-proven at the Proving Grounds on January 7–8, 1931, by Lieutenant Commander Ostrander in the XTSM-1. There were no snags and this vital piece of equipment became standard fitting to all "heavy" dive bombers.

A simpler answer was found for the smaller fragmentation bombs, which was merely to carry such bombs as far outboard under the wings as possible where they could foul no obstruction on release. In any case the value of such small weapons rapidly declined for use on dive bombers in the decade that followed, as such aircraft were built mainly for 500-pound and 1,000-pound bombs. An additional safety precaution introduced at the same time was the slow-arming fuse, which ensured that the bomb was well clear of the aircraft before chance ignition could occur.

Following the testing of the strengthened XTSM-1 in April 1931, the Martin BM-1 was ordered, but this was only a stop-gap, for already the Bureau of Aeronautics were looking ahead at a whole range of designs and options.

The first type evaluated was a two-seater scout and dive bomber. It was this type that was eventually to gain the day at the end of the decade, only to lose it five years after, but in 1932 it was one of many ideas. The designers were required to strive for the following: range with a 1,000-pound bomb of 400 miles; with a 500-pound bomb,

750 miles. As a scouting plane, the range was to be at least 1,000 miles, with the external fuel tanks being substituted for the normal bomb load. This specification led to the Great Lakes XGB-1 and the Consolidated XB2Y-1.

For the development of the alternative one-seat "light" dive bomber, the Curtiss XF11 C-1 and C-2 were produced, both of which were capable of carrying a single 500-pound bomb, and later the XG11 C-3 was ordered. All these aircraft later had their designations changed to BFC-1, BFC-2, and BFC-3, causing some confusion, while the BFC-3 was later to receive the designation BF2C-1.

Thus, by 1932, the U.S. Navy was developing six different types of aircraft to perform three main functions: "heavy" two-seat dive bombers, "light" two-seat fighter dive bombers, tactical scouts, and single-seater fighters.

Of the "heavies," the Great Lakes XBG-1 incorporated many features of the defunct Martin TG-2 torpedo bomber, when that company was taken into the Great Lakes domain in October 1932 and it proved itself superior to the existing BM-1 and the rival Consolidated XB2Y-1. A dozen of the original Martin BM- ls were in service aboard the carrier *Lexington* by July 1932 and they were followed by twenty-one of the later version, BM-2. Highly regarded in service the Great Lakes design was superior, being both smaller with advantages for carrier operating and stowage, and having a higher top speed (188 mph against 145 mph) with a higher ceiling (20,100 feet against 16,400 feet), and thus forty-four of them were ordered, as the BG-1, for the Marines and Navy, entering service in October 1934. A total of sixty were built, but the parent company went out of business in 1936.

With regard to the wider single-seater fighter dive bomber field the situation was similarly resolved. From the Boeing XG6B-1 design the Navy got a 200-mph fighter, which was designed to double as a dive bomber from the start. In this form it was designated the XBFB-1 but their rivals, Curtiss, made the most lasting impression on this particular field in the early and mid-1930s.

The famous Curtiss F11C Hawks were an adaptation of the U.S. Army P-6E Goshawk and as such they featured a Wright 600-horsepower engine. The first navy Hawks appeared in 1932 as the F11C-1, the export version featuring a Wright Cyclone engine of

700 horsepower and, although developed earlier, was designated F11C-2. Both aircraft featured the fixed heavy undercarriage and spats, and both of course were biplanes. In March 1934 this aircraft, originally ordered as a fighter, was redesignated to fit its "light" dive bomber role, becoming the BFC-1 Hawk, similarly the F11C-2 became the BFC-2.

A further refinement of this basic aircraft was the BF11C-3, which had a retractable undercarriage, something quite novel for biplanes. This was also made over to become the famed BF2C-1 Hawk, the export version of which was sold to Argentina and Thailand as the Hawk III. Twenty-eight of these were delivered to the U.S. Navy in 1933 and joined the Navy's crack High Hats squadron embarked on *Saratoga*, but here it served for less than one year.

The impact of the dive bomber was enormous of course in the advancement of the aircraft carrier concept. Now, and only now, the fleet had a fast, handy aircraft that could hurt. The torpedo bomber, although potentially more dangerous against ship targets, was also more vulnerable, for at this time it still had to make a straight low-level run to launch its missile and all warship guns could be concentrated against it. By contrast the dive bomber appeared without much warning in those pre-radar days, from a height to which only the most specialized guns could elevate, and they came in at a speed which limited firing time to seconds. On top of that was its proven accuracy which meant that small ships could be disabled, or even sunk, by this method alone while the battleships could be swamped by a combination of both methods, the dive bomber suppressing the antiaircraft fire to enable the torpedo bomber to close in unscathed. The coordination of these two methods, although ideal of course, seldom proved possible in combat conditions, but when it did work, it was decisive.

With regard to accuracy, the first tests had been impressive and in each further dive bomber trial further improvement was shown. The Curtiss F8C claimed a hit rate of 67 percent on target compared with the horizontal bomber average of 30 percent, while Lieutenant Commander Wagner once claimed that in one test his squadron scored 100 percent hits on a battleship target.

With regard to the ships' defenses, the first feelings were that they had little or no chance of stopping a committed dive bomber by gunfire alone, and Captain Leahy of the Bureau of Ordnance was recorded as saying that this type of attack showed great possibilities. But by 1931, the Bureau of Ordnance was re-asserting its faith in the new generation of close-range weapons to deter dive bombers.

Dive bombing trials against small vessels found that machine-gun bullets could penetrate decks and bulkheads of destroyers, 30-pound bombs could wreck torpedo tubes, searchlights, and boats and that destroyers were very vulnerable indeed and would need heavier antiaircraft weapons and a great many more of them to cope.

Of equal importance, or perhaps more so in the long term, was the discovery of what naval airpower could achieve against land-based aircraft, even as early as the late 1920s. Whereas it was held by RAF authorities that a land-based plane would always be superior to a ship-based one, the U.S. Navy proved in 1929 that this was nonsense. Thus the strategic value of the dive bomber was shown in these early exercises as well as its tactical attributes.

This was largely the work of Reeves, now a rear admiral flying his flag in *Saratoga*. She was part of the "Black" (attacking) fleet in that year's war game, their objective being an assault on the Panama Canal Zone, which was defended by the "Blue" forces. The latter had some 145 aircraft at their disposal for defense, including thirty-seven Army and twelve Navy shore-based planes in the canal zone itself, as well as the carrier air groups from *Lexington*. Against this, "Black" could deploy only 116 aircraft from *Saratoga*, the old *Langley* having dropped out with defects.

Reeves persuaded Admiral William V. Pratt, commanding "Black" fleet, to allow him to use *Saratoga* independently of the battleships for the first time, and she made a high-speed dash through the defenders' screens and flew off her aircraft at dawn. Seventeen torpedo bombers and seventeen dive bombers escorted by thirty-two fighters were dispatched, all of which got through.

Complete tactical surprise was achieved. Canal locks and army airfields in the zone were pummeled with both dive bombing and low-level strafing attacks. When finally engaged by defending Army aircraft, the *Saratoga*'s fighters gave more than they got. Pratt termed the strike and the maneuver that preceded it "the most brilliantly conceived and most effectively executed naval operations in our history."

Another account of this notable day in the dive bomber's history concluded, "In theory the simultaneous bombings blew up the Miraflores and Pedro Miguel locks and damaged the airfields at Fort Clayton and Albright. Nine defending fighters came up from these fields but were hopelessly outnumbered and *Saratoga*'s planes returned with only one technical loss." Truly, the dive bomber had arrived in the U.S. Navy.

CHAPTER 6

Doubts and Hesitancy

Other Nations' Experiments, 1925–32

Chief interest in Britain continued to be shown in dive bombing by the then Royal Air Force-controlled Fleet Air Arm (FAA) flights and the famous "converging" attacks by the Fairey Flycatchers continued to be the most obvious outward demonstration of this policy. However, army cooperation pilots were not averse to conducting their own "unofficial" dives whenever they got the opportunity, even if this was frowned upon by the Air Ministry. H. F. King wrote how "the conniving squadron commanders might well have known better, but they were always first off the stack."

Dives in a Hawker Audax might be breathtaking enough, but it was still the Flycatcher, which represented the British dive bomber *par excellence* at this time. One of the best descriptions of the method was provided by a former pilot famous for his record-breaking feats, Lieutenant Owen Cathcart-Jones, in his book *Aviation Memoirs*. He described practice attacks against stationary targets with four small practice bombs from 2,600 feet. The nose was pulled up into a stall and the aircraft dropped vertically, the target being lined up in the sights. They began to experience the same trouble with bombs hitting the undercarriage, as the Americans were to learn.

A new and more accurate method was then adopted which involved a very steep dive from 2,000 feet down to 150 feet, again with the target lined up in the sights. The aircraft was pulled up sharply at this height and the bomb released within three seconds. Despite the findings at Orfordness earlier Cathcart-Jones recorded that, with practice, this method was very accurate and that direct hits were more common than misses.

The approach and attack saw the flights subdivided into sections of three, in which each circled the target equidistant but apart from each other. Signal to commence the attack was the leader rocking his wings and starting his own dive. As the leader reached the pull-out position the second machine would commence the dive from a different direction and No. 3 would follow in turn from another compass point thus splitting the defensive fire. By the time No. 3 had finished the dive No. 1 would again be in position to attack keeping the target under constant assault.

The incidents of bombs hitting the undercarriage came to a head in Britain in 1932 following an accident at the Sutton Bridge testing range on September 26. While carrying out bombing practice over Holbeach Marsh against a towed target in the Wash, Flight Lieutenant Henry Maitland King, Royal Navy, attached to the carrier *Furious*, was killed when his Flycatcher apparently burst into flames in mid-air and crashed, exploding on impact.

Eyewitnesses told how King had come down from 2,000 feet to 1,000 feet in a 120-mph dive. On straightening out he had dropped two bombs in quick succession. Suddenly, flames burst from the fuselage and a second later the machine dived into the bombing range a few yard from the water's edge. There was a loud crash, followed by the explosions of the bombs still on board.

The subsequent inquest returned a verdict of "death by misadventure," but the truth of the matter came out as follows. The officer commanding No. 401 (FF), Flight Lieutenant Commander R. R. Graham, Royal Navy, stated that the flight was instructed to carry out live bombing. In the interests of safety, he had amended the orders of the previous day's trials, on the twenty-third, to read "that the height from which the bombs were to be dropped was to be *greater* than 500 feet." Flight Lieutenant King had certainly complied with this. He was no novice pilot and, as armaments officer of 404 Flight, had gained experience with live Cooper bombs in August 1930. Graham emphasized personally the danger of diving too low while live bombing before the attack and he was satisfied that all pilots were fully aware of the danger and the orders not to do so. Asked about any orders as to the angle of the dive while bombing, he replied, "In discussing this question with other flight commanders, I gained the impression that the steeper the angle the greater the accuracy." No orders or instructions were issued to the flight on the question of angle of dive. King had reported trouble with his bomb racks on the three practices of September 23, however. Other witnesses gave graphic descriptions of the accident that left little doubt that the bomb had detonated in the air.

AC1 R. A. Blumson of No. 3 ARC was employed on the Range Party at Holbeach and noted that on the whole, FAA flights seemed to dive steeper than other units. Similarly, Sergeant A. Johnstone agreed: "Lieutenant King was diving downwind, i.e., from the north-west. I have noticed that FAA pilots dive more steeply than other single-seater pilots, and I estimated Lieutenant King's angle of dive as between 50 and 60 degrees."

The court of inquiry had no hesitation in deciding that, in their opinion, the bomb when released hit the undercarriage and exploded. They further made recommendations that the method of making 20-pound high explosive bombs "live" should be investigated and the pistol so designed that the bomb could not become "live" until at least ten feet below the undercarriage at maximum diving speed. They further recommended that the position of the bomb rack on the Flycatcher be revised and if possible, set back, and that until this had been done or some alternative found, this form of bomb dropping should be prohibited. The deputy inspector of accidents said that "until remedial measures had been taken, the dropping of bombs from Flycatcher aircraft, when diving, be discontinued forthwith." He added that this type of accident could happen if the aircraft was dived at an angle of about forty degrees.

This hardly was encouraging to further experimentation and action was immediate and widespread, as was shown by a secret telegram dispatched from Air Vice Marshall Dowding at the Air Ministry to Air Marshall Sir John Steel in India: "An accident has occurred in which a live 20-pound bomb released from fuselage rack on a Flycatcher in a steep dive hit the axle and exploded. CAS does not wish to hamper your operations but orders prohibiting diving bombing from fuselage racks with live bombs on single engined aircraft are being issued to other commands."

A minute from the directorate of technical development (DTD) to the air member for supply and research (AMSR) followed in which it was stated that "aircraft for which steep diving bombing is a requirement, the Comb carriers should be so installed that there is no obstruction on the aircraft in the path of the bomb when dropped at any angle of flight from steep climb to vertical dive." This brought a list of modifications to current aircraft.

The deputy chief of the air staff (DCAS) had minuted that "I agree that diving bombing with live bombs from bomb racks under the fuselage of single-engined aircraft should be stopped for the present, but I do not want to stop this form of bombing with practice bombs if it can be avoided, as this will interfere with the special trials now being carried out by Nos. 12 and 40 Squadrons."

The directorate of technological development was able to reply that "the bomb racks on Gordons are on the wings and consequently they are not affected." In the case of the Hart, "one of the racks used for practice bombs is under the fuselage but much further back in relation to the undercarriage than in the Flycatcher. The chance of a bomb from this rack hitting the axle or airscrew in diving is *very remote* and only occurs if the angle of dive is over sixty degrees"—which would seem to confirm that this was not often done in conventional RAF units at that time.

Early postwar German efforts at reestablishment had reached fruition with the secret establishment deep within the Soviet Union for testing designs. A further door was opened with the replacement of the very strict Versailles ruling by the Paris agreement of

TABLE 4: MODIFICATIONS TO ALLOW FORWARD DROPPING ANGLES TO CONFORM TO NEW SAFETY REGULATIONS IN RAF, 1932

Aircraft Types	Forward Dropping Angle	Side Clearances
Fighters	80 degrees	10 degrees
General Purpose	60 degrees	10 degrees
Dive Bomber	60 degrees	10 degrees
Torpedo Bomber	60 degrees	10 degrees
Army Cooperation	60 degrees	10 degrees
Night Bomber	30 degrees	10 degrees

TABLE 5: RECOMMENDATIONS FOR MODIFICATIONS
TO RAF BOMB RACKS, 1932

Aircraft	Details
Flycatcher	It is understood that the necessary modifications is in hand.
Demon	All new aircraft of this type should be modified to allow a clearance of 60 degrees.
Wapiti	No action on aircraft of channel-type carriers. Angle of 55 degrees from carriers under the fuselage can be adopted.
Hart	The light-series carriers only in the first fifteen aircraft of this type should be repositioned to give a forward clearance of 60 degrees.
Hart (India)	No action on aircraft of channel-type carriers. Angle of 55 degrees from carriers under the fuselage can be adopted.
Horsley	No action owing to obsolescence.
Vildebeeste	No action on existing aircraft. All new aircraft to be modified to be clear.

May 22, 1926. Under this amendment the German aircraft industry was allowed to build a restricted number of aircraft on the understanding that these were not to be employed in a military sense, but for flying club use only. They soon took advantage of this.

Obviously, dive bombing aircraft were not a type which was permitted to be studied openly, but nonetheless, between 1925 and 1932, the Junkers company in Sweden and the Heinkel company in Germany were able to make significant advances in this field using the smokescreen of foreign interest and facilities.

Junkers had been early in the field with the production of the successful ground-attack aircraft, the metal frame-worked J-1 of 1917 which was a great advance featuring armour protection for the crew and engine. Two hundred had been built and used successfully, fifty of the two-seater type J10, were also produced as an infantry-support weapon in 1918 so this form of aerial warfare was part of the Junkers tradition well before 1920, although they were not dive bombers as such.

In the early 1920s Professor Hugo Junkers had established a Swedish subsidiary, the AB Flygindustri at Linhamn, near Malmo, as one of the many efforts to get round allied controls. From here came the brainchild of designer Karl Plauth, the K-47, a low-wing, two-seat monoplane fighter. Officially designated as a civilian sports plane and carried under the Swedish civil register as such, it was in fact a very advanced aircraft for its time. Powered by a Bristol Jupiter engine it was specially braced to take the stresses involved in the pull-out from a high-speed dive during fighter operations. Although it proved inferior to biplane types in tests at Lipetzk in 1928 the Chinese authorities had ordered twelve of these aircraft. The Germans themselves rejected it as a fighter and this led to subsequent trials conducted to utilize the K-47's diving capabilities with bomb racks fitted to the machine on sloping struts and, as a dive bomber, the K-47 showed up very well.

Plauth himself was killed in an air accident before the results had come in fully but Swedish Junkers were themselves satisfied enough to continue their development work on the aircraft under a new designer, Hermann Pohlmann, and these efforts resulted in the evolution of perhaps the most famous dive bomber of all time, the Junkers Ju87.

Since the Washington Treaty, it was clear to Japanese leaders that the most likely future opponent in any war would be either the Soviet Union or the United States. The general hostility aroused by their Manchurian operations had emphasized this. To the Navy it was the American threat that loomed largest and the key to attacking Japan across the wastes of the Pacific was sea power, or sea/air power, ships and aircraft of the U.S. Navy. The United States already had a three-to-two superiority in battleships, and when they called for an expansion of their aircraft strength to a figure of 1,000 planes, Japan at once took steps to build up her own strength, in response with the First Fleet Replenishment Program. This included provision for the expansion of her own naval air strength.

In 1931 the Imperial Japanese Navy placed an order with the German Heinkel company for the development of such an aircraft. Basic specification called for a two-seater aircraft able to carry into combat a 550-pound bomb. As well as being stressed for diving it was to be capable of catapult launched operations from warships, and, with the Pacific islands in mind, to be convertible for use both as a carrier plane and a seaplane. Heinkels fitted the bill having already established a good reputation for the latter.

The result was the Heinkel He50aW, completed at Warnemünde in the summer of 1931 as a twin-float seaplane. The original prototype was underpowered with a 390hp Junkers L-5 engine, which was somewhat, rectified with a 490-horsepower Jupiter VI engine in the second land-based prototype, He50aL.

Testing in dive bombing configuration followed, with the second cockpit faired over, the methods used involving the dropping of 1,100-pound blocks of concrete at floating targets in the Breitling near Warnemunde. Another prototype fitted with a 490-horsepower Jupiter engine was produced for the Japanese contract in the autumn of 1932. This featured a redesigned undercarriage and nose section and was designated He50b, also known as the He66 for export purposes.

The first He50 prototype proved incapable of carrying even a 500-pound bomb satisfactorily, but those fitted with the Siemens Jupiter SH22 (later named Bramo 322) engine of 600 horsepower were. Meanwhile the second Japanese prototype was shipped out to the Aichi Tokei Denki KK early in1933. The Japanese, in turn, re-engined it with their own Nakajima Kotobuki II-Kai-1 radial engine of 580 horsepower, and conducted trials in a competition to meet their first dive bomber specification under their 8-Shi (1933) program.

The earliest home produced dive bombers for the Imperial Japanese Navy was the Nakajima D1A1 Type 94 biplane. They saw some combat in the early stages of the intervention in China but were not completely satisfactory. Following the unsatisfactory performance of the Nakajima Type 94 dive bombers, the 8Shi specification called for an improved type of greater robustness. The Mitsubishi DIA2 was one such contender but proved inferior to the Aichi D1A, which was finally selected.

At the conclusion of these trials the He66 export version of Heinkel 's dive bomber was selected for production, the Imperial Navy took up the manufacturer's option and the Aichi company

The earliest home-produced dive bombers for the Imperial Japanese Navy were the Nakajima D1A1 Type 94 biplanes. They saw some combat in the early stages of the war in China but did not perform completely satisfactorily.

was given the contract. This aircraft became Japan's first frontline dive bomber under the designation of the D1A1 Type 94 Carrier Bomber, incorporating several small modifications to undercarriage bracing, tail wheel instead of skid, more sweepback on the wings and other minor changes. Japan was on her way.

Following the unsatisfactory performance of the Nakajima Type 94 dive bombers, the 8-Shi specification called for an improved type of greater robustness. The Mitsubishi D1A2 was one such contender but proved inferior to the Aichi D1A, which was finally selected.

Development of a suitable dive bomber continued slowly in France during the 1920s. Following experimental work in that decade, the Gourdou-Leseurre GL-430B1 was selected as a suitable mount and was given further trials. Its World War I origins are obvious. Despite its poor performance, it was further developed into the GL-432, which was also a parasol-type aircraft. Four were tested between 1936 and 1940.

Meanwhile, back in its country of origin the He50 was demonstrated to the Reichswehrministerium at Rechlin in 1932 and contracts were placed for three aircraft fitted with the Bramo engine. These were also completed in 1932 with a three-bladed metal two-pitch airscrew, a feature designed to enable the pilot to select his airscrew pitch before commencing the dive. As a single-seater dive bomber, the He50 could carry a bomb load of 1,102 pounds (500 kilograms).

As a result of these tests, the German authorities ordered a batch of sixty of the He50L (later redesignated once again as the He50A) for use with the flying-training establishments during 1933, and these formed the nucleus of the planned future dive bomber Staffeln. The He50A had a maximum speed of 143 mph at sea level and a range of 370 miles. In the history of the dive bomber, the He50A deserves a notable place for it provided the basis for the subsequent German and Japanese dive bomber expansion programs. It also saw considerable combat action in China (on both sides) and in Spain.

As in the previous period, all French development was retarded by insufficient funding, although limited trials continued. However, in the early 1930s, France could claim it was ahead of Britain in the fact that it had at least produced an aircraft especially designed for dive bombing. This was the parasol-wing Gourdou-Leseurre GL-430B 1. Powered by a Jupiter 420-horsepower engine it first flew on October 26, 1931, at Villacoublay, but not until 1933 did trials begin to take place in earnest at St. Raphael. It had a maximum speed. of 175 mph at 9,840 feet altitude, but its performance was not outstanding. The GL-430 underwent progressive development, but not until 1935 can we again pick up the French part of our story; the pace was that slow.

CHAPTER 7

Perfecting the Skill

The Accelerating Development of Dive Bombers in the U.S., 1932–40

After the great mushrooming of ideas and experimental aircraft types that followed hard on the heels of the U.S. Navy's conversion to the dive bomber concept, this diversification was more and more restricted as the ideal norm was sought during the 1930s. With the bold adoption of the monoplane by that service years ahead of its rivals, the genesis of the most famous of all American dive bombers, the SBD, was formulated. But the road to that final, memorable design was long and complicated.

The six different designs on hand for study were obviously too many and natural selection eliminated three of them early on. Late in 1933 various designs for two-seater dive bombers, each capable of carrying two 1,000-pound bombs, the XF12C-1, XF3U-1 and the XFD-1, were all converted to scout dive bombers. Of these the XF3U-1 held its acceptance tests, but was then sent back for re-design work and replaced by the XSBU-1. The untested XF12C was redesigned as the XS4C-1 in late 1933, and then became the XSBC-1 early the following year. This conversion involved the replacement of the R-1510 engine with the SR-1820-F, with the installation of a controllable pitch propeller and increased area of the horizontal tail and the release mechanism for a 500-pound bomb. From these designs the US Navy ultimately hoped to shortlist either the XSBU-1 or the XSBC-1 for quantity production as a "standard" type. The Bureau of Aeronautics planned to take on the production models of the winners and incorporate in them the improvements that had been accepted since the original design was initiated. Exactly the same method was to be applied to the development of the XSBF-1 based on the production SF-2 and, from these two parallel developments, the best airplane of the two would be the dive bomber of the future.

Thus, although in 1935 the Boeing F4B4 was still being employed by the U.S. Marines in the dive bomber role, the aircraft designed for the job more and more began to dominate the scene. The biplane was still in evidence at this stage and the Vought SBU-1 was typical of the aircraft in use in 1935. It was the first to be dubbed SB, Scout Bomber, showing how these two functions were hopefully combined in one airframe. As related this was a reworking of the XF3U-1 fighter with a maximum speed of 210 mph capable of carrying a single 500-pound bomb. This Vought dive bomber had a composite construction, all-metal body with fabric covered wings and rear fuselage. Although it was highly aerobatic and could be held firmly in the dive, it lacked speed and firepower and within a year had been relegated to reserve units, although some still remained in service as late as 1940 for training. Its single 800-horsepower Pratt & Whitney R-1535-80 engine gave it a range of 545 miles.

For the 1934 design competitions the U.S. Navy decided that two types were required: the VSB to carry 500-pound bombs and the VB to carry 1,000-pound bombs. The VSB was to have a total

TABLE 6: U.S. NAVY EXPERIMENTAL
DIVE BOMBER DESIGNS

Class	Company	Designation	Notes
VB	Great Lakes Aircraft	XB2G-1	Biplane
VB	Northrop	XBT-1	Low-wing monoplane
VSB	Chance Vought	XSB2U-1	Low-wing monoplane
VSB	Brewster	XSBA-1	Mid-wing monoplane
VSB	Curtiss	XSBC-2	Replacing XSBC-1
VSB	Grumman	XSBF-1	Modified SF-2

A fine aerial view of the Chance Vought SBU-1 Scouting Bombing aircraft in prewar colors. This shot was taken on February 8, 1940, just as this aircraft was being phased out of the U.S. fleet.

weight of 5,000 pounds, the VB 6,000 pounds. It was also stipulated that the lighter aircraft was to have a shorter take-off but in other respects the specification was similar. Both were to incorporate dive brakes and have a stalling speed of 65 mph.

Here it should be noted how the monoplane designs dominated. Despite the Navy's specification and classification, Northrop held firmly that the same design was suitable for *both* requirements. The Chance Vought design was for a biplane version of the SBU-1, but with fully retractable undercarriage. For some reason the Grumman design was not actually submitted to the competition but was proposed anyway. The Brewster company had up to this time merely assembled aircraft but their design had great promise. Unfortunately, the new company was fated never to achieve this in the factory or in the sky, despite promise on the drawing board, a fatal handicap that grew worse and eventually resulted in the biggest foul-up in dive bomber history. Curtiss replaced the crashed XSBC-1 with another aircraft of increased performance to meet the new specifications.

Northrop's foresight was reinforced by the identical conclusions reached by both Chance Vought and Curtiss in June 1935 while their own designs were under construction, namely that the

same design could ably fulfill both functions, and by this time the
Navy itself conceded the advantages of such an idea over their earlier duplication of designs. Both firms put forward modified proposals that their XSBU-1 and XSBC-2 should carry 1,000-pound
bombs or additional fuel, the Navy agreed to this combining of the
VB and VSB roles and the resultant rationalization of aircraft types
at sea. In the case of Curtiss, this meant the replacement of the
existing engine in the XSBC-2 with a more powerful R-1525-82,
and the designation changed to XSBC-3.

Of further considerable interest is the fact that, in addition to
the single-engined designs selected for further development listed
above, the Navy was showing considerable interest in the possible
potential of a twin-engined dive bomber at sea. The Bureau of Aeronautics requested the Naval Aircraft Factory to investigate the possibilities of constructing such an aircraft for dive bombing, with a
higher performance than the single-engined type. However, despite
some study work no prototype was ever constructed, although different parts were mocked up. The proposal advanced no further.

The biplane configuration of the Great Lakes design failed to
meet the tests. It was reworked as a torpedo bomber, the XTBG-1,
but failed in this role also, and with it passed the Great Lakes company, only seven years after taking over Glenn Martin's Cleveland
works.

The Northrop aircraft was an entirely different proposition,
and here was produced the basic design of the later Dauntless.
The Northrop story is, therefore, a unique part of dive bomber
history. John K. Northrop is generally acknowledged it have been
one of the major innovators of aircraft design in the 1930s, found-
ing his company at Inglewood, California, after leaving Douglas in
1932 having already established a reputation with his mail plane
designs. His Gamma mail plane design of 1933 achieved the then
sensational speed of 220 mph but his first foray into the military
field, the XFT-1 fighter for the Navy, failed due in the main to its
high landing speed. His next venture was the remarkable XBT-1.

This was in a great part a progressive development of his earlier
designs for Army attack bombers, like the XA-13 and XA-16 with
fixed undercarriages, which gave strength but caused drag. The
XBT-1 first flew in July 1933 powered by a 700-horsepower Pratt &
Whitney R-1535-66 engine and had a total weight of 1.5 tons. It

reached a maximum speed of 212 mph carrying a 1,000-pound bomb load. After testing throughout the winter it was re-engined with the R-1534-94 of 825 horsepower, with a shortened engine cowling, while the tail fin was redesigned to give a more rounded profile and enlarged. The Navy was sufficiently impressed to place a contract with Northrop in April 1936 for fifty-four BT-1s, while the Army took the A-17 version.

The BT-1 had a speed of 222 mph and a range of 1,150 miles. It had semi-retractable landing gear but did not have folding wings although designed as a Navy plane. When it entered service in 1937-38, it was a significant advance; indeed, it was the *only* plane in the fleet *designated* as a dive bomber. Six embarked aboard the new carrier *Enterprise*, while VB-5 aboard *Yorktown* took further deliveries in 1938. Although the maximum number in service never exceeded forty (in 1940) and all been withdrawn by Pearl Harbor, the BT-1 nonetheless was a great step forward in this field for the U.S. Navy.

Naturally, it had teething troubles. The XBT-1 had difficulties with the new hinged split-flaps attached to the trailing edge of each wing, another Northrop innovation, which, although working well during the dive, tended to cause buffeting of the horizontal tail surface when extended. Numerous provisional alterations had no effect, but the National Advisory Committee for Aeronautics (NACA) solved the problem when Project Engineer Ed Heinemann evaluated the result of a series of large-diameter holes bored in the dive flaps and found that this permitted the flaps to be extended even more in a dive, giving the desired slowing-down-effect, whereas with the flaps shut, these holes made no difference to the lift. The version thus modified became the XBT-2 from which the BT-1 was developed.

The first BT-1s embarked experienced landing difficulties of a most serious nature with the bombers crashing into the barriers or going overboard. The Navy diagnosed this to the shortness of the arrestor hook and also noted that the aircraft tended to "float" when settling down and then to stall violently at the wing tips. This was cured by installing fixed slots in the tips and lengthening the hook. Pilots assigned to the BT-1 underwent a vigorous training program to familiarize themselves with these unhealthy characteristics. The modifications lowered the stalling speed and increased the lateral control, but it was still a tricky aircraft to land on a carrier for all that.

Solving these problems on a small order proved too much for the young firm, and Northrop sold his plant in El Segundo, California, to the Douglas company in January 1938. Luckily, the deal included most of the BT design team, and Heinemann was therefore able to ensure continuity under the new banner.

Although it was Northrop's revolutionary design that was to prove the ultimate base for U.S. dive bomber development, the second half of the 1930s saw the placing of production orders for a number of alternate designs, albeit in small numbers. Strangely, this included an apparent retrogression, in that included in it were numbers of biplanes, despite the general trend to switch to monoplanes everywhere else (save in the artificially retarded Fleet Air Arm of Britain).

TABLE 7: U.S. NAVY PRODUCTION ORDERS, 1935–39

Year	Manufacturer	Type	Notes
1935	Chance Vought	SBU-1	
	Great Lakes	BG-1	Additional
1936	Curtiss	SBC-3	In all cases the production
	Northrop	BT-1	aircraft followed the main
	Chance Vought	SB2U-1	outlines of the experimental aircraft, but with a great increase in weight. In the SB2U-1, for example, these increases involved an extra 9,171 pounds over original contract.
1938	Chance Vought	SB2U-2	
	Naval Aircraft	SBN-2	
	Curtiss	SBC-4	
1939	Chance Vought	SBU-3	
	Douglas	SBD-1	
	Curtiss	SBC-4	Additional

Of these types, a few were notable; others were obsolete on entering service. The SBN-1 was the naval aircraft factory-production version of the XSBA-1. A mid-wing monoplane design, it had the modified dive flaps with Maltese cross type cut-outs instead of circular holes. They were obsolete before delivery, but some operated from *Enterprise* until 1941 before going to training duties. The aircraft had a fully retractable undercarriage. The original Brewster design, the SBA, was powered by a Wright R-1820-4 engine and carried its 500-pound bomb internally for the first time. Thirty SBN-1s were built, ending their days as trainers aboard *Hornet.* The XSBC-4 and the XBT-2 had been ordered in the same year with the same power plant and hydraulic landing gear, but both were outclassed and were stillborn.

The extraordinary story of the Brewster dive bomber spanned two continents and more than ten years and the end result was a huge file, many headaches but few operational aircraft. For a plane that never saw operational service Brewster's long-range "wonder" dive bomber (known as the Buccaneer in the United States and later as the Bermuda in Britain) was to be unique in the annals of aviation history.

The XSBA-1 when it first appeared held out so much promise that the US Navy was captivated at once and rewarded the young company with its patronage. It first flew in April 1936 but this

The Brewster XSBA-1 prototype flight testing on June 2, 1936. Much was expected from this design, but little or nothing resulted with the SBN-1 or the Bermuda for the RAF.

product of the Long Island, New York, design team was from the outset beset by problems, which led to the Navy taking over its design, and the result, the SBN-1, was a failure. However, its successor, the SB2A, promised even more. Whereas the XSBA-1 was the fastest dive bomber in the world when it first flew (at 242 mph), the adoption of the Wright XR-1820 engine with a three-bladed propeller pushed this up to 263 mph in 1937. It was felt that the SB2A could only be better, and throughout 1939–40 the vastly expanded Brewster works, supported by Navy money, prepared itself for the great mass-production they knew must come. And then, in 1940, came the British, newly converted by their desperate plight to their own invention of 1917, and Brewster's future seemed golden.

The strange story of the re-appearance, however briefly, of the biplane dive bomber in the U.S. Navy (deliveries of the F4Bs were still being made as late as May 1938), resulted from the earlier period of wide-ranging trials. The final result of this policy was the production orders for the SBC-3 and SBC-4 series, the world's last dive bombers for naval use built as biplanes. Like the earlier Curtiss

Curtiss SBC-3 Helldivers of VS-3 in an immaculate line on July 19, 1938.

Helldiver, the SBC-3 began its complicated life as a fighter, but whereas the name Helldiver stuck with the earlier model and would do so with its World War II descendant, it never took to the SBC, which is always recalled by its initials and mark numbers.

The ancestor of the SBC was the Curtiss XF12C-1 two-seater fighter. Initial design work began in June 1932, resulting in the AF12C-1, No 9225, a one-off plane that combined a number of new and old concepts in an unlikely marriage. It featured a single parasol wing with a monocoque fuselage, but its all-metal appearance belied the fact that the metal covering for the wings was, unlike the fabric covering of the frame, not a solid affair. The control surfaces and wing flaps remained fabric covered. The dual cockpit was enclosed for streamlining and the undercarriage tucked away into the body housing in the Curtiss style. Powered by a single Wright 625-horsepower R-1510-92 twin-row radial engine with flush cowling, the fact that this aircraft was a monoplane fighter at a time when the Navy still held faith with the biplane made it unique, but, by a strange quirk of fate, it then became a biplane as the rest of the world switched to monoplanes. This came about thus.

Test flying of the XF12C-1 commenced in July 1932, just when the first reactions to the biplane were beginning and resulting modifications slowed down progress. A crash a year later halted it completely and by this time the Navy had lost interest in the two-seater fighter. Curtiss rebuilt it as a scout and tried again, as the XS4C-1 in December 1933 and the next month, as the XSBC1, with a Wright Cyclone R-1820-80 engine.

In September 1934 another crash took place, and by common consent when rebuilding, the parasol gave way to the biplane design, the XSBC-2 (Curtiss Model 77). The leading edge flaps were omitted and the lower wing was fabric covered while the upper remained monocoque making it even more of a hybrid. To add to the confusion, the aircraft retained the same Navy serial number throughout its metamorphosis. As a scout, the second seat was assigned to the rear-gunner, and provision was made for the rear part of the long cockpit to fold down into the fuselage. The engine became again the 700-horsepower Wright XR-1510-2, and with this the "new" aircraft flew in December 1935.Tests resulted in the replacement of the engine with an 825-horsepower Pratt & Whitney R-1535-82 Twin Wasp in March 1936, the machine becoming the XSBC-3. A production order was placed in August that year for eighty-three SBC-3s and delivery began in July 1937 to VS-5 aboard *Yorktown*, followed by VS-3 aboard *Saratoga* and VS-6 aboard *Enterprise* later. Structural changes and the adoption of the 900-horsepower R-1820-22 engine meanwhile resulted in the XSBC-4, and, despite its obsolete appearance no less than 124 of these tubby biplanes were delivered to the navy between January 1938 and August 1939, the last arriving in April 1940 as the SBC-4. Top speed for the SBC-3 was 217 mph and for the SBC-4 232 mph; ranges were 560 and 590 miles respectively; and normal bomb load was 500 pounds, although a 1,000-pound bomb was carried by some variants. VS-2 on *Lexington* took early deliveries of the SBC-4, and the Marines received fifteen, but most subsequently went straight from factory to reserve units, and by the end of 1941 all SBC-3s were ashore. Although the last shipborne SBC-4s served aboard *Hornet* with VS-8 and VB-8 at the time Pearl Harbor occurred they saw no action. But in the interim the European situation had led to a new phase in the SBC story.

Vought SB2U-1 Vindicators on the flight deck of the USS *Saratoga* in February 1938. Their prewar squadron and color markings are shown clearly here.

The Vindicator was given the nickname "Wind Indicator" by Marine pilots who flew it into combat with its peeling fabric patched-up with sticky tape fluttering in the slip-stream during the desperate days of 1942, but five years earlier, when it began to enter service, this aircraft was a welcome addition and much-admired. It was responsible for some notable firsts, being the first monoplane bomber to enter service with the U.S. carrier fleet, and it was fitted with folding wings to facilitate hangar stowage and shipboard usage. It was superior in some ways to its near contemporary, the BT1, although not so advanced aerodynamically. Ordered in October 1934, the XSB2U-1 first flew in January 1935. Its airframe was of composite construction, the wings and all movable tail surfaces being fabric covered. The considerable time lag between the testing of the XSB2U and the introduction of the SB2U-1 into service, despite Navy enthusiasm, was due to two main teething problems. The Navy had been experimenting with a reversible propeller in order to limit diving speeds but, although fitted to the SB2U-1 and SB2U-2, it never worked satisfactorily and was never used. An alternative method was devised by Chance Vought comprising a diving flap fitted to the leading edge of the wings, consisting of a number of spars like a "Venetian blind," which were extended to right angles in the dive. Under test, they in fact proved *too* efficient and full engine power had to be maintained in normal level flight to overcome this drag effect, even though they lay flush with the wing covering in this configuration. The leading edge air brakes caused severe buffeting in use and their weight, 140 pounds, further reduced performance. They also proved slow in operation. The solution adopted in service was therefore to quickly lower the landing gear in the dive and the adoption of a shallower dive than normal to overcome the drag effect. Far more serious a problem was the failure of the R-1535-94 engine during dives

As these were fitted to all the new types of dive bomber then entering service, the whole dive bomber concept was threatened and needed a quick solution, for the SBC-3 and BT-1 were also affected. Under test it was shown that the master rod bearings were failing and the order went out prohibiting the new dive bombers to dive! Single plane tests in 1937 indicated the solution might be the adoption of silver for the manufacture of the bearing and eighteen SBC-3s were thus fitted, but further tests showed that this alone was not the problem. Not until March 1938 was the solution found by Pratt & Whitney who developed silver-lead bearings, and in June these were released for production. Later indium was added to prevent the lead dissolving while the engines were being run in and these bearings were subsequently used throughout the war in US radial engines. The SB2U-2 Vindicator had a maximum speed of 257 mph at 11,000 feet and a maximum bomb load of 1,500 pounds, although 1,000 pounds was the norm. This version could carry two fifty-gallon drop tanks giving a range of 700 miles. A special version (SB2U-3) was developed as a long-range aircraft for the Marines, with extra armour protection and larger extra fuel tanks. A total of fifty-seven of this variant were built; they were, in the words of one historian, "literally a flying fuel tank." Performance suffered accordingly, but this type set another record when the USMC Vindicators made the longest non-stop, overwater mass flight for a single-engined aircraft during a mission to reinforce Midway Island in 1942, when they covered some 1,200 miles. Altogether 240 production Vindicators were built of the three American variants and various foreign adaptations, of which more later, and it proved a rugged and popular aircraft in service. It was as fast as the later SBD in fact, although not so versatile.

The SB2U was in widespread service during 1938–41, and on outbreak of war in December 1941, there were still sixty-two afloat with *Lexington, Ranger, Saratoga,* and *Wasp,* with a further forty-five with the Marines. Most saw very little action before being replaced by the Douglas Dauntless, but the Marines flew their Vindicators into immortality at the Battle of Midway.

Meanwhile, the transition of the Northrop XBT-2 into what was to become the Douglas SBD was proceeding under the design team of Ed Heinemann, now chief engineer of Douglas. In all some twenty-one different sets of tail surfaces and twelve different lateral control variations were tested during this period. The Wright XR-1820-32 engine was adopted and the fuselage redesigned to accommodate it, giving the distinctive SBD profile. These changes not only added some 35 mph to the speed, but also improved handling characteristics. The original Northrop slot arrangement had proved less satisfactory in practice than expected and was complicated to fit, so Douglas therefore developed an alternative wing spoiler, a 1-foot half-round rod attached to the leading edges of the wings 3 feet away from the fuselage. This was fitted in the XBT-2, SBD-1, and SBD-2. The testing of the XBT-2 in the Langley Memorial Aeronautical lab wind tunnels resulted in the smoothing of the BT-1 profile into the genesis of the SBD. When in January 1938 Douglas took over the project it was re-designated as the XSBD-1. The evolution of technique and a careful study of comparative values of dive versus level bombing was to produce the hard facts which further convinced the U.S. Navy that it was on the right track, while, conversely, the U.S. Army continued to blow hot and cold on the subject. The line of thought then developing is reflected in two studies from the late 1930s from which we extract a few relative points.

The ACTS Individual Research Assignment paper by Captain Vernon E. McGee, U.S. Marine Corps, is the first of these illuminating studies. It included the following points. On the origins of dive bombing, he correctly noted that this began in World War I "when it was discovered by ground strafing pursuit pilots that releasing bombs during shallow dives was conductive to greater accuracy." He claimed that little was done during the following decade although a few services toyed with the idea despite the risks involved in terminal velocity dives. He claimed that high-altitude, high-speed dive bombing originated with the U.S. Navy and the arrival of the Curtiss Helldiver of 1930. The general lack of interest shown by the Army was noted: "The Air Corps has conducted some dive bombing experiments with pursuit airplanes in recent years, but has never evolved any tactics for the employment of dive bombers as a class. At present there are no airplanes within the Army Air Force capable of being used as diver bombers." Strangely enough, he claimed that Great Britain and Italy placed "a considerable emphasis on the employment of dive bombing squadrons for coast defense missions" and that their tactics "follow closely those in current use by the U.S. Navy." He could not have been more wrong in his choice; had he picked Germany and Japan, his thesis might have stood up better.

Of more interest and accuracy are his descriptions of the individual and unit techniques then employed by the Americans. The first was the "half-roll." When the target became visible under the trailing edge of the wing, the airplane was rolled slowly into an inverted position and the nose dropped to bear on the target. This

permitted abrupt entry into the dive from minimum speed, facili-
tated smooth control of the airplane during the initial stage of
approach and was well adapted for low altitude bombing of precision targets. Its disadvantage lay in lack of surprise and vulnerability
to antiaircraft fire. The method was considered suitable for individual bombing from column.

Second was the "push-over." This allowed a formation to use
an initial point for entering the dive at considerable distance from
the objective at extreme altitudes. The initial stage was in the form
of a shallow dive, or descending spiral of varying radius and speed.
When the correct position over the target was reached, at an altitude of around 8,000 feet, the airplane pushed over into the final
steep dive for aim and release of bombs. McGee wrote: "This is the
method in current use by the U.S. Navy for formation dive bombing attacks against naval objectives. It is considered flexible as to
direction and angle of approach, and provides the maximum secu-
rity against anti-aircraft gunfire."

He revealed that the usual U.S. Navy practice was to release
the smaller bombs at about 2,000 feet, recovering above 1,000 feet;
with the larger bombs, release was at about 3,000 feet. Column of
sections was the usual bombing formation. In individual bombing
from column approach, the pilots entered the dive at intervals
varying from five to ten seconds and varied the direction of their
approach to avoid the slipstream of preceding aircraft. With formation attacks, the wingmen fanned out as the initial point was
approached and dived with the leader converging on target. The
bombs were released in salvo by sections on signal of the leader, or
when the leader's bombs were seen to clear the racks. Recovery
was made out of antiaircraft range, forming up on the leader once
more and climbing to high altitude.

This detailed paper then describes the methods used in combat, particular emphasis being placed on the destruction of enemy
aircraft carriers, with cruisers, destroyers, submarines, and auxiliaries being secondary objectives. Against battleships the aim of the
converging attack of three or four squadrons of dive bombers was to
confuse and flatten the antiaircraft positions for the torpedo bombers to deliver the *coup de grace.* Softening up attacks in amphibious
landings naturally attracted attention of the Marine pilot and also
the value of the dive bomber in annihilating "sensitive points on the

enemy's lines of communications, beyond the range of supporting gunfire, important supply installations, massive fortifications and heavy gun emplacements." The U.S. Navy viewpoint was that "dive bombers are of particular tactical value against precision and maneuvering targets. The radius of action, and the tactics employed for this class of bombardment aviation are analogous to those prescribed by the Army Air Corps for attack units." Stressing the fact that the need to withstand extra stresses had imposed range limitations on the dive bomber type, McGee stated that, because of this, "the Army has not felt that the advantages of the dive bomber offset the performance limitations heretofore inherent in the design of the airplane. Consequently, no provision for the inclusion of the type in the tactical organization of the Air Force *has ever been made.*" He thought that with the new developments in the pipeline—the Northrop dive bomber in particular—the limitations would vanish. On accuracy McGee produced impressive figures on comparative tests with horizontal bombing showing that on average accuracy was three times as great.

The conclusions reached were obvious: Dive bombing reduced the radial error of horizontal bombing against stationary targets by at least half. Against moving targets, the difference was even more striking: "[T]he dive bomber is *at least four times as effective* as the horizontal bomber carrying the same weight of bombs."

On the debit side was the vulnerability claimed against dive bombing, but because of the agreed truth that "the horizontal bomber at 10,000 feet, flying a steady course and speed to the

---

TABLE 8: AMERICAN COMPARISON OF ACCURACY, DIVE AND LEVEL BOMBING

Type of Target Ship	Percentage of Hits Level Bombing	Percentage of Hits Dive Bombing
Battleship (direct hits)	13.00	40.00
Battleship (within 30 feet)	23.00	53.00
Heavy Cruisers (at speed)	4.24	18.60
Destroyers (at speed)	1.40	7.80

bomb release line, is a better target for the director-controlled guns than is the dive bomber during its erratic, high-speed approach and bewildering final dive," the difference was not as great as the U.S. Army Air Forces—or the Royal Air Force, for that matter—continued to claim.

Even if losses were the same at 20 percent, the dive bomber for this loss would score at least four times more hits than the horizontal bomber, and although McGee did not go into the cost factor of machines and crew totals, it is obvious that both in terms of money and lives, a two-man dive bomber destroyed while scoring four hits is a better return than a seven-man heavy bomber destroyed achieving one hit.

Two years after the appearance of the McGee paper, another attempt was made to analyze the point and counterpoint between the two different methods of bombing. This was the Overfield study on dive bombing versus level flight bombing.

In many of the areas covered, Lieutenant Overfield's study goes over the same ground as McGee. In section 1, which covers equipment, he goes into greater detail, listing the advantages and disadvantages of the two types, dive bomber and heavy bomber, including variations in range and the effect of the endurance on the crews. On this score he concluded that the range of the horizontal bomber was twice that of the dive bomber. However, being carrier based, the actual range was potentially much higher than a

TABLE 9: COMPARISON OF VULNERABILITY TO ANTIAIRCRAFT FIRE, 1937

Type of Attack	Details	Percentage Ratio of Losses Expected
Horizontal Bomber	Above 8000 feet	20
Dive Bomber	Below 2,000 feet	30
Dive Bomber	Converging attacks from several different angles to divide the AA fire	15

machine tied to a shore base, although he did not dismiss this vital point. The stress factor would be proportionally higher for carrier-based dive bombers. He also examined the carrying capacity and range figures for both these types.

On size of bomb carried the dive bomber was restricted, but despite all these considerations Overfield still concluded that the dive bomber was the type that suited the Navy best, for the carrier itself gave it the limitless range the conventional land-anchored heavy bomber lacked. (This point was proven in 1942, for only by flying them from aircraft carriers could Mitchell bombers reach Japan.) On accuracy alone it was the best bet, this factor after all being the ultimate facet on which the whole crux of any battle would rest. Penetration power of bombs against battleship armor was not gone into; here the altitude bomber might have the edge, although the dive process itself added to the terminal velocity (TV) of the bomb, which made for such penetration. Although he admitted that peacetime data made true comparison difficult, Overfield concluded that on what evidence there was, i.e., gunnery

TABLE 10: U.S. NAVY RANGE AND BOMB LOAD COMPARISON, 1938

| | Horizontal Bombing | | | | Dive Bombing | |
	Patrol Bombers	Torpedo Bombers	Fighters		Scout Bomber	Dive Bomber
Range (miles)	1,200	2,020	600	600	650	500
No. of Bombs	2x	2x	2x	2x	2x	1x
and Sizes	1,000	1,000	500	100	100	500
	4x	12x	1x		1x	1x
	500	100	1,000		500	1,000
			12x			1x
			100			1,000

At this time, the load ration of the USAAF long-range B-17 was estimated at approximately 4.8 to 2 over the then-current U.S. Navy patrol bombers.

scores and maneuver rules, the record of the dive bomber was far superior:

> [T]he dive bomber is superior in accuracy when the fire is directed toward precision targets such as bridges, trestles, cross-roads, single ships at sea, etc. The horizontal bomber is effective against these precision targets only by formation bombing when one or more bombs might be placed on the objective by means of salvo fire.

On vulnerability from defensive fire, Overfield's opinions were similar to McGee. Both types could gain invulnerability to a similar degree if surprise was achieved, but the dive bomber was the more likely of the two to achieve it. Predicted and directed antiaircraft fire was more deadly against level bombers, barrage more deadly against the dive bomber in theory. Touching on combat conditions in the Spanish Civil War he mentioned the engine cut-out, glide-approach method as having some possibilities to this end.

> It is quite obvious that the dive bomber has greater freedom of maneuver and, due to its high-speed dive and rapid change in angle relative to opposing guns, is exposed to accurate fire for a lesser period of time.

On actual training methods, Rear Admiral Holmberg, then a young ensign, described how he flew a SBC Helldiver in 1940, and they attacked a spar towed by a destroyer off the west coast of California. Such methods were rudimentary but common the world over.

By this date, the dive bomber was the backbone of the U.S. Navy and Marine Corps air components, along with the torpedo bomber. They had the modern aircraft coming into service, with even better planes planned. They had the experience of almost two decades of experimentation and design behind them, as well as a wealth of expertise. Just as vital as these points, the Navy and its pilots *believed* in dive bombing, and they practiced hard.

CHAPTER 8

A Willful Blindness

The RAF Experience: Trials, Evaluations, and Findings, 1932–39

At the end of 1932, the Sutton Bridge accident caused a temporary halt to the RAF experiments with dive bombing tests until safer measures could be adopted. Once the clearance problems with the bomb racks had been solved by new equipment, modifications, and rules giving shallow dive bombing only as a requirement, the way was clear for further, though limited, experimentation.

In November 1933, tests were initiated at Martlesham Heath to study the effects of dive bombing with mixed bomb loads and its effects on the stability of the aircraft and on the pilot, and to determine to what extent the bomb-aimer, as in level bombing, was able to aid dive bombing, if at all.

The aircraft used was a Hawker Hart (K2466) and special attention was paid to load distribution and weights to see their effect on the plane's centre of gravity. With a bomb load of four 112-pound bombs the Hart's total weight was 4,570 pounds. The limitations of the trials were an angle of dive between 50 and 70 degrees only, calculated by the bubble inclinometer fitted in front of the windscreen. Maximum crankshaft speed was set at 3,300 rpm. In the series of trials carried out in February 1934, no bombs were actually released, only varying loads carried and distributed about the plane to see the effect on a range of tail settings and throttle positions. In each case, four bombs were carried. These were distributed equally, with two bombs on the starboard racks and one on the inner port rack and finally with two bombs on the starboard rack, the port rack being left clear.

The Hart was fitted with a non-adjustable Flettner trimmer strip to the trailing edge of the rudder, set 3 degrees to port, but this was later removed as it was found that the aircraft had no abnormal turning tendency in normal conditions of flight without it, and once removed there was a marked improvement in rudder control at all speeds. Then the whole series of tests, diving only, was carried out with no untoward difficulties being encountered whatsoever, the report stating that "there was no difficulty in operating the tail actuating gear in the dives and no vibration, flutter or control surface instability."

As for the effect on the pilot—dire warnings of which had been made—the report stated that "accelerations of 5.5 Gs occurred in recovery in one or two cases without the pilot experiencing any discomfort. In an angle of 50 degrees at 265 mph 5.5 Gs occurred in recovery with a height loss of 800 feet and a similar blackout from a 70-degree dive at 280 mph resulted in a height loss of 500 feet." This was considered very serious: "[C]are must be taken in the recovery from the dive to avoid the imposition of unduly normal accelerations." It concluded that "it is necessary to allow not less than 1,000 feet for recovery in order that the acceleration shall not exceed 4 Gs."

This was a limitation of the dive bomber, but not final rejection. The next series of tests was conducted in March, and this time, bombs were dropped in singles and groups utilizing the traditional prone-lying bomb-aimer to affect the drop.

All dives were commenced from 10,000 feet, and recovery commenced at 5,000 feet— some 1,000 feet being lost in recovery—so this was really "high" dive bombing compared to U.S. Navy practice at the same period. In dives of 50 degrees, 235 mph was reached; in those of 70 degrees, a speed of 285 mph was attained. In all cases, the maximum crankshaft speed of 3,300 rpm was met by a pre-setting of the throttle.

The first four dives were made in one flight, the aircraft climbing back to 10,000 feet after each release ready for the next, but in dive No. 9, the aircraft landed with bombs on the port wing still in place. It was noted that in all these dives, the release of the bombs had no noticeable effect on the behavior of the aircraft. The prone bomb-aimer, the report stated, was just so much useless weight, for

TABLE 11: RAF TRIALS AT MARTLESHAM HEATH, 1934

Dive No.	Angle of Dive (degrees)	112-pound Bombs Release Sequence —Number of Bombs and Positions
1	50	1—port outer
2	50	1—port inner
3	50	1—starboard inner
4	50	1—starboard outer
5	50	2—port
6	50	2—starboard
7	70	2—port
8	70	2—starboard
9	65	4
10	70	2—one port, one starboard

in dive bombing "the pilot automatically becomes the bomb aimer directing the aircraft towards the target." They noted that there was a strong tendency considerably to over-estimate the angle at which the aircraft was being dived, which could be cured by fitting an inclinometer. Other than that it was suggested that pilots use much shallower angles than those used in the tests. In other words, true dive bombing was out. They also recommended that the bomb-release switch be mounted at the throttle or control column, so that the pilot did not need to take his eyes off the target as he did when it was mounted on the dashboard, and an electrically operated bomb-release switch was necessary.

They concluded that dive bombing depended entirely on the judgment of the pilot to select the correct moment to enter the dive and his own skill at holding the plane on target. Once committed he could not take his eye off the target without seriously affecting accuracy.

The selection of the Hawker Hart for these tests becomes clearer when one examines the design produced by that manufacturer in response to Air Ministry specification G4/31 issued in July 1931. The original specification called for a general purpose light bomber for all-round army cooperation work, with one of the many requirements being the capability to dive bomb. As the Hart was fulfilling just that function and had shown its ability to dive bomb at angles up to 70 degrees, it is not surprising that Hawker came up with what was, in effect, an improved version of that aircraft, both stronger and larger. It had the same bomb load but had greater strength to permit the load to be used in dive bombing. Thus, H. F. King is certainly correct when he states that "this two-seater biplane of 1935 can be regarded as Britain's first specialized dive bomber."

The PV4 first flew at Brooklands on December 6, 1934, by a single 800-horsepower Bristol Pegasus III engine, which was replaced in May 1935 with a Pegasus X of 820 horsepower, and tested at Martlesham between June and October. By the time it appeared, however, the RAF had decided to drop the dive bombing requirement, and this solitary prototype remained the sole example of the Air Ministry's first hesitant step to build a dive bomber as such.

Thus, the RAF continued to view dive bombing as a sideline which any aircraft designed for general army cooperation work could perform when called upon, and Hawker produced several offshoots of the Hart to this effect. Specification G23/33 of 1933, for example, produced the Hardy, a variant of the successful Hart day bomber, and Audax Army cooperation aircraft, with tropical

Some consider the PV4 built by Hawker in 1934 to be the first "purpose-built" dive bomber for the RAF. It was certainly stressed for dive bombing, but although successful, it was not put into production.

The Westland PV7, another RAF dive bomber project that never happened. Shown here without engine or covering, this high-wing parasol bomber never went beyond initial experimentation, and the whole project was dropped as dive bombing fell out of favor with the RAF in the 1930s.

equipment for policing the Empire. Forty-seven of these were built and served in Iraq from October 1934. Strangely enough, they actually became one of the very few RAF aircraft to carry out dive bombing, but this was many years later, with 237 (Rhodesia) Squadron in Italian Somaliland and Eritrea in 1940.

Specification P4/34 was the RAF's biggest step forward in securing a high-performance dive bomber monoplane before the outbreak of war. Fairey and Hawker competed and the best design was the Hawker Henley.

The requirement of February 1934 still did not go all-out for a pure dive bomber, but only called for a light bomber for army support. However it was to be fully stressed for dive bombing with a full bomb load, and a speed of 300 mph was mentioned. As a stable mate of the Hurricane fighter the same power plant was naturally utilized to achieve this, the Rolls Royce Merlin, which, although successful and the logical answer, in effect doomed the Henley for, with limited engine supply and fighters in urgent need, it was not possible to produce both aircraft.

Many of the assembly jigs for the Henley were those used for the Hurricane, but it was not just the shortage of engines but also of the Totol constant-speed propellers. The Henley was a two-seater mid-wing monoplane with capacity for four 500-pound bombs on under-wing racks. The Merlin II engine of 1,030 horsepower gave it a speed of 270 mph and a range of 940 miles, a very advanced aircraft-indeed for its day. The first prototype (K5115) flew in March 1937, but by this time the dive bombing aspect was purely academic for the Air Ministry had dropped this part of the specification towards the end of 1935. A total of 200 Henley's were eventually built, but they were used merely as target tugs while the biplane Hectors went into action.

The promising Henley therefore remained the enigmatic dive bomber that might have been, as the distinguished historian Owen Thetford was to lament: "There will always be speculation as to why the high-performance Henley (of which the RAF had 122 in service in September 1939) was never issued to first-line light bomber squadrons as it could carry 750 pounds of bombs and was much superior to the Battle."

Other designs, which fell by the wayside at this time, included aircraft like the Westland PV7 built to specification G4/31, which called for a monoplane capable of being utilized as a dive bomber *and* a torpedo carrier. The PV7 was a two-seat high-wing aircraft with capacity for two 500-pound bombs and two 250-pound bombs. In view of the trials already described, it is relevant to find that bomb aiming was to be carried out from a prone position below the pilot. Also rejected was the Fairey P4/34. This company had received similar response to their P27/32 design after carry-ing out much study into the problems associated with dive bomb-ing. On the PV4/34 the bomb load was mounted on external wing crutches with the carriers themselves recessed, which did away with the heavy ejection gear for under-fuselage designs.

While the Fairey project was still apparently a viable possibility, the lack of any guidance for private firms on dive bombing from the Air Ministry led to an exchange of letters. Thus, Fairey wrote: "The lack of any staff information in connection with the above maneuver [dive bombing] has led us to initiate a technical investi-gation into the problem."

From experience with the P26/32 and P4/34, Fairey stated that dive bombing with modern high performance aircraft was only possible with the aid of flaps or some other means to restrict terminal speed. For both designs, they proposed incorporating a standard form of split flap to reduce this, "and if it is desired to reduce the diving speed, the obvious course is to make use of the flaps as air brakes." They realized the additional burden of extra tail weight this would entail, but for the P4/34, for example, they pointed out the following: terminal speed with flaps normal was between 450 and 500 mph; with flaps down, it was 230 mph.

The methods employed by RAF Hart aircraft in 1935 were listed as follows:

A. The aircraft entered the dive at 100–120 mph (just below cruising speed) with the throttle left a quarter open in the dive. The tactical approach phase was from 10,000 feet down to 5,000 or 6,000 feet. From there, the final attack dive went in after the aircraft was correctly positioned in relation to the target. The final dive continued down to 2,000 feet when the bombs were released

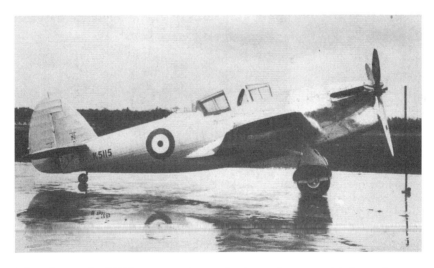

The closest the RAF ever got to producing a first-rate, high-performance dive bomber before the war was the abortive Hawker Henley project, a prototype of which is seen here. The overwhelming prejudice against the aircraft relegated it to the lowly role of target tug while hundreds of the inferior Fairey Battle were built instead.

and pull-out started. Entry was usually sideways not by pushing the nose straight down.

B. Upper limits depended on visibility, cloud base, etc. An undetected approach was the important thing. In clear weather, dives from 10,000 feet to 5,000 feet were found suitable. It was considered that the final attack dive should be as short as possible, with 3,000 feet being the best.

C. On angle of dive, it was stated that "in the approach phase, [the dive angle] is relatively unimportant and is dictated primarily by the need of reaching the required point quickly." A 25- to 35-degree angle was taken as the mean. In the attack, the dive should not be too steep as this led to magnification of any initial error, "and thus may easily lead to over-the-vertical dives." Conversely, too flat an angle made it harder to keep the target in view. A sarcastic dig at the U.S. Navy methods is found here: "There appears to be no advantage in the so-called 'hell-dive' vertically over the target for this reason among others." This point is important to understand subsequent RAF attitudes.

D. The duration of the dive depended on the speed attained; in the Hart, it was 280 mph, which meant 3,000 feet. The shortest time possible was recommended for future work.

E. 2,000 feet was recommended as the best height for bomb release, although it was admitted that "accuracy falls off rapidly as height of release increases."

F. Speed in the dive was "an unnecessary factor since no additional penetration worth consideration can be acquired by bomb dropping by this method. Speed affected vulnerability but a speed of 300 mph was considered suitable to cover this factor."

Mention of penetration power is interesting, and we shall return to that point in due course. The minute concluded as it had begun, on angle of dive considerations: "If this feature can be examined, it may be found that future dive bombing [sic] attack will allow flatter angles of dive at speeds of say 350 mph, thus easing the loads due to TV speeds and pull out conditions."

All these points were subsequently incorporated into a memorandum by the Scientific and Technical Branch, which was subsequently modified and amended over the years. The DTS found it "a very useful paper." More important were his subsequent remarks: "It is a great disappointment to me that the Vickers 027/34 was cancelled, as this promised to be a really high speed Aeroplane, and we should have been able to solve many of these problems with it in a full scale manner." He did not fully share ops opinion of dive bombing. "I have always held the view, which was confirmed as the result of the numerous discussions during my visit to the United States, that really a dive bomber must be *designed* as such. That is, one cannot just take any aeroplane and expect to use it as a dive bomber. The Americans were emphatic about this, and I am sure they are right." He continued: "Our new Medium Bombers, such as the Battle and Blenheim, cannot be looked upon as dive bombers." He would have liked to have had the chance of pushing ahead with the development of a true dive bomber to explore all the problems involved: "But for lack of design capacity, and the crowding up of other requirements, I think I should have done this." He expressed the hope that developments in the Fleet Air Arm would compensate for this lack.

However, the DTS viewpoint was a minority one, and subsequent developments in this field in the RAF proceeded exactly the opposite to his recommendations with the medium bombers, especially the Battle, which was grossly overproduced just as it would be in the years ahead, being constantly tried out as a makeshift dive bomber, despite his warning that it would not work. A specialized dive bomber was therefore abandoned. Again, the lectures delivered at Camberley Staff College between 1931 and 1934, and later expanded and published in book form by Wing Commander Slessor, more accurately reflect the official RAF line on this subject.

Slessor's main thesis was that the airplane was not a battlefield weapon. On dive bombers, he did at least make an important distinction of the type:

Assault action, however, should not be confused with dive bombing. The latter is a special technique, wherein the bomber makes his attack coming down from a considerable height at a very high speed, aiming the airplane at the target, and releasing the bomb at a relatively low altitude—from 500 to 1,500 feet; it is a method which is likely to become increasingly popular for engaging strongly defended objectives where the presence of anti-aircraft artillery makes accurate precision bombing from a height a matter of increasing difficulty and danger; but it is a method quite distinct from assault action.

In April 1936, a further detailed paper was submitted, and it is interesting to note how true dive bombing is hardly considered at all, and when it is, it is usually treated as something undesirable or impractical. This paper began by stating that, with the advent of high-speed aircraft of clean aerodynamic design, it was necessary to reconsider the technique of dive bombing attacks. The current position with regards heights and angles was re-examined, bomb release and speed were listed, and the following data were recorded accurately after recently conducted trials against the Chatham Float target. These were compared with data on the dive bomber fighter designs submitted for the 027/34 specifications for the Navy. "Some very accurate bombing was obtained in these trials, and it would appear that angles of dive between 30 and 65 degrees in these trials should cover all contingencies of attack in the future."

On penetration by the SAP bombs then in use, it was estimated that at high speed, a 45-degree dive was the *least* which would bring the bomb within the required angle of strike when released at 1,500 feet. The conclusion reached after considering the tactical aspects of diving with the flaps lowered or normal was "with great reluctance, that in diving attacks, aircraft of clean aerodynamic

TABLE 12: COMPARISON OF DIVE BOMBER DESIGNS
FOR THE RAF, 1936

Flap Setting (from 5,000 ft)	Aircraft Speed (mph)	Angle of Dive (degrees)	Speed Attained (mph)		
			Vickers	Blackburn	Avro
Normal	200	30	282	270	255
Normal	200	45	297	300	320
Down	150	70	231	240	215
Increase in weight due to flaps (in pounds)			70	150	150

TABLE 13: FAIREY BATTLE DIVING TESTS
USING SPLIT FLAPS, 1936

Angle of Dive in Degrees	Pullout Height (ft)	Speed at Pullout (mph)	Height Lost in Recovery (ft)	Height on the Regaining of Level Flight (ft)
30	3,000	280	230	2,770
30	2,500	296	260	2,240
30	1,500	320	280	1,220
45	3,000	292	590	2,410
45	2,500	308	640	1,860
45	1,500	338	760	740

design will reach too high a velocity to make recovery from 1,500 feet reasonably safe and certain, and that it will be necessary to apply some form of air brake to check speed." This meant utilizing flaps or lowering the undercarriage as the Americans found later with the Vindicator. It was admitted, however, that the steeper the dive—within reason, without a substantial increase in speed—the better was the sighting view, which in turn led to increased accuracy of bombing.

It was recommended that in any future aircraft designed with dive bombing in mind, it must be capable of making retarded dives from 5,000 feet, commencing at 200 mph, to 1,500 feet at an angle of 65 degrees without exceeding an airspeed of 260 mph. Trials with a medium bomber produced estimated effects of using split trailing edge flaps, which opened equally above and below the chord of the plane and eliminated the torsional stresses. In view of earlier remarks about their unsuitability, it is interesting to note that the following figures refer to the Battle.

On April 9, the ninth meeting of the Bombing Committee was held at the Air Ministry, and dive bombing was on the agenda. Some revealing statements were made and future policy guidelines issued, from which we shall extract a few of the more notable ones.

Although the bombing trials against the target ship *Centurion* had
shown great improvement over those of 1935, Group Captain
Guilfoye put this down mainly to the lower release height of the
bombs, the flexibility of the methods used, and good leadership.
Discussing the time interval between individual aircraft, Wing Commander Walker, who had led No. 57 squadron in the 1934 trials,
stated that he tried for three seconds and No. 33 squadron practiced on the same scale. Flexibility was the main consideration, and
instead of the normal three-flights-of-four formation, or the newer
four-flights-of-three, Walker asked that six flights-of-two be considered. The Admiralty representatives said that this would certainly
make defensive fire more difficult.

On diving angles, it was stated that No. 801 (FF) squadron with
Nimrod and Hart aircraft were more flexible than No. 33 squadron
and that their angle of dive was a little steeper. They also favored
attack in succession from astern of the target ship rather than No.
33's converging attacks by each half of the squadron from opposite
directions. On training, it was stated that a pilot could attain his
maximum efficiency after having dropped a hundred bombs in
dives. The maximum angle of dive was given as 70 degrees, but the
DCAS Air Vice Marshall C. L. Courtney believed this could be
reduced, "as aircraft would very rarely dive at such an angle." It was
therefore agreed that the new maximum angle laid down for the
RAF should be only 50 degrees. This obviously ruled out true dive
bombing.

Lowest limit for bomb release was fixed at 1,500 feet, and as for
sighting, the RAF still thought that "anything in the nature of a
complicated sight for dive bombing was impracticable," according
to Mr. F. W. Meredith. He recommended a simple method utilizing
two foresights, one to indicate direction of aircraft and the other
where the bomb would go. A signal lamp linked to the altimeter
would give bomb-release indication, and the method would be limited to downwind bombing. While agreeing this was better than no
sight at all, the Navy representative held out for a more elaborate
sight and a subcommittee was set up accordingly.

Also recommended was an angle-of-dive recorder and a height
recorder. The three Navy men still felt, however, that "there was a

necessity for a more thorough analysis and correlation of the various factors affecting a successful dive bombing attack." It was stated that "dive bombing attacks were regarded with some concern by the Army, whereas from the Naval point of view such attacks were considered easier to repel than those from high altitudes." This was a rather different viewpoint than that being expressed elsewhere in the Navy at this time. Captain Stephen Roskill, himself an antiaircraft gunnery expert, cites the C-in-C Mediterranean at this period, for example, who recognized that the Navy had no effective defense against the dive bomber. Hard experience in 1940-42 would appear to bear this latter view out.

The use of the Aldis sight again came up, despite the findings of the 1918 trials. Since then, the Air Ministry had restricted its use against ground targets below 1,000 feet, but in 1937, there was a flurry of exchanges on the issue. One wing commander wrote in February that "as diving bombing aircraft pull out of their dives above 1,000 feet, authority is requested for pilots to use Aldis sights during these dives." The Director of Training noted that as "high diving" bombing release was in fact about 2,000 feet, there was no objection, while the commanding officer of No. 2 (Bomber) Group stated flatly that the use of the Aldis sight for dive bombing was not considered to be of any practical advantage. He pointed out that accurate dive bombing depended on knowledge of the correct angle of dive, characteristics of the bombs, and the estimation of wind strength, which was a matter of experience that could not be judged prior to commencing the dive. The use of the Aldis necessitated a predetermined point of aim, and this would prevent pilots from observing their position relative to the target. In dive bombing, therefore, the use of the Aldis sight "would render dive bombing more inaccurate."

Further "urgent trials" in dive bombing were held by the Special Duty Flight (K1999) and an Audax (K3080). Using LC 250-pound bombs, the tests were

1. Dive bombing from 6,000 feet for release at 2,000 feet.
2. Diving from 2,000 feet to 250 feet, pulling out, and releasing bombs when level.

The bombs were carried on the inner carriers only, and diving speed was kept below 290 mph or an engine speed of 3,300 rpm. On December 18, 1937, Wing Commander Training made amendments to standing instructions with regard to the break-away phase on completion of dive bombing:

1. On pulling out, pilots were not to climb away but flatten out at ground level into a gentle turn, taking advantage of topographical conditions to keep as low as possible to void giving antiaircraft defense a nil-deflection shot.
2. Straight flight in these conditions was to be avoided and no climb made until well clear of defenses.

In 1936, four Hind squadrons carried out high dive bombing tests with angles of dive up to 70 degrees, and the average result was an error of 41 yards. In 1937, eleven Hind squadrons carried out high diving bombing with the angle of dive restricted to 50 degrees as a method of preliminary training for the advent of monoplanes. The average mean error went up to 70 yards.

Since monoplanes that were in no way designed for dive bombing were all that were available because of earlier policy decisions, in 1938 six Fairey Battle squadrons carried out high dive bombing tests. The average error bounded up to 130 yards. The same year, two Blenheim squadrons carried out shallow dive bombing (i.e., at an angle of dive under 50 degrees). The average error went up yet again to 146 yards. When two other Blenheim squadrons tried out high dive bombing, they brought the average error back to 121 yards, but this was still three times that achieved three years earlier with more traditional methods. The bankruptcy of the RAF policy to discard the building of designed dive bombers was obvious to all.

On February 4, 1938, a meeting was held at the headquarters of No. 1 (Bombing) Squadron at Abingdon, chaired by Wing Commander E. R. Openshaw with representatives from No. 15 (B) Squadron and the Royal Air Establishment (RAE), together with Air Ministry officials. Squadron Leader C. D. Adams described the method of dive bombing used by No 1. Squadron during the special trials of 1937–38. He re-emphasized that as no syllabus of training or any sort of theory existed, they had evolved their own methods on the spot.

TABLE 14: RAF DIVE BOMBING TRIALS
WITH HAWKER HINDS, 1937–38

Type of Target	Angle of Dive	Release Height (ft)	No. of Bombs	Average Error (yds)
Stationary	Steep	1,000	135	35
		2,000	459	54
		3,000	142	82
	Shallow	1,000	99	38
		2,000	303	61
		3,000	102	98
Armored Motor Boats	Shallow			
(straight course)		2,000	35	44
(avoiding action)		2,000	63	40
Radio-Controlled Battleship	Shallow			
(straight course)		2,000	44	82
(avoiding action)		2,000	31	53

Their theory incorporated keeping the altitude of the aircraft constant and determining aiming marks on the ground to allow for the drift of the aircraft during the dive and the "fall away" of the bomb, and they extended the principal to cover moving targets.

In turn the RAE representative, Mr. Meredith, gave an account of the way they were approaching the same problems. They dived their aircraft in such a manner that the projection of its track on the ground passed through the target at a given height (indicated by a light operated by a contacting altimeter). The bomb was released by a gyro-operated mechanism after the aircraft had pulled out through the angle necessary to compensate for the "fall away," and they used an inscribed grid on the pilot's windshield.

The final suggestion was for a combination of both methods, RAE theory and No. 15 Squadron's practical experience, and a Hind was equipped for a month-long trial period with a graticulated

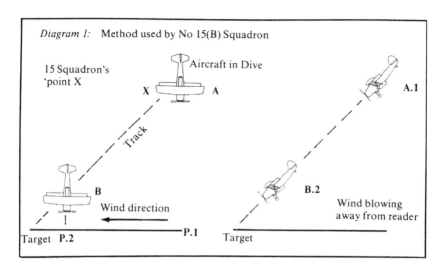

Diagram 1:   Method used by No 15(B) Squadron

The aircraft is placed at X (starting point of dive) and aimed at P1, which is a predetermined distance upwind from the target. Wind was then allowed to blow the aircraft toward the target. During the entire dive, the aircraft is *heading* in a vertical plane but *tracking* toward the target at an angle dependent on wind strength.

windscreen, sensitive altimeter, and indicator lights with an automatic release controlled by gyro. Following these tests, the first RAF *Theory of Dive Bombing* was compiled and issued.

Since 1932, the minimum height regulation for diving attacks had been 1,000 feet, but in June 1938, permission was sought for this to be lowered to 500 feet "as this form of training is carried out by Hind squadrons." As late as July 1939, there was an effort to stop camera gun practices involving diving close to airfields, but the majority of groups were against this ban until various trials then underway with shallow dive bombing had been completed, it being pointed out that "if low level and shallow dive bombing is to be permitted, high level bombing might also be allowed, in which case present practice would continue with the exception of high dive bombing which is now practically obsolete."

Hitler was now doing more or less as he pleased in central Europe, and he had made no attempt to hide the strength of the Luftwaffe during the occupation of Czechoslovakia or in Spain. At the time of the Munich crisis of 1938, the following appeared in a

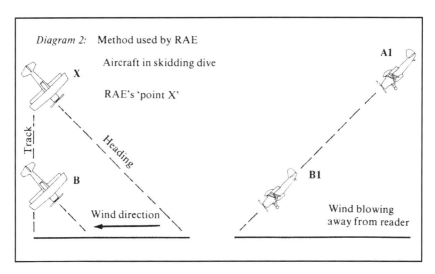

Diagram 2:   Method used by RAE

Aircraft in skidding dive

RAE's 'point X'

The aircraft is placed at a point in the same vertical plane as the target. The nose is then pointed at P1, which is indicated by a graticule on the pilot's windscreen and must be kept in position so that it cuts the target during the whole dive. The aircraft then *tracks* toward the target and *heads* at an angle sufficient to counteract the wind blowing it away. The aircraft is then in a skidding dive tracking toward the target.

minute from headquarters of No. 2 (Bombing) Group: "It is pointed out that low dive bombing does not form part of the syllabus in any kind of bomber aircraft. . . . It is appreciated that shallow dive bombing is still in the experimental stage for the monoplane type medium bomber."

As the last year of peace ran out, the RAF spent a great deal of time and effort trying to devise a system in which its single- and twin-engined medium bombers, never designed for the job in the first place, could conduct a limited form of shallow dive bombing, despite earlier doubts on both sides of the Atlantic about the wisdom of such a policy.

True dive bombers continued to be rejected officially by the Air Ministry until the eve of war. Extracts from the first meeting of the Bombing Policy Sub-Committee on March 22, 1938, revealed some interest in dive bombing, but despite practical experience in the U.S., Germany, and Japan, the RAF was still convinced that the technique would not be possible for them. C-in-C Bomber Command, for example, stated that it appeared as if recent developments had put steep dive bombing out of the question. He went on to say that although he would certainly like to have aircraft capable of steep diving, as this method had many advantages, he understood that, for technical reasons, it was impracticable without complicating aircraft and losing other important characteristics and advantages. If this was in fact the case, he did not think it worthwhile to follow up.

The directorate of technological development then outlined three methods that were being developed to allow steep dive bombing to be tried again:

1. Use of special flaps to retard speed of dive as with the Blackburn Skua.
2. A new type flap being fitted to the Battle, which obviated necessity for any increase in strength of tails or wings.
3. An airscrew, which would get to a very fine pitch in order to retard speed of dive.

Shallow dive bombing was examined and found to be more their taste, although it was stated that it still required full investigation from the technical standpoint, in the hope that they could use existing light bomber types. The C-in-C said that "he was not clear whose job it was to initiate these investigations or what establishment should undertake them." It was agreed that tests should be carried out under scientific investigation, but the directorate of technological development and the directorate of defense research and development DDRD stated that although trials had been on the Martlesham program for some time, no progress had been possible, "*owing to lack of high speed aircraft.*" The italics are in the original and made at a time when the Hawker Henley was in production as a target tug.

Finally, they found that it was, even at this late stage, "impossible to reach any solution or conclusions on the tactical or technical advantages or disadvantages of shallow dive bombing consequently recommendations as to the extent to which it can take the place of steep dive bombing attacks are not yet feasible."

What proved to be the final meeting on dive bombing in the RAF took place in September 1938 with war only twelve months away. The committee painstakingly went over the ground covered by the earlier meetings, but their ultimate conclusions were much the same. These are best summarized thus:

1. Steep dive bombing should not at present be regarded as a requirement for modern RAF aircraft in view of the special devices necessary and the difficulties of bomb release in a steep dive.
2. Shallow dive bombing should be continued without special devices and sights, and the most satisfactory methods should be evolved at the Armament Training Camps.
3. The dive bombing type trials of new aircraft done at A & AE Martlesham Heath were sufficient, and no special dive bombing armament trials are required.

In other words, the RAF—luke-warm at best for twenty years and finding insurmountable problems other nations had solved a decade earlier—totally rejected dive bombing. Indeed, having decided there was no place for the type or the method, they attempted by legislation to purge the very language of the concept, and it was recommended that "this type of bombing should in future be termed 'Losing Height Bombing.'" And that, as far as the RAF was concerned, was that.

Except, of course, that dive bombers would not conveniently vanish overnight. Training Command, for example, did not seem to share the view that dive bombing was either no longer relevant or that the problems could not be overcome. After first repeating yet again that "no instructions explaining the theory and principles [of dive bombing] have ever been circulated," they reiterated that a compromise might still be possible. For example, modern aircraft like the Battle, they felt, "can dive successfully at an angle up to approximately 60 degrees, [and] it is very strongly suggested that the AGA dive bomb sight referred to by Squadron Leader C. D. Adams in his report on his attachment to the Swedish Air Force this year should be purchased and suitable tests made immedi-

TABLE 15: RAF COMPARATIVE SHALLOW DIVE BOMBING TESTS WITH LIGHT BOMBERS IN 1938

Type of Aircraft Tested	Battle	Blenheim	Wellesley	Harrow	Whitley
Indicated Air Speed (mph)	308	285	240	220	220
Engine RPM (one-third throttle)	3,000	2,750	2,600	2,600	2,450
Engine RPM (open one-third)	3,600	3,120	2,925	2,925	2,940
Max Angle at which Bombs Clear	80	30	54	30	30
Controlling Factors of Dive Angle	Engine RPM	Engine RPM or Bombs Fouling Structure	Engine RPM or Wing Stiffness	Engine RPM	Engine RPM
Height at the Start of Dive (ft)	5,000	5,000	—	—	5,000
Height of Bomb Release (ft)	2,000	2,000	—	—	2,000
Dive Angle (one-third throttle)	17	18	—	—	20
Dive Angle at which Target Closed	—	—	—	—	25
Speed at Entry	150–180	120–160	—	—	120
Speed at Bottom of the Dive	240–285	215–160	—	—	215–220
Height Lost	500–900	500–900	—	—	500

ately." They supplied figures to support their case, although the angles used hardly justified the term dive bombing.

The subject was returned to on October 20 when it was stated that although the Air Ministry thought dive bombing was obsolete, not everyone shared that opinion in the RAF. It was suggested that the officials might not be aware of the capabilities and possibilities of dive bombing: "It may not be realized that Battle aircraft can dive at 60 degrees without difficulty and within the limitations laid down. It will be seen, therefore, that if the Swedish sight was obtained and the dive bomb reports of No. 15 (Bomber) Squadron circulated that we should have very accurate bombing on this type of aircraft in a reasonably short time."

Further backing was given in a memo of November 1938. The points made were that shallow dive bombing was valueless, despite the RAF's concentration exclusively on that type, and the angle of dive to be efficient had to be at least 45 degrees. The overwhelming advantages of steep dive bombing from 6,000 feet were considered to be so great as to justify its retention, if a suitable aircraft could be obtained. Finally, if it was shown that even the Battles could be dived steeply, then all Battle squadrons should be trained in this technique.

But it was all too late. By rejecting a purpose-built dive bomber with the Henley or the other alternatives of 1934–35, the RAF had committed itself to the rejection of true dive bombing, and everything else was compromise. The overwhelming power in the upper echelons of the heavy bomber lobby carried all other considerations before it, and by the eve of the war, the equally neglected fighter arm was crying out for what spare design and building capacity there was in order to make good its own deficiencies. There was no room, even if the Air Ministry had been willing—which was far from the case to add a dive bomber program at this late stage. And so the ill-conceived Battles went to their doom in low flying suicide en masse in those desperate hours during the Battle of France in May and June 1940. Years later, Sholto Douglas admitted that the prewar policy of the RAF had been wrong: "It would have been so much better, if, some years earlier, we had developed a dive bomber along the lines of Ernst Udet's Stuka, instead of devoting so much of our resources to the design, development, and the production of those wretched Battles."

CHAPTER 9

Against All Odds

Naval Dive Bombing: The British Experience, 1932–39

The result of having the air arm of the Royal Navy under the control of the RAF between 1918 and 1938 was an absolute disaster. This is best illustrated by contemporary comparisons of strength between the principal navies of Great Britain, the United States, and Japan. By as early as 1933, the Admiralty, which in 1918 had established an overwhelming lead in sea and air power, was bemoaning the fact that Japan, the most likely enemy in any foreseeable naval conflict at that date, was, after twelve years of peace, far ahead of Britain. The British lead in 1918 in aircraft, men, carriers, and expertise had been allowed to wither away through lack of funds and interest.

A minute from the director of the naval air division (DNAD) revealed the sorry picture at the end of November 1933. "It is desired to draw the attention of the Board to the situation regarding Japanese naval aircraft which will arise when certain expansion programs now proposed for the future are completed." The facts showed that with regard to shore-based naval aircraft the program of seventeen squadrons for Japan was completed in 1932, while the 1st Replenishment Program proposed to increase that total by a further fourteen squadrons, which gave the total number of combat aircraft estimated to be in service with the Imperial Japanese Navy (IJN) by April 1937 as 472. Nor was this all, for the 1934–35 program provided for a further eight new squadrons on top of these, giving the IJN a grand total of 590 shore-based aircraft by 1938.

With regard to ship-carried aircraft, the IJN would have 329 by April 1937, including reserves. Two new carriers were under construction, and aircraft provided for in the same estimates would give them a total of 500 shipborne aircraft of all types by 1938. The DNAD report continued: "The full measure of the weakness of our air power in the Far East will be realized when it is pointed out that our one carrier in China has a capacity of only twenty-one aircraft, and that the total of ship-borne aircraft is only twenty-six on that station. At Singapore there are only four flying boats and twenty-four bombers of the RAF (not under naval control)."

Should war break out over China, the result of such a state of affairs was not difficult to predict: "[A]ir superiority, with all its great advantages will go to the Japanese fleet. This will entail continuous T/B and dive bombing attacks." Admiral Rawlings was very prophetic, and he warned that "these figures showed we cannot afford any further to delay the development and expansion of the FAA."

Nor was the Admiralty any less alive to the developments taking place across the Atlantic. Comparisons of strengths and methods were produced in January and December 1936, which showed that the gap was increasing in relative strengths of naval aircraft.

It was further estimated that the U.S. Navy had some 1,218 aircraft on hand against a Royal Navy allocation (requested only) of 305. More important, the British figure included no specialized dive bombers at all. The Admiralty was pressing for such aircraft, indeed strongly recommending them, but not getting them. In a minute of 1933, the DNAD made some very sound recommendations: "In general, sufficient evidence is available to indicate that dive bombing is likely to be far more effective than high level bombing against any target, and 'B' [bombs designed to explode underwater creating a "water equals hammer" effect] development is likely to accentuate this since, owing to the increased time of flight high level bombing with 'B' bombs will be the easiest type of attack to avoid unless complete surprise is achieved."

The minute continued: "So long as the FAA has no aircraft capable of really effective dive bombing attack with heavy bombs, the torpedo is the only weapon of attack which can be pressed home sufficiently to obtain results commensurate with the effort and probable losses. It cannot at present be anticipated that any developments in dive bombers, even with 'B' bombs, will entirely supersede

TABLE 16: COMPARATIVE STRENGTHS OF NAVAL
AIRCRAFT, UNITED STATES AND GREAT BRITAIN, 1936

Date	Service	Carrier Based (All Types)	Land Based		
			F/B	Scouts	T/B
1/1/36	Great Britain	180	34	—	36
	United States	455	154	31	42*
12/1/36	Great Britain	198	40	54	40
	United States	475	158	31	45*

* In both cases, this figure included eighteen fighter dive bombers.

the torpedo." On the other hand, "the torpedo is not the most effective initial weapon of attack on enemy carriers, which will usually be our primary objective. At least in the first attack, which is designed to stop all flying operations, there is little doubt that dive bombing with SAP bombs should form the main part of the attack."

The Royal Navy cannot therefore be faulted in their correct appreciation of sea/air warfare as it actually took place in combat ten years later, and their thinking was on a par with American and Japanese ideas. Obtaining suitable aircraft from the RAF was something else again, as Admiral Sir Dudley Pound later explained: "[T]he navy only receive from the RAF in the way of services that which the RAF is prepared to give. Symptomatic of the latter was the failure of the RAF—who had no interest in dive bombing—to produce a dive bombing sight at the Admiralty's request in the six years between 1932 and 1938."

The most important development for the Royal Navy in attaining the kind of aircraft it required to catch up with foreign rivals was initiated at a meeting held at the Air Ministry in November 1934. The chairman, Air Marshal Sir E. R. Ludlow Hewitt, deputy chief of the air staff, expressed the view that "a considerable change of policy was involved in the Admiralty proposal to introduce a fighter dive bomber, and that as far as he knew no official letter on this aspect of the matter had been sent to the Air Ministry. The question had in fact arisen out of the discussion, which had been going on with regard to the Osprey replacement. It had not been considered by the Advisory Committee." He went on to reveal that he had only discussed the matter informally at the Admiralty the day before and he then outlined the Navy's reasoning behind it for the benefit of the Committee, which is of considerable interest for it reveals how the Royal Navy was viewing the dive bomber in the mid-1930s.

They felt that there was insufficient room aboard carriers to provide for both the defensive and the offensive aircraft needed in required numbers. The proposal was an attempt to secure protection against air attack by an aircraft that might combine both duties but, as he emphasized right at the start: "The first of these was dive bombing against hostile carriers, the second was the attack of enemy aircraft in the air."

On the feasibility of producing an aircraft that would be an effective fighter as well as a good dive bomber, Mr. J. S. Buchanan of DDTD said that because of the weight problem and the need for high wing loading, the radius of turn would be very poor as a fighter. The replacement envisaged for the Demon fighter would not fit the role as the requirements were different, but the Hart replacement might fit the bill as the aircraft would be able to do dive bombing and fly at 250 mph. But after discussion it was rejected as unsuitable. Since it was a fighter, moveable front guns or a very powerful armament of front guns were asked for, but Buchanan stated that if four were required, there would be great difficulty in finding room for them, and they would be heavy.

The chairman stated that it was no good giving the fighter dive bomber adequate armament unless it had the performance necessary to engage the enemy. The essential factor was therefore performance, and this was what they also wanted from the dive bomber point of view. He was inclined to conclude that there was no particular difficulty in producing a dive bomber with the necessary performance, a somewhat different viewpoint than that being expressed at the Air Ministry at the time (see chapter 8). He continued: "It was quite clear that in any one aircraft it was impossible to combine high qualities as a dive bomber with equally good qualities as a fighter." (Eight years later, the Air Ministry was arguing the opposite as a reason for not wanting dive bombers.)

The naval representatives then made it crystal clear that if it was to be a choice, they would prefer dive bomber qualities to be emphasized rather than fighter qualities. Buchanan said that the experimental aircraft could not be expected before about the middle of 1936 and that no service unit was likely to be re-equipped with them before 1938. The Committee finished with a series of decisions with regard to the new aircraft, which can be summarized as

1. To recommend the issue of the specification of this aircraft, with a view to adoption, if successful, in place of present fleet fighters.
2. To include in the specification a suitable description of the purpose and function of the aircraft.
3. To specify two front guns only.
4. To leave it to contractors whether it be biplane or monoplane, in either case wing-folding must be as rapid as possible.
5. To have landing speed of not more than 60 knots.
6. An overall length of not more than 36 feet, with 33 feet as ideal.
7. To leave the remainder of the specification as previously drawn up by the two staffs.

The concept of the "light" fighter dive bomber was the only one to hold sway in the British forces in the 1930s, and the Fairey Flycatcher tradition was continued with the Hawker Nimrod, shown here being rocket-assisted off the flight deck of a carrier.

It can thus be seen that from the very start, the Skua was to be designed as a dive bomber *first* and as a fighter only secondarily. This is a fact that is frequently ignored in the postwar evaluation of this aircraft, which is invariably judged on its fighter performance rather than as a dive bomber. This unfounded criticism of its capabilities continues up to the present day.

One historian did, however, get the right perspective; the former editor of *Flight International* stated that "it was the first specialized dive bomber to enter British service and has been accorded (the present writer feels) less than its deserved acclaim."

This major point of emphasis of role was restated in the resulting full specification (027/34) issued on December 12, 1934. The main details agreed were

1. It was to be a single-engined ship-plane either monoplane or biplane for FAA, to operate from carriers, and its role was defined as
   (a) to disable the opposing FAA be dive bombing attacks on hostile carriers and other vessels and to undertake such other dive bombing as may be required.
   (b) to engage hostile aircraft in the air.
2. Dimensions were a height of 14 feet, 9 inches; a length of 33 feet; span of 46 feet, with wings folded this to be 16 feet only. Half a minute was given as time to fold mainplanes.

On the tendering for the aircraft, Mr. Buchanan recommended to the air member for supply and research on December 13, 1934, that only three firms be asked to tender, and tenders to be due one month from date of issue. The most suitable firms were Hawker and Fairey, followed by Gloster, Vickers, Blackburn, Westland, Bristol, and Armstrong, but because of other commitments, this list was whittled down to Blackburn, Hawker, and Vickers, while Armstrong —who had already submitted proposals for an aircraft of this type fitted with the Hyena engine—could have their aircraft evaluated in the same tests.

In the interim period before the arrival of the dive bomber proper into service, a hodge-podge of aircraft continued to be utilized by the Fleet Air Arm for "light" dive bombing work. Although the much-loved Flycatcher had continued in service with the Royal Navy, it was finally declared obsolete in April 1935. Its successor was the trim and pleasing Hawker Nimrod, first introduced in 1932. A single-seater biplane with all-metal structure but composite wings, it was powered initially by a 525-horsepower Kestrel II MS and later by a 640-horsepower Kestrel V engine. Based on the RAF Fury, but with a greater wingspan as well as the extra naval equipment, the Mk1 had a top speed of 181 mph, the Mk2 195 mph at 14,000 feet. It was originally called the Noorn and came down by way of the Hornet and the Hoopoe. The Nimrod was fitted with either the Aldis or the ring-and-bead sight, and they were interchangeable. Dive bombing capability was limited by the provision of light series carriers under the starboard wing in which four 20-pound bombs only could be stowed. With such weapons, its role could only continue to be the limited one of the disruption of enemy warships' antiaircraft fire—this at a time when in the American Curtiss Goshawk was taking four 116-pound bombs into action.

Deliveries of the Hawker Nimrod to the FAA began in 1932. In the same year, it was joined by the Hawker Osprey, a two-seat derivative of the Hart, the later RAF workhorse in dive bomber trials. Like all FAA aircraft, the Osprey was intended to fulfill a number

One of the early Blackburn Skuas, K5178, on the ground with the old-style cockpit, 1937.

of functions ranging from fighter to light bomber. It had folding wings and, powered by a Kestrel V engine, reached a maximum speed of 176 mph at 13,210 feet. In 1938, the Nimrod and Osprey joined the new carrier *Ark Royal* on her maiden voyage.

These were the two main types in use in the mid-1930s, but mention should also be made here of the two Fairey stalwarts that came along at the end of that decade, the Swordfish and the Albacore. Although their principal forte was torpedo bombing, they had, by necessity, to double as dive bombers from time to time and for that reason deserve passing mention. The Swordfish, of course, became immortalized in its designed role, but tests utilizing this aircraft as a dive bomber were carried out in 1939 against the target ship *Centurion*, with quite reasonable results while embarked on the carrier *Glorious* in the Mediterranean.

During the war, the Swordfish was frequently called upon to perform in a dive bombing role, mainly because of the lack of anything more suitable afloat at that time. As for the Albacore, emphasis was placed in its original design on limited dive bombing capability, and was not just an afterthought, and as H. F. King remarked, the Albacore should be thought of as a complementary aircraft to the Swordfish, rather than as its replacement. The Swordfish outlasted the Albacore in operational use, but nonetheless, postwar judgments are often harsher on this aircraft than they need to be. Although

TABLE 17: DIVE BOMBING TRIALS
WITH FAIREY SWORDFISH, 1939

Height of Release	Angle of Dive	No. of Bombs Dropped	Average Error (yards)
1,200	70	61	94
1,300	70	54	49
1,700	60	72	80
1,500	70	72	95*
1,800	60	54	44*
1,200	67	53	75*

* Target ship taking avoiding action.

obviously obsolete compared with every foreign contemporary, the Albacore could dive bomb well, even if this fact was rarely acknowledged. For example, in the Western Desert operations of 1942, Albacores of No. 821 and No. 826 Squadrons worked with great effect in this role, making 471 sorties between June and November. One historian noted how "their accuracy in dive bombing was proverbial. Yet swamped by the numerically much greater effort put up by the RAF, and ignored by the Admiralty, who were moved at one point to enquire to what extent they were being employed, it was hardly known they were there."

Despite the (perhaps unsuspected) merits of these two contenders, it is a fact that it was on the Nimrod, Osprey, and, later, Skua, that the Royal Navy's experience of dive bombing was based in the immediate prewar years of 1935–39. Firsthand accounts by the pilots themselves stress that the constant practice of this method achieved very good results with all three types. Damage to enemy carriers remained a priority, although, when the Skua entered service with its more powerful bomb load, serious thought was given to just how effective dive bombing might be on heavily armored warships. Any thought of sinking battleships, of course, was merely postwar bravado because of the many factors involved in penetrating the armored decks of such vessels, but severe damage could be done to upperworks and gun turrets of the lighter weapons carried by such ships, while other surface ships, from heavy cruiser downward, stood to be badly damaged by dive bombing as it had by then developed.

A great deal of study before the war went into the effects of bombs on battleship armor, and a whole series of tests was conducted up to the outbreak of war. The ABE Committee was set up in October 1936 to study this question, and was known as the "Sub-Committee on Bombing v Battleship Experiments," which in March 1938 changed to "Sub-Committee on Bombing and AA Gunfire Experiments." The Admiralty constructed a full-scale model representing one part of a section of a modern battleship—it became known as the "Chatham Float"—and this was used for trials from 1934–35 onward in the River Medway. RAF aircraft attacked this with 250-pound and 500-pound bombs, and the FAA used "B" bombs. One result from this was that no bomb ever penetrated four inches of armor.

**TABLE 18: HEIGHTS AT WHICH DECK ARMOR COULD BE
PENETRATED BY BOMBS**

Armor Thickness (inches)	2,000-pound AP Bombs	1,500-pound AP Bombs	1,000-pound AP Bombs	50-pound AP Bombs
7	9,000 ft	13,000 ft	immune	immune
6	7,000 ft	10,600 ft	15,000 ft	immune
5	5,000 ft	7,800 ft	10,500 ft	immune
4	3,000 ft	5,000 ft	7,000 ft	12,000 ft
3	1,000 ft	2,500 ft	4,000 ft	7,000 ft
2	—	—	2,000 ft	3,200 ft

Penetration depended on impact velocity and terminal velocity. Terminal velocity is the maximum speed any object achieves after accelerating at about 32 feet per second per second, when the air resistance drag eventually balances the force of gravity. In practice, the terminal velocity of almost all bombs was never reached, as this would have necessitated dropping them from over 50,000 feet. Impact velocity is the speed that each bomb reaches on striking the target. Dive bombing added some initial velocity of the aircraft, but not enough, in the Air Ministry view, to be worth the effort. Again, the attacks delivered at angles of less than 40 degrees, although accurate, would greatly increase the chances of the bomb "skidding off the armor decks because of its shallowness. Major C. S. Parsons, Bsc, came to different conclusions in his later study. He found that in comparison to horizontal bombing with a 40-degree dive, the impact velocity from 1,200 feet was 173 percent greater. At 400 feet, it was 250 percent greater. With a 60-degree dive, the figures for the same heights were 215 percent and 349 percent, respectively. There is no doubt, therefore, that dive bombing was more effective with the same weight of bomb than any level method at that time, and it would have been far more accurate.

The tests themselves incorporated both high level and dive bombing and were also carried out for accuracy estimation by the squadrons embarked aboard the *Glorious*, although for the tests

TABLE 19: COMPARISON OF DIVEAND LEVEL
BOMB VELOCITIES

Dive Angle: 75 degrees
Speed: 420 mph
Initial Velocities: 595 ft/s vertical
                   249 ft/s horizontal

Height (ft)	Time of Flight (s)	Target Distance on Release (ft)	Horizontal Distance Traveled (ft)	Distance of Impact from Target (ft)	Vertical Impact Velocity (ft/s)
1,200	1.95	322	485	+163	657
1,000	1.63	268	406	+138	647
900	1.47	241	366	+125	642
800	1.31	215	326	+111	637
700	1.15	188	286	+98	632
600	0.99	161	246	+75	627
500	0.83	134	207	+73	622
400	0.67	107	167	+60	617

they were disembarked and operated from Hal Far airfield in Malta. The Nimrod and the Swordfish were used by the FAA (see tables 17 and 20).

Among the conclusions reached by the Admiralty and RAF from these figures was that a very marked improvement in the standard of dive bombing was apparent. It was noted how pilots who had bombed the same target ship the year before at once showed not only superior results to those only trained against splash targets, but also over their own previous figures. Those pilots unaccustomed to bombing such a large target as a battleship were deceived by the great size of *Centurion*, which they imagined would be an easy target after small armored motor boats, but they found this was not so until they had learned the trick of selecting a small point of aim rather than the whole ship, which improved their accuracy. Pilots of No. 812 and No. 823 Squadrons were instructed not to dive below 1,000 feet, but those of No. 825 Squadron had

TABLE 20: DIVE BOMBING TRIALS
WITH HAWKER NIMRODS, 1939

Height of Bomb Release (ft)	Angle of Dive	No. of Bombs Dropped	Average Error (yd)
2,400	62	48	84
2,000	65	48	67
2,400	65	48	72*
2,000	66	47	54*
2,300	67	48	64*
2,300	67	48	73*
2,000	68	44	51*

* Avoiding action being taken by target ship.

only a 600-foot limit, "as this is the minimum height allowed in war." In view of earlier comments, it is interesting to note that the report stated that while this restriction was observed at first, pilots tended to disregard it in the later series. This resulted in an increased number of hits, several of which should be discounted.

On steepness of the dive, there was a variance of opinion. One commanding officer stated that "it was noticed that those TSR pilots who favored a steep dive angle did not get such good results as those who favored a more shallow dive," while another said that "the steeper the dive the less skill is required to judge the exact moment of release." The obvious conclusion was arrived at, that a compromise between these two extremes would probably produce the best average results.

On the vexed question of bomb release height, the summary of these tests read:

While the accuracy of dive bombing increases as the height of release is reduced, there must be a height for any given target in which the increase in percentage hits obtained is over-balanced by the casualty rate suffered. This height will depend on the variations in accuracy with height of release, and will vary with the extent of the AA defence and the degree to which surprise is achieved, but it is obvious that a lower height of release is possible and desirable when attacking a small lightly defended ship, such as a destroyer, than when attacking a capital ship or a carrier. In attacks on capital ships or aircraft carriers the release should not be nearer than at 1,000-yard slant range from the target, in present circumstances.

These figures, obtained with biplanes, were similar to the results of dive bombing tests conducted by aircraft of No. 100 (TB) Squadron, RAF, in the Far East during October 1938. Their old Vildebeest biplanes were the approximate equivalents of the FAA aircraft in appearance and capability, on paper anyway, and reflect another area of neglect. Dive bombing carried out by this squadron was studied but considered of little value in assessing the dive bombing capability of modern light bombers:

The maximum angle of dive laid down in F406 (1939) for medium bombers is approximately 30 degrees according to the limitations of the aircraft. It seems therefore that this method of attack carried out in the Vildebeest does not to any extent simulate the 'shallow' dive bombing of twin-engines aircraft. If the correct angle of dive is maintained the high speed must, of necessity, be sacrificed and the angle of dive is such that, in a Vildebeest, the practice becomes normal dive bombing.

The RAF's conclusion was that "it is intended that all aircraft should carry out dive bombing at the angle most suited to the type." Since they had no true dive bomber, the matter ended there.

CHAPTER 10

Achtung—Stuka!

Germany Re-enters the Field, 1932–39

Initial buildup for the German Air Force had begun with the introduction of the He 50a, and this was to be an interim measure until the second stage of the planned expansion could be implemented. All this initial work was well in hand prior to 1933 and the advent of the Luftwaffe as such, but with the arrival of Hitler and Goering on the scene in January of that year, the increase in all armament research again gained new impetus, and the tempo of the programs was rapidly increased.

In October 1933, the fighter unit Jagdgeschwader 132 (Fighter Wing 132) was given prime responsibility for dive bombing training. They were already equipped with Arado Ar65 and He51 fighters and, to carry out their new duties, were allocated the first He50as off the production line.

In a further expansion initiated on January 1, 1934, another fifty-one of these aircraft were ordered, and although these were mainly for service with the flying training schools, they did form part of the equipment of the first German dive bomber unit to be established, Fliegergruppe Schwerin (Air Group Schwerin). With further ambitious expansion planned, even these were in short supply, and the He51 was also utilized in this role for a short period. A British report of 1936 pointed out that "the He51 forms the equipment of No. 132 (Richthofen) Wing (nine squadrons) and also as a temporary measure of No. 162 (Immelmann) and 165 (six and three squadrons, respectively) Wing, which are intended for low attack of Dive bombing."

So pressing was the need for such aircraft that at one point in 1935 export models for the Chinese Air Force were held over for Luftwaffe use for a six-month period. The 1st Group of the 162nd Stuka Wing (*Stukageschwader*, or StG) was formed from Air Group Schwerin in April 1936; its 2nd Group was formed at Lubeck-Blankensee; and the 1st Group of StG165 was formed at Kitzingen, three He50As being allocated to each squadron at this time.

Although the He50A then began to be phased out to the training schools, they did see operational use during the occupations of the Rhineland on March 7, 1936, when 1st Group, StG165, moved two Staffeln to Frankfurt/Main and the third to Mannheim soon after this reorganization. As Hitler's bluff worked, these half-trained infant dive bomber units were not called upon to go into battle, which was just as well. Nonetheless, the Luftwaffe's first dive bomber soldiered on well, remaining in the training role as late as 1943, and even seeing combat later in the war on the Eastern Front when an Estonian-manned night ground-attack group (*Nachtschlachtgruppe*, or NSGr) used these elderly biplanes against the advancing Soviet forces until October 1944.

In order to act as an operational stopgap in squadron service, the next stage of the dive bomber plan initiated a requirement for aircraft capable of this role, which would be both cheap and, more important at that time, quick to produce. The basic design was for a single-seater biplane of all-metal construction and the two aircraft proposed in response to this specification were the Fieseler Fi98 and the Henschel Hs123. Very similar in some respects, they were to have widely differing fates.

Designed by Reinhold Mewes for the Fieseler Flugzeugbau—which was the firm of Gerhard Fieseler, a contemporary of Ernst Udet, and had Udet's enthusiastic backing—the prototype Fi98a flew for the first time in early 1935. Powered by a 650-horsepower BMW 132A-3 radial engine it had a maximum speed of 183mph and was fitted to carry four 110-pound bombs under the lower wings. Of conventional construction, the Fi98 was flown at Rechlin and performed well enough, but its rival was considered ahead in design and performance. The second prototype was never built, and after attempts to interest the Japanese had met with similar lack of interest, this one-off dive bomber passed from the scene.

By contrast, the Henschel Hs123 was the greatest success. The Henschel Flugzeugwerke had only come into being in March 1933, with Erich Koch as Chief Engineer and Friedrich Nicolaus as Chief Designer under Oskar Henschel, their factory at Schonefeld near Berlin opening in December 1935. Nonetheless, the design the young company came up with was outstanding. Although employing the same power unit as the Fi98, the Hs123 featured some radical advances, the most obvious feature being its clean aerodynamic design, which, unlike the strut-cluttered Fieseler, showed only as a single streamlined interplane strut with no external bracing. In the original prototype, the BMW 124A-3 engine (a license-built version of the Pratt & Whitney GR-1690 Hornet), was encased in a large-diameter, smooth cowling and had a fixed, spatted undercarriage like the Fi98.

It was in performance that it showed up against its rival to advantage. The first prototype, Hs123 V1, was put through its paces at Johannisthal, near Berlin, only three days after it had been unveiled, on May 8, 1935. The man putting the machine through a series of stiff dives was Udet himself, and in his hands the plane performed gloriously, attaining a maximum speed of 220 mph at 4,000 feet, although without any armament aboard at that time.

Enthusiasm was such that two more prototypes quickly followed that summer, the Hs123 V2 with the long smooth cowling replaced by the distinctive short cowl with eighteen little blisters enclosing the valve gear, and the Hs123 V3, which had a three-bladed, adjustable-pitch airscrew. Prolonged testing followed at Rechlin, which ended in tragedy when two of the aircraft broke up in midair, due to the diving stresses being too much for the center-section struts. Both pilots were killed, and it appeared that the Luftwaffe dive bomber program, already in the doldrums, faced termination. However, considerable strengthening of this weak area was made on the Hs123 V4, and when this prototype was tested in 80-degree dives at Rechlin that autumn, it came through with flying colors.

The future of the Hs123 was therefore assured, and a small preproduction batch of Hs123 A-0s for evaluation showed little change from the V4. In 1936, the Hs123 A-1s began to roll off the assembly line, joining squadron service the following year. Main alterations in these were the adoption of the 880-horsepower BMW 132Dc engine, tailplane struts instead of bracing cables as in the Hs123 V4, and a completely metal-skinned fuselage of oval cross-section. As a dive bomber, it could lift a single 550-pound bomb in a crutch and four 110-pound bombs under the wings. The Hs123A had a maximum speed of 248 mph and a range of 530 miles. It was not, of course, fitted with dive brakes and had a designed diving speed of 350 mph.

It should not be thought from this brief description of the German dive bomber program up to 1936 that the proponents of this form of bombing had things all their own way at the RLM (*Reichsluftfahrtministerium,* the Reich Air Ministry). There were many in Germany who held the same viewpoint as the British air chiefs and were vehemently opposed to vertical attack for the same reasons. One of the chief opponents was also the man in the position to do the most to retard development. Wolfram von Richthofen was appointed head of the technical office, and he harbored grave doubts all along. He believed that for any aircraft to dive below 6,000 feet in the face of heavy antiaircraft fire would be nothing less than suicide. He felt that the return in terms of accuracy would not be compensated for by the enormous casualties such aircraft would incur.

His viewpoint must be taken in the context of the state of the art, both for offense and defense, and in the mid-1930s, it had some validity. At that time, the cost-effectiveness of producing cheap dive bombers, able to do with accuracy what a whole squadron of expensive horizontal bombers could only achieve by saturation of the target, was very alluring in terms of manpower and speed of production. Bombsights were primitive and would remain so for almost another decade, and Germany had no need for long-range aircraft, as all her immediate potential enemies were on her doorstep. Richthofen always assumed that the enemy armies would deploy their antiaircraft batteries in the same density and with the same attention to mobility as did the Luftwaffe's own flak arm, but this proved illusory. Both in terms of accuracy and power, German light automatic weapons and heavy antiaircraft artillery remained supreme throughout the war.

Be that as it may, the German Stuka Program several times came close to termination in the 1930s, and the fact that it was saved must to a large extent be credited to the intervention and single-mindedness of one man, Ernst Udet.

This colorful character has been the subject of several books, so only the salient details of his involvement need to be restated here, along with the demolition of the myths. Of the latter, it would seem that Ullstein correspondent Walther Kelffel was the first German to bring back detailed word of American progress in dive bombing in the air shows of 1930. After seeing the Helldiver in action, he submitted a report to the Air Travel Department praising its virtues. The German dive bomber program was already under consideration at this time, and no doubt Kleffel's report provided more food for though.

It was not until the Cleveland demonstration of 1931 that Udet was similarly impressed and was allowed by the Americans to try the Helldiver himself, being given *carte blanche* by Doolittle and the Curtiss-Wright Company after the U.S. Army had rejected the Helldiver themselves. The American company offered to sell Udet one aircraft for $14,000 in talks soon afterward, and on his return to Germany in October 1931, he took up the championship of the dive bomber with some fervor, but as a civilian, his arguments did not carry much weight. He discussed it with Goering, who did not then have the power to help him.

Eighteen months later, it was a different story, and Goering was not only pressing Udet to join the Nazi party but the new Luftwaffe as well. On March 25, 1933, Udet, as an honorary Air Vice Commodore of the German Sports Flying Club, had a position, and that summer, he was back in the United States. The U.S. Navy's Bureau of Aeronautics had given permission for further demonstrations and sales, and on October 19, 1933, two crated Hawks arrived at Bremerhaven as Udet's personal property. They were named *Iris* and *Ilse*, manufacturer's Nos. 80 and 81, respectively, and had cost Goering $11,500 each in the end—an expensive indulgence, but one he no doubt considered worthwhile, for the end result was that Udet joined the Luftwaffe and became the chief "prophet" of the dive bombers already undergoing evaluation.

Udet himself flew the Hawk in a demonstration at the Rechlin Test Center in December 1933 and then at Staaken. But his audience of high-ranking officers, including Erhard Milch, state secretary of RLM, watched his performance in stony silence. The Hawk performed well in four power dives, but the observers remained unenthusiastic, and the planes were released back to Udet, flown to Tempelhof, and put in storage. One later crashed in 1934, and the other ended up in the Berlin Museum before the war, its final resting place being the Air Museum at Krakow in Poland.

There seems little doubt then that the Hawks themselves had little or no effect on the Luftwaffe's dive bombing policy at that time—which, as we have seen, was already set on its predetermined course with indigenous machines. But in gaining Udet, the Luftwaffe had also obtained a man who now put every effort into seeing that the dive bomber program was a success, often at the risk of his newly obtained job and upsetting his superiors. Thus, at the age of forty, Udet became a Luftwaffe colonel with the post of Inspector of Fighters and Stukas in January 1936. Here he found two men who shared his enthusiasm, Major General Walter Wever, Chief of the Air Staff, and Colonel Wilhelm Wimmer of the Technical Branch. Richthofen was still opposed, but when Wever died in an air crash at Dresden in June of that year, Udet took over Wimmer's position at the Technical Office and was then in a position to really push the dive bomber program ahead.

Two things resulted from this: one was his flight testing of the Fw56 Stosser and the growth of a legend-within-a-legend; the other was a competition to initiate stage three of the German air armament program and the first full-scale production of a satisfactory dive bomber for the Luftwaffe.

One of the first aircraft Udet examined in his new role was the Focke Wulf Fw56 Stosser, also known as the Falcon. Its origination is well documented in the story of its designer, Kurt Tank, but it was never a dive bomber. Tank became Technical Director in 1933, and the Fw56 was his first major aircraft for the company. It was designed as a fighter for home defense and first flew in November 1933. The Fw 6 was an advanced design monoplane, featuring the parasol wing, but initial prototypes were shown to have weaknesses here, and the V3 was much strengthened. With the Fw56 V4, dive brakes were first introduced to improve performance as a fighter, but thereby it became a suitable vehicle in Udet's eyes as a dive bomber trainer. He flew the second prototype when he visited Johannisthal and was impressed with the Stosser's diving performance—its speed of 300 mph and the ability of pulling out of a terminal dive from 6,500 feet. He therefore requested that the Fw56 V2 be modified so that further diving trials could be held.

This was done, the aircraft being fitted with the vane-operated variable-pitch airscrew and with light underwing bomb racks capable of carrying six 22-pound smoke bombs. In this configuration Flight Captain Wolfgang Stein held a series of trials in which an average of 40 percent of the bombs hit the target. Udet, according to one biographer, did rather better with cement bombs, scoring 50 percent direct hits. Nonetheless, despite its attractive diving ability, the Fw56 was rejected as a dive bomber trainer and saw service solely as a fighter trainer.

During this time, the Junkers team had been pressing on with their own experiments after their K47 experience. Development was still continuing when Henschel and Fieseler competed, but by the end of 1935, satisfactory progress had been made with the first prototype of the Junkers Ju87 designed by a team led by Herman Pohlmann. In fact, the year before, the RLM had given their sanction for the construction of three prototypes and, in January 1935, issued their official *Sturzbomber* (dive bomber) specification, drawn up heavily around the Junkers proposal to other firms. These, however, went their own ways in their interpretation of what was required, and the Ju87 remained unique.

The Ju87 V1 was ready by March 1935 at Dessau and embodied most of the radical features called for in the definitive stage of Germany's three-part program. From their long experience in the field, Junkers introduced innovations of their own within the basic concept. The finished design was a single-engined, two-seater monoplane featuring the inverted gull-wing, and a very sturdy undercarriage enclosed in a trouser-type fixed fairing, similar to the racing aircraft of the day.

The distinctive wing, which was to become the hallmark of the Stuka, had its center part built integral with the oval-section fuselage of all-metal construction and was again built for strength. The

first prototype had a twin tail to give the rear gunner a clear field
of fire, and the crew was housed back-to-back under a spacious
canopy, which gave an outstanding all-round view. It was powered
by a Rolls-Royce Kestrel V, a twelve-cylinder water-cooled engine
rated at 525 horsepower for takeoff, driving a two-bladed fixed
pitch airscrew of wooden composition. Air brakes were to be a feature of the design, but were not ready when Ju87 V1 undertook its
initial trials at Dessau in the summer of 1935. This probably contributed to the vibration suffered during diving tests, which culminated in the collapse of the tail section, and the aircraft crashed.

As a result, the tail section was redesigned as a single-fin unit,
and the aircraft now featured under-wing dive brakes that consisted of a hinged slat that could be turned to 90 degrees during
the dive, effectively keeping the speed of descent down to about
375 mph, which was the limit the Pohlmann team felt the aircraft
could withstand. The Ju87 V2 also had a new power plant, the
Junkers Jumo 210A 610-horsepower engine with a three-bladed
variable-pitch airscrew. The third prototype was almost identical,
but the engine was lowered to improve pilot visibility, while the tail
fin was enlarged and fitted with small endplates. The radiator was

One of the unsuccessful contenders against the Ju87 during the
Rechlin trials to select Germany's dive bomber type in June 1936 was
the Arado Ar81. Tests with the V-1 showed that more strength was
required, so the second prototype, shown here, had bracings to the
tailplane. This still proved insufficient.

also enlarged to combat heating problems, and the basic profile of the Stuka was complete.

All was now set for the comparative trials, but on June 9, 1936, von Richthofen issued a confidential memorandum recommending the immediate halting of dive bomber development in one last attempt to reverse the current policy. He was thwarted in this by the fact that the very next day, Udet took over his job and immediately cancelled his predecessor's instructions. The program went ahead as planned.

Although the Ju87 was the most favored contender for the position of Germany's final phase of dive bomber program, comparative tests were held in June 1936 to evaluate it in competition with several rival designs. The main contenders were the Heinkel He118, the Arado AM, and the Blohm und Voss Ha137, the last of which was something of an outsider. Whereas the specification had called for a two-seater, the Ha137 was a single-seat aircraft. Nonetheless, it included some advanced features that appealed to the Richthofen concept of ground attack rather than dive bombing, and so the Ha137 was allowed to compete.

Of all the designs considered, the Arado probably stood the least chance of all for selection as the new Luftwaffe's next *Sturzkampfflugzeug* (dive bomber aircraft)—or Stuka, as it was subsequently abbreviated around the world. The Arado design presented a rather hodge-podge appearance, as if spare parts from a number of aircraft had been thrown together. An equispan biplane, it had a fixed undercarriage and a twin-fin tail. The two-man crew was seated in tandem behind a long nose, which housed a Jumo 210C engine driving a three-bladed airscrew. The Ar81 had a span of just over 36 feet and a maximum speed of 214 mph and could carry a single-crutched 550-pound bomb on the swing arm mounting to clear the airscrew like the latest American designs.

Despite its odd appearance, the Ar81 was, of necessity, a strongly built aircraft, but its old-fashioned struts and bracings stood out in marked contrast to the sleek designs of its rivals. The Ar81 began its flight tests late in 1935 and encountered similar stability problems with the twin-finned tailplane that had beset the Junkers prototype. The Arado Ar81 V2 featured a brace tailplane section with inverted vee-struts, although subsequent testing showed this was insufficient.

As a result, the third prototype featured a redesigned rear fuselage and tail assembly and a deeper, stronger body with a Jumo 210Ca engine driving a two-bladed, variable-pitch airscrew.

The Blohm und Voss Ha137 had not grown out of the Sturz-bomber Program as such to start with, credit being given to designer Richard Vogt for initiating it as a test-bed for his new wing form, the inverted gull-wing configuration which he had pioneered while working in Japan on the Kawaski Ki-5 fighter. Indeed, Blohm und Voss was not even asked to tender for the final stage of the program. Nonetheless they pressed on with their own concept in the hope that the inherent strength of the new tubular wing form would attract attention.

Not surprisingly, then, the Ha137 presented a similar outward appearance to the Ki-5 and was also a single-seater design, the final choice of power plant being the Pratt & Whitney Hornet radial built under license. The result was an attractive low-wing mono-plane of all-metal construction with heavy trousered undercarriage fairings and an inverted gull-wing similar to the Ju87, but other-wise, it was very different in appearance and conception.

The Ha137 presented a rakish appearance and was aerody-namically cleaner than either the Junkers Ju87 or the Arado Ar81. It featured an open cockpit, and the BMW 132A3 engine gave it a maximum speed of 205 mph, less than its rivals. It could carry only a light external load of four 110-pound bombs on underwing racks, although provision was made for the fitting of 20-millimeter cannon for the ground attack role more favored by the Richthofen faction at the RLM.

The first prototype flew at Hamburg in April 1935. Although the Ha137 V2 followed quickly, the unpalatable fact that a two-seater was required meant that this aircraft never really stood a chance in the tests. Vogt knew that to redesign it would cripple its performance, but the RLM continued to give backing to the project with a view to utilizing it in the ground attack role which had many supporters, and an additional three aircraft were built. They were powered by the Kestrel V, this version being designated Ha137B. A two-bladed, variable-pitch airscrew replaced the three-bladed metal one at the same time. Tests in the autumn showed that the aircraft performed

The most serious contender to the Stuka's crown at the Rechlin trials was the Heinkel He118. Shown here is the first prototype, V-1, fitted with the Rolls-Royce Buzzard engine.

quite well and the Ha137 V3 was selected to take part in the test program the following year.

The most advanced design of all was the Heinkel He 118, and to many people, it was a mystery why this aircraft was passed over for the Ju87, which it outshone in almost every way.

The designers of th He118, Walter and Siegfried Gunter, prepared the drawings for their dive bomber hand-in-hand with their new fighter design, the He112, and this showed up in the sleek and graceful product that finally emerged. Advanced features were apparent everywhere. A clean monoplane designed to the latest concepts in construction, with an oval-section all-metal fuselage carrying a crew of two in a semi-enclosed tandem cockpit, the He118 featured such innovations as an internal bomb bay capable of housing a single 1,100-pound bomb if flown as a single-seater, or a 550-pound bomb if both crew members were carried; a fully retractable undercarriage, which was also fully enclosed; and an aerodynamically clean silhouette, marred only by a small chin radiator, designed to complement the new Daimler-Benz DB600 twelve-cylinder liquid-cooled engine. It looked, and acted, like the thoroughbred it was. Like the Hawker Henley in Britain at the same time, this completely deserving aircraft was shunted to the sidelines by an official policy that ignored its virtues and emphasized its faults.

It was a larger aircraft than its rivals, having a span of 49 feet, 6.5 inches and a total weight of 9,082 pounds. This was deliberate policy in order to ensure sturdiness, and it was anticipated that the new engine would more than compensate. In fact, the maximum speed for the version fitted with the DB600 was a good 245 mph at 19,685 feet—far in excess of the others.

The first prototype, however, featured not the DB600 but an imported engine, the Rolls-Royce Buzzard of 845 horsepower, and it flew in the winter of 1935-36, some time behind the other contenders. However, the He 118 V2 carried the designed engine and quickly joined in the trials, claiming speeds of 270 mph in level flight, which seemed then to indicate Heinkel had found a winner. This was sufficient to narrow the pretrial choice down to the Heinkel He118 and the more well-established Junkers Ju87, the Ar81 being retained as a back-up, with the Bv137 more or less out of the running before the trials commenced. A more powerful engine, the DB600C, was fitted to the He118 V3, and orders for ten preproduction aircraft were placed at once. A modified tailplane assembly was introduced, and a reduction in wingspan was achieved by clipping the original elliptical design somewhat. In this form, the Heinkel was ready for the contest.

Some people are convinced that the trials were only a showpiece and that the result was a foregone conclusion. Certainly the

The second prototype of the Heinkel He118.

odds were heavily weighed in favor of Junkers, who had a long head start, but in the event, the choice was narrow.

The Ha137 was no longer a serious contender, and with Udet's sudden takeover from Richthofen, any hopes Blohm und Voss might have had for a dramatic change of policy in favor of the fighter type ground attack design were dashed, Vogt being informed that they were not being awarded any production contracts. The last faint anticipation that this aircraft might be adopted for carrier purposes when the laying down of the *Graf Zeppelin* for the navy was announced was also short-lived. The Ha137 did not have the range considered necessary for maritime operations.

The Arado Ar81 performed well during the tests reaching a speed of 373 mph during its dives and pulling out without ill effects, and its accuracy and general performance equaled—indeed, outshone according to some reports—the other aircraft in the role for which it was intended. Its outmoded design was however a fatal handicap, and the Ar81 was doomed by its late arrival for the tests; by the time it was performing, the die had already been cast, and the Arado followed the Ha137 into oblivion.

The He118 entered the lists with great hopes based on its earlier superlative performance. However, its reputation had been based on overall figures, and although advanced as an aircraft, the He118 fell down in the vital role for which the whole program had been created, dive bombing. Flown by Flight Captain Heinrichs, the He118 did not exceed 50 degrees in any of its dives, whereas the Ju87 went in almost vertically. This was the factor above all else that decided the competition in Junkers' favor, but it was not the cut-and-dried decision often claimed.

The final decision was still in doubt when Udet himself elected to give the He118 a last chance to prove itself—with himself in the cockpit. On June 27, 1935, he took off in the third prototype from Marienehe to put it through its paces. Fitted with an interconnection of the airscrew pitch change with the flaps/dive brakes, which was still not perfected, the He118 required careful handling. Before the flight, chief test pilot Nitschke had explained that before going into the terminal dive, the airscrew must be changed to a coarse pitch, but Udet, impulsive as ever, sped down the runway without apparently taking this fact in. The result was predictable. The

He118-Vs was thrown joyously into a dive by Udet, who forgot to carry out this simple procedure. Coming down from around 13,000 feet, the propeller took off on its own, taking the reduction gears with it. The tail broke off, and managing to get out, Udet followed the plunging bomber down to earth in a more dignified manner by parachute. His fault or not, the hopes of Heinkel went up in flames with the funeral pyre of his He118.

This was not quite the end of the He118, however, and Heinkel, who had been selling his designs to Japan since 1935, was approached, quite separately, by both the Japanese Navy and Army on the potential of this aircraft. We shall follow its fortunes in the next chapter.

With the elimination of the He118, the selection of the Junkers Ju87 for the last phase of the Luftwaffe's prewar buildup already underway was initiated at Dessau. Indeed, all preparations had been made in 1936 when the first ten preproduction machines were ordered. The most significant part of the German dive bomber story now began, for with the outbreak of the Spanish Civil War, the new aircraft and the "new" techniques were to be given a perfect setting to evaluate their merits.

The Ju87 V4 differed from earlier prototypes by having a swinging bomb crutch as in the Ar81, designed to lower the bomb clear of the airscrews before release. The crutch could take either a 550-pound bomb with normal crew of two or, with the aircraft flying as a single-seater, a 1,000-pound bomb. In preproduction batches, the Jumo 210C replaced the earlier engine, and a more simplified wing construction to facilitate rapid assembly was introduced.

In 1937, the first of the production models, the Ju87 A-1 (Anton), started to roll off the line and join squadron service. The first unit to replace their Hs123As was the 1st Squadron of the 162nd Stuka Wing (Immelmann) in the spring of 1937. It saw its first service during the occupation of Czechoslovakia and differed from the preproduction Ju87A0s in that it had the Jumo 210Da engine of 635 horsepower, which in turn was replaced by the Jumo 211 late in 1937. After some 200 Antons had been completed, this version was phased out, and a complete reworking of the basic design was initiated, resulting in the Ju87B (Bertha), all the Antons having been relegated to training units by September 1939.

The "Little Angel." The Hs123B was so dubbed by the Spanish pilots who flew it during the Spanish Civil War. The Germans used them in World War II in a ground attack role, not as true dive bombers.

After the establishment of the Condor Legion, a Kette (a flight of three aircraft) of Ju87As was dispatched to Spain from the 163rd Stuka Wing. Although only three of these aircraft were used, their crews were rotated so that a constant supply of battle-trained veterans returned to the Reich to pass on their knowledge. There was still uncertainty about the precise role of the dive bomber, but it was felt to be more a weapon for back area bombing than for close support, although combat soon proved it was suitable for both roles. Evaluations were made by the He50A and He51 fighters, the Hs123 as well as the trio of Ju87As in this theater.

The He51 soon found herself outclassed as a fighter, and these aircraft—which had already doubled up once in the dive bombing role during the earlier buildup phase—were again fitted with racks to carry ten 22-pound bombs for low-level attack. The Hs123 was fitted up to carry out similar duties after the appointment of General Richthofen as the Legions Chief of Staff, and five Hs123s arrived in Spain in December 1936 at Seville for use in their dive bomber role, but it was mainly as ground attack aircraft that they were employed. Rugged, reliable, and able to absorb punishment from ground fire, simple to operate and maintain, the Hs123 proved very popular. Franco's airmen were equally delighted, dubbing the aircraft *Angelito* ("Little Angel"). In response to their requests, another eleven were shipped out, and in 1940, the surviving fourteen from both batches were handed over to the Spanish Air Force, where they remained in service for many years. The Hs123 equally commended itself to German pilots in this role, and although its replacement by the Ju87 continued unabated, it was to earn new acclaim both in Poland and France in 1940 and was resurrected from training schools to serve on in the grim wastes of the Eastern Front until 1944.

The Ju87 A1 was no angel; indeed, its crews promptly gave it the sobriquet of *Jolanthe*, after the pig in a German stage comedy of the time, and a pig was duly painted on the wheel spats of both the Ju87 A1s and, subsequently, the early Berthas, which arrived in Spain later. The pig motif remained the Stuka mascot throughout the war also, but this name did not reflect on its flying qualities, for it was a joy to handle, being very sensitive to the controls and rock-steady in a dive; further, it had a wide all-round vision that delighted those flying it after the cramped cockpits of earlier types.

As a combat aircraft, the Stuka was efficient, accurate, rugged, and totally reliable. Although the Hs123 claimed to be one of the few dive bombers that could really be dived vertically, the Ju87 was equally at home at ninety degrees and soon proved herself in action, seeing combat at Teruel and Ebro, as well as in the Catalonian campaign. In Spain, too, its accuracy found reflection in attacks on shipping targets—at which, of course, the dive bomber excelled. Strangely enough, this feature seems to have passed unnoticed by the Royal Navy, which was very active around the Spanish coast at the time. The ship-killing capabilities of the Stuka appeared to come as a nasty shock to the Royal Navy in the years ahead.

In October 1938, the new Ju87B arrived in Spain, and special Bomber Group K/88 conducted operations with it with increasingly good results, five aircraft being the permanent establishment. A modified Ju87 A1 formed the basis of the B series, being fitted with the Jumo 211 engine early in 1938. This was followed by the Ju87 V6 with altered airframe and ten preproduction machines and the new jigs were assembled at Tempelhof. By the autumn of 1937, the first aircraft were coming off the line. The Ju87 B0 featured an entirely new body line and cockpit, and it had the clumsy undercarriage fairings replaced by spats.

The increased lifting power of the new engine enabled the 1,100-pound bomb to be carried with a normal crew, an alternative load being a single crutched 550-pound bomb with four 110-pound bombs on underwing racks. In parallel with the enormous growth of the Luftwaffe, production of the Stuka rose from 395 in 1938 to 557 in 1939. A rapid change in organization had taken place in these years to accommodate this expansion.

A total of nine Stuka Groups were equipped with the Ju87B by September 1939. They were divided into twenty-seven squadrons with an establishment of forty aircraft. The 2nd Dive Bomber Squadron of the 1st Training and Demonstration Wing had twenty-five aircraft. In addition to these were the modified Ju87Cs (Caesar) allocated for the navy's future air arm as the 4th Stuka Squadron of the 186th Carrier-Based Stuka Group 4, and the thirty-six Hs123s forming the 2nd Squadron of the 2nd Ground Attack Training and Demonstration Wing at Alt-Rosenburg.

This impressive force was ready for action when war broke out with Poland on September 1, 1939, and with Britain and France two days later. Only one untoward incident marred the remarkable growth of the German dive bomber force, and it proved a sobering blow.

In a final period prior to moving up to their war stations, General Richthofen—who, although still harboring some misgivings about dive bombers, had nonetheless been appointed to lead them into battle—had planned on a demonstration for the benefit of assembled Luftwaffe leaders, including Hugo Sperrle, who had commanded the Condor Legion in Spain, and Bruno Loerzer. This was to take place at the Neuhammer training ground with a mass Stuka attack using smoke bombs. Three squadrons were to take part, led by Captain Sigel of 1st Group, 76th Dive Bomber Wing, followed by the 1st Group of the 2nd Dive Bomber Wing, both units attacking in sequence.

The ill-fated Stukas had been instructed to approach the target at 12,000 feet, then to dive through a cloud layer reported to be lying between 2,500 and 6,000 feet (although there is some doubt whether the reports of the latter were ever transmitted), and to

TABLE 21: GROWTH OF GERMAN DIVE BOMBER UNITS, 1935–39

Month/Year	Units in Service	Equipment
August 1935	I/StG162 (Schwerin)	Hs123
August 1936	I/StG162 (Schwerin)	Hs123
	I/StG165 (Kitzingen)	
	II/StG165 (Wertheim)	
April 1937	I and II/StG162	Ju87A
	I/StG262	
	III/StG165	
	I/StG165	Hs123
	II/StG165	
September 1939	I/StG1	
	Ju87B	
	I, II, and III/StG2 (Immelmann)	
	III/StG51	
	I/StG76	
	I and II/StG77	
	II (Sturzkampf)/LG1	
	4(St)/TrGr186	
	II (Schlacht)/LG2	Hs123

release their bombs at 1,000 feet. The official version was that the doomed groups of the 76th Dive Bomber Wing failed to realize that a ground mist had formed and they dived into this, mistaking it for the higher cloud layer, which had subsequently dispersed. Whatever the truth, one whole formation of Ju87s tore straight into the ground at full speed. Only a few aircraft from the second flight realized the error in time and pulled up, and many of these failed to clear the surrounding trees. In seconds, the testing ground was littered with the exploding debris of thirteen Stukas as they hurtled down to their destruction at Neuhammer. Nonetheless, after landing and a brief rest, their compatriots carried out the scheduled attack later that day on the direct orders of Richthofen. Within a fortnight, the survivors of this carnage were spearheading Germany's opening attacks on Poland and the start of World War II.

CHAPTER 11

The Rising Sun

The Expansion of the Japanese
Naval Arm, 1932–39

With the adoption into service if its first dive bomber, the Nakajima Type 94 D1A1, the Japanese Navy soon began to flex its
muscles. Their relationship with Heinkel in Germany continued
throughout the 1930s, but the Japanese always adapted the German
designs to fit their own special needs. Although dive bombing did
not form a very large part of the requirements of the Japanese
Army Air Force, they too maintained a continued interest in new
designs, completely separate from the navy, which gives good insight into interservice relations.

The Nakajima 94 was soon taken afloat aboard Japan's growing carrier fleet, and sea trials began in earnest. From what they
learnt from these tests, the D1A-1 was further developed into the
Type 96. Largely similar to the original He50A Japanese version, a
two-seater biplane with a 550-pound bomb-load, it was re-engined
with the 600-horsepower Hikari engine to improve performance,
giving it a top speed of around 140 mph, becoming the D1A1.

Joined by the Mitsubishi Type 96 by the outbreak of the so-
called Sino-Japanese incident of July 1937, which led to the start of
permanent Japanese expansion on the mainland of China, the dive
bombers were serving with the fleet in reasonably large numbers.

These units saw extensive action for the next three years in the
China theater. The development of expertise in the dive bomber
arm of Japan followed that of the general trends elsewhere but with
the added degree that Japan was the first nation—other than the
U.S. Marines' small-scale activities—to test their men and machines

TABLE 22: JAPANESE DIVE BOMBER UNITS IN SERVICE, JULY 1937

Carrier or Unit	Equipment	Complement
Ryūjō	Nakajima Type 94	15
Kaga	Nakajima Type 95	12
12th Air Corps (Shanghai)	Nakajima Type 94	12
13th Air Corps (Shanghai)	Mitsubishi Type 96	12

in hard action, which no exercise, however extensive, could hope to simulate sufficiently. It is not surprising, therefore, that Japan's naval air arm was a superb weapon by 1941–42, for they had had six years of combat experience to perfect their techniques.

A large proportion of Japanese air effort was solely devoted to the direct support of land operations. This was especially notice-able with the Army Air Service, but the navy also carried out this type of warfare. In fact, an overproportionate percentage of what long-range bombing existed was carried out by the Mitsubishi G3M "Nell" bombers of the Japanese Navy flying missions, averag-ing 1,250 miles from both Formosa and Kyushu, Japan, against city targets like Shanghai, Nanking, and Hangchow.

For attacks on ships a report stated: "It is not possible to say whether the Japanese prefer the torpedo or the bomb as a weapon against ships. Pilots are trained to use both. Much attention has been given to dive bombing practice, and the Naval Air Force have had considerable experience in China of both dive and level bombing against stationary targets."

With regard to attacking enemy seaborne trade, it was admitted that "the Japanese have shown themselves to be particularly ruthless during the China campaign, and there is little doubt that they would make air attacks on enemy sea-borne trade, without regard to the safety of the crews of the vessels they attacked." It was naively worded, but still highly accurate. With regard to the tactical employ-ment of aircraft in cooperation with the army, the report goes on: "The Japanese evidently consider this method of employing aircraft to be useful and effective." The surprised tone is apparent, contrasting as it did with RAF doctrine of the time. All types of aircraft were employed thus, and all types of tactics were used: "Level bombing from medium or low altitudes, dive bombing and low flying tactics with light bombs and machine guns are the normal practice. Aircraft are frequently used as an adjunct to artillery in the bombardment of enemy strong points or artillery positions."

The analysis of dive bombing is worth quoting in full:

> Dive bombing is carried out by light bombers and fighters and is particularly favored when no AA resistance is expected. One of three methods may be adopted; single aircraft attacks, attacks by two aircraft, or attacks by flights in "V" formation or in line astern. Against moving targets on land such as motor vehicles or mobile guns, two aircraft are normally employed; the first dives and opens machine gun fire causing the abandonment of the target; the second aircraft then makes a dive bombing attack on the then stationary target. Dives are normally made at an angle of about 60 degrees, and bombs are released at about 800 feet.

But it was not only small-scale targets that were selected for the dive bombers' attention in this campaign. For example, during the Japanese assault on Nanking, which commenced on September 18, 1937, it was the dive bombers of the Second Combined Air Flotilla, commanded by Rear Admiral Mitsunami, that, heavily escorted by Mitsubishi ASM "Claude" fighters, carried out repeated raids on the city, which was defended by Chinese pilots flying all manner of foreign fighters. The success achieved by the dive bombers of the Imperial Japanese Navy is even more worthy of note when it is remembered that their training was designed for use against warship targets at sea, not land targets. Nanking had fallen to the Japanese by December.

The importance the Japanese Navy attached to the dive bomber is illustrated by the fact that some 428 Aichi "Susie" aircraft were built at a time when the U.S. Navy was ordering dive bombers in batches of only twenty-four to forty and the Royal Navy still had no real dive bombers at all in service.

In the summer of 1936, the Imperial Japanese Navy had issued its next expansion program included in which was the II-Shi specification for a dive bomber to replace the "Susie." Although Aichi, Nakajima, and Mitsubishi all submitted their tenders, having all built models for the fleet, Mitsubishi was passed over because of its heavy commitment in the field of the Zero-Sen fighter, and so the navy placed orders for two prototypes from each of the other two companies.

If the Type 94 had derived from the ideas of the Heinkel Company, then it can be claimed, to a lesser extent, that the Heinkel He70 Blitz influenced the design of the Aichi D3A or Type 99 "Val." Indeed, the navy had purchased an example of the He70 earlier, flying it under the designation LXHe1, but no further orders had followed.

Nonetheless, when the Aichi team of designers under Tokuichirou Gomei commenced work on the new specification for the Am-17, a few features of the He70 attracted them even though their finished product was completely dissimilar in appearance. Once more, the design called for ruggedness and strength, common factors in all specialized dive bombers and particularly so in those designed from the outset to operate from aircraft carriers.

The first prototype was completed and flew in January 1938—a single-engined monoplane with fixed undercarriage that gave it a superficial resemblance to the Stuka from some angles, but this was merely coincidence. The power plant selected was the 710-horsepower Nakajima Hikari 1, a single-row nine-cylinder radial, but this proved to be insufficient once serious trials commenced. External dive brakes were fitted under each wing, hydraulically operated, but the original design did not prove outstanding. The crew of two was seated in tandem and a single 550-pound bomb was carried in the by-now normal crutch with provision for bombs under each wing. It was the first mainly metal dive bomber constructed for Japan, although the control surfaces were covered with fabric.

Because of the relatively poor showing of the first prototype considerable reengineering was done on the second aircraft. For a start the Hikari 1 was replaced by the 810-horsepower Kinsei 44 fourteen-cylinder radial engine. The wing and tailplane were increased and an improved type of dive brake was incorporated. This improved

Japan took advantage of previous close connections with the Heinkel company when both its navy and army expressed interest in the He118, despite its rejection by the Luftwaffe. Here the V-4 prototype is seen assembled in Japan for trials. The type was not further developed but may have formed the genesis of the later Yokosuka D4Y dive bomber concept.

version was designated D3A1 and in the usual comparative trials proved itself winner against the Nakajima D3N 1. Aichi was therefore awarded the contract for the Type 99 carrier dive bomber, and six preproduction models were ordered forthwith.

Meanwhile, Heinkel had appeared on the Japanese scene more with his big He118. It had already been rejected by the Luftwaffe, but the RLM had given the Heinkel team permission to try to sell the He118 abroad, and with his previous connections, Heinkel naturally contacted the Japanese naval attaché. It appeared the right moment for such a move, and once again, it seemed that success was assured, for the Imperial Navy was already looking beyond the Type 99 into the future. The Army Air Force, by this time no doubt influenced by events in China, also indicated interest in the Heinkel design and separate negotiations were conducted in the "normal" manner with both services by the German company. The result was that both placed orders for single aircraft, the navy for delivery in

February 1937 and the army for October of the same year. The navy also acquired the manufacturing license for the aircraft without waiting for evaluation tests. This proved somewhat premature, but they had already paid out 530,000 Reichsmarks.

In the event, it was the He118-V4 that was shipped out on the freighter *Kagu Maru* from Hamburg on February 1, 1937, and thereafter reassembled at Yokosuka under the designation DXHe1 for flight-testing. The He118-V4 was powered by a DB601A engine, with a 1,175-horsepower takeoff rating. Great things were expected of it. Preliminary plans were made for the Hitachi Seisakusho to undertake manufacture. Then came the tests.

These proved to be as big a blow as had those conducted at Rechlin the previous summer. Again, although the He118 showed a superlative turn of speed in level flight (260 mph), it crashed during further evaluations, breaking up in midair. For the second time, Heinkel had lost out. Although the He118-V5 was shipped out on September 15, 1937, for similar trials by the Japanese Army, nothing further resulted, and the He118 dive bomber—outstanding in everything *except* dive bombing—had reached the end of the road.

It is doubtful whether the Heinkel company derived much satisfaction from the fact, but the Japanese Navy were still impressed with some of the design features of the ill-fated He118, but whether it influenced the final design of the Yokosuka D4Y is open to question. At all events, they decided to go ahead with their own interpretation of what was required.

At the First Naval Air Technical Arsenal in Yokosuka, a special design team was assembled under Masao Yarmana to translate the navy's future requirements into an advanced dive bomber for the fleet. The specifications called for a top speed of over 280 mph and a range of some 800 nautical miles with a 550-pound bomb. This materialized in November 1940 as the D4Y1 Suisei (Comet) prototype, a really first-class dive bomber by any standard.

An all-metal, low-wing monoplane, the D4Y had a retractable undercarriage, internal weapons bay with the crew of two seated in tandem under a streamlined canopy affording good all-round vision, which was important for both dive bombing and deck landings at sea. With a span of 37 feet, $8^3/_4$ inches, the new bomber was compact enough to dispense with the complicated folding wing

Japanese Navy Vals taxiing out for a sortie on an island airstrip, April 23, 1943.

structure, and this added to its strength. The diving brakes were of the electrically operated slotted flap type, fitted forward of the landing flap. Its total weight was 8,047 pounds. Originally, it was intended to fit a license-built version of the DB601A, the Aichi Atsuta, but this was not ready in time, and a 960-horsepower DB600G engine was imported. Four later prototypes carried the same power plant.

The D4Y1 first flew in December 1940, and hopes were high that full-scale production would quickly follow to allow the replacement of the "Val" now that the war clouds were darkening, but this was not to be. Diving tests had shown up weaknesses in the wings under stress. Although limited production continued, the new dive bomber, like the earlier American Vindicator, was not allowed to carry out its main task, and was used for reconnaissance missions only. Another three years were to pass before the "Judy," as it was code-named by the Allies, was able to take its place in the battle line of the Imperial Japanese Navy. Much had happened in the meantime.

No such hold-ups were affecting the Aichi "Val," however, and with production lines in full swing, this aircraft rapidly replaced the other types at sea and in frontline units in China. September

1940 saw the first combat mission of this dive bomber with the 12th Air Corps. This unit launched the first air raids against Chungking deep in the heart of China, from their base at Ichang on the afternoon of September 3, 1940, heralding an even deeper penetration of Japanese forces into the heartland of China. Part of their immunity was attributed to the fact that the sky was clear of Chinese aircraft, for with the arrival of the Zero-Sen, or "Zeke," fighter in the skies above the battlefields, all opposition was annihilated, and the Vals were able to cruise to their targets and carry out their precision attacks undisturbed by anything other than Chinese flak.

Fresh targets in southwestern China also became available to the Aichi D3A when the Vichy French Government allowed the Japanese to operate from French air bases in Indochina. The Vals of the 14th Air Corps began flying in October. On the seventh of that month, Kunming airfield was brought under dive bombing attack, four Chinese aircraft being destroyed on the ground while the escorting fighters disposed of those that ventured aloft. No dive bombers were lost.

This pattern was repeated on December 12 when ten D3As raided Siangyun with similar results. At sea, the new dive bombers joined their squadrons aboard the carriers after detailed deck trials earlier in 1940 aboard the *Akagi* and *Kaga*. In September 1941, however, all D3As were pulled out of China. Events were rapidly building up to the long-forecast showdown with the United States, and the navy's frontline dive bombers were put in a period of intensive training against ship targets. There was no doubt that the really vital decision, when it came, would find the D3A operating against this type of opposition, a somewhat different proposition than the poorly defended Chinese airstrips.

The Japanese Army Air Force continued to show interest in dive bombing from time to time. The events in China and the continued tension with Soviet Russia along the Manchurian border, which led at times to all-out, if undeclared and unpublicized, war, gave them further pause for thought in the late 1930s, and designs were finally pressed forward for a dive bomber of their own. Two widely different designs resulted.

The Mitsubishi Type 99 Guntei was born directly out of combat experience in China and was the brainchild of the long-distance record holder, Captain Yuzo Fujita. He saw considerable action in a ground-support role and was eventually killed in combat. He saw the need for a small bomber that could be mass-produced to carry out the combined functions of tactical reconnaissance in advance of the forward troops, coupled with dive bombing ability to offer immediate pinpoint support against strongpoints which it had spotted which might delay any advance. To carry out such a combined mission, it had to be agile enough to avoid enemy fighter opposition, but at the same time, it had to be sufficiently stressed to carry out dive bombing. It seemed an illogical combination, but the resulting Mitsubishi design fulfilled both roles well.

The Ki51 was a two-seater, low-wing monoplane and carried its bombs externally under each wing, but, in its primary role as a scout the bombs were light. It was powered by a single 900-horse-power Kinsei Ha26 engine. Its forte was its good performance at low altitudes and for this it was fitted with small slats on the leading edge of each wing. Its radius of turn was around 500 feet. Designed to operate close up with the leading troops from improvised

Dive bombers over China. The sturdy, stubby shape of the Mitsubishi Type 99 Guntei was built as a cheap, short-range dive bomber to operate in the rugged terrain of mainland China. Code-named Sonia by the Allies, it saw extensive service during the war.

airstrips, it featured a takeoff distance of only 540 feet and a landing distance of 910 feet.

Over 1,470 of these aircraft were eventually built by Mitsubishi and Kawasaki, production continuing until July 1944. Its main operational use was in China. Code-named "Sonia" by the Allies, the Ki51 was a very successful type in its limited dive bombing role, even when used in the more mountainous regions of central China.

An attempt to improve on its performance led to the Manchurian Aircraft company producing an experimental version of the Sonia, the Ki71, powered by the Ha112 engine. It featured a retractable undercarriage and was armed with fixed machine-guns in the wings as well as ten small bombs. The fuselage was elongated and the wing featured a straight centre section with a dihedral angled outer section. However the Army showed no interest in this version. In common with older types, it found a limited employment as a suicide bomber at the end of the Pacific War, but it was really too slow for effective operational use. Although outclassed by most contemporaries and not a true dive bomber, the Sonia deserves this passing note in our story.

Of more interest was the army's concept of the large, twin-engined dive bomber conceived at the same time. This was drawn up in response to the Army's need for a more powerful aircraft with a descent range to tackle the very likely possibility of war with Soviet Union along the Manchurian border. Not originally conceived as a pure dive bomber type, but termed the Ki48 light bomber, the specification called not only for an internal bomb bay capable of housing 880-pound bombs but was to feature a mid-lower gun turret for ground strafing as well.

Powered by two 1,000-horsepower Ha25 engines and with a crew of four, the Ki48 was a mid-wing monoplane. The initial trials took place between July and November 1939, during which extensive flutter was encountered. To alleviate this, the tailplane was raised by $15\frac{1}{2}$ inches, and the rear fuselage was considerably strengthened. The result was the Model 1, and some 550 of this type were built between July 1940 and 1942. Although it was used extensively in China, it was not a great success in this form, being too heavy for its power plant. As a result, the model 21A was brought out, featuring two of the improved Ha115 engines. This version first appeared in

April 1942, but of particular interest to our story was the model IIb, which was specially designed as a dive bomber variant.

Air brakes were added to each wing and with these this heavy aircraft was capable of diving at 60 degrees, which was satisfactory from the Army's viewpoint. A fin was added in front of the tailplane for further strength in this role in some of the later models. Code-named "Lily" by the Allies during the Pacific War, the Kawasaki Type 99 was one of the very few twin-engined dive bombers to see extensive war service (the others being the German Junkers Ju88 and the Soviet Pe2). The Ki48 served in both China and the Pacific, but it was not an especially effective aircraft, its maximum bomb load of 1,000 pounds being low for an aircraft of its size. About 2,000 were built before production terminated in October 1944. Both of these types were not built originally as dive bombers but were adapted later. Experimentation continued by the army, and war experience showed that the need for dive bombers was valid. The result was the experimental Ki66.

The first directive for initiation of design and construction of the Army Air Force's first real dive bomber was issued in September 1941, after extensive studies of the Navy dive bombers. The Army decided, as in the case of the Ki48s to opt for a twin-engined aircraft. As this was the first such aircraft Japan had produced to be fitted with air-brakes, extensive wind-tunnel testing was carried out and, as a result, a multi-strip, semi-retractable air brake was

TABLE 23: JAPANESE NAVY DIVE BOMBER STRENGTH, DECEMBER 1941

Carrier Based	No. Embarked	Shore Based	No. on Strength
Akagi	18	Yoksuka Air Corps	12
Kaga	18	Saeki Air Corps	16
Hiryū	36	Usa Air Corps	36
Soryū	36		
Shōkaku	27		
Zuikaku	27		

selected for use. These were both effective and stable, and one was fitted under each wing.

Work proceeded slowly with the outbreak of war. The first Ki66 was not completed until November 1942, when it underwent a two-month test program. Joined by a second and third prototype, it was sent to the Army Experimental Command in February from which the aircraft emerged as an entirely satisfactory dive bomber but sadly deficient in speed.

Two further prototypes of a more powerful and faster version were commenced, but in October 1943, all work was halted after a total of six aircraft had been built. This was not the final Japanese Army interest in dive bombers, but on the eve of the Pacific War, the main strength of Japanese aircraft of this type rested with the navy. By December 1941, this had reached a formidable degree of expertise.

CHAPTER 12

Conversion to Accuracy

Other Nations' Developments and Operations, 1932–40

Interest in the dive bomber not only encompassed the major naval powers like Britain, the United States, Japan, and the new Luftwaffe of Germany, but it also spread to other nations who experimented in their own ways during this period. The other two major powers that adopted dive bombers in limited form were France and Italy, while Soviet Russia failed to develop any interest until very late in the day. Lesser nations either copied or bought versions of the main types available, but some, like Poland and Sweden, carried out their own research into the problem and came up with some novel answers.

In France the testing of the Gourdou-Leseurre GL430B 1 continued throughout the mid-1930s, and at the end of 1935, this company received a small order from the French Navy for four aircraft derived from this design, these being designated as the GL432. The GL432 was a single-seat, parasol-wing monoplane like the earlier experimental machines and could carry a single 330-pound or 500-pound bomb under the fuselage instead of the 110-pound missile of the prototype. Designed for carrier work, it had a wingspan of under 43 feet, thus eliminating the need for folding wings aboard France's only operational carrier, *Béarn*. This aircraft flew for the first time on January 28, 1936, and trials continued into the war, the last flight taking place on May 7, 1940.

Four prototypes were constructed, and a great number of tests were conducted in a four-year period, but aircraft were never actually embarked aboard the *Béarn*. Their ultimate fate is obscure, but one was captured at Orly by the Germans and then destroyed, while another was seen at Bretigny at the beginning of 1946.

A further development of this design with a more powerful engine was the GL521, which had a maximum speed of 186 mph. The first prototype of this version arrived at Villacoublay in March 1937, but during subsequent testing at St. Raphael, it crashed into the sea. A second model was accepted in December 1938, and additional trials led to a new aircraft altogether.

It can thus be seen that between the wars the French Navy had put a great deal of thought into the dive bomber with nothing to show for it. Subsequently, the only attack aircraft embarked aboard the *Béarn* between the summer of 1927 and the autumn of 1939 were Levasseur torpedo bombers, which doubled as limited dive bombers from time to time. Among these were the Levasseur PL7 and PL101, both of which were three-seater biplanes with poor performance and capable only of shallow diving.

Like most army air forces, the French flirted on and off with the dive bomber concept between the wars, but they were never really convinced of its potential until too late. Typical of this attitude was their attack bomber Breguet 690. A twin-engined two-seater with clean lines, it was originally designed as a three-seater fighter, making its first flight in March 1938 and joining squadron service as the Br691AB2 in October 1939. After the Polish campaign, there was a re-study of the dive bomber in most air services, and an investigation was conducted into the feasibility of converting this aircraft to the dive bomber role as the Br698, but France's collapse terminated all such projects before they had progressed very far.

And so it was that France's naval air branch (*Aéronavale*) alone continued to seek a satisfactory dive bomber of their own before the war. The design for a modern aircraft came from the Societe Anonyme Loire-Nieuport designer M. Pillion. His earlier two-seater, shipboard fighter for the Nieuport company, the Ni140, had not entered service, but he gained insight into the special problems of the navy during its development, while his single-seater land fighter, the Ni161, although similarly not adopted, gave him expertise in stress problems.

Work on the first prototype LN40 commenced in 1937, and it flew for the first time in June 1938. At casual glance, it owed a good

The second prototype LN40 dive bomber for the French Navy. It was later designated the LN401.

deal to the Ju87, featuring similar gull-wing configuration, but it was much more advanced and had a fully retractable undercarriage. Powered by a 690-horsepower Hispano-Suiza 12Xcrs engine, it was an aerodynamically clean single-seater. The lower portions of the single rudder were split vertically, dividing right and left and serving as additional dive brakes. Six preproduction models were ordered in 1936, and after trials, this was increased by a production order for the LN410 for the navy.

Meanwhile, events in Spain had aroused the army's interest, and a land-based version was built, the LN411. In fact, the French Army Air Force (*Armee de l'Air*) ordered three LN40 prototypes in August 1938; the initial navy order for seven LN410s followed on August 26, and the following year, on July 3, the navy ordered another batch of thirty-six. The army order for the LN411 came in September 1939, but almost at once, they decided it was under-powered for their requirements and required an engine of at least 1,000 horsepower to make it viable in their eyes. In the event, they turned to American builders for their dive bomber needs.

But it was not just the LN411 that the Army Air Force could not decide upon, it was the dive bomber as a whole. Indeed, despite the purchase of foreign aircraft being approved, the Army Air Force came out quite firmly against dive bombing on September 14, 1939, and reaffirmed this policy even after the fate of Poland and on the eve of their own lesson on April 25, 1940.

Of the forty LN411s ordered and completed, thirty-nine were handed over to the navy when all army interest officially ceased at that date. The solitary remaining exception was retained by the army, which planned to develop it further. Work continued for a while until surrender forced it to be hidden away. The original airframe was fitted with the 1,100-horsepower HS12Y-51 engine and had a redesigned wing structure. Not until after the liberation did the solitary LN42 prototype, as it was designated, continue development. The decision to hand over the LN411s to the navy was taken on October 13, 1939, and welcomed by the navy, which was still critically short of modern aircraft, their own modest orders being only slowly fulfilled. In fact, by the time of the French surrender in June 1940, only twenty-eight had been completed, in addition to the three LN40 prototypes. In September 1939, there were just three LN410s in service.

With its own program in total disarray as war drew closer, the French Navy urgently cast around for a solution. They found it in the Chance Vought SB2U Vindicator. Although the Vindicator was in service with the U.S. Navy as its first monoplane dive bomber and was popular and well tried, by late 1938 it was beginning to be phased out as the new Douglas SBD came along. Both the U.S. Navy (and the Vought company) were wondering what to do with surplus aircraft in the near future. This dilemma coincided with the French need, and both came together at the Paris Air Show of November 1938 with the V-156 (as the export version of the Vindicator had been designated).

The plan was to take the V156 around Europe after showing it in December at the Sâlon Aéronautique International, but when the French expressed interest, this plan was dropped. The French government had decided as early as May 1938 that the Vought V156s were necessary and planned to order ninety of them (although only forty were ultimately delivered). The prodding behind this decision by the navy was the fact that the whole LN401 program of tests was coming apart at the seams, airframe failures had developed in those aircraft that got off the runways, and production problems and accidents were multiplying.

The American sales team of Lyman Bullard and Earl Irwin spent two months at Orly airfield, while technical changes were itemized for the Vindicator to fit in with French service requirements and handbooks were translated. In February 1939, they returned to the Chance Vought plant at Stamford, Connecticut, with the prototype. Here the company was already hard at work turning out production models of the V156F to French requirements.

The actual modifications were few, the French version featuring a reverse operating throttle, finger-type diving brakes (the Americans were lowering their undercarriages during dives because of the failure of their own dive brake system), and instruments graduated in the metric system. A French radio was fitted, plus French machine guns (which had an alarming habit of jamming after twenty rounds). Although the standard U.S. Navy bomb-crutch was retained, capable of lifting bombs up to 1,000 pounds, the French rarely used such large missiles for their dive bombers.

The first deliveries began just before the outbreak of the war. Five Vindicators were shipped out to Orly for re-assembly in July 1939. Ensign Boone T. Guyton had left the U.S. Navy and joined Chance Vought that month as a test pilot. With his vast expertise of Vindicator operations, he was a natural choice as the liaison test pilot, and he went to Orly to join Captain Gerald Mesny, the French project officer, in getting the aircraft operational.

The French V156 first flew over its homeland on August 6, 1939, and by the outbreak of war, six were ready and tested. After September 3, 1939, the United States' neutrality laws caused complications, but a compromise agreement enabled Guyton to go on flying and testing the dive bombers as manufacturer's property before they were officially handed over to France. After nineteen had been handed over, assembly work moved to Brest for safety, and the first squadron formed under Captain Mesny, followed by a second at Cherbourg. By April 1940, the first batch of forty V156Fs had joined the French Navy, and the American technicians left, since there was no immediate sign of the second group of fifty arriving. In fact, they never arrived in France.

Meanwhile, the decision had been taken to replace the American bomb-crutch with the bigger French Alkan type. This involved modifications to the fuselage to enable the bomb to clear the propeller arc, but by May 1940, this had still not been carried out, so in true dive bombing runs, only underwing bombs could at first be used. The heavier bomb load could therefore be utilized only in a more shallow dive with consequent lack of precision. The French Navy's V156Fs carried a single 1,000-pound bomb under the body, or else two or three 330-pound bombs (one under each wing and one amidships), on their combat missions.

With the formation of the first units, elementary exercises commenced, and since the navy never had modern equipment, the exercises had to start almost from scratch. In November 1939, the first aircraft went to their war stations, although the sole French aircraft carrier *Béarn* was rarely used operationally. In September 1939, she had aboard nine Vought 156Fs and four LN401s but, of necessity, had to land them to ferry other aircraft from the United States. In March 1940, following several such trans-Atlantic trips, the *Béarn* was employed in conducting deck landing trials off Toulon; as a result, the French Navy's dive bombers were used mainly as land-based combat planes.

TABLE 24: FRENCH NAVY DIVE BOMBER STRENGTH, APRIL 1940

Unit	Commander	Aircraft Type	Complement
Escadrille AB-1	Lt-de-Vaisseau Mesny	Vought V156F	12
Escadrille AB-2	Lt-de-Vaisseau Lorenzi	Loire LN-410	12
Escadrille AB-3	Lt-de-Vaisseau Pierret	Vought V156F	12
Escadrille AB-4	Lt-de-Vaisseau Laine	Loire LN-410 & 411	12
Escadrille AB-5	Lt-de-Vaisseau Dupont	Loire LN-411	12

Out of the first batch order of forty V156Fs, only twenty-four were eventually operational, and they were organized in five *Escadrilles* (squadrons) with the available LN401s and LN411s.

Of these, the fifth *Escadrille* had been formed at Houtin in April but was still not equipped and trained. Five more Vought V156Fs were at Hyeres in southern France awaiting the return of *Béarn* for deck trials, but she never came. The reason for her absence was the additional order of dive bombers made by the French Army Air Force during one of their earlier bursts of temporary enthusiasm for the type.

Although even more outdated than the Vindicator, the Curtiss SBC4 was still in production for the U.S. Navy in 1939 for reserve units. Early in that year, the French Army Air Force had placed an order for ninety Curtiss 77s (the export version of the SBC4) to be delivered as quickly as possible. The U.S. government had sanctioned the deal, despite the many complications involved regarding neutrality, and in order to speed up delivery, the U.S. Navy took fifty of their own SBC4s out of service, and Curtiss refurbished them to French requirements. The U.S. Navy deficit was to be made up from the last fifty aircraft of the French order later.

Modifications, which were carried out at Wright Field in Dayton, Ohio, to these SBC4s were simple: installing a new seat to fit the French type parachute B and fitting of French machine guns. The aircraft were then flown to Houlton, Maine, for shipment by road across the Canadian border to Dartmouth. This devious route was used to avoid infringing neutrality laws too obviously. From Canada, the dive bombers were transported to Halifax, Nova Scotia, and loaded aboard the *Béarn* for ferrying to France.

This all went almost according to plan. Of the fifty aircraft duly refitted, one was lost in a snowstorm en route (NXC21), and its American pilot, B. R. Wallberg was killed. The remaining forty-nine reached the border intact and were duly wheeled over to Dartmouth, fully camouflaged and with French nationality markings already painted on. However, the *Béarn* could only accommodate forty-four aircraft, and these were duly embarked in June 1940. The remaining five aircraft (NXC48, C49, C51, C53, and C54) remained at Dartmouth until August, when they were taken over by the British. On February 17, 1941, these ex-French SBC4s were delivered to Rissington airfield in the United Kingdom for training FAA engineers after the RAF had tested them and stated that they were unfit for European combat. These machines were allocated the British serials AS467-471.

To conclude the story of these French dive bombers, after the German invasion of France, *Béarn* was diverted to Fort-de-France, Martinique, and there all forty-four SBC4s were disembarked under the control of the Vichy French authorities. The aircraft were parked out in the open and slowly rotted away in the humid temperature. By 1942, the majority were unserviceable, but when the island finally went over to the Allies, pro-Vichy individuals blew many of them up with explosives.

Italian experience largely followed that of France in belated attempts to produce an indigenous dive bomber. All aeronautical development was in the hands of the Italian Royal Air Force (*Regia Aeronautica*), and the navy had no say in the matter, so dive bombing languished. It was not until the sanctions and possibility of war with Great Britain in 1935 over the invasion of Abyssinia that the need for a precision bomber to attack the British Mediterranean Fleet initiated a fresh look at this neglected form of bombing attack in Italy.

As a result of this crisis, preliminary plans were put in hand for the rapid development of a dive bomber by the Air Force General Staff (*Stato Maggiore dell'Aeronautica*) to the SIAI Marchetti Company. Their specification called for a single-seater dive bomber to carry an 1,100-pound bomb and the airframe was to withstand stability tests in dives from 40 degrees to 90 degrees. Alessandro Marchetti thought that an aircraft fitted with two 460-horsepower Piaggio PVII engines should be able to conform to these instructions, and design work commenced at once on "Program R."

The first result was the prototype SM85 (MM374) that first flew on December 19, 1936. It was a twin-engined monoplane with a cantilever wing and retractable landing gear. It featured a very simple box-type fuselage with a marked upward sweep to nose and tail and earned it the unofficial title "Flying Banana." A single-seater,

The first Italian SM85 dive bomber. Its wooden box fuselage and unmistakable shape can be seen. It suffered from poor pilot visibility and was grossly underpowered despite having two engines.

the original had an enclosed cockpit housed well forward with a simple fairing behind it and had a very restricted view. First flown by test pilot Adriano Bacual, this aircraft was delivered to the Furbara test center on April 27, 1937. Designed to operate against an enemy fleet, the early trials held that spring were against warship targets. Many high-ranking air force and navy officers attended, as did Mussolini himself, because it was he who was pressing hardest for such an aircraft to advance his ambitions at this time.

Two further prototypes (MM385 and MM386) joined the first at Furbara, and these were flown in March and April 1937. Both featured small improvements and a better-designed cockpit. Although not too impressive in its performance, an initial production order was placed for ten (Type B), and this was followed by a second order for another twenty-two (Type C) in which visibility for the pilot was increased by completely redesigning the cockpit as a raised "bubble" type forward with a "glasshouse" extension aft.

These first S85s (redesignated in June 1938 as the SM85) were delivered to the experimental Italian dive bomber unit (*Reparto Sperimentale Volo a Tuffo*), commanded by Captain Ercolani, for evaluation and development of techniques. After repeated testing, they discovered that although the S85 handled well enough in horizontal flight, its speed was insufficient in the dive to be effective and listed among the many other faults found by this unit during the next year was insufficient power, weak landing gear, and the need for variable-pitch airscrews. In short, the plane was not a success, and although proudly displayed as an operational dive bomber to visiting officials like Germany's Erhard Milch in March 1939, it was never likely to be. However, Benito Mussolini expected a dive bomber squadron to show the world, so one was formed.

This was the 96th Dive Bombing Group (*Gruppo Bombardamento a Tuffo*, or BaT) established on March 20, 1940, with two squadrons (*Squadriglie*), 236 and 237, and a total strength of nineteen aircraft. However, all SM85 production had ceased after the thirty-sixth aircraft in December 1939, and on Italy's entry into the war in June 1940, this independent group was transferred to the island of Pantelleria to await its chance to attack the British Fleet.

The improved SM86 was a direct development of the SM85. It is true to say that many of the lessons learned from the earlier effort were put right in the prototype (MM397)—for example, stronger landing gear, better vision, and the like—but it was no more a success than the SM85. More powerful 600-horsepower Walther Sazitta

A one-off refinement of the "Flying Banana" was the SM86. It incorporated many refinements over the SM85.

engines were the major refinements, driving three-bladed variable-pitch propellers, but the drive system remained the same.

This prototype was delivered to the 1st Experiment Center (*Centro Sperimentale*) at Guidonia on May 10, 1940, by test pilot Elio Scarpini after its maiden flight had taken place at Vergiate on April 8, 1939. Testing by the experimental group pilots resulted in very luke-warm reports about this aircraft's capabilities. Not satisfied with the adverse reactions, Savoia asked the ministry to test the aircraft in combat. The SM86, piloted by Scarpini, was therefore sent to join 96th Group at Comiso, along with several Ju87s, arriving on September 4, 1940, to await its chance to prove itself, flying with 236th Squadron.

Apart from these custom-built dive bombers, Italy conducted other experiments and learned from combat in the Spanish Civil War. Italian participation in that conflict was more widespread than that of Germany; Italian aircraft were early in the field on Franco's side, among them being a section of Breda 65s serving with the 65th Assault Squadron (*Squadriglie Assalto*) based at Puig Moreno. The Breda 65, designed by Giuseppe Panzieri and Antonio Parano, was one of the most important designs of the prewar Italian Air Force in that it introduced to that service all-metal construction and retractable landing gear. Of some interest to this story is the fact that during the Aragona offensive of July 1938, three of these aircraft were employed as dive bombers. They carried out their attack on the bridges at Flix across the Elbro River in dives of 80 degrees and succeeded in destroying these very important targets outright. In all, eighteen Breda 65s were used in Spain; only two were lost.

In early 1939, an Italian aviation team visited Germany and observed the aircraft being produced by Junkers and Heinkel, including an impressive tour of the Ju87 assembly lines at Dessau. They returned with new demands for the Italian industry to develop the dive bomber, and a competition was set up. They also recommended that the Stuka itself be tried out for the Italian Air Force. Whether or not the Stuka design impressed itself upon Italian manufacturers as the ideal at which to aim is not certain, but certainly, the design ultimately produced by the Breda team of Vittorio Calderini and Mario Pittoni bore a marked resemblance to that aircraft.

It was on August 28, 1939, that the Italian Air Ministry announced the competition for dive bomber designs open to either single or twin-engined aircraft. The single-engined Breda 201 was more streamlined than the Ju87, but it featured the inverted gull-wing configuration. It was powered by a Daimler-Benz DB601 engine and had a retractable undercarriage and slotted dive brakes of the Northrop principle on the inner surfaces of the trailing edge of each wing, with small underwing dive flaps on the inner edges. The tail wheel was fixed. Piloted by Mario Acerbi, the Breda 201 first flew on July 3, 1941.

Caproni's entry to the competition was the Ca335 Tuffo, designed by Cesare Pallavicione. It was developed in conjunction with the Ca335 and powered by a single Isotta Fraschini IF Delta RC35 of 700 horsepower. The Ca335 Tuffo was a single-seater of all-metal construction, had retractable landing gear, and could carry a single 1,100-pound bomb. Flown by test pilot Ettore Wengi, this prototype was evaluated during January 1941 and delivered to Guidonia for testing, but no orders resulted.

The CANSA Fc12 was really designed as a dive bomber trainer and was a private venture by Fiat's CANSA subsidiary. A monoplane, it was fitted with dive brakes under each wing, fully

The Italian Breda Ca65 was used by the Italians during the Spanish Civil War in a dive bombing role, though it was not built for it.

retractable landing gear, and a light bomb rack under each wing. It first flew at Cameri in 1939 and underwent trials until 1940, but it was never evaluated by the Air Force.

Another design was the IMAM Ro41. A single-seater fighter, this aircraft was serving with 5th Assault Flight (*Stormo Assalto*) and was used to conduct a special study of ground attack utilizing a diving angle of 45 degrees by 98th Squadron, 7th Group, 5th Flight, when they formed the Dive Bombing Center (*Nucleo Volo a Tuffo*) under Captain Ercolani. It was used as a dive bomber trainer during the war.

The IMAM Ro57bis was originally conceived as a twin-engined fighter and designed by G. Gala550. Powered by two 870-horsepower Fiat A74 RC38 engines, the prototype (MM407) was modified as a dive bomber at Guidonia in the summer of 1940 by the addition of two dive brakes under the wings, a bomb rack for a 1,100-pound bomb under the fuselage and an extra bomb-aiming window cut in the fuselage. With these alterations, it underwent testing at the hands of Aldo Ligabo and Commander Mantel. Although, as a dive bomber, it was really underpowered and of limited range, the Ro57bis was nonetheless offered to the air force, and 200 (subsequently reduced to ninety) were ordered in 1942. Although far from outstanding, the Ro57bis is worthy of note, for it was to achieve the only big Italian success in dive bombing with its own aircraft during the war.

Another contender for the competition was the twin-engined Piaggio P122 dive bomber powered by the Piaggio PXI RC40 radial engine rated at 1,000 horsepower. It was developed from the P108 through to the P133, but was not accepted into service. The Italians, like most other nations, tried to adapt existing aircraft to perform dive bombing of various types. Prewar experiments of this kind included the Fiat Cr42 AS Falco. This famous little biplane fighter (the Italian equivalent of the Gloster Gladiator) was adapted to a ground-attack role in 1940. The possibility of it carrying 550-pound bombs was investigated, and during the Greek campaign, a few were used as glide-bombers with anti-personnel bombs (*spezzonti*).

At Guidonia in the autumn of 1940, dive brakes were tested on the Caproni Ca310 in the somewhat optimistic hope that it would thus somehow transform itself into an Italian equivalent of the Ju88. The brakes used were the Ballerio SCA, but not surprisingly, the results were abortive.

Similar thoughts were entertained with the Breda Ba88, with perhaps a greater chance of success. A number of these twin-engined, high-wing monoplanes were modified as a dive bomber trainer. Tested in diving missions in 1940, they were further modified with enlarged wing areas, more powerful Fiat A74 engines, and all defensive armament removed. Dive brakes were fitted under each wing, but the aircraft were not successful and were used operationally only for a brief period.

Additional experiments of a similar nature were tried later in the war and will be described in their proper place, but it can be seen that, if anything, the Italian Air Force was even less well equipped for dive bombing than either Britain or France at the outbreak of World War II. It is little wonder then that they quickly turned to Germany for help to solve their problems in this field.

In Poland, we have already seen how the final commitment to a ground-attack policy had resulted in the PZL P23A Karas aircraft which entered service in the Polish Air Force and was replaced in the same role by the improved P23B, but this was by no stretch of the imagination a dive bomber, nor was there any call for one initially. World events, however, influenced Poland as they did other nations, but the original thought behind Poland's first dive bomber design was the replacement of the P11 single-engined fighter. Seeking to remedy a deficiency in both these types led the Polish Department of Aeronautics to study the possibility of combining the functions of both as a quick and economical answer on the lines of the FAA Skua. The result was the P38/39 concept.

The idea was not exactly the same as the Skua; instead, the Poles planned to produce a basic airframe that could be completed either to perform as a two-seater fighter (the P39) or as a dive bomber, while another version of the same aircraft would be completed as an attack plane or long-range escort fighter. It is the former that we are concerned with here, for the P39 designation was later dropped, and both versions were designated the P38, later given the name *Wilk* (Wolf).

The P38 was, in fact, a remarkable aircraft for such a nation as Poland, not rich or technically advanced, to produce for itself. It was an all-metal, cantilever monoplane with retractable undercarriage. It was originally to be powered by either the Hispano-Suiza or the Foka V-type engine, but these plans fell through. It was felt undesirable to produce the Hispano-Suiza in Poland, and their own Foka engine in turn proved unreliable in testing during development work.

Instead, the Gnome-Rhone double-row radial engine was selected, but negotiations for the license to manufacture dragged on until 1938, while the plans to adapt the P38, redesigned the P38-Lampart, were even more sluggish. As it was, the Ranger-powered Wilk second prototype was not completed until the spring of 1939, and neither of the two aircraft produced had even conducted their trials when war broke out on September 1, 1939.

Therefore, the only aircraft found by the advancing German forces that resembled dive bombers in Poland were some 250 PWS26 single-engined biplane trainers. They had been hastily adapted to carry two 26½-pound bombs on underwing racks, but in the event, there was not time for them to be used in combat.

Dive bombers of various kinds and adaptations served with most of the minor powers before the war. Probably the most active were those employed in China and Spain.

In 1934, the Chinese Central Government had placed orders with Heinkel for twelve He50a biplanes—similar to those used by the Luftwaffe, but powered by the more reliable Jupiter VI engine and designated He66aCH. These dive bombers were shipped out that summer. A repeat order was placed for another twelve a year later, and these had the SAM22B radial engines as in the Luftwaffe version. Known as the He50bCH, these machines were completed in the spring of 1935, but they were held up for six months because of the Luftwaffe's own shortages in this type of aircraft. They finally arrived in China in January 1936.

These He50bCHs were assembled at Peking in the summer of 1937 and had their tail surfaces painted yellow to avoid confusion with the Japanese D1A1, but they saw active service for only a short period before being relegated to training duties.

The use in Spain of the Hs123 has already been mentioned, and known as Angelitos, they performed well. Another aircraft, the British Hawker Fury fighter, also saw limited service in the same conflict. Three of these biplane fighters were ordered in 1935. Powered by a single Hispano-Suiza 12 X-Brs engine, they were first flown under Spanish colors in July 1936 and actually arrived in that country on April 11, 1936, in company with an Osprey from the same company.

A week later, the Civil War commenced, and the Fury aircraft (4-1, 4-2, and 4-3), became split between the opposing forces, two being flown by the government and No. 4-2 by the Nationalists. They appear to have changed hands from time to time before being written off, but one (4-3) was reported to have been used as a dive bomber before being finally destroyed in 1938.

Away from Europe, Argentina took delivery of the Hawk III, the export model of the U.S. Navy's BF2C-1, while Thailand also purchased a number of Hawk III dive bombers before the end of the war and may have used them against the Vichy French in their brief conflict during 1941.

But of the smaller nations, it was Sweden that made the greater strides, initiated the greatest research, and evolved the most advanced theories of the dive bomber idea during the 1930s and 1940s. Their detailed studies resulted in the AGA dive bomb sight which aroused even the interest and admiration of the RAF when Squadron Leader Adams served as liaison officer with the Royal Swedish Air Force in 1938–39.

The Royal Swedish Air Force (*Flygvapnet*) had not been formed as a separate service until July 1, 1926, and by 1931, it had reached an establishment of only 80 aircraft, instead of the planned 229. This state of affairs continued until further agitation led to reorganization under the 1936 Defense Resolution when the Swedish Air Force finally became truly independent of the army and navy.

During this period, Sweden relied on the import of foreign aircraft for most of its front-line strength, and in 1934, it purchased

A wing of Royal Swedish Air Force B5 license-built Hawker Harts,
which formed the basic dive bomber strength of this neutral nation.

three Hawker Hart day bombers from Britain, along with some
Ospreys for naval cooperation work. At the same time, talks were
opened on the possibilities of the manufacture of these aircraft
under license at the ASJA Linkoping, at the forerunner of SAAB,
at the AB Gotaverken, at Gothenburg, and at the CVN (Central
Maintenance Depot) at Malmslatt—under the designation S7.
With the receipt of intelligence of dive bombing developments
abroad, Major Gyllenkrook of the Swedish Air Force sought to
silence continued naval opposition to the air force's expansion
plans by practical demonstration of the accuracy of dive bombing
against naval targets, and the three Harts were selected as suitable
aircraft for this purpose.

The first dive bombing trials were conducted by No. 4 Wing at
Fröson in northern Jamtland and showed that the Hart was both
capable of withstanding such dives and of hitting the targets. "Sensational Swedish Dive bombing" ran one press headline at the
results. The tests were expanded by No. 4 Wing during the early
spring of 1935. Of interest during these trials of 1934, however,

was the fact that the German Junkers team was testing the K47 at Fröson at the same time as the first Hart trials there. The Limhamn-assembled K47 was conducting rocket-bombing tests, and the Swedish and German teams had the opportunity to study each other's tests in detail.

During February and March 1935, comparison trials with horizontal bombing and dive bombing were conducted here too, and again the dive bomber results came out far superior. All three British-built Harts were used in these trials, which were led by Captain Paul af Uhr from F3 Malmslatt, and among other experts in attendance were Captain Alf Svenzén and Captain Hugo Svenow, while the more notable junior lieutenants were Ragnar Carlgren and Nils Selander. At the same time, they were redesignated as the B4 Light Bomber, and delivery of fifty license-built Harts from the Linkoping ASJA factory were well advanced. These Harts were fitted with the 590-horsepower Nohab Mercury VII radial engine built under license at Trollhattan.

The initial tests proved very satisfactory. Lieutenant Carlgren reported that after intensive training, he could maintain a diving angle of 80 to 85 degrees. In the summer of 1935, therefore, the F1 Light Bomber (Attack) Squadron was set up at Vasteras under the command of Carl Bergstrom with dive bombing as its main program. More training in this form of attack continued the following winter, and in all, fifteen to twenty pilots were put through the course. Swedish dive bombing was therefore well established. We shall return to the Swedish developments in this art in later chapters.

CHAPTER 13

The Warbirds Prepare

The Main Contenders before the War: Aircraft, Training, and Tactics, 1939–41

The six principal dive bombers in service with the major powers on the eve of World War II were the German Ju87 Stuka, the American Douglas SBD Dauntless, the Japanese Aichi D3A1 "Val," the British Blackburn Skua, the French Loire-Nieuport LN-410, and the German long-range Junkers Ju88, which was just entering service. The American Curtiss SB2C-1 Helldiver and the Japanese Yokosuka D4Y "Judy" were under development.

The only true British dive bomber in service at the outbreak of World War II, the Blackburn Skua, deserves special attention for that very reason. From the original confusing specifications, the company, beset by enormous difficulties, produced a very good dive bomber whose fighter performance was—and was always intended to be—a secondary consideration.

The design team led by G. E Petty at Blackburns quickly responded to the order issued by the Air Ministry in April 1935. The first prototype (K5178) flew in 1937 and was shown at Hendon display that same year. The second prototype (K5179) soon followed, differing only in having an elongated nose. Both were powered by the Bristol Mercury XII radial engine, and with these, they conducted their trials.

As a result of quantity production orders placed by the Air Ministry for 190 Skuas to a modified 25/36 specification in July 1936, a major change in these aircraft from the initial pair was the adoption of the lower-powered Bristol Perseus XII sleeve-valved engine, and these became Nos. L2867-L3056. The first Skuas began to join

TABLE 25: BASIC DETAILS OF THE SIX MAIN DIVE BOMBERS IN COMBAT SERVICE, 1939–41

Aircraft	LN410	Skua II	D3A1	Ju87B	SBD	Ju88A-1
Country	France	Britain	Japan	Germany	U.S.	Germany
Engine (hp)	1 × 690	1 × 905	1 × 990	1 × 1,100	1 × 1,010	2 × 1,200
Span (ft)	45'11.75"	46'2"	47'7.25"	45'3.5"	41'6"	59'10.75"
Length (ft)	32'.75"	35'7"	32'4.75"	36'5"	32'2"	47'1"
Height (ft)	11'5.75"	12'6"	12'7.5"	13'2"	12'7"	15'11"
Max Speed (mph)	220	225	240	238	253	280
Weight (lb)	6,250	5,490	5,309	5,980	5,903	22,500
Ceiling (ft)	31,168	20,200	30,050	26,250	29,600	27,500
Range (miles)	746	760	915	370	860	1,553
No. of Bombs	1	1	1	1	1	4
Bomb Load (lb)	496	500	551	1,100	1,200	3,969
Crew	1	1	1	1	1	4
Designed Base	Carrier	Carrier	Carrier	Land	Carrier	Land

squadron service with No. 800 Squadron at Worthy Down in the autumn of 1938; six were sent initially.

The main features of the Skua are of interest. The fuselage was of metal monocoque structure in two sections which were joined forward of the fin. Alclad frames, stringers and special sections riveted together, held the flush-riveted plating surface. Special attention was paid to buoyancy in the event of ditching in carrier operations at sea. Two water-tight compartments were built into the main structure, one forward under the pilot's floor and the other aft behind the cockpit.

The whole after section of the fuselage carrying the tail unit and tail wheel was detachable and built in the same manner as the main section to which it was bolted. A light metal fairing was carried underneath for the fixed tail wheel. The tail unit was fixed and cantilever. The elevators had inset hinges and trimming tabs with irreversible controls operated from the cockpit. The cantilever fin was detachable from the fuselage. The rudder was horn-balanced with inset hinges and the balance tab operated automatically.

The wings were in three sections, center and two outer. The center section was former detachable, being bolted under the fuselage so the upper surface formed the bottom of the front watertight compartment of the fuselage. The wing tips were upswept at the tips and watertight compartments were built into each wing. The flaps were all-metal. The undercarriage retracted outward and upward into recesses in the other main planes. The hydraulic system operated the retractable undercarriage units and the flaps on the wings. The pneumatic system comprised an engine-driven compressor, air reservoir, oil reservoir and trap, air filter, and pressure gauge.

The flying control surfaces were operated by a normal system of cables, pulleys and levers; the control-column had a knuckle-joint so that lateral movements of the upper portion controlled the ailerons.

The Bristol Perseus XII air-cooled, sleeve-valve, radial engine was fitted with a controllable pitch three-bladed airscrew. It provided 830 horsepower for takeoff and was rated at 745 horsepower at 2,400 rpm at 6,550 feet. It was cowled by a fairing ring, and the cooling was controlled by gills.

The crews were accommodated in a long enclosed cockpit with a transparent cover. The pilot was over the center section and had an excellent view in all directions, especially for landing, in a heated cockpit. The observer-gunner was seated well abaft the wings, the glass was strengthened and special frames protected both from rolling-over accidents.

The Skua was fitted with fixed machine guns in the leading edges of the wings firing forward outside the airscrew disc, and a single moveable machine-gun on a special mounting at the back of the cockpit. Provision was made to mount a camera gun on the starboard side of the center section controlled, like the wing guns, by the pilot.

The method and details of a typical Skua attack plan are illustrated in diagrams 3-5 and are based on sketches made for the author by Skua pilots. Again, these varied according to a number of conditions including weather, type of target, bomb load carried, whether surprise was achieved, and the like.

Given this aircraft in sufficient numbers the FAA was confident of showing just what up-to-date dive bombing could achieve at sea. They quickly got their chance.

The Luftwaffe's dive bomber units had, by the autumn of 1939, completely reequipped with the Ju87B-1. The establishment totaled 336 aircraft, of which 288 were immediately available for operations. At this time, the B-2 replaced it on the production line at the Weser works.

Refinements over the B 1 were restricted to minor items, the chief of which was a broad-bladed airscrew, while the maximum bomb load could rise to 2,200 pounds, with the second crew member deleted and other modifications. Variants of this subtype included: Ju87B-2/U2 with improved radio communications equipment. Ju87B-2/U3 incorporated additional armour protection. Ju87B-2/U4 was an experimental modification with skis instead of wheels; it was not a success.

The intended strike group for the aircraft carriers Germany had under construction or planned was to be equipped with the Stuka, and special preproduction models stressed for catapult launch and fitted with arrester hooks were designated the Ju87C (Caesar). A further refinement of this type with folding wings and

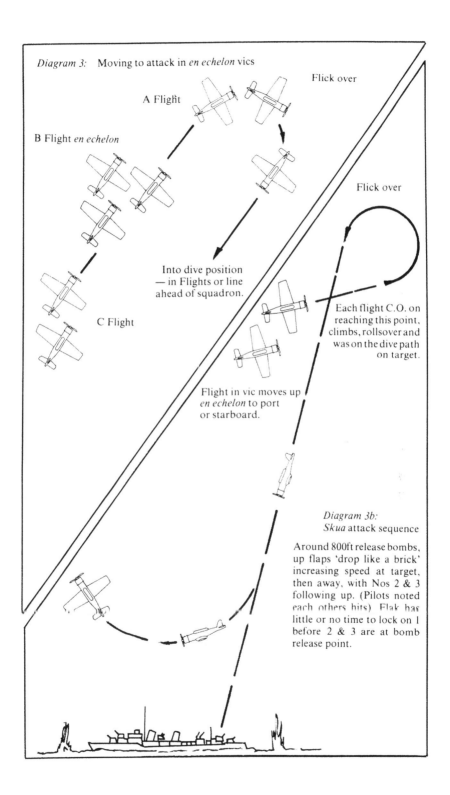

Diagram 3: Moving to attack in *en echelon* vics

Flick over

A Flight

B Flight *en echelon*

Flick over

Into dive position — in Flights or line ahead of squadron.

Each flight C.O. on reaching this point, climbs, rollsover and was on the dive path on target.

C Flight

Flight in vic moves up *en echelon* to port or starboard.

Diagram 3b:
Skua attack sequence

Around 800ft release bombs, up flaps 'drop like a brick' increasing speed at target, then away, with Nos 2 & 3 following up. (Pilots noted each others hits) Flak has little or no time to lock on 1 before 2 & 3 are at bomb release point.

Diagram 4:   Lining up target vessel with electronic ring and bead sight. Gunsight used for dive bombing.

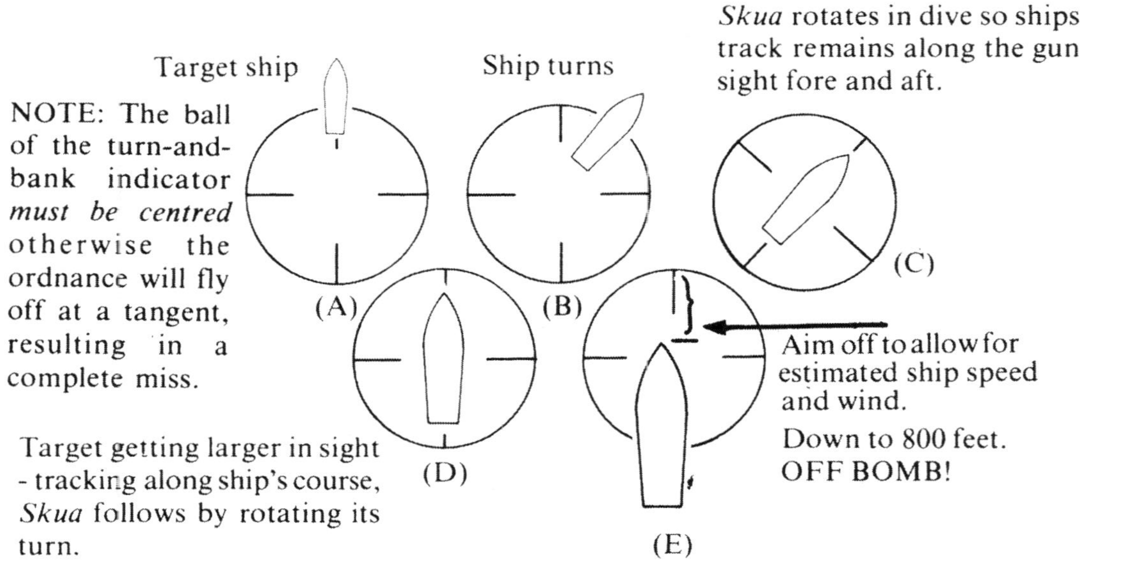

Target ship

NOTE: The ball of the turn-and-bank indicator *must be centred* otherwise the ordnance will fly off at a tangent, resulting in a complete miss.

Ship turns

Skua rotates in dive so ships track remains along the gun sight fore and aft.

(A)

(B)

(C)

Target getting larger in sight – tracking along ship's course, *Skua* follows by rotating its turn.

(D)

Aim off to allow for estimated ship speed and wind.

Down to 800 feet. OFF BOMB!

(E)

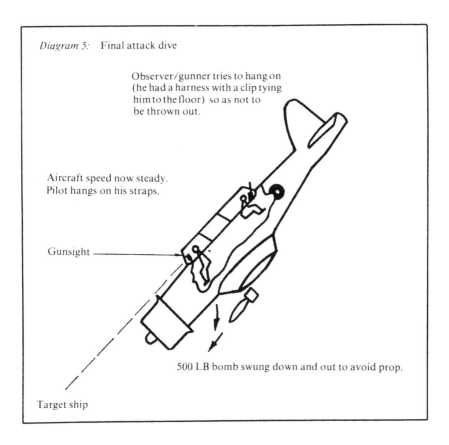

Diagram 5: Final attack dive

Observer/gunner tries to hang on (he had a harness with a clip tying him to the floor) so as not to be thrown out.

Aircraft speed now steady. Pilot hangs on his straps.

Gunsight

500 LB bomb swung down and out to avoid prop.

Target ship

jettisonable undercarriage for sea ditching became the Ju87CT (*Trägerflugzeug*, carrier aircraft). When the project was later cancelled and work stopped on the *Graf Zeppelin*, most of these carrier Stukas were reconverted back to the standard Ju87B-2.

Another development that paid handsome dividends was the Ju87R (Richard), which, like the above variations, was introduced early in 1940. It was a long-range modification for anti-shipping strikes and featured drop tanks and extra radio equipment, while the R2 was a further improvement on this type.

Training for Stuka crew was tough and detailed in order to produce first-class air groups for precision work. The first *Stukaschule* (Stuka school) was set up at Kitzingen, and later, *Stukaschule* 2 was established at Graz in Austria. As a temporary measure, there were also *Stukavorschulen* for preliminary Stuka training, but these were disbanded on November 17, 1942. All operational units had advanced training squadrons (*Ergänzungsstaffeln*), replacement sections deployed mainly at the home base in which new personnel were trained to operational readiness as far as possible. From November 17, 1942, these sections were organized into *Ergänzungsgruppen,* one for each Stuka wing.

Familiarization training in 1939 was done with the Hs123 and the Ju87A, during which formation flying, fighter tactics to elementary standard, and dive bombing were carried out, each averaging about thirty sorties in all or just over fifty hours actual flying time.

Whereas the dive bombers of most other powers were naval weapons first and foremost and hence concentrated their training on anti-shipping tactics, the exact reverse was the case in Germany. Nonetheless, specific training against ship targets was carried out, especially in the units destined for carriers. A wooden cross anchored offshore was one basic target in order to assimilate crews with the special difficulties of estimating height and wind-drift at sea.

Just prior the outbreak of war, the existing formations of nine dive bombing wings were authorized to be expanded to twelve—in addition to Carrier Groups I and II of the 186th Wing. The first carrier group was formed at Burg near Magdeburg, and the second was in the process of formation at Kiel. This was never completed, and the naval units were reconverted back to normal Stuka duties early in 1940, but not before they had seen action in Poland.

Each wing (*Geschwader*) was divided into a staff flight (*Stab*) and three or four groups (*Gruppen*). A group comprised three squadrons (*Staffeln*) of nine operational and three reserve aircraft each, with airborne squadrons subdivided into flights (*Kette*) of three aircraft each. Typical attack formations during this period were stepped-up echelon and similar basic methods common to all air forces.

Apart from the Stukas, which formed the backbone of the dive bomber forces in Germany in 1939, the most advanced German twin-engined attack bomber was undoubtedly the Junkers Ju88, dubbed the "Wonder Bomber" by Goering. It was far in advance of its rivals in both Germany and around the world, and great things were expected of it. The Ju88 did indeed prove itself the main workhorse of the Luftwaffe. It was adaptable in the extreme, and an enormous number of derivations were evolved from the same basic airframe over the years. It was as a dive bomber that it first made its mark, however, and this is the role in which the Ju88 excelled and which concerns us here.

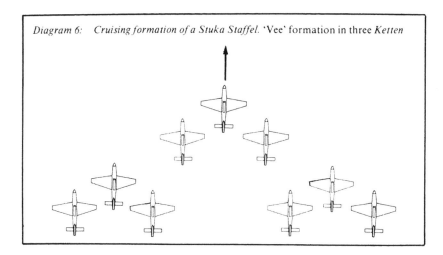

Diagram 6: *Cruising formation of a Stuka Staffel.* 'Vee' formation in three *Ketten*

Diagram 7: Approach period - *Staffel* adopts triple *Ketten* en echelon

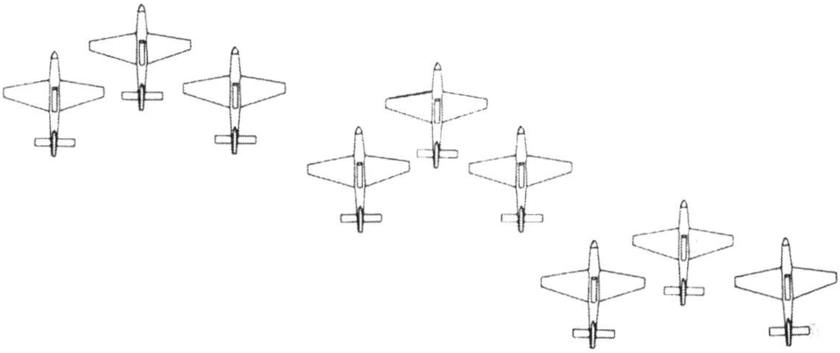

Diagram 8: Over Target ready to commence Dive. *Staffel* is stepped up echelon. Following signal from *Kettenführer* each aircraft peels off into the attack dive.

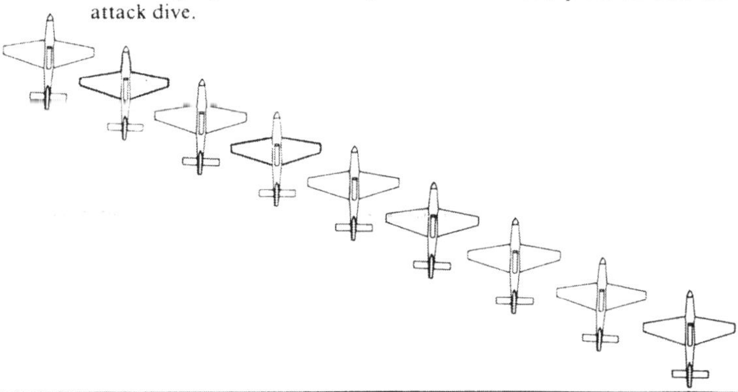

The Ju88 stemmed from a 1935 requirement for a *Schnellbomber* (literally, "fast bomber"), a hard-hitting medium bomber that could outpace any fighter then being conceived. Design work by W. H. Evers and Alfred Gassner, who had gained considerable experience in the American aircraft industry, commenced in January 1936. The original project studies were designated Ju85 (with a twin fin/rudder assembly) and Ju88 (with a single fin/rudder), and detailed design work on the selected version started at once. The first Ju88 prototype was completed in record time and was first flown by test pilot Kindermann on December 21 of the same year. The design was an obvious success and was developed through several further prototypes. Once the early teething troubles had been overcome, no time was wasted to demonstrate the potential of this new bomber to the world, and in March 1939, the specially modified fifth prototype (Ju88-V5) established a new world speed record of 321.25 mph over a closed 621-mile circuit carrying a 4,409-pound payload. Of course, the initial production series, completed early in 1939, was not nearly as fast, but nevertheless, it returned excellent performance characteristics. Series production of this new bomber was initiated at several plants, by which time the decision had been taken to adapt the Ju88 for dive bombing. Apart from some restressing, this involved the fitting of slatted underwing dive brakes outboard of each engine nacelle. These brakes hinged under the front spar and initially caused some problems in such a highly stressed aircraft when extended.

A special unit, *Erprobungskommando* 88 (Operational Test Commando 88), was set up in summer 1939 to test the new bomber under service conditions and provide the initial trained crews. The first operational unit, the 1st Group of the 25th Bomber Wing, was formed in August 1939, and redesignated the 1st Group of the 30th Bomber Wing in September, was soon in action. Because of the unexpectedly slow deliveries of the Ju88A-1 series, this unit included several pre-production and test aircraft to bring it up to strength.

—— ⊨◊⊟ ——

In the United States, the Douglas XSBD-1 was accepted by the U.S. Navy in February 1939, and two months later, the naval authorities placed orders with the parent company for 144 Dauntless dive bombers, of which fifty-seven SBD-1s were for the marines and eighty-seven SBD-2s for the navy. The navy version differed from the initial series principally by having an additional machine gun in the rear cockpit, bulletproof windscreens, and some armor protection for the crew. The production-model Dauntless was also fitted with self-sealing rubber-lined fuel tanks and provision was made for two 65-gallon fuel tanks in outer wing panels for increased range. The offensive load was augmented by adding underwing racks for 100-pound bombs.

Contrary to normal practice, it was the marines rather than the navy who took the initial deliveries of the new dive bomber, and June 1940 saw the first SBD-1s entering squadron service with Marine Air Group (MAG) 1 based at Quantico, Virginia. The first Dauntless dive bombers joined the navy in November of the same year, and all eighty-seven had entered service by May 1941. The first carrier air group to completely re-equip with the Dauntless was VB-2, commanded by Lieutenant Commander H. D. Felt aboard *Lexington*. With the new aircraft, this unit participated in the annual army maneuvers held at Lake Charles, Louisiana, and also took part in a mock attack on Oahu in May 1941.

Further variants entered service from 1942 onward. These were the SBD-3 and SBD-4. The SBD-3 had been ordered in June 1940, by which time the power of the dive bomber had been strikingly demonstrated in Europe. One hundred seventy-four aircraft were asked for, and deliveries began to the navy in March 1941. The new version featured such improvements as twin guns in the rear cockpit, self-sealing fuel tanks and extra armour. The power plant was the major modification with the adoption of the Wright R-1820-52 engine, which gave a maximum speed of 250 mph. The electrical system was modified at the same time. This version was to be the major type used in the Pacific campaigns of 1942. After Pearl Harbor, 500 additional SBDs were ordered.

The SBD-4 came in much later and differed in the installation of extra radio equipment, radar, and the fitting of a Hamilton Standard Hydromatic constant-speed propeller. Some 780 of this type were ordered; deliveries commenced in October 1942 and continued until the following April.

Normal prewar training in the U.S. Navy consisted of fifty practice dives, or ten flights with five dives in each sortie. Automatic pull-out devices were not used, although tested at the Patuxent River Center in 1944. They were not popular with the crews however. The U.S. Navy used the eighteen-plane squadron formation with three divisions of two three-plane sections. The normal cruising altitude was 18,000 feet. Attack dives were initiated by the leader from down-sun and upwind, and the push-over was made from 15,000 feet, with peel-off commencing from top of the stack and followed down in sequence. An unbraked Dauntless would achieve a speed of 425 mph, but the air brakes held this to a normal speed of 276 mph. The SBD was stressed up to 4 Gs, and normal angle of dive was 70 degrees.

The diving sequence for the Dauntless compares interestingly with the Stuka method. The leader signaled the moment of attack not by waggling his wings, as was the British practice, but by kicking his rudders. The pilot then throttled back and lifted the nose of the SBD slightly above the horizon to stall position. The lever marked "D" at his right hand was then operated, opening the dive and landing flaps. The plane was then pushed over on its side towards the peel-off direction of the leader, and at a 70-degree angle, it dived toward the target. The crutch gear was released, swinging the bomb out and down to clear the propeller arc.

In the approximately thirty seconds of the descent, the target was lined up in the crosshairs of the sight, wind deflection and drift being calculated and then translated into action by a touch on the ailerons to regain alignment selected by the pilot's judgment. The engine was kept revving over, just sufficient to ensure instant pick-up when required. At the selected height, usually between 1,500 and 550 feet, the manual bomb release was operated for either the fuselage bomb or the entire bomb load including the wing racks. This was done either manually or electrically, this extra equipment being fitted later in the war. Most pilots also operated the manual gear to make quite certain of release.

On release of the bomb, the throttle was opened up and the stick pulled back, the dive brakes retracted and the SBD hurtled out and clear of the target to reform away from the action zone.

Pilots at this stage were experiencing 5 Gs or more. Although, as Holmberg explained, automatic pull-out devices were scorned in the U.S. Navy, the Luftwaffe, in contrast, had tested these in the 1930s and had fitted their aircraft with the Askania autopilot, tested by Melitta Schiller on the ten preproduction Ju87A-0s. This could be overridden by the pilot manually and was not fitted to later marks, presumably for the same reason as in the United States.

Although considered by some postwar critics to be obsolete before America entered the war in December 1941, the Dauntless was the most modern dive bomber available, equipping two-thirds of the carrier groups and steadily replacing the Vindicator in the others during the first half of 1942. Like the Ju87, it was to make its mark in no uncertain manner in the years that followed. In all, some 6,000 were built.

The U.S. Army's interest in dive bombing had been practically nonexistent from the 1920s onward. The strategic doctrine of Hugh Trenchard and others dominated everything else, as in the RAF. But the stunning work of the Stukas led to some hasty rethinking while others remained blinkered throughout. As a result, policy resembled a seesaw over a number of years. One convert to dive bombing was General George C. Marshall, then Chief of Staff, and he initiated a crash program to equip the army with no less than sixteen dive bomber groups in the great expansion programs of 1940.

The bulk of the first order was for a variant of the Dauntless, known as the A24 Banshee, an appropriate name for a dive bomber. However, almost at once, the Truman Committee, set up in 1941 to study future requirements, reversed this policy, recommending that in the Army Air Force, the dive bomber did not merit funding to any large extent. The U.S. Navy wisely ignored this banality, but the army—no doubt influenced by the RAF, boasted to have "exploded the myth of the Stuka" in the Battle of Britain—decided to abandon the complete program, and General Orvil A. Anderson deleted the entire project.

The vacillation continued. General Marshall was not impressed by Anderson's claims that although fighters could dive bomb, dive bombers could not fight. It was perfectly true, of course, but he was

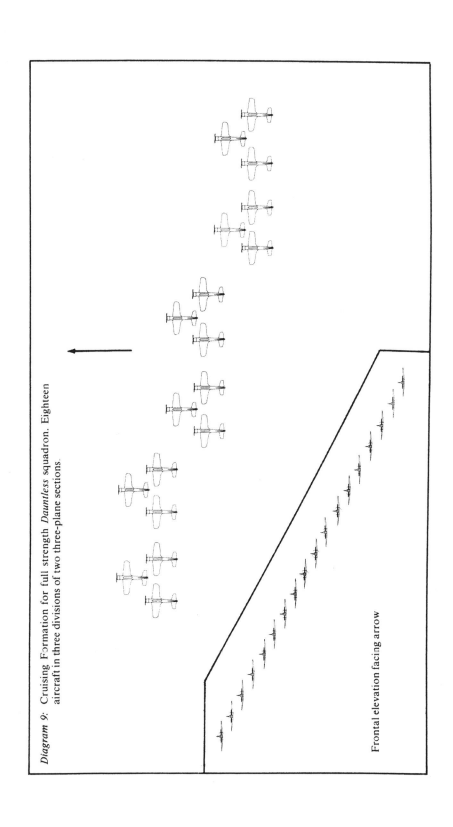

Diagram 9: Cruising Formation for full strength *Dauntless* squadron. Eighteen aircraft in three divisions of two three-plane sections.

Frontal elevation facing arrow

more impressed by what dive bombers were actually doing in the Balkans, the Mediterranean and Russia in 1941, than by what fighters might be able to do at a later date. Therefore, he restored the program, and the production of the Banshee went ahead; the first seventy-eight were the equivalent of the Navy's SBD-3.

Unfortunately, the army was to find that you did not just need the hardware to construct a good dive bomber force, you had to have the enthusiasm and expertise as well, and they just did not have this. To catch up on twenty years' neglect of the type, they called in navy and marine airmen to advise the newly forming groups.

The first batch of Banshees, called A-24s, differed little from the navy SBD, except that the arrester hook was removed and the solid rubber tire was replaced by a pneumatic one. A further ninety A-24As (SBD-3As) were converted from existing Navy orders. The first unit to take delivery for Army service were the 27th Bombardment Group in the Philippines, to whom some fifty-two were shipped out in November 1942. But they never reached their destination.

Meanwhile, the new dive bombers ordered in response to the navy's August 1938 specifications were on the drawing boards to replace the Dauntless. These were the Curtiss SB2C Helldiver and the Brewster SB2A Buccaneer. Unfortunately, although both designs

A head-on shot of the French Navy Loire-Nieuport LN dive bomber shows its twin tail fins, three-bladed prop, spatted undercarriage, and inverted gull-wing configuration. Little wonder that both friend and foe alike mistook them for Stukas in 1940.

promised the ultimate in engineering and refinements—internal bomb bays, increased speed and range, air-cooled radial engines of greater power and reliability, retractable landing-gear, de-icing equipment, armor protection, and so on—they were having great difficulty in transferring these ideals from drawing board and factory floor to sky and squadron service. Both designs were big aircraft by dive bomber standards of that time and were beset by totally unforeseen snags that meant delay after delay.

In January 1939, the go-ahead was given for the two companies to proceed with the development of the XSBA-1 and the XSBC2-1, and contracts were awarded in May. The Brewster plant was expanded but could never settle in its enlarged status. Problem after problem cropped up on the shop floor and dragged on.

The XSBA-1 weighted 3,695 pounds when completed, and with the Wright XR-1820 engine, it reached 242 mph. This was not good enough, and the machine went back to the factory to be fitted with the improved XR-1820-22 engine and a three-blade propeller. This improved performance to a top speed of 263 mph, making it the fastest single-engined dive bomber in the world at the time. All seemed set, and the subsequent enormous British orders that followed this impressive display in 1940 appeared to indicate clear sailing for the new company. But the Buccaneer's problems were not in the air but on the ground.

Curtiss was no more fortunate, although its problems were the reverse of Brewster's; after all, they had built dive bombers before while Brewster had not. It was when the Helldiver was aloft that the problems started. A new plant was laid out at Columbus with the latest equipment, and the navy and army placed order after order for the Helldiver, but the "Big-Tailed Beast" would not cooperate. Already a hefty animal, the replacement of the magnesium alloy by aluminum was necessitated early on, and the weight still went up. Changes in the cannon armament called for the redesign of the wings, and wind-tunnel tests resulted in a large increase in wing area—despite the fact that the original specification called for two Helldivers to be accommodated on the 40-foot-by-48-foot lifts of the new *Essex*-class carriers then being built. The carriers could not be altered.

The XSB2C 1 made its maiden flight on December 18, 1940, at the hands of test pilot Lloyd Childs, and trials ran through to February 1941, terminating abruptly on the ninth of that month when the plane crashed and broke in half. Rebuilt in May and tested at an increasing tempo with the orders multiplying that summer, many changes were made in the design, and not until November were the first dive tests made. Then a second crash in December halted the entire development.

At this stage, December 1941, a total of 578 Helldivers were on order for the navy, but after Pearl Harbor, this was increased to 3,000, of which 450 were be built under license in Canada for the RAF. In addition, the army had ordered its own version as the A-25, but the first production model, SB2C-1, did not take to the air until June 30, 1942. Two more followed, and testing continued throughout the summer and autumn. More aircraft followed, as well as more tests and modifications, and it was not until 1943 that the first Helldiver joined a combat squadron, VS-9, aboard the carrier *Essex*. Even then, the tale of woe was not at an end. We will

Fixing one of the small bombs on the underwing racks of the French Navy's Voughts in France, 1940.

return to the Helldiver/Buccaneer saga later in our story. Perhaps it was fortunate that across the Pacific, the Japanese were having no better fortune with their replacment for the Aichi D3A "Val," the Yokosuka D4Y "Judy."

As mentioned earlier, the prototype Yokosuka D4Y flew in the last month of 1940, and hopes were high that it would replace the Aichi D3A before outbreak of war. But like the Dauntless, the Val was destined to soldier on and carry the bulk of the air-sea war in the Pacific on its own. The reasons were very similar to the American difficulties.

The testing of the five Yokosuka D4Y prototypes fitted with the Daimler-Benz engine had shown marked wing flutter and structural weaknesses when diving. Such was the urgency of the program, however, that the production line was kept in operation, but a strict embargo was enforced on actual dive bombing by this aircraft. The first D4Ys therefore went to war as reconnaissance machines and not in the role for which they had been designed. Even so, only two dozen of this type, the D4Y1-C, had been completed by late spring 1943. It was in March of that year that the wings' structural problems were finally resolved and the first Suisei (Comet) dive bombers joined the fleet. They were fitted with the Aichi Atsuta 21 engine (Japanese-built version of the German DB601) as the Model 11 Carrier Bomber.

In order to fill the gap, the Aichi D3A had to be stretched and this was achieved by fitting the 1,300-horsepower Kinsei 54 engine and larger fuel tanks. A few modifications to the fuselage were also incorporated and the new version began entering service as the D3A2 (or Model 22) in the autumn of 1942, after 478 D3Als had been completed. Sub-contracted to the Showa Company as well, a total of 1,016 Model 22s were produced up to the end of the war.

An even more advanced dive bomber development intended to replace both the Val and the Judy was the Aichi B7A Ryusei (Shooting Star), dubbed "Grace" by the Allies. Another very big bomber by carrier standard, the Grace had a span of 47 feet, 3 inches, and was powered by a 1,670-horsepower Nakajima Homare

23 engine, which gave it a maximum speed of 352 mph; and the bomb load was 1,760 pounds. We will return to the development of this powerful aircraft in a later section.

And so the dive bomber went to war.

CHAPTER 14

Blitzkrieg!

The War Years: Germany, 1939–40

Germany commenced hostilities against Poland at 4:45 A.M. on September 1, 1939, but the first dive bomber mission actually preceded this by some minutes, as three Ju87Bs under Bruno Dilley carried out a surprise assault on the bridges at Dirschau on the River Vistula some time before this. The three aircraft from 3/StGI were given the task of cutting the detonation leads by which the Poles hoped to destroy the bridges and hold up the German advance. So the first true bombing mission of World War II was a dive bombing one.

The Polish campaign was the first demonstration to the world of the blitzkrieg technique, with fast, mobile forces spearheaded by armored units and dive bombers, blasting their way through the defenses and old-fashioned military units of the enemy, encircling them and destroying them piecemeal. The pattern that developed was to become a familiar one.

The initial strikes were directed at the airfields and ships of the Polish Navy. Misty weather conditions and the dispersal of Polish fighters to hidden airstrips somewhat nullified the first attacks, but soon the dive bomber was striking hard with telling effect. Two groups of the 77th Stuka Wing (StG 77) under Colonel Schwarzkopff were ready at Neudorf, west of Oppeln, and they initially attacked Lublinitz. The 1st Group, 76th Stuka Wing (StG 76), led by Hauptmann Sigel, struck Wielun. The 2nd Stuka Wing (StG 2) struck at a variety of airfield targets; those its 1st Group, under Colonel Dinort, were assigned the airfield at Krakow but aborted their mission and instead hit smaller airfields closer to the border, tangling with

Polish fighters and losing one dive bomber while destroying one of the enemy in return.

The 1st Group of the 1st Stuka Wing (StG 1) attacked the radio stations of Babice and Lacy but found it difficult to destroy the masts by bombing alone. To deal with the warships of the Polish fleet, strikes were mounted for several days against the Bay of Hela and other ports by the naval Stuka unit 4/186 and the 1st and 2nd Groups of the 2nd Stuka Wing, reinforced by the 4th (Stuka) Group of the 1st Training and Demonstration Wing (LG 1). The first success was the sinking of the torpedo boat *Mazur* by Hauptmann Kogl at Okswie. The minelayer *Gryf* was hit and burned for two days before sinking. The only casualty was the aircraft of Oberst Czuprina, which was destroyed, although others were damaged. The next day, the *Gdynie* and *Gdansk* were sunk in the Gulf of Danzig by the 4th Group of the 1st Training and Demonstration Wing, and on September 3, attacks by 4/186 went in against the destroyer *Wicher* and minesweeper *Mewa* at Hela, and both Karl-Hermann Lion and Oberleutnant Rummel scored direct hits on the destroyer. Both vessels sank, and they were joined on September 6 by the gunboat *General Haller*, while her sister ship, *Kommandant Pilsoski*, was badly damaged and had to be scuttled later.

And so it continued. The minesweeper *Czapla* and *Jaskolka* were sunk by Stukas on September 14, and the remaining warships were either forced to flee to England or neutral ports, while others were captured intact. The accuracy and power of the dive bomber, first demonstrated in Spain against ships, was shown to be deadly.

On land, the close cooperation between the armored columns and the dive bombers was also demonstrated. Liaison officers kept up with the advance and directed Stuka strikes against strongpoints, artillery, bridges, and troop concentrations, crippling the enemy and restricting his movements. On the first day of battle, the 1st Group, 2nd Stuka Wing, found a Polish cavalry unit at Wielun, and the thirty Stukas destroyed it. On September 2, the 77th Stuka Wing inflicted similar carnage on an infantry column at Radomsko, and 1st Group of the 2nd Stuka Wing and the 1st Group of the 76th Stuka Wing wiped out a disembarking troop train at Piotrkow. The 2nd Training and Demonstration Wing (LG 2) hit Dzialoszyn with similar effect, and then the dive bombers were switched with high

This photograph of the Ju87B was later altered to recreate an incident when a navalized Stuka jettisoned its undercarriage during the Polish campaign of 1939. The incident happened, but the picture was fake.

speed to the southern front where they bombed Polish troops at Tschenstochau.

Some losses were sustained when unescorted Ju87s ran into Polish fighters on September 5. The Polish 114th Fighter Squadron intercepted fifteen Stukas and shot down two of them. By the end of the week, this unit had claimed ten Ju87s, and similarly, III/Dyon was credited with destroying three Stukas on September 4 and three or four others over Torun bridge on September 6. But the whole campaign cost Germany a total of only thirty-one dive bombers—a minimal loss against the results they achieved.

At the Battle of Ilza on September 8-9, Richthofen sent in 135 Stukas in nonstop attacks on the Polish army trapped there. Repeated assaults with 110-pound fragmentation bombs and machine-gun fire decimated the Polish ranks, and they surrendered on the thirteenth. A last-ditch attempt by the Poles to inflict a defeat on the German armies took place during the Battle of Burza between September 9 and 12. Massed dive bomber attacks were mounted from forward airstrips at Tschenstochau and Krusryna, and the newly formed 2nd Group, 51st Stuka Wing (StG 51) moved up in support. The Kutno pocket was dive bombed endlessly, and the Poles were forced to retreat back across the Vistula in confusion, 170,000 of them laying down their arms by the nineteenth and opening the way to Warsaw itself.

By September 25, the city was surrounded, and to prevent heavy street fighting, some 240 Ju87s were employed in round-the-clock dive bombing in Operation Seaside. They were reinforced by Ju52/3m transports dropping incendiaries. The attacks lasted the whole day, by which time Warsaw was in flames. On the twenty-sixth, its surrender was offered. The garrison at Modlin still held out, but the Stuka groups dropped 318 tons of bombs on the fortress on September 26–27, and the Poles gave up on the twenty-eighth.

It had been a remarkable vindication of the dive bomber. For the loss of thirty-one Stukas—eighteen of them to fighter attack—Poland had been brought to her knees in less than a month. The Germans had learned a great deal from the campaign and now planned to put those lessons into effect on the Western Front, but bad weather postponed this until the spring of 1940. Meanwhile, dive bomber production was substantially increased.

The larger long-range dive bombers, the Ju88s, had also had their baptism of fire. Several dive bombing attacks were conducted against the main British fleet anchorage at Scapa Flow and in the Firth of Forth, during which several cruisers and destroyers were hit and damaged, including the *Norfolk, Edinburgh,* and *Mohawk.*

The next test of these units came with the German invasion of Norway in April 1940. Only one Ju87 unit was involved—the 1st Group of the 1st Stuka Wing under Hauptman Hozzel, which operated at first from Holtenau near Kiel. Their first mission was to bomb the fortress of Oskarsborg and Akershus, which guarded the seaward approaches to Oslo. Twenty-two Ju87s attacked the fortresses, which were carved out of solid rock in places, and scored many direct hits. The Stukas then moved into Fornebu field itself, close to the Norwegian capital, and April 9, they were ready to cooperate in the drive north by the German army.

Employing a degree of flexibility the Allies were never able to match, this unit moved up the coast, first to Sola near Stavanger and then Vaernes near Trondheim. Again, their close-support effect was vital, blasting the stumbling Allied columns in the snow around Namsos, Aandalsnes, and finally Narvik. In order to improve their effect, they were reinforced by some of the new long-range Ju87Rs, which were brought in in May. With their two 66-gallon drop tanks, they had a radius of action of 400 miles—compared with the 156 of the Ju87Bs—and they quickly proved their worth.

Some British Gladiator fighters were hastily flown in and operated from a frozen lake before the Stukas found them and destroyed them, but the Ju87s lost three or four of their number in this action. The main Allied reaction could only come from the sea, and the Ju87s and Ju88s quickly found themselves in action with the navies of Great Britain and France off the coast. They hit and heavily damaged the heavy cruiser *Suffolk* on April 19 after she had bombarded Sola, and many attacks were made on the battleships and carriers of the Home Fleet; the destroyer *Eclipse* was badly damaged.

The greatest impact was made by the dive bombers on the smaller ships that were operating in the restricted fjords, and young aces like Hozzel, Grenzel, Mobus, and Schaefer all earned the Knight's Cross in the attacks on Allied shipping at this time. During the evacuation of Namsos on May 3, two large destroyers, the British *Gurkha* and the French *Bison*, were sunk by Stukas. Two days later, the large Polish liner *Chrobry* was hit amidships by Stukas with a 550-pound bomb, which started large fires, and the liner had to be sunk. On May 30, the AA sloop *Bittern* had her entire stern blown off by a Stuka bomb and also had to be sunk.

Before Norway finally fell, however, the main dive bomber actions were taking place far to the south. For the decisive battle in the West in 1940, the Luftwaffe had a total of 324 Ju87 dive bombers deployed.

The story of the Stuka's role in the Battle of France was a repeat of their success in Poland, for the Allies had learned little, while the Germans had made improvements to their technique, which led to even greater efficiency. After the normal pinpoint attacks against airfields and fixed fortifications, and after lines had opened up the Allied front at selected points, the panzers roared through the gaps. It then became the dive bombers' role to keep the enemy paralyzed, pulverizing his troops and artillery, cutting his supply lines, pounding his reserves, and smashing any force that seemed to be making a stand.

The advanced troops had wireless contact with the Stuka control near headquarters, and by reference to a map grid, any strongpoint could be neutralized within a short while, and then the troops would press forward once more. An additional factor was noticed at this time. The effect of a dive bomber in a steep dive was found to have a numbing effect on unseasoned troops not experienced in being on the receiving end or trained to cope with it. In April 1940, the 1st Group of the 2nd Stuka Wing at Cologne-Ostheim airfield fitted makeshift sirens to the legs of their aircraft to enhance this noise, and so successful was it that it was adopted official by all Stuka units. The Germans called this device the "trombones of Jericho."

The initial dive bomber attacks were at airfields and fortresses near Liege in Belgium. Fort Eben Emael was taken by shock troops after a Stuka assault, and the defenses of the River Maas were forced. At Moerdijk, Stukas struck at defense works and antiaircraft positions over the Diep from the tenth through to the twelfth. Then they suddenly vanished. They were moved south to support the panzer thrusts as Sedan.

TABLE 26: STUKA ORDER OF BATTLE, MAY 10, 1940

Luftflotte and CO	Army Group and Area of Ops	Fliegerkorps and CO	Unit and Type of Aircraft
2	B	VIII	StG1 — Ju87
Kesselring	Belgium and Netherlands	Von Richthofen	StG2 — Ju87
			StG77 — Ju87
		IV	LG1 — Ju88
		Keller	StG3 — Ju87
3	A	II	II/StG1 — Ju87
Sperrle	Luxembourg and the Meuse	Loerzer	IV/St/LG1 — Ju87

On May 13, some 700 aircraft were in the air over Sedan, of which 200 were Ju87s. They saturated the French defenses, flying 200 sorties on that day. Both the 2nd and 77th Dive Bomber Wings were involved, and they quickly opened up the bridgehead so that Hoth's armored columns could pour through. Losses were light except for one fierce action when five Curtiss Hawk fighters of the French air force caught a Stuka force dive bombing a motorized column in the Ardennes on the twelfth and claimed to have destroyed no less than sixteen of them. This amounted to a quarter of the Stuka losses for the entire campaign. But by the end of the day, the German tanks were over the river and racing through hordes of fleeing French soldiers who abandoned their guns and threw away their rifles whenever Stukas appeared.

The short range of the Ju87 made it essential for the Stuka groups to move their forward bases almost daily, but their ground organization was up to the task. From May 15, the Stukas were constantly on the move across northern France. Allied counterattacks were delayed and, even when delivered, lacked the power to burst through like the German Stuka-tipped wedges. On May 17, the French 4th Armored Division, commanded by Charles de Gaulle, made one such attempt to cut the long corridor the panzers were using. With 150 tanks, de Gaulle thrust north toward Montcornet on the River Serre. They made initial gains and then were bogged down under continual dive bombing. On May 19, they struck out against Laon toward the Serre, now only nine miles away, but they were brought to a grinding halt by evening.

It proved difficult actually to destroy individual tanks by bombing, but the Henschel 123 came into its own in a classic attack on May 22 near Cambrai. Commanded by Hauptmann Weiss, the 2nd Group of the 2nd Training and Demonstration Wing attacked a French column of forty tanks and 150 trucks at low level with 100-pound bombs and quickly knocked out five tanks. Further attacks stopped the French in their tracks.

When the British attacked south from Arras, it was the Stuka attacks that brought them to a standstill in a short time, and by the next morning, the town was in German hands. As the Allied northern armies withdrew to the Channel ports of Boulogne, Calais, and Dunkirk, the Stuka units moved up to deliver the coup de grace, occupying St. Quentin on the twenty-third. On May 25, the 1st Stuka Wing was in action at Amiens, and the 77th Stuka Wing operated with good effect against French artillery around their new forward base.

The next phase was the elimination of the fighting garrisons at these ports. On May 25, the 2nd Stuka Wing mounted heavy attacks on Boulogne, which fell that same morning. At Calais, the British were fighting hard, and the 1st Stuka Wing devoted its entire strength to crushing this resistance. Off the coast, the destroyers of France and Britain were bombarding advance German units, and the dive bombers were called upon to deal with them also. At Boulogne, dive bombers had already dispatched the French destroyers *L'Adroit* and *Orage* and crippled the *Frondeur*. Stukas operating at the extreme length of their range also sank the tankers *Salome* and *Niger* and the troopship *Pavon*. In the north, the Dutch also suffered, losing the destroyer *Jan Van Galen* and the gunboat *Johan Maurits Van Nassau* to dive bombers, while the British destroyers *Valentine* and *Whitley* were sunk and *Winchester* and *Westminster* damaged off Holland by the same units.

By May 24, eight Ju87s had been shot down over the coast in attacks on warships, but in return, they had damaged the British *Vimiera* and the Polish *Burza* and sunk the *Wessex* off Calais on the same day.

At dawn on May 26, German general Heinz Guderian prepared for his final attack on Calais, which was held by the stubborn British 20th Division. More than 100 aircraft from the 77th Stuka Wing and the 2nd Stuka Wing attacked in waves throughout the day, reducing the old town center to rubble. The port surrendered on the same evening.

The next day, VIII Air Corps, which contained the bulk of the Ju87s, began to direct its full attention to the perimeter of Dunkirk, where the British were evacuating their forces. At 0740 hours, the first Stukas arrived over the town and the beaches and sank the French troopship *Cote d'Azur*. On the following day, the big dive bombers of the 1st Training and Demonstration Wing, Ju88s, sank the largest merchant ship there, the 6,900-ton *Clan MacAlister*, and at 1600 hours, a massed Stuka assault was launched on the harbor area. They found many ships crammed with troops alongside the mole and dived to the attack. The paddle steamer *Fenella* was hit by a bomb, while another exploded on the dock alongside, riddling her hull and troop-packed superstructure. She listed quickly and went down.

The destroyer *Grenade* took a heavy bomb, which penetrated inside before exploding, turning her slender hull into a slaughter-house. Parting her moorings, she swung into the channel with huge fires raging from stem to stern as her ammunition exploded. She managed to get clear before she went down, her few survivors being picked up by a drifter, which in turn was hit and sunk almost immediately.

The destroyer *Jaguar* was hit, but not so seriously, and she got clear, as did the personnel ship *Canterbury*, which was also hit by a bomb. The paddle steamer *Crested Eagle*, fully laden with survivors from *Fenella*, was hit by a Stuka bomb just as she cleared the mole, and was beached and burnt out. Two trawlers were sunk outright, *Polly Johnson* and *Calvi*. The French destroyer *Mistral* caught the full blast of a near miss and her upperworks were completely wrecked. Nor was this all. Two Southern Railway ships, *Namannia* and *Lorina*, were hit and sunk, as was the paddle steamer *Gracie Fields* with 750 troops aboard.

Casualties in the Ju87 units that inflicted this carnage amounted to a total loss of eleven from all sources. British fighters claimed to have destroyed sixty-nine German aircraft this day. A Defiant squadron claimed no less than nineteen Stukas alone. This was typical of the fantasy-figures toted by the RAF and British media, but the true total loss was really only eighteen of *all* types.

Bad weather on May 30 brought some respite, and although two Stuka groups got airborne, their missions were aborted as the rain closed in. But on June 1, the dive bombers were back over the beaches at 0720 hours. The minesweeper *Skipjack* was hit and sank like a stone. The destroyer *Keith*, with only thirty rounds of ammunition left was attacked again and again. Three near misses brought her to a stop. Another attack saw a Stuka place a bomb straight down her after funnel. Listing and covered in clouds of steam, she took another direct hit on her bridge and sank.

In the same attack, Ju88s hit the tug *St. Abbs*, and the tiny vessel disintegrated, while farther along a Stuka planted a heavy bomb in the destroyer *Basilisk*, damaging her so much that she had to be sunk next day. Two other destroyers, *Whitehall* and *Worcester*, were damaged; the gunboat *Mosquito* was hit, set ablaze, and abandoned; and the minesweeper *Salamander* was also hit. The dive bombers hit the destroyer *Ivanhoe*, which was towed away. At 1300, the French destroyer *Foudroyant* was set upon and, according to the French report, "submerged in a cloud of Stukas." She was hit by several bombs and went down in an instant. The personnel ship *Scotia* was attacked by twelve Ju87s that afternoon while leaving with 2,000 French troops. Three bombs hit the ship, including one that went down a funnel. The troops, panic-stricken, rushed the boats, and the destroyer *Esk* drove off another attack to pick up the few survivors.

The Stuka attacks continued in mounting fury throughout the afternoon. The paddle minesweeper *Brighton Queen* was hit in the stern and sank with 700 French and Moroccan troops aboard. A small convoy of French auxiliaries was set upon at 1600 hours by eight Ju87s, and they quickly dispatched the *Denis Papin*, *Venus*, and *Moussaillon*.

Again, German losses were only twenty-nine aircraft of all types this day, although the RAF boasted it had shot down seventy-eight. The last dive bomber mission against Dunkirk was on June 2, and it was directed against fortifications and bridges as well as Fort Vallieres, which was destroyed by precision bombing. Eight Stukas attacked two RAF launches off Gravelines at 1530 that afternoon, sinking the 243, while the railway ships *Paris* and *Worthing* were also sunk. The final stage of the Battle of France commenced on June 5, and within three weeks, it was all over. Britain was now on her own with invasion expected at any time. As if to confirm this, the Stuka groups began to gather on airfields close to the Channel coast. The reorganization is given in Table 27. Under the newly appointed Kanalkampffuhrer Fink, the Luftwaffe used their dive bombers to clear the English Channel of British shipping while the army and the heavy bombers got ready for the next stage.

The final evacuations from Europe had seen the Ju87s inflict further heavy casualties on shipping. The troopship *Lancastria* was sunk with heavy loss of life off St. Nazaire, and the destroyer *Bulldog* and personnel ship *Bruges* had been damaged. The British stationed a destroyer flotilla, the 4th, at Dover and continued to run their coastal convoys up the Channel. To draw out the British fighters, the Stukas and Ju88s were now dispatched against these targets and soon achieved results.

On June 10, nine Ju87s attacked the destroyers *Boadicea* and *Bulldog*, which were operating off the French coast. Each ship was hit by three bombs and heavily damaged. The next target was the big convoy OA168 that two Stukagruppen caught off Portland. Four large merchant ships were sunk (a total of 16,000 tons), and nine others were damaged severely (40,000 tons); those sunk were the *Britsum*, *Dallas City*, *Deucalion*, and *Kolga*. The big merchant ship *Aeneas* was also sunk by Ju87s, and in attacks on Portland itself, the auxiliary AA ship *Foylebank*, bristling with guns, was dive bombed and sunk. The whole attack cost StG2 just one aircraft.

Targets now became scarce as the convoys were routed mainly at night, but on July 7, Stukas attacked gun positions on the Isle of Wight; on the ninth, they sank the coaster *Kenneth Hawksfield* off Sandwich, and on the tenth, Ju88s joined in raids on Falmouth and Swansea. On the eleventh, a big effort was mounted by Stukas of the 2nd and 77th Stuka Wings in the Portland area, but this was broken up by fighters, and they sank only the patrol ship *Warrior II*.

TABLE 27: ORGANIZATION OF GERMAN DIVE BOMBER UNITS, JULY 1940

Units	Area	Notes
I, II, and III/StG1	Angers/St. Pol	Incorporated the former III/StG51 and TGr186
I, II, and III/StG2	St. Malo/St. Omer, St. Tron, and Lannion	
I, II, and III/StG77	Caen	Incorporated the former I/StG76
I/StG3	Dinand/Fleurtuit	Stab unit forming
IV (Stuka)/LG1	Tramecourt	
7/StG51		Forming, and later became 4/StG1

On July 13, they were back in force attacking a convoy off Dover, and the next day, the 4th (Stuka) Group of the 1st Training and Demonstration Wing caught another convoy off Eastbourne, sinking the coasters *Betswood* and *Bovey Tracey*. On July 18, the Stukas found the Channel clear of shipping, and the only ships at sea were patrol vessels. These were duly dive bombed and machine-gunned to good effect. The following day, Dover harbor was hit, and on July 20, the Stukas found convoy "Bossum" ten miles off the same port. The 2nd Group of the 1st Stuka Wing, led by Keil, penetrated a fighter screen to sink the collier *Pulborough I* and damage several other ships, including the destroyers *Beagle* and *Brazen*.

Dover was hit again on July 20, but the climax came five days later with the attacks on convoy CW8 that was found off Deal by the 1st and 3rd Stuka Wings, with thirty Ju88s of the 4th Bomber Wing (KG 4) in support. Five ships were sunk outright: *Ajax, Coquetdale, Empire Crusader, Henry Moon,* and *Summity* (totaling 5,117 tons). Another six were badly damaged for the loss of two dive bombers. The next day, the destroyers *Brilliant* and *Boreas* came out of Dover to attack E-boats and were pounced on by Stukas; both destroyers took two direct hits.

On July 27, Ju87s and Me110 Jabo fighter-bombers attacked Dover harbor, sinking the destroyer *Codrington* inside and damaging the *Walpole*, while Ju87s savaged the "Bacon" convoy off Swanage; the 1st Group of the 77th Stuka Wing carried out attacks. Meanwhile, a force of fifteen radar-directed Me109 and Me110 Jabo fighter-bombers had caught the destroyer *Delight* off Portland and sank her. Destroyers had been forbidden to sail by daylight in the Channel by the Admiralty, but the local commander thought he knew better and paid the price. They also sank the patrol ship *Gulzar*. Four Stukas were lost.

The last battles fought by the German dive bombers in this phase were between August 9 and 11. Convoy CW9 was the first victim, when massed Stuka assaults accounted for sinking six ships (70,000 tons) and damaging six more. Waves of Ju87s continued the assault, but for the first time, they met strong RAF fighter resistance by Nos. 43 and 145 Squadrons. The 3rd Stuka Wing's 1st Group lost three aircraft, and the 1st and 3rd Groups of the 2nd

Stuka Wing lost one each, while the last formation over the target, the 2nd Group of the 77th Stuka Wing, was badly knocked about, losing three aircraft shot down and five damaged.

On August 12, the 4th (Stuka) Group of the 1st Training and Demonstration Wing under Hauptmann von Brauchitsch attacked a convoy in the Thames estuary, damaging two more ships. The next day, *Adlertag*—"Eagle Day," the German code-name for the main attack on Great Britain—opened in earnest. The Battle of Britain called for the Stuka units to switch their targets away from the coastal convoys and their tactical role, for which they well designed, to a strategic role, for which they were not. The Ju87s were thus misused and thrown away in needless sacrifice against top-class fighter opposition. Their hitherto relative immunity received a severe blow, as did their reputation in Britain.

The battle commenced officially on August 13, but weather conditions delayed the big attack until the afternoon when VII Fliegerkorps swung into action. The 2nd Group of the 2nd Stuka Wing mounted a twenty-seven-plane strike against Middle Wallop airfield, and the 77th Stuka Wing contributed fifty-seven dive bombers to an attack on Warmwell. The 4th (Stuka) Group of the 1st Training and Demonstration Wing went to Detling. The results of these attacks were mixed. Major Enneccerus's formation was jumped by Spitfires over Lyme Bay, losing six aircraft, while the 77th Stuka Wing, although suffering no losses, failed to locate its target. Detling was hit hard, however, and twelve Blenheims and Ansons were destroyed on the ground.

The 2nd Group of the 1st Stuka Wing and the 4th (Stuka) Group of the 1st Training and Demonstration Wing participated in the second day's attacks, which spread along the south coast, but on August 15, there came a day of disaster for the Stukas. The main targets this day were Hawkinge airfield and Portland harbor. At first, they were successful; both Hawkinge and Lympne airfields were badly damaged by heavy and accurate dive bombing and put out of action by the 2nd Group of the 1st Stuka Wing under Hauptmann Keil and the 4th (Stuka) Group of the 1st Training and Demonstration Wing under Hauptmann von Brauchitsch—the latter losing five aircraft, the former none.

The Ju88s of the 30th Bomber Wing (KG 30) joined in, dive bombing Driffield, losing six aircraft, but destroying twice that number and four hangars. In the afternoon, the Stukas put in a second blow as the 1st Group of the 1st Stuka Wing and the 2nd Group of the 2nd Stuka Wing cooperated with Ju88s of the 1st Training and Demonstration Wing. They were intercepted by RAF fighters, but managed to bomb Worthy Down and Middle Wallop. Fighting reached a new high on August 16–18. The 2nd Stuka Wing bombed Tangmere on the first day, losing eight aircraft but causing widespread damage. All the hangars were destroyed, and workshops, stores, and a pumping station were pulverized, while three Blenheims and seven Hurricanes were destroyed on the ground.

Sunday, August 18, was a black day for the Stuka wings. All four were sent out and duly attacked the airfields of Ford, Gosport, and Thorney Island, again with good effect; many British aircraft were hit on the ground, and installations were wrecked. But once more, the British eight-gun fighters were waiting for them in hordes, and they decimated the Stukas before the German fighters could intervene. Hardest hit of all was the hitherto lucky unit StG77.

Among their targets was Poling radar station. While over Selsey Bill, they were intercepted by no less than four fighter squadrons, and in the ensuing massacre, the 1st Group of the 77th Stuka Wing lost no less than twelve of its twenty-eight aircraft, with six more damaged; among the casualties was Hauptmann Meisel. Four more Stukas from the 77th's other units were also lost. Despite the severe damage that they had inflicted, the loss rate of thirty destroyed or damaged was clearly prohibitive.

It was decided to save the Stukas for the proper role, supporting the actual invasion landings themselves. Accordingly, they were moved north to the Pas-de-Calais area behind the 16th Army, and discussion began with the commanders of the leading infantry and tank units that were to carry out the landings on how best to coordinate forces on *Der Tag* ("The Day").

For Operation *Seelöwe* ("Sea Lion," the land invasion of Britain), it was decided that the Ju87s should concentrate their efforts in supporting the army around Dover, Folkestone, and Sandgate; two complete wings were allocated for this. At the same meeting, held on September 13, a specially equipped squadron was decided upon to destroy the suspected nest of heavy gun batteries located at Dungeness. Two other groups were allocated for the support of VII Corps, while the 1st Group of the 3rd Stuka Wing was to be held in reserve in Brittany for opportune use once the soldiers ashore called for further assistance.

Thus by early September, the 2nd Group of the 1st Stuka Wing (Pas-de-Calais), the 2nd Group of the 2nd Stuka Wing (St. Omer), and the 4th (Stuka) Group of the 1st Training and Demonstration Wing (Tramecourt) were ready with the other units refitting and retraining. The 77th Stuka Wing had suffered such heavy losses that it needed a much longer period of respite to rebuild, and during this period, it was virtually non-operational. But they waited in vain for the order to begin the invasion.

With the final outcome of the aerial battle decided in favor of the RAF and the heavy bombers employed in night attacks on London, the Stukas were dispersed. Many were dispatched to Italy and Germany in readiness for the campaigns planned in southeast Europe, but the Ju87s had not completely vanished from the skies over Britain.

Convoys had recommenced into the Thames, and it was decided to update the anti-shipping data by mounting a series of selective dive bombing attacks before all the Ju87s moved off to their new combat zones in the spring. With a large number of ex-navy crews among its personnel and with experience in this form of warfare, the 3rd Group of the 1st Stuka Wing, under Mahlke, was selected to conduct these during November.

Dive bombing attacks took place against these convoys on November 1, 8, and 11, and these proved quite successful. No Stukas were lost in the first three attacks, and the casualties they inflicted were significant. These larger ships proved more difficult to actually sink, but many were damaged.

The Germans estimated that they had destroyed a far greater tonnage in these attacks than they actually had: 18,000 tons on the first, 21,000 tons on the eighth, and 37,000 tons on the eleventh. The final attack took place on November 14, and the RAF met them with a strong force of fighters. Subsequently, the British claimed to have inflicted wholesale slaughter on the German dive bombers, but in fact, this was not true. On finding the skies full of fighters,

TABLE 28: RESULTS OF DIVE BOMBING ANTI-SHIPPING OFFENSIVE, NOVEMBER 1940

Date of Attack	Ship Bombed	Tonnage	Result
November 1	*Letchworth*	1,317	Sunk
November 8	*Catford*	1,216	Damaged
	Fireglow	1,568	Damaged
	Ewell	1,350	Damaged
November 11	*Colonel Crompton*	1,495	Damaged
	Corduff	2,345	Damaged
	Corsea	2,764	Damaged

the attack on the convoy was called off, so the CO of the German fighter escort diverted the dive bombers to targets in the Dover area. He prudently declined to join them, and the Stukas were heavily engaged. Only one Stuka was actually shot down, that of Oberleutnant Blumers, and three more crash-landed on returning to France. Only one Ju87 was undamaged, but most got safely back to their home airfields.

During the winter of 1940–41, the few remaining Ju87s in France conducted a series of pin-prick harassing raids over the Channel on southern coast towns. The damage they inflicted was slight, and by the New Year, most had been withdrawn south. A new chapter was to open in the Mediterranean, but first let us examine Allied dive bombing attacks, commencing with the destruction of the *Königsberg*.

CHAPTER 15

A Muted Riposte

The Sinking of the *Königsberg* and Allied Operations, 1940

The background to the attack on the *Königsberg* was that a powerful German naval force had penetrated the defenses of the Norwegian harbor of Bergen on April 8, 1940, and landed troops, which occupied the town. It was one of a series of such attacks that in one swoop took the major ports of Norway and left the British with the task of ejecting them. Aerial reconnaissance had shown that two of the German cruisers still lay in Bergen harbor, and a force of twelve Wellington and twelve Hampden bombers was dispatched to sink them. They failed to score a single hit, and one of the cruisers returned to Germany. The other, the light cruiser *Königsberg*, which had been slightly damaged by three shells from a Norwegian fort earlier, remained afloat, and plans were put in hand to attack her again, but this time with a more effective force.

At the beginning of 1940, following German air raids on Scapa Flow, three squadrons of Hurricanes were based at Wick to defend the fleet anchorage. As their parent aircraft carriers were employed elsewhere, this duty had been taken over by two squadrons of Skuas that were based ashore at HMS *Sparrowhawk*, the Naval Air Station at Hatston. These squadrons were No. 800, commanded by Captain Richard Thomas Partridge, Royal Marines, and No. 803, commanded by Lieutenant William Paulet Lucy, Royal Navy.

The senior observer of No. 800 Squadron, Lieutenant Commander Geoffrey Hare, Royal Navy, had been sent to the RAF Coastal Command squadron to be employed in watching the Norwegian harbors the Germans had occupied, and he had been aboard the plane that had overflown Bergen early on the April 9. It was Hare who had identified the two German cruisers of the *Köln* class then in harbor, and on his arrival back at Lossiemouth, he lost no time in transferring to a transport that whisked him back to Hatston, Kirkwall, to report to his unit. Already the news of his sighting had led the CO of *Sparrowhawk*, Commander C. L. Howe, Royal Navy, to request permission to use his two Skua squadrons in an attack, and this was granted. Planning commenced at once.

The main problem was the distance to the target, for the limited range of the Skua meant that the fuel situation was bound to be extremely tight. It was essential to have first-class navigation to make precise landfall, and having just been over the target, Hare was obviously an essential part of the mission.

A secondary problem—although it was one that did not seem to enter the heads of the eager young pilots presented with a real target at long last—was the lack of current training in dive bombing. There had been little or no opportunity for the squadrons to carry out any recent practice, a fact commented upon later by the Director of the Naval Air Division. Both risks were willingly accepted, and the plan, formulated and pushed forward to top speed, went ahead even though all were rusty.

The departure of the *Köln* had, unknown to the pilots at Hatston, left them with one target ship on which to concentrate their attack, the 6,600-ton light cruiser *Königsberg* commanded by Captain Ruhfus. He was left in an unenviable position after the departure of his senior officer and was eager to follow him back to Germany without further delay. What was keeping him at Bergen was not the three shell hits, which were not serious, but the unreliable machinery of his vessel.

She carried only light armor protection and mounted three triple 5.9-inch gun turrets (one forward, two aft) and twelve torpedo tubes. Her AA defense consisted of six heavy guns (3.5-inch) and a light automatic-weapons battery of eight 37-millimeter guns and four 20-millimeter guns—a battery, incidentally, far superior to that mounted by equivalent British warships at this time. Her waterline protection was only 2 inches thick, and against air attack, her deck armor was a puny quarter of an inch maximum, although her turrets and barbettes had $1\frac{1}{4}$-inch armor. Her weakness made her an ideal dive bomber target.

There was no doubt that ships of light cruiser size and under were vulnerable to bombs of the 500-pound SAP type, provided that accuracy could be achieved. *Königsberg* was 570 feet long overall with a maximum beam of 50 feet; she presented a reasonable target, especially since she was stationary. This area was cut down, for the turret roofs were the most heavily protected part of the ship. This left the bows and quarterdeck as the obvious aiming points, with the clutter of the bridge, funnels, and amidships superstructure as secondary ones, for the AA weapons were concentrated here.

However, the magazines, ready-to-use ammunition, and large machinery spaces below decks gave this amidships portion a high degree of vulnerability if fires could be started by hits or near misses. There was the additional advantage that, as she was motionless, no aiming-off was required. Also, as she lay alongside a jetty this would offer firm resistance to her hull if it tried to move away and absorb the water-hammer effect of close misses alongside. Its resistance would increase their effect enormously. The greatest advantage of all, however, was undoubtedly the surprise they could achieve, which would keep the flak to a minimum. There was little to fear from fighter defense at this stage; the nearest German fighters were at Sola/Stavanger airfield 150 miles to the south.

Although recognition would present little problem to Royal Navy and Royal Marine flyers, Hare noted for the crews that their target would probably have a white band on both forecastle and quarterdeck and a white band with a Swastika painted on the turret.

Königsberg had in fact moved her anchorage since Hare's first sighting the day before, and she now lay alongside the Skoltegrund Mole, her starboard side secured, facing east toward the shore.

The plan of attack was a straightforward one. The distance to the target ruled out anything other than a straight "in-bash-out" mission. But even so, the planning of the best route across the North Sea up to Bergen to the target without raising the alarm and then out again called for careful timing. All depended to a great degree on the expertise of the two senior observers, Hare and Lieutenant Michael Hanson, Royal Navy. Tribute was later

paid to the meticulous work of the Air Staff Officer, Lieutenant
Commander Aubrey St. John Edwards, Royal Navy, and indeed, it
cannot be faulted.

Aircraft available for the sortie consisted of eleven Skuas of No.
803 Squadron and five of No. 800 Squadron. They were to operate
in two groups of nine and seven aircraft, respectively, but in the
event, one aircraft lost touch during the outward flight, and the
actual composition of the force was 9-6-1, with the odd aircraft
doing its own accurate navigation and carrying out its own separate
attack some ten minutes after the others.

Takeoff was to be at 0445 hours on April 10, to arrive over the
target at first light to achieve maximum surprise. The weather conditions on that day put back the actual time of departure to 0515,
but this did not, in the end, jeopardize the mission.

The plan called for the two groups to take their departure
point from Auskerrey and make a course of 074 degrees (true) for
Marsten, crossing the Norwegian coast in latitude 60.09 north at a
height of 12,000 feet. The two groups were at all times to remain in
visual contact with each other and, once inside the coastal islands,
were advised that a track of 360 degrees would lead them up the
fjord. If their landfall was to the southward of this datum, it would
still lead them to Bergen, but if it was north to the open sea once
more, it would lead them westward.

Strict radio silence was to be maintained throughout the outward track, and IFF equipment was not carried. The W/T fre-
quency was given as 366, and the silence was only to be broken
after the attack to transmit a brief report.

On completion of the attack, the fuel situation was to be examined. All aircraft which at that stage had under 50 gallons in their
tanks were given permission to land in Norway, but well clear of
Bergen itself. Should the aircraft come down in serviceable condi-
tion, the Norwegian authorities were to be consulted in order that
the return flight could be resumed next morning. But if the aircraft was immobilized because of damage, it was to be destroyed.

The rendezvous point for the reassembly for the return flight
was fixed over the island of Lyson on the coast, some 270 miles
from the target area. The crews were told to wait here for ten min-

utes and only then take track 260 degrees for Sumburgh. Again, strict wireless silence was to be maintained on the return leg, only to be broken when 60 miles from Sumburgh when the ETA was to be signaled by either group leaders or single aircraft. Any aircraft arriving over Sumburgh with less than 30 gallons of fuel was to land there as refueling facilities had been laid on. In the event, none of the aircraft needed this emergency service.

A final note of caution was imparted. Aircraft were strictly forbidden to land with their 500-pound bombs aboard. With their enthusiasm, there seemed little likelihood that this would arise, and indeed, it did not.

At 0515 hours on April 10, all sixteen Skuas, fully laden with fuel, took off from Hatston into the dim, murky half-light and formed up as arranged in two groups before setting off on track 074 for Norway. The weather was good for their mission with 5/10th cloud at 8,000 feet to give them protection from the ground and visibility for 20 miles. The wind was northwest at 16 knots.

The Skuas winged east on their course in two groups except for White Leader. Lieutenant Taylor later reported that he could not gain touch with the main party, but he nonetheless navigated successfully on his own and was the last aircraft in over the target.

The Skuas approached Bergen harbor from the southeast, and after a brief pause to scan the area where the two cruisers were last reported, they identified "a cruiser of the *Köln* class" at her new berth alongside the mole. At 0720 hours, the sections formed line astern to begin the final phase of the approach dive to clear the thin layer of cloud at 8,000 feet. Below it, visibility was excellent—at least twenty miles. The German defenses, moreover, were caught flat-footed as the long line of Skuas barreled in toward them out of the sun.

Most of the aircraft released their bombs at 2,000 feet from the final dive point of 6,500 feet, and the majority went in at a 00-degree angle of dive, but there were, of course, variations to this norm. Several released at 2,500 feet, and two—Rooper and Harris—released at 3,000 feet. Hanson and Spurway pressed in to around 1,500 feet before releasing. Even more coolly, Church, having made his vertical dive down to the target, did not release

TABLE 29: FAA ATTACK ON *Königsberg:* ORDER OF BATTLE

No. 800 Squadron

Yellow Leader	Capt. R. T. Partridge, RM; Lt. Cdr. G. Hare, RN
Yellow 2	PO Amn. H. A. Monk; Ldg. Amn. L. C. Eccleshall
Yellow 3	PO Amn. J. Hadley; Ldg. Amn. M. Hall
White Leader	Lt. E. W. T. Taylor, RN; PO Amn. H. G. Cunningham
Spare Section	Lt. K. V. V. Spurway, RN; PO Amn. C. J. E. Cotterill
Spare 2	Acting PO J. A. Gardner; Naval Amn 1st Class A. Todd

No. 803 Squadron

Blue Leader	Lt. W. P. Lucy, RN; Lt. M. C. E. Hanson, RN
Blue 2	Capt. E. D. McIver, RM; Ldg. Amn. A. A. Barnard
Blue 3	Lt. A. B. F. Harris, RN; Ldg. Amn. G. S. Russell
Green Leader	Lt. H. E. R. Torin, RN; Midshipman(A) T. A. McKee
Green 2	Lt. L. A. Harris, RM; Naval Amn. 1st Class D. A. Prime
Green 3	Lt. W. C. A. Church, RN; PO Amn. B. M. Seymour
Red Leader	Lt. B. J. Smeeton, RN; PO Amn. B. M. Seymour
Red 2	Lt. V. H. Filmer, RN; Naval Amn. 1st Class F. P. Dooley
Red 3	Acting PO T. F. Riddler; Naval Amn. 1st Class H. T. Chatterley

because of bad positioning. Not satisfied, he pulled up and around and made a second attack from stern-to-bow in a shallow run at 40 degrees, dropping his 500-pound bomb from 200 feet, then clawing away through flak up to 3,000 feet. Considerable tracer from a now wide-awake flak ship followed him. This highly audacious assault was ended with nothing more serious than "one large hole in mainplane close to fuselage."

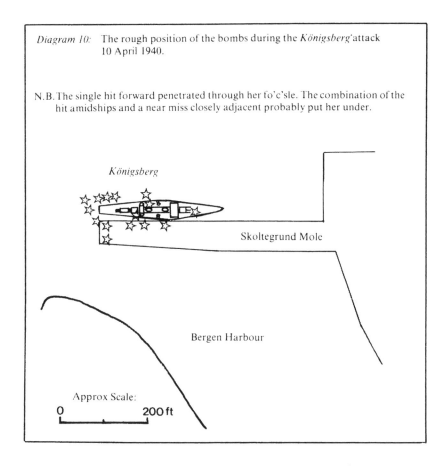

Diagram 10: The rough position of the bombs during the *Königsberg* attack 10 April 1940.

N.B. The single hit forward penetrated through her fo'c'sle. The combination of the hit amidships and a near miss closely adjacent probably put her under.

Königsberg

Skoltegrund Mole

Bergen Harbour

Approx Scale:

0   200 ft

Again, the angle of dive varied—60 degrees being the norm—but several aircraft went in at 70 degrees and some at 50. The final run was bow-to-stern along the full length of the target and the majority of bombs hit aft the ship.

The complete surprise achieved in this attack can be seen by the slowness of the German reaction—about half the aircraft had completed their dives before the first guns opened up—and by the accuracy of the bombing. Only a single AA gun of large calibre appeared to be manned aboard the *Königsberg*; most pilots reported a solitary gun aft firing shells at five-second intervals that were bursting around the dive bombers. The light weapons opened fire later, from both the target ship itself and nearby vessels, in particular one ship described, presumably because of the weight of fire, as a "flak ship." AA guns ashore were also noted to be in a position about a mile southwest of the target vessel, but no crew reported that these in any way affected their approach or aiming.

As the bombs screamed down, the cruiser was enveloped in smoke and flames, which made aerial observation and confirmation difficult. Two hits were claimed amidships and one on the forecastle, in addition to at least one near-miss. The bombs that hit alongside on the mole—of which there were five, four of them very close—threw up dust and clouds of rubble, which increased the difficulty of spotting.

The majority of pilots reported that they could not clearly estimate the damage, although a few seem to have had a better view. Riddler, for example, stated that his bomb missed the ship altogether and set fire to a building on the jetty. Spurway reported his bomb bursting internally producing clouds of smoke and debris, while Russell reported that Harris's bomb was a hit on the cruiser's forecastle, which caused a large black hole from which flames and white smoke poured.

MacIver scored a direct hit amidships between the two funnels, and this was probably the most lethal strike of all. All the bombs were very close; in fact, the DNAD report estimated that the mean error was approximately 50 yards, which compared "very favorably" with a 1939 practice, which averaged 70 yards.

The *Königsberg* soon started sinking by the bows with flames leaping 100 feet into the sky as she sank deeper and deeper. Her stern cocked up exposing her screws, and some 50 minutes after the attack she rolled over and capsized.

Petty Officer Gardner, the last pilot over the target, reported that the target appeared to have been hit badly, but her final end was witnessed by an American captain aboard the *Flying Fish*, which was also in harbor.

The striking demonstration of the power of the dive bomber made a deep impression, but unfortunately, the next attack carried out by the FAA Skuas lacked all the essential requisites for such a mission. They were sent in against a target they could not possibly have sunk, the German battle cruiser *Scharnhorst*, and they did not have the vital element of surprise. The result was a disaster.

Aerial reconnaissance had revealed the presence of the German fleet—*Scharnhorst, Admiral Hipper,* and four destroyers—in Trondheim Roads on June 12, 1940, and plans were at once made to strike at them with the dive bombers embarked aboard the carrier *Ark Royal.* A feature of the planning was the provision for a preemptive strike, which was to be mounted by RAF Beauforts against the fighter airfield at Vaernes, to take place not earlier than 0200 hours on the thirteenth. Long-range Blenheim fighter escort for the attack and return flight was also supposed to be laid on by the RAF, but this failed to materialize at all. The Beaufort attack did, in fact, take place, but it had exactly the opposite effect as intended, for far from destroying enemy fighters on the ground, it merely stirred up the hornets' nest too late and resulted in German fighters being airborne ready and waiting when the Skuas arrived over this target area.

The German flak defenses were also similarly warned by this strike. The Fleet Air Arm's major asset, surprise, was thrown away by the RAF. As it was a 20-minute flight from the head of the fjord to the target, it is possible that German coastal observers would have had the same effect anyway. Be that as it may, they were not caught napping this time but were fully prepared. Under such circumstances, the DNAD later considered that the FAA Skua attack had a right to expect only one hit and a 25 percent chance of a second, with 30 percent casualties from flak and another 30 percent from fighters. His figures proved to be only too accurate.

Ark Royal arrived at her flying-off position undetected and prepared a strike force of fifteen dive bombers, six from No. 800 Squadron and nine from No. 803 Squadron. This number was governed by the following considerations:

1. Of the Skua pilots available, only these fifteen had previous experience with dive bombing in the Skua.
2. The standing air patrol over the fleet limited the number available for the strike.

3. With the light winds then prevailing, fifteen was the maximum number that could be flown off with a full bomb load
in one range.

The force flew off the carrier at 0002 on June 13, each armed
with a 500-pound SAP bomb. It was led by Lieutenant Commander
Casson, Royal Navy, and Captain "Birdy" Partridge, Royal Marines.
They crossed the Norwegian coast at 0123 and split into two formations in readiness for their attack. They found the weather clear and
the fighters and flak waiting. No. 800 Squadron made shallow dive
bombing runs in line astern down to 8,000 feet from the north,
being met by heavy antiaircraft fire. No. 803 Squadron attacked
from south to north, bow to stern of the battle-cruiser, save for the
last section.

As the Skuas bored in, the German fighters closed with them,
Me109s and Me110s tangling with the dive bombers early on and
others waiting for them to complete their runs. Despite the inferno
into which they flew, the survivors pressed on down and were
rewarded with two direct hits and several near misses according to
contemporary reports, although the Germans only admit to one.
Tragically, this bomb was a dud that failed to explode.

But they paid a very heavy price for this minimal damage. No
fewer than eight of the fifteen Skuas were destroyed, and the few
survivors managed to escape only by hugging the deck in the mist.
The RAF fighters that were supposed to protect them appeared only
after it was all over and they were on their way back to the *Ark Royal.*

Scharnhorst duly sailed for Germany with her efficiency unim-
paired. The RAF launched a series of attacks on her while she was
off the coast on June 21, when Bristol Beauforts carried out shallow
dive bombing attacks at 200 mph from a height of 1,500 feet. But
although these attacks were most gallantly pressed home, only GP
bombs were carried; they were virtually useless against the deck
armor of the battle cruiser, which was $4\frac{1}{2}$ inches thick in places.
This showed a complete misunderstanding of the problems
involved in attacking large warships, and aircrews were sent out to
their deaths on an impossible mission with no chance of success.
This fuzziness was a hangover from the prewar days when dive
bombing had been scorned by the RAF and early war experience

had taken time to seep through. That the performance of the German Stuka in Poland had influenced the RAF's thinking a little is shown by correspondence in February and March 1940, just before the Norwegian campaign broke. Here we see the first hints of concern with regard their attitude. SASO wrote to Group Captain Training as follows:

> [I]n the order of priority of training in methods of bombing, dive bombing is placed in a low order. In view of the increased importance of the role of the Battle squadrons in support of the Army, and in view of the likelihood of Battles being employed in operations against military road movements, I think that the order of priority of dive bombing of the type envisaged in our Command Tactical Memorandum No. 8 should be placed in high order.

Meanwhile, a Secret Memo from ACAS to SASO, Bomber Command, revealed that DGRD was of the opinion that no concessions could be made on the speed limitations. "He is of the opinion that the figures laid down in the Pilots' Handbook represent

TABLE 27: ORGANIZATION OF GERMAN DIVE BOMBER UNITS, JULY 1940

Units	Area	Notes
I, II, and III/StG1	Angers/St. Pol	Incorporated the former III/StG51 and TGr186
I, II, and III/StG2	St. Malo/St. Omer, St. Tron, and Lannion	
I, II, and III/StG77	Caen	Incorporated the former I/StG76
I/StG3	Dinand/Fleurtuit	Stab unit forming
IV (Stuka)/LG1	Tramecourt	
7/StG51		Forming, and later became 4/StG1

the extreme concessions which the technical experts are prepared to make without further investigations." Further trials had been arranged "as a matter of urgency" and were in progress.

The report on these trials was duly submitted in March 1940. The types of dive bombing investigated were to commence between 7,000 and 8,000 feet with bomb release at between 4,000 feet, emerging from the dive between 3,000 and 4,000 feet. Owing to adverse weather conditions, these trials were limited to single aircraft. Seven pilots carried out attacks, dropping fifty-six bombs. Moreover, as there were no observation quadrants at Perpignan where the trials were conducted, no accurate assessment of the results was possible. "It appeared, however, that the average bombing error from the experimental heights was double that from normal heights." The CO of the Advanced Air Striking Force summed up the attitude to these small-scale experiments, which seemed only to confirm the RAF's already deeply-held opinions on the matter: "It cannot be said that these trials provide sufficient data on which to base any final conclusions. It is regretted that training requirements of a more urgent nature prevent further trials being carried out on high dive bombing in the near future."

And for the time being anyway, that was that as far as the RAF was concerned. The Norwegian campaign produced another flurry. A Secret Memo dated May 5 stated that "the dive bombing successes obtained in Norway by the Skuas and Junkers have raised in the minds of the Air Staff the suspicion that perhaps the prewar policy of neglecting the dive bomber was not entirely sound" and that "probably the dive bomber will be put forward as a future Air Staff requirement." But further reflection was that "the problem of making our existing bombers do steep dive bombing is a formidable one, and is probably insoluble as a short-range project. I am therefore reluctant to embark on it until we have enough evidence to show that it will be worthwhile."

With the blitzkrieg in France and the Low Countries, such attitudes were shown to be bankrupted. The low-level methods utilized by the RAF proved fatal, and battle losses were ghastly. If the RAF had no dive bombers, then the French had a few—though pitifully low in numbers compared with the Germans. They did what they could. Only fifty-two Vought V-156Fs were on hand in May, and twelve of these were destroyed on the ground in a single attack at Boulogne-Alprech airfield. The replacement aircraft for this unfortunate unit, AB-3, did not arrive until May 23—far too late. AB-2 survived a similar attack with only slight damage. AB-4, equipped with the Loire dive bomber, had been the last to equip, and they moved to Berck on the evening of May 17.

Missions with both Voughts and LNs took place from May 15 onward with French Naval Air Force dive bombers operating against targets at Walcheren Island with some success on the following three days, with few losses. On May 19, word arrived that French troops were encircled in the forest of Marmal, and AB-2 and AB-4 were sent in to help them, fielding eleven and nine dive bombers, respectively. At 1800 hours, they made their approach in Vics of three. Unfortunately, the promised fighter cover failed to show up. Nonetheless, the Loires deployed to the attack as instructed, diving from 6,000 feet to 1,000 feet before releasing their bombs. They were met by very heavy flak, and no less than ten of the LNs were shot down over

The French Navy was re-equipping with the export version of the American Chance Vought Vindicator during early 1940, but deliveries had not been turned into full combat squadrons before the blitzkrieg of May and June. This V156F of AB-1 is given a final check on its home base.

the target. The survivors—six from AB-2 and four from AB-4—returned to base at 2030 hours. Of these, only three remained airworthy, having been holed by flak and by their own bomb splinters. They had, however, caused some damage to the German armor, and considering that they had received no training in this type of targeting, they had done wonders. They were now no longer operational as a fighting unit and were out of the action for two days refitting.

In a desperate gamble to stem the flood of German armor across the River Oise, every available dive bomber was dispatched against the Origny-Ste. Benoite bridge on May 20. Captain Mesny led eleven Voughts of AB-1, with one Loire of AB-2 and two of AB-4. RAF Hurricanes failed to provide the cover promised, and they were jumped by Me109s some distance from the target. Five Voughts were destroyed, and the others failed to attack accurately. The three LNs managed to slip through, and although one was shot down by flak, PO Hautin scored a direct hit with a 330-pound bomb, which destroyed the bridge.

Their ranks thus decimated, only token strikes could now be mounted by the French Navy dive bombers. It is to their lasting credit that they fought on to the end. On May 21, the only two surviving Loires went out again against enemy targets on the River Aisne, from which only one came back. Meanwhile, the five serviceable Voughts of AB-1 were evacuated from Boulogne the day before it was overrun and flew to Dunkirk. All its ground staff and damaged aircraft were captured by the Germans. AB-2 and AB-4 likewise moved out of Calais as the panzers surrounded it and flew to Cherbourg. They had four aircraft left fit for operations, and one of these from the total of thirteen dive bombers was shot down over Rouen. The Dunkirk aircraft were also joined to the others at Cherbourg on May 22, carrying out an attack on enemy tanks near Abbeville.

With the Germans attacking the perimeters of the Boulogne defenses, the remaining Voughts of AB-1 were again thrown in to bomb the German-held Fort de la Crèche that afternoon. They made two attacks and lost another plane to flak. For the second attack, the four V-156s were joined by three more from a maintenance unit; all seven got back safely, but one crashed on landing.

By now, all northern French airfields were in danger of being overrun, and AB-1 pulled its six Voughts out of Cherbourg to Britain, landing at Tangmere. On June 1, these French dive bombers took off from this British airfield to strike at German forces near Furnes. This mission was carried out without loss, but they became dispersed. Four landed at Cherbourg, one back at Tangmere, and one at Hawkinge.

With the arrival of reserve aircraft, AB-1 was built up to six Voughts, and these were dispatched against targets at Gravelines. They missed the rendezvous with their fighter escort, and the mission was aborted forthwith; the aircraft landing at Cherbourg were still bombed up.

By now, the end was very near. On June 3, AB-2, AB-3, and AB-4 began to move their equipment out and shifted their base far south to Hyeres once more on the Cote d'Azur. Some ten Voughts and fifteen LNs survived to carry out this operation, but during the transfer, they lost one LN-401 to an attack by a Polish fighter pilot in a Morane 406 who thought it was a Stuka. Of the five

A very rare photograph of a camouflaged French Navy Vought. Squadron markings on the fuselage side were overpainted and replaced with a small-diameter cocarde.

Voughts left on strength of AB-1 at Cherbourg, still more sacrifice was asked. On June 9, they attacked a German column at Rouen successfully, losing one aircraft to flak damage and a crash landing. On June 23, they joined the remaining French dive bombers in the south, for by this time, Italy had joined the war against the Allies. With the fall of Cherbourg imminent, the squadron had operated briefly from Brest with four Voughts, and when Brest in turn went under on the nineteenth, they shifted to Hourtin near Bordeaux. They carried out their last mission on the twenty-first, destroying a bridge over the Loire without loss.

Italy entered the war on June 10, and the three squadrons, freshly equipped, took the war to the new enemy. On June 13, four Voughts of AB-3 attacked an Italian submarine off Albenga, dropping five bombs and inflicting some damage, but that same afternoon, one Vought was destroyed by an Italian fighter. Further losses were suffered when six Voughts of AB-3 were destroyed on the ground at Cuers-Pierrefeu. More decimation followed with an attack mounted on the night of June 18–19 against Imperia and Novi-Ligure by thirteen Loires of AB-2 and AB-4. Two were hit by flak over the target, and two more were lost in bad weather over the Alps; one crash-landed.

With the armistice, Captain Mesny set out with four Voughts for the south, as related, but two turned back because of bad weather, and only two arrived. The remaining aircraft of AB-2 and AB-4 were evacuated to Corsica and were there made unserviceable. Thus passed the French dive bombers for the time being. Reports that captured Voughts were put into service by the Luftwaffe for testing and even used operationally in attacks on Dover Harbour in July 1940 have not been confirmed, despite efforts by this author.

Meanwhile, the prewar reputation of the RAF's light attack bombers having vanished together with the bulk of the Fairey Battles in futile sorties and severe losses, British counterattacks were no more effective than those of the French Army Air Force in restoring the situation. The rapid progress of the German armies was watched and monitored as they pounded across France, but little in the way of effective opposition could be offered after the first four days.

Not having a dive bomber of its own, the RAF was forced to call on any type of aircraft it could lay its hands on to perform this function. The true cost of its prewar stand against dive bombing was made apparent by the pressing into service of such antiques as FAA Swordfish and obsolete Hawker Hector biplanes to perform this function as the crisis rose.

Eleven Swordfish from No. 812 Squadron were sent on a dive-bombing mission against German troops at Gravelines on May 26, armed with 250-pound bombs. They claimed the destruction of three tanks for the loss of one Swordfish. The RAF continued this dive-bombing support for the Calais garrison throughout the twenty-seventh, not knowing for certain that it had surrendered. A large variety of aircraft were utilized in this role. Six Westland Lysanders were dispatched on the twenty-fifth to dive bomb a German battery without observing results. On the twenty-sixth, six Hectors of No. 613 Squadron dive bombed the same battery, led by Squadron Leader A. F. Anderson. They went back the next day with six Hectors and nine Swordfish; one Hector failed to return.

The Skuas of the FAA saw a great deal of action at this period over France. No. 801 Squadron flew into RAF Detling during the second half of May, just in time to start helping cover the collapse of France and the German thrust into Belgium. As well as some reconnaissance work over the channel ports, they attacked bridges, barges, and land targets. They found themselves targets for both the Luftwaffe and the RAF fighters and had to fight their way both to and from their targets. They attacked German batteries at Cape Gris Nez as well, but working under RAF Coastal Command, they found little appreciation of dive-bombing work—targets or problems—among their new masters.

Working from the *Ark Royal* during the Dakar fiasco in September 1940, FAA Skuas and Swordfish conducted dive-bombing attacks against the Vichy French battleship *Richelieu*. This was an even more futile exercise than the attacks on *Scharnhorst* in June, for the French giant's armor was of even greater thickness, and she was completely unscathed.

CHAPTER 16

Death from the Sky

Axis Reorganization and Mediterranean Operations, 1940–42

We have seen how the early Italian experiments had resulted in the production of the SM85 and the prototype of the SM86, with neither aircraft performing very well. Nonetheless, with the Italian entry into the war in June 1940, these were the only available dive bombers on hand for the Italian Air Force to carry out Mussolini's demands to sweep the Mediterranean Sea clean of the British Royal Navy.

Thus, on May 29, 1940, the 96th Dive Bombing Group was formed, the first and only Italian-built and Italian-manned dive bomber unit. It consisted of eighteen SM85s and the solitary SM86, under the command of Captain E. Ercolani, with 236th and 237th Squadrons led by Lieutenant E. Marcozzi and Lieutenant F. Malvezzi, respectively. Named the Independent Group (*Gruppo Autonomo*), this unit was transferred from Rome's Ciampino airfield down to the island of Pantelleria in the middle of the Sicilian Channel, close to Malta, in readiness for its chance of a contest with the ships of Admiral A. B. Cunningham's Mediterranean Fleet. The transfer was completed by June 5, 1940.

Their opportunity soon arose, for on July 19, the naval battle of Calabria was fought. The British fleet chased the Italian fleet back within sight of its home ports before losing contact. Here, with an enemy fleet within biscuit toss of the Italian airfields, were plum targets for the Italians' taking—three battleships and an aircraft carrier with no fighters aboard. But unfortunately for their hopes, the Independent Group never even made contact, let alone carried out any dive bombing attacks.

The damp, humid conditions at Pantelleria were just too much for the wooden structure of the "Flying Banana." During the whole of June and July, the SM85s managed only two recce sorties from the whole group, and then they were retired to Rome once more with a zero war efficiency rating. Although refurbished and based for a while at Comiso in Sicily, all these dive bombers were soon broken up.

The solitary SM86, still being flown by test pilot Scarpini for the makers, *did* make one solitary combat flight against Malta (in company with some Ju87s) on September 15, during which it dropped its single 1,100-pound bomb on Hal Far airfield. But the Italian Air Force was not impressed and had by this time, as in so many other things, turned to its Axis partner for the solution to its dive bomber problems, although many experiments continued to be conducted to find a suitable Italian-built dive bomber in the subsequent years.

A special mission was dispatched to Germany by the Chief of the Italian Air Staff, General Pricolo, after he had studied reports of the SM85 failure. General Urbani and Colonel Teucci, air attaché in Berlin, held talks with Reichsmarschall Hermann Goering, which resulted in the purchase of batches of Ju87Bs and Ju87Rs, while provision was made for the training of pilots at the 2nd Stuka School at Graz in Austria; the first fifteen pilots started in July, with another fifteen in August. The Stukas purchased by Italy were tropicalized by having sand filters fitted and desert survival equipment added for use by the new dive bombing groups. Despite repeated rumors that the Italians built Ju87s under license in Italy, the fact remains that this is not the case; all were brought in from Germany.

The first Stukas arrived in Sicily on August 21, where they formed the 96th Group under Captain Ercolani, with thirteen aircraft of 236th and 237th Squadrons, led by Lieutenant Malvezzi and Lieutenant G. Santinoni at Comiso airfield.

Similar arrangements were also made to equip dive bomber units of Germany's other allies. The *Magyar Kiralyi Legiero* of Hungary formed the dive bomber group *I Onálló Zuhanöbombazö Osztaly* with two squadrons of Ju87B2s, and these were replaced by Ju87Ds two years later when it finally became fully operational. The Romanian air force formed *Grupul 6 Picaj* with Ju87Bs, having three nine-plane squadrons ready by 1941 in time for the invasion of Russia. Bulgaria took small batches of Ju87B2s—and later Ds—during the same period, as did the Slovakian air force.

The only home-built dive bomber to serve with the Bulgarian Air Force during the war was the DAR10F, which was a modified version of the DAR10 fighter-bomber with structural strengthening. The dive bomber modification was influenced by events in France in 1940 and first flew early in 1941. Only a limited number of DAR10s were so modified for front-line service however before they were replaced by Ju87-D5s supplied by Germany. However, the DAR10Fs still surviving by that time found some useful combat service in the anti-guerilla operations in Yugoslavia until late in the war.

The DAR10F was a low-wing monoplane, with fixed spatted undercarriage and a crew of two. It was powered by a 960-horsepower Fiat A74 RG38 engine, which gave it a top speed of 282 mph at 16,400 feet and a range of 870 miles. This little bomber had a wing span of 41½ feet, a length of 32½ feet, and was armed with two fixed 7.92-millimeter MG17 machine guns, two 20-millimeter MG FF cannons in the wings, and a flexible MG15 in the rear cockpit.

The Romanian IAR81 and IAR81A were modified versions of the IAR80 and IAR80A fighters, respectively. They featured an increased wingspan of 34 feet, 5½ inches, a length of 29 feet, 2½ inches, and a height of 11 feet, 10 inches. The fitting of bomb racks under the wings for four 110-pound bombs and under the fuselage for one 551-pound bomb was supplemented by four 7.99-millimeter cannon in the IAR81A. It was powered by a single 1,025-horsepower IAR (Gnome-Rhone) 14 K 115 engine, which gave it a top speed of 317 mph at 13,120 feet and a range of 584 miles. This single-seater adaption was further supplemented in the dive bomber field by the IAR81C, a fighter/dive bomber version that featured two 20-millimeter MG151 cannon; it could also carry bombs. A total of 260 of the A and C series were built—along with the B, which had no dive bombing potential—and were used on the Eastern Front.

More potent for the Mediterranean theater of operations was the transferring of the German 2nd Stuka Wing, with more than 100 aircraft as part of X Air Corps, to airfields in Sicily. Here they were to pose a great threat to Malta, Egypt, and the Royal Navy. Their first and most spectacular attack took place on January 19, 1941. The 1st Group of the 1st Stuka Wing, led by Major Enneccerus, and the 2nd Group of the 2nd Stuka Wing, led by Hauptmann Hozzel, attacked the British fleet in the Sicilian Channel. They scored one hit on the battleship *Warspite* in return for the loss of one Stuka shot down by the battleship *Valiant*, but their main target was the aircraft carrier *Illustrious*, and in a precision assault they hit her with no fewer than six heavy bombs while three more were near misses. Heavily damaged, the only thing that saved the ship was her armored deck. The next day, another attack sank the cruiser *Southampton*, and damaged the *Gloucester*. Not for more than eighteen months did heavy ships attempt to dispute these waters again.

A Ju87R-2 of the Italian 101st Dive Bomber Group on patrol over Greece in 1941. The long-range fuel tanks can be seen clearly here.

Repeated attacks were made on Malta, with both the dock-yards and airfields being the targets, and in these, the German Ju87s were joined by the growing numbers of Italian dive bombers. Additional units moved into desert air strips to support the Axis attacks through Libya and into Egypt and took a major part in the subsequent campaigns in the years 1941–42 as the tide of war flowed up and down the North African coast. Other targets for both German and Italian Stukas and Ju88 units were the convoys from Gibraltar and Alexandria, which attempted to lift the siege of Malta during the same period. It is no mean boast by the Ju87 crews that they inflicted more damage on the Royal Navy in this period than the entire Italian Navy and Air Force combined. During the evacuation of Greece and the Battle of Crete in April and May 1941, the Ju87s took on the Mediterranean Fleet in earnest and inflicted heavy casualties, while further losses of smaller war-ships became a regular feature of operations off Tobruk and other North African ports. The successes of the Stukas against warship targets in the Mediterranean theater during this period are sum-marized in Table 30.

TABLE 30: ROYAL NAVY WARSHIPS SUNK OR DAMAGED BY JU87S IN THE MEDITERRANEAN, 1941

Date	Ship	Type	Result
January 10	*Illustrious*	Aircraft Carrier	Heavily damaged
January 10	*Warspite*	Battleship	Slightly damaged
January 11	*Southampton*	Cruiser	Sunk
January 11	*Gloucester*	Cruiser	Damaged
January 16	*Perth*	Cruiser	Damaged
January 16	*Illustrious*	Aircraft Carrier	Damaged
January 19	*Illustrious*	Aircraft Carrier	Damaged
February 22	*Terror*	Monitor	Sunk
February 24	*Dainty*	Destroyer	Sunk
April 27	*Diamond*	Destroyer	Sunk
April 27	*Wryneck*	Destroyer	Sunk

TABLE 30: ROYAL NAVY WARSHIPS SUNK OR DAMAGED BY JU87S IN THE MEDITERRANEAN, 1941 (*cont'd*)

Date	Ship	Type	Result
May 21	*Ajax*	Cruiser	Damaged
May 22	*Greyhound*	Destroyer	Sunk
May 22	*Gloucester*	Cruiser	Sunk
May 22	*Fiji*	Cruiser	Sunk
May 22	*Carlisle*	Cruiser	Damaged
May 22	*Naiad*	Cruiser	Damaged
May 23	*Kelly*	Destroyer	Sunk
May 23	*Kashmir*	Destroyer	Sunk
May 26	*Formidable*	Aircraft Carrier	Damaged
May 26	*Nubian*	Destroyer	Damaged
May 28	*Ajax*	Cruiser	Damaged
May 28	*Imperial*	Destoyer	Damaged (sunk later)
May 29	*Hereward*	Destroyer	Sunk
May 29	*Decoy*	Destroyer	Damaged
May 29	*Dido*	Cruiser	Damaged
May 29	*Orion*	Cruiser	Damaged
May 31	*Napier*	Destroyer	Damaged
June 1	*Calcutta*	Cruiser	Sunk
June 24	*Auckland*	Sloop	Sunk
June 29	*Waterhen*	Destroyer	Sunk
July 11	*Defender*	Destroyer	Sunk
July 12	*Flamingo*	Sloop	Damaged
July 12	*Cricket*	Gunboat	Damaged

It will be recalled that the first Italian dive bomber unit to re-equip with the Ju87 arrived at Comiso, Sicily, in August 1940. Their first mission took place on September 2 with an abortive search for a reported convoy near Malta. It was finally located the next day, and at 1425 hours, five Ju87s of the 96th Group went into action against it with an escort of six Macchi 200 fighters. Although they subsequently claimed to have hit a cruiser, no hits were made. A

A formation of Ju87R-2s of the 101st Dive Bomber Group returning to their airfield at Trapani Milo in Sicily after an attack on Malta. The distinctive Monte Erice can be seen to the left.

second raid with four Stukas made the same claim and a third attack added another cruiser plus a carrier damaged, but again, this was over-confidence, and no hits had been scored on any vessel. On September 5, five Italian Stukas dive bombed Malta.

More attacks followed, and on September 17, the Italian 96th Group suffered its first loss when twelve Stukas attacked Mikabba airfield in a dive. They were intercepted by Hurricanes of No. 261 Squadron and lost Sergeant Catani from 237th Squadron, who became a prisoner of war. On September 27, the Italian Stukas transferred to Lecce airfield in readiness for the invasion of Greece, but eight of these aircraft subsequently returned to Comiso on November 11 to form the nucleus of the second Italian unit.

The first actions of the 96th Group over Greece took place with attacks on Janina, Presba, and Florina airfields on November 5, 14, and 16, 1940, and on December 7, they were joined at Lecce by the 97th Group. The 96th was brought back for a period in January 1941 to take part in the *Illustrious* action, but they aborted their mission. Both units continued to support the hard-pressed

Italian troops on the Albanian front into the New Year, with some successes and a few losses. On March 5, a third Stuka group was formed, the 101st.

Both these units were joined by the other four squadrons at Lecce, the 208th during March 7–8 and the 209th on March 17. The Italians were taking a bad beating from the Greeks at this time and were hard-pressed to hold Valona itself, so great demands were made on the dive bomber crews, and as a result of bad weather conditions in the mountains during the winter and the poor state of the landing grounds, the attrition rate was high.

In February 1941, the first Italian Stukas joined the Germans in North Africa. The 96th Group transferred to Benghazi airport in stages beginning on February 1, as they were replaced by the 101st Group in the Balkans. Thee 236th Squadron under Captain E. Malvezzi was the first and was later joined by five Ju87s of the 237th Squadron under Captain G. Santioni. These were soon in action over Tobruk.

The solitary SM86 prototype was attached to th 96th Group to prove itself in combat. It was flown by Scarpini and made an attack on Hal Far with a single 1,100-pound bomb. When the 96th moved to Lecce-Galatina for the Greek operation, a dive bombing attack was made by Scarpini in this aircraft on Greek positions at Giannina. However, on December 21, Scarpini was shot down while flying a Ju87, and the SM86 was relegated to a hangar at Galatina and forgotten.

In the summer of 1941, this aircraft was dismantled, but a second prototype (MM398) fitted with two IF Gamma RC351 engines was tested at Vergiate by Commander Guido Nobili. The initial flight took place on August 7, and trials continued until December, but nothing much ever came of it.

For their own training the Italians modified three Caproni Bergamasca API, which had a fixed landing gear. These had been built for Paraguay, but were never paid for, so the Regia Aeronautica took them over and the Nucleo Addestramento of Lonate Pozzolo (Varese) modified them as dive bomber trainers. They were fitted with Junkers-style dive brakes made of wood under the wings, and stripped of nonessential gear. As such, these three API

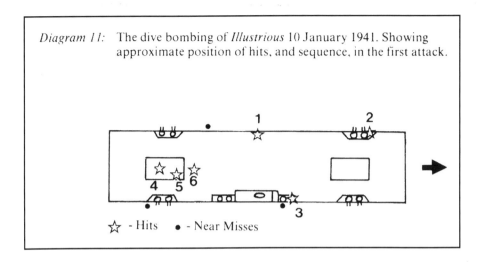

Diagram 11: The dive bombing of *Illustrious* 10 January 1941. Showing approximate position of hits, and sequence, in the first attack.

☆ - Hits   ● - Near Misses

were used sparsely during 1941–42 but were not a success, and in June 1942, they were scrapped.

In North Africa, StG3 moved into Castel Benito, Sirte, and Arco Philernorum airfields in January 1941, and were joined a month later by 1st Group, 1st Stuka Wing. Both units provided the spearhead of the newly formed Afrika Korps. The first German Stuka lost was shot down over Agheila on February 6, 1941. By April 1941, 3rd Group, StG1, had moved over from Sicily also. Those that remained continued to pound Malta constantly. They were reinforced by the larger long-range Ju88s, and yet another group was moved out of France to reinforce them during the same month, leaving only sixty Ju87s in that country.

In order to remove the threat of British bombers operating against his vital Romanian oil fields from Greek bases, Hitler was determined to get Mussolini out of the mess he was in in Greece and eject the Allies from Europe for good. He tried diplomatic means first, but when Yugoslavia threw out its government, German plans were hastily recast. The Stuka units already earmarked for the invasion of Russia—Operation Barbarossa—were quickly moved into forward bases in the south of Austria and Romania instead for another blitzkrieg demonstration. The 1st and 3rd Groups of the 77th Stuka Wing, now refitted and refurbished, moved into Rumanian bases; the 1st and 3rd Groups of the 2nd

Stuka Wing, the 1st Group of the 3rd Stuka Wing, and the crack 2nd Ground Attack Group of the 2nd Training and Demonstration Group moved into ready-use strips on the Bulgarian border as part of VIII Air Corps, and the 2nd Group of the 77th Stuka Wing lay ready in Austria, with the Italian units outflanking them at Albania. The Axis forces jumped off on April 6, 1941, and achieved complete surprise.

Once more, the combination of Stuka and Panzer was irresistible, as Hitler had predicted. The 2nd Ground Attack Group of the 2nd Training and Demonstration Wing wiped out the tiny air base of Prilep on the first day, then swung into their classic role of breaking up troop columns. The Yugoslav army was on par with the Polish army of two years before in bravery, but also in obsolescence and the effects on it were just as devastating. The 77th Stuka Wing cooperated in the massive attack that gave Belgrade the Warsaw treatment, while the Staff Group of the 3rd Stuka Wing and the 2nd Group of the 77th Stuka Wing blasted their way into the northern part of the stunned country. The 2nd Ground Attack Group of the 2nd Training and Demonstration Wing moving at

In an effort to bolster the Italians against the British Mediterranean Fleet and in attacks on Egypt and Malta, the Luftwaffe moved powerful forces into the area, including a wing of Stukas and some Ju88s. Here Italian airmen examine one of the first Ju88s to arrive in Sicily in early 1941.

breakneck speed, put in heavy attacks around Skopje, Servia, and over into Greece itself. Yugoslavia sued for terms on the fourteenth, but the panzers had thrust on into Greece without stopping, and within a few days, they had done what Mussolini's legions had failed to do all winter—thrown the Greek Army into hasty retreat along with its British allies. Athens capitulated on April 27, and German paratroopers crossed the Corinth canal, turning the last defensive line left to the Allies.

Almost incidentally, the Luftwaffe turned on the ports and harbors of Greece, sinking, among others, the old battleship *Kilkis* in dock, the destroyer *Hydra*, nine lesser warships, and forty-three merchantmen totaling 63,975 tons. The Ju87s contributed in full measure to these losses. A heavy toll was taken among transports evacuating the British forces, and in addition to the warships, the transports *Hellas, Pennland, Costa Rica,* and *Slamat* were sunk with heavy loss of life among the troops aboard. The long-range dive bombers, Ju87Rs, also struck across the water to Suda Bay, Crete, hitting the already damaged heavy cruiser *York* and finishing her off.

The surviving Allied troops reached Crete and began methodical preparations against the attack they daily expected against that now isolated island. Over in the western Mediterranean at this time, Stuka operations, both German and Italian, were more limited. The main mission was undertaken against the "Tiger" convoy bringing tanks and troops through from Great Britain via Gibraltar and Malta. An attack on May 8 by Ju87s was frustrated by Fulmar fighters from *Ark Royal* and by heavy cloud cover; no ships were hit.

dive bombing operations were stepped up on Malta. A heavy raid was mounted on April 14 with both Ju87s and Ju88s. The bulk of the fighting, however, lay in the eastern basin as the Axis armies swept east along the North African coast and isolated the port of Tobruk. The 5th Group of the 1st Stuka Wing under Hauptmann Joachim Rieger, an anti-shipping expert, was kept busy attacking the warships keeping the port provided.

Meanwhile, the Stuka units had been regrouping in readiness for the assault on Crete itself, Operation Mercury (*Merkur*). For the first three weeks of May, they were busy preparing forward airfields in southern Greece and the southeast Peloponnesian islands for the dive bombers and troop-transporting Ju52s. Into the newly created airstrips at Melos, Lulaoi, and Scarpanto flew the Stukas. They now had the range to cover all the seaward approaches to Crete. The 2nd Stuka Wing had its groups ready by May 20, with two at Molai and Mycene and a third at Scarpanto. At Eleusis, the longer ranging Ju88s of the 1st and 2nd Groups of 2nd Training and Demonstration Wing settled in under Hauptmann Hoffmann and Kollewe.

They were eager to face the British fleet, but their first task was to soften up the islands' defenses to pave the way for the airborne troops. In order to increase the killing power of their bomb loads, which tended to explode upward on contact with the rocky surface, new fusing systems were adopted by the Stuka crews themselves to give a more lethal lateral spread against concentrations of troops. This involved fitting a metal rod with a 3-inch-diameter disk at the end to the bombs; the bomb was thus detonated some 12-inches above the ground, giving a high scatter effect. It was named *Zünder-abstandstäbe* or *Dinortstabe* after Dinort, whose unit was the first to use them.

The battle for Crete opened on May 20, 1941, and initial dive bomber targets ashore were the defenses around Maleme and Canea airfields, especially the antiaircraft batteries. An hour after these attacks started, the first gliders arrived over these fields and at the Akrotiri Peninsula overlooking the main harbor area of Suda Bay, and strong and continuous dive bomber sorties were flown all day in support.

The Mediterranean Fleet was at sea in strength to deal with the expected seaborne landings, and during the days that followed, they were subjected to an unprecedented scale of air attack by the Stuka units. Although on the twenty-first, the dive bombers were still mainly preoccupied with supporting the troops ashore one Italian group was allocated to deal with the British warships at daybreak. Attacks were made at first light, and the cruiser *Ajax* was hit and damaged. Just as important was the scale of expenditure of the warships' antiaircraft ammunition, and after one day of non-stop dive bombing, the fleet found itself dangerously depleted in this respect for the next days combat.

On May 21, the destroyer *Janus* was sunk in a combined attack by Italian Cant bombers and the Stukas of 3rd Group, 2nd Stuka

Wing, under Hauptmann Brucker, which hit her at 1239 hours with three bombs. The first two struck aft, wrecking her boiler room and engine rooms, while the third exploded her after magazine. A photograph taken by the Italian Stuka unit, the 210th Squadron, which also attacked, shows her blowing up.

The pattern was repeated during the following days. The Ju87s more and more were switched to take on the warships. At 0630 hours on the twenty-second, the cruisers *Fiji* and *Gloucester* were both near-missed without serious damage. Attacks by the 1st Training and Demonstration Wing damaged the cruisers *Carlisle* and *Naiad*. At 1320 hours, the destroyer *Greyhound* was detached from the fleet to sink a solitary fishing boat between Pori and Antikithera islands, and she was set upon by eight Ju87s, which hit her at 1351 hours. A 550-pound bomb fell directly on her solitary 3-inch AA gun, and the two 110-pound bombs were also hits. *Greyhound* sank in four minutes with heavy loss of life. This was bad enough, but the error was compounded by the detachment of two more destroyers to pick up her survivors, with the *Gloucester* and *Fiji* in support. These ships steamed away from the protection of the battleships' AA fire and into the arms of the Stukas. By the time they were recalled, it was too late. Already low on ammunition, *Gloucester* was soon reduced to firing practice shells at the waves of dive bombers that pounced on the squadron.

Having survived numerous attacks by Ju87s and Ju88s, *Gloucester* was hit at 1527 hours by at least two bombs. The first exploded in the gunroom flat, damaging a boiler room and extinguishing all lights; the second hit the after antiaircraft director and demolished the main topmast. Another attack resulted in several near misses, and then another hit was received on her port torpedo tubes, and yet a fourth detonated on her port pom-pom mounting. Heavily on fire, the cruiser slid to a standstill, and still the bombs rained down. Three more explosions rent her hull at 1545 hours; she listed over to port and finally sank at 1715, her death throes being recorded on film by the victorious airmen.

Fiji did not long outlast her. Continuously near-missed during the afternoon, her AA armament all but depleted, she was finished off by a single direct hit after a Me109 Jabo of 1st Group, 1st Training and Demonstration Wing, had brought her to a halt earlier with a 550-pound bomb that blew in her plating amidships. After a second hit, she rolled over at 2015 hours.

During the course of the day, the battleships *Warspite* and *Valiant* were both hit, as were, again, the cruisers *Carlisle* and *Naiad*. During the following night, the same errors were repeated, and three destroyers were detached to bombard Maleme airfield. At dawn on the twenty-third, they were located while withdrawing by the 1st Group, 2nd Stuka Wing, under Hauptmann Hitschold. The *Kashmir* was hit first and quickly sank. Then the *Kelly*, turning hard under full helm at high speed, was struck by a heavy bomb, which capsized her. This was at 0800 hours. Survivors from these two ships were picked up by the *Kipling*, which herself survived several heavy attacks that left her trailing oil, but she reached port.

In attempts to limit the scale of Stuka attacks ashore, where the fighting had reached a critical stage, it was decided, in the lack of any RAF contribution, to launch a carrier attack on Scarpanto airfield from the *Formidable*. This was done on the night of the May 25-26, but although some slight damage was done to a few aircraft, the losses inflicted were negligible, and the price paid was exorbitant. Although the fleet withdrew beyond normal Stuka range quickly, they overlooked the fact that Stukas were still operating from Libya also. Thus, they were caught by the 2nd Group, 2nd Stuka Wing, under Major Enneccerus at 1320 hours. The twenty Ju87Rs were operating at the extreme edge of their range when they picked up the fleet, and they made their attacks immediately. Penetrating the barrage, the Ju87Rs scored two direct hits on the carrier, damaging one of the 4.5-inch turrets and hitting the carrier on the starboard side aft, blowing out the ship's bulkheads and starting large fires. Eight Stukas had attacked *Formidable*, while the others turned their attentions to her consorts. The destroyer *Nubian* was hit by a bomb, which blew her stern off, but she managed to limp home. Subsequent attacks by the Ju88s of the 1st Training and Demonstration Wing scored one hit on the "Y" turret of the battleship *Barham*. On the same day, the evacuation of Crete began.

At 1700 hours on May 28, a force of three cruisers and six destroyers heading to embark soldiers was located about 90 miles from Scarpanto and subjected to nonstop dive bombing until nightfall. The destroyer *Imperial* was near-missed, as was the cruiser *Ajax*, which had to be sent back damaged. By 0255 hours, the remainder had finished loading and again stood out to sea with 4,000 troops aboard. At 0345 hours, the rudder of the *Imperial* jammed and she had to be sunk by another destroyer. By 0600, while clearing the Kaso Strait, the force was located and the dive bombing commenced. *Hotspur* was attacked by six Ju87s but survived. Not so fortunate was the *Hereward*. Attacked at 0625, she was hit close by her fore funnel by a Stuka which dived below 1,500 feet in a determined attack. She was crippled, left behind, and later finished off.

Next to be damaged was the destroyer *Decoy*, her engine room taking splinters from a near-miss that fractured her turbine feet and reduced her speed to 25 knots. This was at 0645 hours. The promised fighter cover never materialized, and at 0735, Stukas machine-gunned the cruiser *Orion*, wounding her captain. A near-miss reduced her speed to 21 knots. At 0815, the Ju87s planted a direct hit on the cruiser *Dido*. It is thought that this one hit—on "B" turret—killed twenty-seven sailors and eleven soldiers, with many more wounded. Eight close misses were counted around her at this time.

The ordeal continued. At 0900 hours, the *Orion* was also hit, on "A" turret, by a Ju87 that onlookers mistook for a suicide attack, so low did the aircraft dive before release. The Stuka failed to recover and crashed into the sea just off the bows of *Dido*. It is possible that the pilot was badly wounded and determined to sell his life dearly. The whole armored casing of the ship's turret was torn away, and the guns were destroyed, while "B" turret next to it was also heavily damaged.

At 0930 hours, *Orion* was near-missed, and at 1045, eleven Stukas delivered another concentrated attack on her about 100 miles south of Kaso Strait. She was immersed in the spray of numerous near-misses, and one bomb hit her hard. It passed straight through her bridge and sick bay and exploded deep inside her, demolishing the stokers' messdeck, which was packed with troops. This single bomb killed 107 sailors and 155 soldiers, wounding 300 more. The scene below defied description.

A similar ordeal awaited a second squadron of warships on the thirtieth when the cruiser *Perth* was hit behind her bridge by a bomb that penetrated to her foremost boiler room at 0930 hours.

TABLE 31: FIRST FOUR ITALIAN STUKA UNITS OPERATIONS, 1940–41

Group	Commander	Strength	Squadron	Commanders	Date
96th	Capt. Ercolani	13	236th	Lt. Malvezzi	August 1940
			237th	Lt. Santinoni	
97th	Col. Moscatelli	14	238th	Lt. Bertuzzi	November 1940
			239th	Lt. Genni	
101st	Maj. Donadio	16	208th	Capt. Bertuzzi	March 1941
			209th	Capt. Romanese	
102nd	Capt. Genni	20	209th	Capt. Stringa	May 1941
				Lt. Bigoni	

She was also near-missed in a later attack, as was the destroyer *Jaguar*. Some fighter cover appeared after this, driving off one heavy attack by Ju87s and Ju88s, and no ships were actually sunk.

During the same day, the destroyer *Kelvin* was so damaged by three Ju88s that she had to be sent back, and the next morning, twelve Ju88s damaged the destroyer *Napier*. The transport *Glengyle*, escorted by three cruisers and six destroyers, embarked 6,029 soldiers that night without loss, but the final drama of the Crete campaign took place the next day. The antiaircraft cruiser *Calcutta* was sent to help escort her but was herself caught by surprise by two Ju88s diving out of the sun at 0917 hours, despite radar warning. The second aircraft straddled *Calcutta* with a perfect stick, two bombs striking the old vessel, which sank rapidly within a few minutes. Thus ended the Battle of Crete, perhaps the Stukas greatest victory at sea.

Although the bulk of the Stuka units were almost immediately transferred back north in readiness for the postponed assault on Russia, a number of units remained in the Mediterranean, and these, in cooperation with the Italian Stukas, were instrumental in giving the British army more bitter lessons. By now the Italians had built their strength up to four units as shown in Table 31.

The dive bombers that remained were fully committed to supporting Rommel's thrust east to the Egyptian border, which left Tobruk cut off. The supplying of this garrison gave the depleted Mediterranean Fleet a further chore, and one in which the dive bombers were able to take good advantage of. Heavy attacks were also made on Tobruk itself.

The German units employed in 1941 in North Africa were 1st Group, 1st Stuka Wing; 2nd Group, 2nd Stuka Wing; and 1st Group, 3rd Stuka Wing. The main assault had broken earlier, in April, but the garrison had withstood it well. During the quick German advance, the dive bombers had performed well in their textbook drill of army cooperation. One observer noted, "On April 7, the GAF struck in considerable strength at the Derna defiles, which were chock-full of retreating vehicles. inflicting much damage and seriously delaying the withdrawal."

Between April 11 and June 24, 1941, no less than forty-six Stuka missions were made on Tobruk and its harbor. Many of the attacks were directed at AA positions, and the heaviest assaults occurred on April 14 (40 Ju87s), May 29 (60 Ju87s), and June 2 (60 Ju87s). Out of 959 aircraft who flew the missions, the defenses claimed the destruction of fifty-four Stukas by the heavy and light AA batteries of the garrison, proving that well-trained gunners could inflict damage on dive bombers if they stood their ground. At sea, losses were heavy.

On May 25, the Italian 239th Squadron, led by Commander Genni, attacked warships off Tobruk at 1720 hours, sinking the merchantman *Helka* (3,741 tons) and her escort, the sloop *Grimsby*. On June 24, Stukas sank the sloop *Auckland*, and so it went on. Between April 12 and December 9, the Royal Navy lost twenty-six naval vessels, including the brand-new minelayer *Latona*, which was sunk in a night dive bombing attack. Six merchant ships were also sunk, and many others were damaged.

As 1941 turned into 1942, the dive bomber was making an impressive mark on the North African desert campaign, but the Allied response was weak or nonexistent. Let us turn to Britain and see why this was so.

CHAPTER 17

War in Whitehall

British Limited Operations and Disagreements, 1940–42

The massive and decisive defeat of France and the conquest of the whole of Western Europe in the same manner as the overrunning of Poland the year before rammed home the lesson of the power and effectiveness of the dive bomber, both as a battle-winner and economical force. With Great Britain penned into her home islands and daily expecting an invasion, a hasty reexamination of the hardware with which they might expect to repel such an invasion emphasized the complete lack of any type of dive bomber in the RAF for army cooperation work. This caused much adverse comment from Winston Churchill, and the new Minister for Aircraft Production, William Maxwell Aitken, 1st Baron Beaverbrook, quickly set to work to try to rectify the situation.

The RAF, having set their faces against the type for many years, and with no quick way of obtaining a dive bomber from home factories, countered with the oft-repeated paper arguments that varied from time to time but remained always, in essence, firmly opposed to the dive bomber and more and more deeply committed to the long-range heavy bomber. It was not the German armies they wished to destroy but the German cities, and this they felt would be all that was required to win the war anyway.

General William Edward Ironside had been one of the senior army officers who had foreseen the need for close air support in the same manner as the German Army used the Stukas. He had strongly advocated an Army Air Arm long before the war, much to the distaste of the air marshals. He maintained that for such a job,

specialized aircraft and aircrew were needed, attuned to the requirements of land warfare. The air chiefs would have none of this, maintaining their faith in general-purpose light bombers to carry out the
tasks; the only specialized role to which they catered was the provision of spotter aircraft in the form of the Lysander, which was totally
unsuitable for the type of mechanized warfare which had broken
over Ironside's troops in May 1940. As his biographer subsequently
noted, "The opening stages of World War II, with German dive
bombers preparing the way for armored columns, now proved Ironside right."

No less an impact had been made on his successor at Dunkirk,
General Alan Brooke, who noted, "After seeing yesterday the ease
with which a dive bomber can sink a destroyer, it is an unpleasant
feeling." His biographer noted that "a subject to which Brooke
devoted almost as much time was air cooperation with ground
troops. His experience in France had made him fanatical about
this." But he was not to get much farther than his predecessor in
convincing others for the need for it.

An American historian noted that "the RAF and French Air
Force also began the war with little in the way of an effective,
trained air arm for close cooperation with ground forces. In the
1940 crisis in France, this cost them dearly." Too late, the French
acknowledged the truth of this: "Even though the Stukas had
already shown their worth in Spain, and though General
Vuillemin, at General Milch's invitation in 1938, had watched an
impressive display of dive bombing, our High Command, both air
and army, did not see fit to adopt this type of warfare."

Even Churchill himself, a staunch defender throughout the
war of the RAF line in Parliament and public, from time to time
allowed himself to vent his frustration at the lack of British dive
bombers and the will to produce one. The RAF view was upheld in
the many debates that followed by Sir Archibald Sinclair, air minister. Beaverbrook was convinced of the need for dive bombers even
if the air staff was not, and a bitter conflict of priorities existed
over the years between the two rival ministries, who failed to see
eye-to-eye on many topics—not least the dive bomber. Being a
Canadian, Beaverbrook took a broader trans-Atlantic view. He saw
the untapped resources of the United States as a safe base upon

which the immediate needs of Britain in the air could be built up, and although the British Purchasing Commission had already been established in the wake of the original Anglo-French team, he went right over their heads through Maurice Wilson of the Royal Bank of Canada to get the aircraft he considered necessary.

In April 1940, the French had ordered 192 of the Brewster 340 dive bombers through the Anglo-French Agreement. This being a modification of the U.S. Navy Buccaneer dive bomber, prepared by the same corporation. With the collapse of France, this contract was taken over by the British government under the terms of the Purvis Block-Laine agreement. The contract contained an option to order an additional 150 aircraft, and this option was exercised by the British Purchasing Commission on July 27, 1940.

At that date, Brewster offered a further option of 100 aircraft, and this option was also exercised by the commission on November 1, 1940, bringing the total number of Bermudas (as the RAF renamed them) dive bombers on order to 450. On November 2, a new contract was created to cover the supply of another 300 aircraft of this type. Delivery was to be made of the full 750 beginning in January 1941, to be completed by March 1942.

But between the taking over of the original French order in July and the placing of the November orders, a great deal had happened. With the formation of the Ministry of Aircraft Production, still more orders were placed in the United States that cut across these arrangements. On June 16, 1940, Sir Henry Self sent a telegram to the Ministry of Aircraft Production, which contained an offer of 200 Vultee Vengeance dive bombers; a decision had to be made by June 21. Beaverbrook consulted with War Secretary Anthony Eden, and the details were shown to the Air Ministry, who approved the order. On June 28, Eden wrote to Sinclair, confirming the order of 200 Vengeance aircraft and suggesting that the general and the air staffs should consider the organization of units together. Sinclair agreed.

Meanwhile, the subject of dive bombers had been raised by John Moore-Brabazon, the minister of transport, in a private capacity. His idea was to build dive bombers under license in new factories in Canada. The availability of American types with the promise of early delivery overrode this idea, and further orders were placed in the United States instead. As Lord Beaverbrook wrote to Sinclair later, "we ordered in the United States, as you know, because prior to July 1940, no one at the Air Ministry had included dive bombers in their requisitions, nor had anyone even ordered a prototype. So we had none on home stocks and the quickest way to get them was in the United States."

Historian A. J. P. Taylor recorded the upshot of the July order thus: "In July 1940, he placed a large order for dive bombers in Canada and the United States. Eden, then secretary for war, was enthusiastic. The Air Ministry protested and refused to supply or train pilots."

On August 2, a meeting took place between the air staff and the general staff, with the threat of invasion looming large over them. The Air Ministry viewpoint prevailed although the final salient features agreed on for a new "close-support" aircraft were as follows: "A single engined dive bomber (light or medium type, with a crew of two primarily for operating by day; in consequence it must be adequately armed and protected against air and ground opposition. In this respect it should be armored underneath while the majority of its gun armament should be in self-defense against fight attack mainly from above." The suggested bomb load was 700 pounds. "In addition to the normal qualities of a dive bomber, the aircraft should be suitable for flying at a very low altitude to achieve surprise." An optimum top speed of about 300 mph was required, as was a maximum range of 700 miles. The aircraft was to be constructed with a view of ease of maintenance. All well and good, but the Air Ministry had the last word: "The technical specifications of an aircraft to meet these requirements is a matter for the air staff to decide." Just what this meant was revealed later. "While a steep dive bomber was *not essential*, the aircraft should have as steep an angle of dive as possible without prejudice to other essential requirements." This proved to be the "out" they required to guarantee that the plane would not be a true dive bomber. The RAF was not talking about a dive bomber at all, but rather the allocation of the Blenheim to the close-support role. Meanwhile, more orders were placed by the Ministry of Aircraft Production for American-built dive bombers, but the heady promises of the builders soon fell short, and deliveries were increasingly delayed as teething and shop floor problems delayed the program month after month. By May 1941, a revised estimate of delivery dates for the Vengeance and Bermuda was submitted.

Beaverbrook again raised the question of dive bombers with Sinclair in February 1941 and was duly informed that no more orders for this type of aircraft were going to be placed. In despair at this attitude, Beaverbrook tried another tack and directly approached David Margesson, who had succeeded Eden as War Secretary. The reply he got left no doubt that the War Office had been weaned away from their original stated specifications of the previous summer. "While we were deeply impressed with the capabilities of aircraft used in this manner, we are not convinced that the so-called 'dive bomber' is the most suitable aircraft to use. Hence, we have abandoned the use of the term 'dive bomber' and have spoken of a 'close support' bomber."

As a further step, the priority given to existing orders was further downgraded. A memo of February 25 reduced the dive bomber in priority from third to bottom place, behind the heavy and medium bombers, fighters, and army-support types. The Air Ministry went still further after a meeting with American general Henry "Hap" Arnold, then chief of the U.S. Army Air Corps, on April 23. On April 26, the Air Ministry notified the Ministry of Aircraft Production that "the Air Ministry confirms that the additional orders

TABLE 32: REVISED DELIVERY FORECASTS FOR U.S.-BUILT DIVE BOMBERS FOR RAF, MAY 1941

Type	Date	Number	Type	Date	Number
Bermuda	June	1	Vengeance	June	1
Bermuda	July	12	Vengeance	July	1
Bermuda	August	41	Vengeance	August	2
Bermuda	September	70	Vengeance	September	9
Bermuda	October	86	Vengeance	October	20
Bermuda	November	90	Vengeance	November	32
Bermuda	December	90	Vengeance	December	44
Total		390	Total		109

for dive bombers are not wanted unless such orders are necessary to enable the Brewster, Northrop, and Vultee plants to be switched later on to types which are needed. If there is no such need or intention, the Air Ministry suggests that the expenditure of labor and materials on these order is wholly unjustified."

Despite such statements, additional orders were placed by the Ministry for Aircraft Production for 300 Vengeances on April 9 and another 300 on June 17 under the Lease-Lend Agreement; this was in addition to the 200 ordered on February 25, before Lend-Lease had been enacted. When Churchill asked why no dive bombers had yet entered service in the RAF, despite the pressing need for them, he was told that "a dive bomber, which of necessity would be inadequate for any other role, was a luxury which we could not afford." So two years after the Ju87s had shown what could be done, Britain was still arguing about the need for such aircraft, with France, Norway, Greece, and North Africa behind them. In September 1941, a total of 1,400 Vengeance and Bermuda dive bombers were on order. It was then stated that the RAF hoped to equip ten squadrons with Bermudas starting in February 1942. The Vengeance dive bombers were to equip squadrons in the Far East, Australia, India, and Canada.

In May 1942, a further review revealed that no Bermuda aircraft had yet become available from production. Deliveries were now expected to start in July. Only one Vengeance had been delivered in March and twenty-three more in April; of these, five were being shipped to Australia. Total aircraft accepted on May 12, 1942, were nineteen from Vultee, fifty-one from Northrop (which was subcontracting). The fact that the latter were ahead in supply was because they had concentrated on the Vengeance, whereas Vultee was still working on modifications to the basic design; as a result, the planes from the two plants were virtually different types. The Northrop version lacked fittings for the F24 camera, fixed-gun heating, long-range fuel tanks, and other extras.

The RAF had insisted on a number of improvements following initial trials, the chief of which were strengthening the undercarriage, redesigning the elevators, changing the propeller blade, and modifying the fuel system. It was planned to equip nine squadrons in Australia, two in Canada, six in India, and one in South Africa.

A camouflaged Skua II with Bristol Perseus XII enging L2928 over England. After Dunkirk, Skuas operated under RAF Coastal Command and carried out many hazardous missions across the English Channel.

Earlier offers of Dauntless dive bombers from the United States had been rejected out of hand by the RAF, as the SBD was considered obsolete.

Meanwhile, the last Skua dive bombers of the Royal Navy had been disbanded; most of them were replaced by Fulmar fighters. The new Fairey Barracuda, which combined a principal role as torpedo bomber with strong dive bomber potential, had been delayed by replacement of the power plant. The last operational dive bomber unit with the British forces, other than experimental units, was No. 810 Squadron, which still operated under Coastal Command, though it sometimes embarked aboard carriers to conduct strikes against coastal shipping and land installations off Norway with the fleet. This was now a hard-flying, tough unit that had developed a sturdy independence and pioneered many new dive bombing innovations off their own backs. They still came up against a wall of ignorance as to how their aircraft could be properly employed and suffered much frustration; they were given missions and tasks impossible to carry out in safety. Their end came

abruptly when the Luftwaffe attacked their base at St. Eval and
destroyed many Skuas parked near the control tower. It is on
record that many of the crews openly cheered and applauded this
destruction of their aircraft, so bitterly did they feel they had been
mishandled by their new masters. It was a sad end to what could
have been an invaluable unit.

In contrast to the British abandonment of dive bombing and
the continued expansion of Axis uses of it, it is interesting to see
the developments taken to fruitition by one small neutral state in
the European theater during this period to see what conclusions
they had reached. Because Sweden was not involved in the war,
her independent train of development is of considerable interest
as it was free of any bias. It will be recalled that the first batch of
CFM license-built Harts (B4s) was delivered starting in July 1936.
These deliveries continued from July 1938 to May 1939, with the
balance of the CVM and ASJA contracted 134s, a total of forty-five
in all, until May 1939. The three original Hawker Harts (S7s) were
kept in service for a number of years, being phased out of service
between 1940 and 1947, one with 1,284 flying hours on the clock.
All the B4s built in Sweden served through the 1930s until 1940–
41, and some continued until 1946–47, clocking up 1,100 to 1,235
flying hours.

Meanwhile, anti-shipping tactics had been developed by the
Swedish dive bomber groups. The basic attack plan was based on
the nine-plane squadron attack. By 1939, the Swedish dive bombers
had been organized with F4 Jamtlands at Fröson (near Ostersund
in Northern Sweden) and F6 Vilstgota at Karlsborg west of central
Lake Vattern. With F4, the Harts served operationally from January
1938 until October 1940, although a couple of Harts were in use
after that date for minor duties until December 1943. The F6 Wing
received its first Harts in February 1940 and the type served operationally until November 1941. From 1940–41, the light bomber
units were re-equipped, but during the Winter War of 1939–40
between Soviet Russia and Finland, a few Swedish Harts saw limited
combat when in early 1940 three (and later four) B4As served with

the Swedish Volunteer Flight F19, a mixed squadron of fighters and light bombers sent to aid the Finns in the north. Losses in this brief campaign consisted of two Harts, which collided on January 12 over Markajarvi-Salla, and a third was shot down by Soviet fighters soon afterward.

During 1940–41, their replacements arrived. These were SAAB B5s, a license-built version of the American Northrop 8A-1 light attack bomber. Powered by a single Bristol/SFA Mk XXIV 980-horsepower engine, the B5 was a great step forward. It had a top speed of 205 mph and a range of 1,056 miles with a bomb load of 1,100 pounds. Even so, this was only an interim type, and in 1942–43, the introduction of the SAAB B17 began.

Dive bombing in Sweden, as in other nations, was meant to utilize the element of surprise, and attacks were usually mounted from 4,900 to 6,500 feet using cloud cover if available. "The pilot must localize his target with the utmost rapidity and at once like a thunderbolt from a clear sky, dive down onto it," read one account. "When starting the dive, the flying speed is usually less than 125 mph, in the almost vertical plunge it accelerates quickly to about 250 mph."

Meanwhile, the main Luftwaffe effort from mid-1941 was directed against the Soviet Union, but limited and renewed use of the dive bomber continued to dominate their war effort in the Mediterranean theater as 1941 gave way to 1942. Long-range dive bombers—Ju88s of LG1, for example—carried out a mission against Suez itself from their bases in Crete on July 14, 1941, during which they hit the liner *Georgic* (27,751 tons) and set her afire; she became a total loss.

Night dive bombing operations continued on a limited scale, and some took place over Britain in the autumn of 1941. Although only training units remained in northern France, the experience gained led to a series of small-scale night "tip-and-run" raids, which were launched against southern coastal towns to gain additional combat experience. Operating from Pas-de-Calais airfield, some thirty Ju87s were used, and attacks were made on Margate and

This Northrop 8 A-1 dive bomber was purchased by the Royal
Swedish Air Force to replace its old Harts.

Ramsgate (September 7–8) and Dover (October 1–2 and 2–3),
resulting in some civilian casualties.

Back in the Mediterranean, the arrival of the 2nd Air Fleet
(*Luftflotte*) in Sicily in November 1941 heralded a renewal in German intentions to force the issue over Malta. Although many of the
Stuka units initially allocated had to be retained in the Russian theater to hold the Soviet winter offensive, Ju87D strength reached its
peak in the Mediterranean in 1942.

With the arrival in Sicily of the Advanced Training Group of the
1st Stuka Wing in December 1941, the attacks were renewed on
Malta. Their aims then were two-fold: to reduce the island as a base
for offensive operations by the Royal Navy and to soften it up in
preparation for its invasion and occupation (Operation Hercules),
which was planned for the summer of 1942. The success of the first
part, conversely, led to the abandonment of the second prema-
turely, and Malta was to survive.

The 1st Group, 3rd Stuka Wing, was already in the area, and
the two new units were reorganized in March 1942 to form a complete wing with the 1st Group, 1st Stuka Wing, becoming 2nd
Group, 3rd Stuka Wing; the 2nd Group, 2nd Stuka Wing, was redesignated as 3rd Group, 3rd Stuka Wing. With more than seventy
Ju87D1-Trop Stukas and the long-range Ju88s of the 1st Training

and Demonstration Wing operating from Crete after undergoing an intensive anti-shipping course, the stage was set. Cooperating were the Italian 209th and 239th Squadrons of the 102nd Group. Captain Giuseppe Tamborra of the latter unit was killed over Malta on May 30, and his replacement, Lieutenant Fulvio Papalia, in turn was shot down by a Spitfire on July 12. These units operated from Gela from May 1942 onward. The 3rd Group, 3rd Stuka Wing, converted to Doras at Biscari–San Pietro in March.

The assault that broke over Malta during the first four months of 1942 was the heaviest concentration of bombing to date, and enormous damage was done to the dockyards and airfields. But in the interim the island's defenses had been improved with numerous heavy and light AA batteries and the establishment of strong forces of Spitfires with better facilities. Constant reinforcing of these fighters was carried out by aircraft carriers of the Royal Navy, with the USS *Wasp* also making two such ferry trips as well. Thus, the battle was much more evenly joined than before, and dive bomber losses were severe. They retained their effectiveness, however, and the warships based at Malta took such heavy losses they had to withdraw.

On February 9, 1942, Stukas operating from the desert badly damaged the destroyer *Farndale* off Mersa Matruh during a convoy operation, and in the aftermath of another convoy, Ju88s destroyed the supply ships *Clan Campbell*, *Pampas*, and *Talabot*, as well as the naval auxilliary *Breconshire*, between March 23 and 26. During the same period, Ju88s also hit the destroyer *Legion* south of Malta. She joined the destroyer *Kingston* in dry-dock, and there both were subjected to violent Ju87 attacks. *Legion* was finished off on March 26.

In April, dive bomber assaults on the harbor grew to a high intensity. On April 9, the destroyer *Lance* was wrecked in dock, and on the eleventh, *Kingston* and the already damaged destroyer *Gallant* were hit and wrecked. The light cruiser *Penelope* was damaged but escaped to Gibraltar despite several attacks by Ju88s. Among other ships sunk by the dive bombers in this period were the submarines *Glavkos*, *Pandora*, and P36, the tanker *Plumleaf*, and the minesweeper *Abingdon* on the fifth. South of Crete, the Ju88s of the 1st Training and Demonstration Wing caught the destroyers *Jackal*, *Kipling*, and *Lively* on May 11 and sank them all.

Attacks on relief convoys continued unabated. In June, a double operation was mounted by the Royal Navy: Harpoon from the west and Vigorous from the east. In the narrows, the Axis dive bombers attacked the former on June 14 without success, but the next day, Stukas sank the *Chant* (5,601 tons) and *Burdwan* (5,600 tons) and disabled the tanker *Kentucky*, which was later abandoned. Vigorous fared even worse, as Stukas operating from Crete and the desert airfields were switched to this target. This saved the retreating troops of the 8th Army but decimated the ships.

On June 12, Major Walter Linke led a Ju87 attack that so damaged the transport *City of Calcutta* that she had to turn back to Tobruk. The Dutch freighter *Aagterkerk* developed engine trouble and was also sent there, but an attack by forty Ju87s outside the harbor sank her on the fourteenth and damaged the corvette *Primula*. The 1st Training and Demonstration Wing's Ju88s under Captain Helbig attacked the same afternoon, sinking the *Bhutan* (6,104 tons) and damaging the *Potaro* (5,410 tons). The next day, the 3rd Stuka Wing mounted a saturation attack, sinking the destroyers *Airedale* and *Nestor* and damaging the cruiser *Birmingham* before the convoy turned back to Alexandria.

A B17 on patrol over Swedish forests in 1943. The first Swedish-built, Swedish-engined dive bombers were the SAAB L10s, designated as the B17 dive bomber. They began to enter service in 1943.

In August, the biggest Malta convoy was mounted via Gibraltar in Operation Pedestal. It was given the protection of three aircraft carriers, two battleships, and a host of smaller warships. On the evening of August 11, Ju88s near-missed the carrier *Victorious,* and on the twelfth, Ju88s of the 1st Group, 54th Bomber Wing in Gerbini; the 606th and 806th Bomber Groups in Catania; the 2nd and 3rd

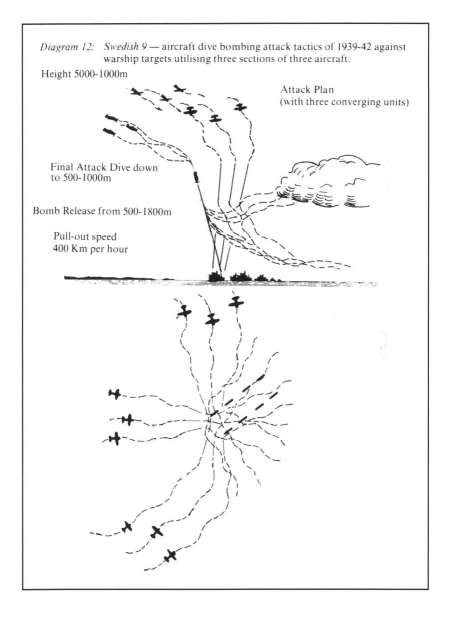

Diagram 12:   *Swedish 9* — aircraft dive bombing attack tactics of 1939-42 against warship targets utilising three sections of three aircraft.

Height 5000-1000m

Attack Plan
(with three converging units)

Final Attack Dive down
to 500-1000m

Bomb Release from 500-1800m

Pull-out speed
400 Km per hour

During the blitz on Malta in spring 1942, German and Italian dive bombers joined forces to drive out the British navy. Shown here is a Ju88A-4 of Bomber Wing 77 over Sicily en route to Malta.

Groups of the 77th Bomber Wing in Comiso and Gerbini; and the 1st Training and Demonstration Wing, which was flown in from Crete to Gerbini, mounted a succession of heavy attacks. A heavier assault by thirty-seven Ju88s at midday damaged the freighter *Deucalion* (7,516 tons). By 0635 hours the next day, the convoy was in Stuka range, and a combined attack by twenty Ju87s of the 3rd Stuka Wing from Trapani and nine Italian Stukas from the 239th Squadron broke through the defenses. Near-misses were scored on several ships, including the battleship *Rodney*, while the carrier *Indomitable* was hit by two heavy bombs and near-missed by three others. She had to withdraw badly damaged and heavily on fire.

On the evening of August 12, a strong attacks by thirty Ju88s sank the *Empire Hope* (12,628 tons) and *Glenorchy* (8,982 tons). The following day, twelve Ju88s sank the *Waimarama* (12,843 tons), and Italian Ju87s hit the *Dorset* while German and Italian attacks hit this ship again, as well as the *Port Chalmers* and the tanker *Ohio*. Then Stukas hit the *Rochester Castle*, while *Dorset* (10,624 tons) was finished off by Ju87s, fourteen of which concentrated on her that evening. Another Stuka crashed into the *Ohio*.

In June, the 3rd Stuka Wing conducted heavy dive bombing attacks, which crushed the defensive line held by the Free French at Bir Hacheim, and soon afterwards, heavy Stuka assaults led to the fall of Tobruk itself. This further success led to a motion of censure on the government, in which Churchill had to defend the anti-dive bomber policy of the RAF. But in truth, such were the delays to the promised American-built Vengeance and Bermuda types that even if the air marshals had somehow been forced to admit that they had been as wrong in 1942 (as they were in 1940, 1935, and 1918), they would have been unable to do much to rectify matters.

Not only in the Mediterranean had the dive bomber achieved a lasting mark on events in 1942. By now, the war was worldwide, and in Russia and the wastes of the Pacific and Indian Oceans, other nations' dive bombers were dictating the course of events.

CHAPTER 18

Clash of Giants

The Eastern Front, 1941–42: German and Soviet Developments

While everyone was busily writing off the Ju87 on paper in Britain, the Germans were developing a new mark of this aircraft that incorporated many wartime lessons. This was the D (Dora) series, the most widespread mark to be built. In essence, the Dora was a cleaned-up Bertha with a redesigned cockpit and improved armor protection for the crew. The defensive armament was modernized with the fitting, initially, of the twin MG17 and then of the MG81 gun. The power plant was the new Jumo 211J-1 engine developing 1,400 horsepower for takeoff. After initial teething troubles with this engine had been surmounted, causing delays in production, the Doras soon began to leave the assembly lines. Bomb load was a much-improved 4,000 pounds. Thus, the new 2,205-pound SC-1000 GP bomb or the armor-piercing 3,086-pound PC 1400 bomb were both to feature in their operations. As time went by, the outer wing racks, capable of carrying an assortment of 110-pound, 550-pound, or 1,100-pound bomb loads, were also adapted to carry a wide variety of specialized weapons packs, like the Waffenbehalter WB81 with six 7.9-millimeter MG81s for ground-strafing troop concentrations, or the paired 20 millimeter MG FF cannon for tank busting. Although designed initially as an interim aircraft, its continued handiness and the lack of a successor with its all-round abilities and utility meant that the Stuka continued in production on a large scale throughout 1941–43; production totals were 476 and 917, respectively, for the first two years.

The experimental Ju87 V-21 and V-22 first flew in February 1941, being joined by two more prototypes in May and June. The fifth, Ju87 V-25, was a tropicalized version. Production at the Bremen-Lemwerder factory was well in hand with orders for more than 1,000 D1s when the Russian campaign got underway, but re-equipping the units took time, and the first Dora did not make its debut until January 1942, with the 1st Group, 2nd Stuka Wing, in northern Russia. Another variant, the Ju87D-2, was identical except that it featured a strengthened rear fuselage and tail wheel and carried a towing hook for ferrying cargo gliders.

Meanwhile, the bulk of the Ju87 dive bombers that took part in the opening stages of Barbarossa remained the Berthas, along with some Richards, all of which had been secretly transferred to their eastern airstrips in record time after their victories in the Balkans in May 1941.

Preparations for the long-cherished annihilation of the hated Soviet empire had been taking place with painstaking care ever since October 1940, when the blitz was still in full swing against London. Under the Eastern Building Program, German construction units and material had been steadily moved into Poland, and throughout the winter of 1940–41, airfields and support facilities steadily mushroomed along the uneasy eastern frontier. This program was greatly increased in the spring of 1941 and the first flak units moved in to take up positions. During the Balkan campaign, the first active steps were taken for the speedy reception of the squadrons themselves, but the actual movement of the units was delayed as long as possible to avoid detection. Training schools were set up openly in areas then secretly moved west and replaced by the administration train of the operational units. Even so, the move, when it did come in the wake of the hard-fought Crete campaign, was a masterpiece of organization, especially for the Stuka spearhead of VIII Air Corps under von Richthofen. They had to move at the greatest speed from their forward airstrips in the Greek islands and Crete itself, northward across the primitive terrain and poor communications network of the Balkans, into Germany and then, after a short period of refurbishing, into their newly prepared airfields.

All this was done with complete success, and absolute surprise was achieved. By June 1, the first units were entraining in Romania for Germany, while their ground staff flew north to Poland in Ju52/3m transports. Other units were also moving in from France, and in less than three weeks, 2,500 aircraft were established on their jump-off fields in readiness.

On the opposite side of the border, we have seen how almost the entire Soviet Air Force interest in army support roles had been concentrated on their very efficient *Shturmovik* units, and despite their interest in early German dive bomber trials before the war, they had not followed this line of development themselves. It was not until the Spanish Civil War awoke them to the potential of the dive bomber that they began to cast around for a suitable aircraft for themselves.

The brilliant designer Vladimir Mikhaikovich Petlyakov had been in the forefront of a high-altitude bomber concept and had produced a sleek machine in answer to that requirement, the Vysotnyi Istrebitel, VI 100, which was adapted to bomber requirements as a three-seater.

With the instruction to change its specification yet again to produce a dive bomber, Petlyakov's design team kept the main features of the VI 100, including the twin M105R engines, all-metal construction and retractable undercarriage, and made modifications including the fitting of slatted dive brakes. The result was the Pikiruyuschii Bombardivrovshchik, the PB100, the first prototype of which flew for the first time on December 22, 1939, with test

TABLE 33: GERMAN DIVE BOMBER DISPOSITIONS, JUNE 22, 1941

Air Fleet	Air Corps or Location	Stuka Units Allocated	Number of Aircraft
2	VIII Air Corps	II & III/StG1	87
	I & III/StG2	83	
	II Air Corps	I, II, & III/StG77	122
5	Kirkenes, Norway	IV (Stuka)/LG1	42

pilot P. M. Stefanovskii. Tests continued through to June 1940, and by that time, the aircraft had proven itself an ideal dive bomber. It should be noted how the Russians, with little or no previous experience in dive bomber design, produced a first-rate aircraft of this type the first time round.

Apart from its high landing speed, and a tendency to spin, coupled with a famed landing characteristic of bouncing on heavy touchdowns, the PB100 was an extremely advanced aircraft for its day. It had a span of 56 feet, $3\frac{1}{2}$ inches and a length of 41 feet, $6\frac{1}{2}$ inches, making it a large aircraft for a dive bomber, but its performance was superb. Its engines gave it a top speed of 335 mph, thus overcoming the main limitation of all other foreign dive bombers, for it could outpace most fighters. The fact that it could attain such high speed and still dive bomb perfectly should give pause for thought, and one finds it hard to understand why twenty years of prewar study in Britain should have concluded that such a combination was impossible.

It was a three-seater and had an armament of two fixed, forward-firing machine guns when it was put into production as the Pe2 in 1940. The rear defensive armament was a flexible 12.7-millimeter gun, and a non-retractable central gun of the same caliber was fired by means of a periscope gunsight. Heavy protective armor was installed from 6 to 9 millimeters in thickness, and other refinements included a fully automatic dive recovery system as in the German Junkers Ju88. It had a range of 932 miles and could carry a bomb load on underwing racks of up to 2,200 pounds, although 1,320 pounds was a normal combat loading.

It was an impressive aircraft by any standard and brought enthusiastic comment by RAF Squadron Leader Lapraik when he tested it in 1942, but the RAF ignored this. Unfortunately for the Soviets, in June 1941, although production had been underway for some time, few of these dive bombers had reached frontline service when the Germans opened their attack all along the 1,000-mile front.

One other Soviet dive bomber was in limited service at this time. This aircraft was an adaption to dive bombing profile of the Tupolev SB2 bomber, a three-seater, with a span of 66 feet, $8\frac{1}{2}$ inches, and a length of 40 feet, $3\frac{1}{4}$ inches, and designated the SBRK or Ar-2. The Ar-2 was powered by two 1,100-horsepower

In the Soviet Union, A. N. Tupolev started designing a high-speed bomber with dive bombing capability. The SB-2 was still under test in 1941, but some 200 were completed as three-seat dive bombers with the M-105R engine and dive brakes. They were given the designation SB-RK and were commonly known as the Archangelsky Ar-2 and saw combat in 1941–42.

supercharged M-105R engines and featured a reduced wing area over the SB2bis from which it was modified. Only some 200 dive bomber versions were built.

The requirement for the Samolet-103 bomber, which A. N. Tupolev began designing in 1938, called for a high-speed bomber with the speed of a fighter, capable of horizontal and dive bombing, but prototypes were still under test at the outbreak of the war with Germany.

The SB-2, however, powered by two M-100 in-line engines behind frontal radiators, went into mass-production in 1936. It was a three-seat monoplane and could carry a bomb load of 1,320 pounds. Each M-100 was of 860 horsepower, giving the aircraft a maximum speed of 263 mph at 13,120 feet, with a range of 608 miles. Some 200 were completed as dive bombers with the M 105 engine, and wing brakes under the designation SB-RK or Ar-2, and these saw combat in 1941–42.

The German assault on Russia opened in dramatic style with huge losses being inflicted on the Russian air strength and gains of hundreds of miles being made within a short while. Whole armies were surrounded and surrendered.

Of the initial air strikes, more than 4,000 Soviet aircraft were destroyed for the loss of only 150 German aircraft, of which a mere twelve were Ju87s. On the combination of Stuka and Panzer much has been written. Close cooperation reached new stages of perfection with liaison officers actually riding in tanks and calling up the Stukas to break the strongpoints. The farther they penetrated into the vast Soviet hinterland, the worse communications became, but the Luftwaffe was a leader in this field and managed to keep the Stukas supplied as they leapfrogged ever farther east, until they were within 65 miles of Moscow itself.

Farther north, Leningrad was besieged, and the vast Soviet fleet lying at Kronstadt was the objective of an all-out assault by the Ju87s of the 1st and 2nd Groups of the 2nd Stuka Wing; the assault was brought up in haste from the central front to their new base of Tyrkowo. Unfortunately, the new heavy armor-piercing bombs did not arrive at first, but the attacks, launched with some panache between September 21 and 24, 1941, achieved great success. Led by Dinort again, repeated dive bombing resulted in the sinking of the battleship *Marat* by Hans-Ulrich Rudel and the damaging of the cruiser *Kirov* by the death dive of Captain Steen, commander of the 3rd Group, 2nd Stuka Wing. A second battleship, *Okt-yabrskaya Revolutsiya*, received slight damage from six bomb hits, and the destroyer *Steregushchi* was hit and capsized. Other ships damaged included the destroyers *Gordy*, *Grozyashchi*, and *Silny*, the depot ship *Smilny*, and the submarine *Shch306*. On September 23, the cruiser *Kirov* was hit and damaged again, as was the cruiser *Maxim Gorki* and destroyer *Grozyashchi*. The destroyer *Minsk* was hit and sunk along with the patrol vessel *Taifun*, and the submarine *Shch302* was damaged before the attacks were called off because of the pressure of the land battles developing again in the south.

The German armies were switched from the Moscow front toward Kiev, and the Stukas operated from the Konotop region in support of the 4th Panzer Army in this offensive, resulting in another great victory. But now the Russian winter was setting in, and the resumed offensive against Moscow, Operation Typhoon, was brought to a halt just short of its target. The Russians counter-attacked in strength. Serviceability among the Stuka units fell to an all-time low in the severe conditions. Many units were pulled out to refurbish; others were switched south to the Mediterranean theater. Attacks in the south on the Crimea against the fortress of Sebastopol on December 17 and in the north at Litsa against the vital Murmansk rail link—both supported by dive bomber forces—ended the same way. Brought to a dead stop by the combination of the Russian weather and their extended lines of communications the Germans were almost overwhelmed by the massive counterattacks with fresh Siberian troops in the winter months. Only heroic fighting by the troops on the ground and the firm orders of Hitler to stand fast and not panic, saved the day.

The Stukas did much to help by attacking Soviet tank forces whenever they broke through, and they often had to fight for their own advanced airstrips as the marauding T-34 tanks threatened to overrun them as was the case at Kalinin with 2nd Group, 2nd Training and Demonstration Wing, and 1st Group, 2nd Stuka Wing. Meanwhile, the 4th Stuka Group of the 1st Training and Demonstration Wing was redesignated the 1st Group, 5th Stuka Wing, under Hans-Karl Stepp, and this unit was moved south for a while to coordinate attacks with the 1st Stuka Wing led by Walter Hagen on the Leningrad Front. They began to re-equip with Doras, as did the 77th Stuka Wing with the same aircraft at Boblingen.

When the spring thaw came preparations were put in hand for a renewal of the German offensive, which for 1942 were to be mainly directed towards the south. At first, though, preoccupations with the northern areas saw the Ju87s fully extended. At exactly the same time as their compatriots were pounding the warships of the Royal Navy in their base at Malta, the Ju87Ds on the Eastern Front were opening up more heavy assaults on the Russian fleet at Kronstadt, with a view to immobilizing it before the thaw was completed. Sixty-two Stukas of the 1st Stuka Wing under Hagen spearheaded this attack, supplemented by the 1st and 2nd Groups of the 2nd Stuka Wing and the thirty-three Ju88s of the 1st Bomber Wing, commanded by Angerstein. Walter Hagen had been the original leader of the 1st Aircraft Carrier Group and had a first-class anti-shipping record behind him (210,000 BRT sunk). A total of 596 sorties were made during Operation Ice Push (*Eisstoss*) during which the battleship *Oktyabrskaya Revolutsiya* was hit four times, the cruiser *Maxim Gorki* seven times, and the cruisers *Kirov* and *Petropavlovsk* and destroyer *Silny* seriously damaged, while the minelayer *Marti*, the destroyer *Grozyashchy*, and the training ship *Svir* were also damaged.

In May, VIII Air Corps was moved from the central front to new airfields in the Crimea after the forcing of the Kerch Peninsular had left the massive fortress of Sebastopol isolated the previous month. In preparation for the German assault, a larger number of dive bomber sorties were flown against the many strong forts and gun positions in the area. Into this attack, the whole of the 77th Stuka Wing was thrown in a round-the-clock offensive.

Between June 2 and 6, 1942, the 77th Stuka Wing flew some 600 sorties per day against Sebastopol, delivering pin-point attacks on such defensive positions and among other prime targets destroyed by the Ju87s were the giant "Maxim Gorki" guns, 12-inch monsters. Only direct hits could damage such dug-in weapons, but the 77th managed to put them out of action. Other targets calling for the greatest precision were pumping stations and power stations of the garrison's water supply, as well as the endless lines of field works and gun-pits. The Ju87s and Ju88s also carried out numerous sorties against the port and shipping bringing reinforcements to the fortress across the Black Sea. On June 10, Ju88s sank the transport *Abkhaziya* (4,727 tons) and the minesweepers *Svobodny* and T413 in the harbor, and the next day, the transport *Gruziya* (4,857 tons) was also sunk there. On the eighteenth, the destroyer *Kharkov* was hit and damaged, and on the twenty-sixth, the destroyer *Bezuprechny* was sunk. The destroyer *Tashkent* was sunk with many casualties among her wounded evacuees on the June 27.

The 1st, 2nd, and 77th Stuka Wings were all fully committed in the classic role as the final blitzkreig got under way in July 1942, and the field-grey soldiers and panzers moved over the endless dusty steppe through Voronezh, across the Rivers Tim and Don, ever eastward, smashing south past Rostov towards the Caucasus and the distant oilfields of the Caspian Sea.

This advance finally ran out of steam on the foothills of the Caucasus and in the rubble of the city of Stalingrad on the River

Volga. Here, determined Soviet troops clung to their strongpoints among the ruins of factories and rail yards and for some reason the German army under Paulus became immersed in a vicious and intense street fight, from house to house, floor to floor, instead of merely bypassing the city in the hitherto efficient German manner. The Ju87s of the 2nd Stuka Wing became adept at attacking targets a mere block or less from their own front-line troops, whose positions among the debris could only be made out by flying with map in hand.

Despite the utmost efforts of the dive bomber pilots, who were forbidden to release their bombs until certain of their targets, the small eastern part of the city held out against all attacks and the German divisions were fed in and ground down piecemeal. Then, on November 19, fresh Soviet armies massed on their flanks, broke through north and south of the city, crushing the Italian and Romanian armies holding those sections and encasing the German 6th Army in gigantic claws. Attacks by the 2nd Stuka Wing from Karpovka failed to stop them, and at Oblivskay, the Stukas were hardput to prevent their own airfield from being overrun. The German offensive was over.

Meanwhile, up on the edge of the Arctic Circle, the 1st Group, 5th Stuka Wing, based at Kirkenes, under Major Hans-Karl Stepp, was operating in bad conditions supporting the further attempts to cut the Belomorsk-Murmansk railway. They made frequent attacks on lines and rolling-stock, but it proved impossible for the German troops under General Dietl to advance across the tundra and take the major supply port of Murmansk itself. The dive bombers' efforts were therefore turned toward attacking that base and the ships and convoys from Britain approaching it with vital American war supplies. The Ju87s lacked the range to attack the Arctic convoys for anything but the last few miles of their long journeys, but the 1st Group did achieve much success in anti-shipping sorties around the Kola Inlet area.

On May 15, 1942, they dive bombed Murmansk harbor, badly damaging the Soviet submarine *Shch403* and the American freighter *Yaka* (6,187 tons). On June 1, Ju87s sank the British freighter *Empire Starlight* (6,850 tons), and on June 25, they caught a flotilla of British minesweepers in the Kola Inlet and sank the *Gossamer*. Their other achievements included a dive bombing attack on a convoy that had just reached Murmansk, on February 27 and 28, 1943, during which they scored direct hits on three freighters totaling 11,341 tons. On March 6 and 13, 1943, they sank one merchant ship and damaged another.

The main dive bombing attacks on the convoys of Allied merchantmen carrying tanks, aircraft and munitions to north Russia, were carried out by the Ju88 units based at Banak and Bardufoss. The three groups of the 30th Bomber Wing were the most notable in these operations, especially the 3rd Group under Captain Klaus Nocken. On March 28, 1942, a storm scattered convoy PQ15, and the dive bombers of the 3rd Group were able to attack isolated merchant ships with ease, sinking the *Raceland* (4,815 tons) and *Empire Ranger* (7,007 tons). On April 11, the same unit attacked and sank the *Empire Cowper* (7,164 tons) from the homeward bound convoy QP10 and the *Harpalion* (5,486 tons). A greater victory came on May 14 when the 3rd Group dive bombed a British cruiser squadron in the Barents Sea and scored hits on the cruiser *Trinidad*, which was so damaged that she had to be sunk.

Against the convoy PQ16, 3rd Group, 30th Bomber Wing, mounted an attack with six aircraft on May 25, damaging the freighter *Carlton* (5,127 tons), while on the twenty-seventh, 111 sorties were flown, resulting in the sinking of the *Alamar*, *Mormacsul*, *Empire Lawrence*, and *Empire Purcell*. Four other freighters were damaged, one of which, the *City of Joliet*, later sank. Against the ill-fated PQ17 convoy, even greater slaughter was executed. Again, the ships were left without escorts after the convoy scattered. This left easy pickings for the Ju88 crews, and they sank—or in some cases finished off ships crippled by U-boats—the freighters *Washington* (5,564 tons), *Bolton Castle* (5,203 tons), *Pankraft* (5,644 tons), *Peter Kerr* (6,476 tons), and *Fairfield City* (5,685 tons), as well as the rescue ship *Zaafaran*. They also hit and damaged the freighters *Paulus Potter*, *Earlston*, *Empire Byron*, and the fleet tanker *Aldersdale*, all of which were finished off by U-boats later. Hunting down the few survivors later, the three groups under Kahl, Stoffregen, and Herrmann sank the *Pan Atlantik* (5,411 tons) on July 6.

Against the better-protected PQ18 convoy in September 1942, they fared less well. It had the escort carrier *Avenger* in company, and most of the dive bombing attacks were directed against her rather than the convoy. Despite many near-misses, she survived. The 30th Bomber Wing's only successes were the blowing up of the ammunition ship *Mary Luckenbach* (5,049 tons) on September 14 and the *Troubador* (6,458 tons) on the eighteenth.

On November 4, attacks against independently routed ships by the 1st Group of the 30th Bomber Wing sank the Soviet *Dekabrist* (7,363 tons), while the 2nd Group scored a hit on another two, one of which, *William Clark* (7,176 tons), was finished off by U-boats on the fourth, while the other, *Chumleigh* (5,445 tons), was similarly disposed of on the sixteenth.

The last major battle in the East in which the Ju87 participated in large numbers in their dive bombing role, after the holding actions of 1942–43, was Operation Citadel (*Zitadelle*) against the Kursk salient. This was also the last great German offensive of the war on the Eastern Front. The following units took part, supplemented by the Hungarian Stuka unit, 102/1.

The decline of the Ju87 took place after this battle, and an indication of the future role of the aircraft was given by the inclusion in one squadron of each of the first two groups of the "Kanonvogel" Stukas, each equipped with a tank-busting Flak 18 37-millimeter cannon under each wing. This interesting development, however, falls outside the scope of this study. Conversely, as the dive bomber declined in the Luftwaffe, it increased in usage

TABLE 34: STUKA UNITS
AND COMMANDERS,
BATTLE OF KURSK, 1943

Unit	Commanding Officer
1st	Colonel Gustav Pressler
2nd	Colonel Dr. Ernst Kupfer
77th	Colonel Helmut Bruck

and value in the Soviet Air Force. The Petlyakov Pe2 increased in stature with the development of new techniques. Some 460 had been ready as early as June 1941, but their pilots lacked expertise in the dive bombing technique. A. G. Fedorov of 9th Bomber Air Regiment conducted a detail survey on the Pe2 in 1942 analyzing its combat record. Meanwhile the famous Col L. S. Polbin of the 150th Bomber Air Group was developing his own techniques for attacks in this aircraft after early experience at the Battle of Smolensk in July 1941. Another leading pilot flying the Pe2 was Col V. E. Nestertsev of the 23rd Bomber Air Division, which featured in the winter fighting of 1941–42.

It was Polbin who evolved the classic dive bombing technique known as the "dipping wheel," or *Vertushka,* which he used during the Stalingrad counteroffensive and had perfected by the time of Kursk, and on July 7, Soviet dive bombers inflicted heavy casualties on the panzers with these methods. With full and complete fore-knowledge of the German plan of attack betrayed to them, the Soviets were not only able to hold the German thrusts but, within days, had launched their own counteroffensive at Orel on July 11. Before this onslaught, the Germans in many places were forced back. Nonstop dive bomber missions by the Ju87s were launched to stabilize the front in many places, and this setback was not the disaster that Stalingrad had been; nonetheless, it was a massive defeat and the turning point on the Eastern Front. From now on, it was the Soviet Pe2 that dominated the dive bomber scene in this vast area while the Germans switched over increasingly to dive bombing

TABLE 35: TRANSITION FROM STUKA WINGS
TO GROUND ATTACK WINGS, OCTOBER 1943

Original Designation	New Designation	Area of Operations
StG1	SG1	Eastern Front
StG2	SG2	Eastern Front
StG3	SG3	Balkans
StG5	SG5	Norway
StG77	SG77	Eastern Front

by high-performance fighter aircraft—Jabo units equipped with the FW190 aircraft.

The increasing vulnerability of the ageing Ju87 was now recognized, and although production continued, it was more as a specialized tank-buster and night bomber that it was used in this theater. This change was emphasized with the change of title of the dive bomber units from Stuka wings to ground attack wings, which now took place. It was a transition to be reflected also among the Allied air forces at this time.

CHAPTER 19

Dive Bomber Arena

The Pacific War, 1941–42: American and Japanese Operations

War between the United States and Japan, long simmering, broke out with the attack on Pearl Harbor on December 7, 1941. The strike was made with carrier-based dive bombers and torpedo aircraft and was directed against the fleet in harbor and the military airfields. The planes took off from the six big carriers of Japanese admiral Chuichi Nagumo's strike force, Kido Butai, and achieved considerable surprise. The first wave included fifty-one Aichi D3A1 Vals led by Lieutenant Akira Sakamoto, and their target was the two main American fighter bases. Sakamoto himself led twenty-five Vals in a dive bombing attack on Wheeler Field, dropping the first bomb of the Pacific War at 0755 hours. A second group of twenty-six Vals under Lieutenant Kakuichi Takahasi hit Hickham Field and the seaplane base on Ford Island. To their regret, their original targets, the American carriers, had been reported as missing. Each Val in the first wave carried 250-pound fragmentation bombs to destroy parked aircraft.

A second wave followed and consisted of seventy-nine D3A1s led by Lieutenant Commander Takashige Egusa, the prewar dive bomber ace. Their target had been the carriers, but in their absence, they turned their wrath upon the battleships that had survived earlier attacks. In return for the loss of one Val from the first wave and fourteen from the second, the Japanese dive bombers hit the battleships *Nevada* and *Pennsylvania* and hit and wrecked the destroyers *Cassin* and *Downes* in dock and *Shaw*, whose magazines exploded.

Some ninety-two navy and ninety-six army aircraft were destroyed on the ground.

On their way back to Japan after this strike, forty-two Vals were dispatched against Wake Island, and on December 21, eighteen of them were dispatched, but thick cloud aborted their mission. A second strike led by Lieutenant Heijiro Abe, also of eighteen dive bombers, went in the next day, and on December 23, the Vals covered the landing, which took this island.

After a brief respite in Japan, Nagumo's remaining four carriers were sent to the southern area of operations to assist in crushing any opposition to the invasion forces that were swarming all over that area. After refueling at Truk, they launched a ninety-plane strike at Rabaul on January 20, but found little in the way of opposition and fewer worthwhile targets. The Vals sank a solitary merchant ship in the harbor.

On January 21, a strike was mounted against Kavieng, Lae, and Salamuaua on the eastern coast of New Guinea, with similar results. Rabaul was again dive bombed on the twenty-second before the force returned to Truk. Here, two Japanese carriers were detached to patrol off Japan following the U.S. carrier strikes against the Gilbert and Marshall islands, but they failed to locate the American force.

Meanwhile, the *Hiryū* and *Soryū* had also come south, and their dive bombers launched attacks on the naval base of Ambon in the Celebes on January 24 and 25, 1942. On February 4, Japanese Navy bombers, operating from the airfield at Kendari, attacked an Allied naval squadron south of Kangeon Island, badly damaging the American light cruiser *Marblehead* and hitting the heavy cruiser *Houston* on one of the after 8-inch turrets, putting it out of action, to the north of Bali.

Thus far, it had been the Japanese dive bombers that had made most of the running, but in January and February, two small American task groups built around the carriers *Enterprise* and *Yorktown* made tip-and-run raids on Wotje, Maloelap, and Kwajalein on February 1 and on Jaluit, Mili, and Makin.

Although the Dauntless had received its blooding at Pearl Harbor, when several *Enterprise* planes had been destroyed, the strike that was launched from the same ships by SBDs against Roi at 0445

The terror of the Allies in the Pacific in 1942: the Aichi Val dive bomber. It was the standard Imperial Japanese Navy dive bomber from Pearl Harbor to Guadalcanal.

hours on February 1 was its debut as a dive bomber. Unfortunately, surprise was not achieved, and Commander Hopping's Scouting 6 was met by heavy flak and fighters. Thirty-six SBDs took part in this raid, which at 0700 hours dropped the first bombs of the war to hit Japanese territory, but Hopping himself was shot down. Another dive bombing attack on shipping in Kwajalein harbor resulted in the loss of five more SBDs with scant results, one transport claimed sunk and nine damaged. A later raid on the airfield destroyed hangars and several bombers for the loss of another Dauntless.

Further missions were launched. *Lexington* flew Dauntless raids against Rabaul, which was now in Japanese hands, on February 20, and *Enterprise* hit Wake on the twenty-fourth and Marcus Island on March 4. Attacks by dive bombers from *Lexington* and *Yorktown* on Lae and Salamaua claimed the sinking of a minesweeper and two transports.

If the results of the U.S. Navy's Dauntless strikes in early 1942 were disappointing, then the activities of the A24 units of the U.S. Army Air Force in the same area were more so and confirmed the army's long-held conviction that dive bombers and dive bombing were a pointless and costly exercise.

At the time of Pearl Harbor, it will be recalled, the U.S. Army had on order a large number of the A24 Banshee and had placed further contracts for the A25A, the army equivalent of the Curtiss SB22 Helldiver. Not content with this, immediately after the outbreak of the Pacific War, the U.S. Army, seeking a faster way to supplement their strength, cast their eyes on the British dive bombers being built in America, and as a result, some 492 of these were appropriated by the U.S. Army Air Force in January 1942: 300 Vengeance aircraft and 192 Bermudas (the U.S. Navy's Buccaneer). Beaverbrook wrote to Sinclair that "the Arnold/Portal agreement increased the number of these which we surrendered, and sanctions the seizure from our orders of 300 Vengeance dive bombers, 158 of these were ex-contract for which we had paid in full hard cash and 142 were from Lend-Lease."

However, in actual combat conditions, those dive bombers the U.S. Army already had proved a disappointment to them. Operations by the 91st Bombardment Squadron in the Dutch East Indies achieved little or nothing, while the 8th Bombardment Group based in northern Australia were no more successful. The Army pilot's verdict was that the Dauntless was too slow, unmanoeuverable and obsolete. The principal action in which they participated

The U.S. Army Air Force equivalent of the Dauntless was the Douglas A-24. It was offered to Great Britain in 1940 but rejected by the RAF. The U.S. Army used it in the southwest Pacific in 1942, though not as successfully as the U.S. Navy.

was an attack by the 27th Bomb Group (Light) with seven A24s on a Japanese naval squadron off Java on February 29, 1942, in which they claimed, falsely, several hits on a cruiser. Two dive bombers were lost.

Further dive bombing missions were undertaken in April 1942, against Laue and Salamaua, but the next operation was a complete disaster, for in a raid on Buna on July 29, six out of seven A24s were lost, and thereafter, the Army withdrew them from combat.

Although the bulk of the Aichi D3Als were operating from carriers during this period, land-based dive bomber units were set up by the Japanese on February 1 to assist the army's operations during the conquest of the Philippines and Celebes.

Sixty-eight Vals were in reserve in Japan at the outbreak of the war, and from these, the 31st NAC was formed and undertook dive bombing missions during the final drive on the fortresses of Bataan and Corregidor. Similarly, the 33rd NAC was set up at Saeki and transferred to Macassar on March 2 from which it participated in the conquest of Java.

The Nagumo force reformed round the carriers *Akagi*, *Kaga*, *Hiryū*, and *Soryū* at Palau in mid-February 1942 to strike at the only major port and supply base in Australia capable of reinforcing the hard-pressed Allied troops in the southern zone. On February 19, from a position in the Banda Sea, these aircraft carriers flew off a strong strike force of 188 aircraft, reinforced by fifty-four land-based planes, and this mass hit Port Darwin without warning.

Seventy-one Vals were included in this formation. Only eight defending fighters managed to get into the air, and these were quickly overwhelmed; fifteen more were destroyed on the ground. The Vals were then turned loose on the mass of shipping in the harbor with good effect, meeting hardly any opposition. In the precise dive bombing that followed, seven transports were sunk (43,429 tons), including one spectacular hit on an ammunition ship, which ignited its cargo of 200 depth charges and caused widespread destruction. Also sunk was the American destroyer *Peary* while among the many ships damaged to varying degrees were the American aircraft tender *William B. Preston*, the Australian sloop *Swan*, and six large freighters. Numerous small auxiliary craft were destroyed, and the whole port was rendered unusable for weeks.

A similar raid was launched against Tjilatjap on March 3, sinking two freighters and damaging fifteen more which were later scuttled when the port was evacuated.

Next, the Nagumo force—with five carriers, four battleships, three cruisers, and nine destroyers—sailed from Staring Bay in the South Celebes on March 26 to launch air strikes at the known naval bases of Colombo and Trincomalee in Ceylon (Sri Lanka), in the hope of catching the new British fleet under Admiral Somerville. Having been sighted earlier, the Japanese launched a strike force at Colombo on April 5, which included thirty-six Aichi D3A1s, but they found the harbor empty of shipping. In the ensuing air combat, twenty-five RAF and FAA aircraft were destroyed for the loss of seven Japanese. The bombers scored hits on the armed merchant cruiser *Hector* (11,198 tons) and the old destroyer *Tenedos*, the latter having her stern blown off. Both were sunk.

Meanwhile, two British heavy cruisers, *Cornwall* and *Dorsetshire*, which had been detached from the main fleet in an error reminding one of Norway and Crete, were located by the Japanese steaming south to rejoin it. Soon after midday, a powerful force of eighty Vals under Lieutenant Commander Egusa were dispatched to attack them. At 1330 hours, this force had found the two ships, and ten minutes later, they commenced their attack dives, splitting themselves equally between the two targets. Their accuracy was phenomenal despite the violent twisting and turning of the cruisers and the barrage from their combined antiaircraft armaments of sixteen 4-inch guns and many smaller weapons. The *Cornwall* took fifteen bombs in seven minutes and sank. The *Dorsetshire* was pulverized in the same manner, one bomb penetrating her magazine, which exploded. Within eight minutes, she too had gone under.

Having failed to find the main British fleet at Colombo, Nagumo turned next to Trincomalee. On April 9, another strike force was dispatched, which included thirty-six Vals. They were met by Hurricane fighters from No. 261 Squadron and Fulmars from the FAA No. 273 Squadron, who claimed to have inflicted a smashing defeat on the Japanese. In truth, the Japanese lost only nine aircraft in all, while the British lost nine Hurricanes and one Fulmar.

The dive bombers continued in and found few worthwhile targets, so they contented themselves with hitting the monitor *Erebus*

and sinking the transport *Sagaing*. All the other ships had been
cleared from the port and sent south without any protection at all.
They were soon sighted by the Japanese and their position radioed
to Nagumo. On receipt of this news, Egusa was launched with his
eighty D2A1s to deal with them, and at about 1300 hours, they
located their prey steering frantically toward the coast and broad-
casting plaintive appeals for fighter cover. It never came. Instead
came the redoubtable Egusa with the Vals deploying in their clas-
sical style and commencing their dives.

Their targets were the aircraft carrier *Hermes*, without planes
embarked; the Australian destroyer *Vampire*; the corvette *Hollyhock*;
the naval auxiliary *Atheltone*; and the tanker *British Sergeant*. Naturally, the carrier was the prime target.

At her maximum speed of 23 knots, the *Hermes* sought to
evade her fate, opening fire with her pitiful AA armament, two 4-
inch guns and some Oerlikons, but in the first pass by ten dive
bombers, most of these weapons were wiped out by hits. One of
the 4-inch guns was blown over the side with its entire crew. The
forward lift was hit and blown 20 feet into the air before falling

The first aircraft carrier to be sunk by dive bombers was the British
Hermes in 1942 off Ceylon. Caught flat-footed by Vals of the Nagumo
Task Force without air cover or planes of her own, she quickly went
to the bottom of the sea after a large number of direct hits.

back into the hangar well killing all those inside. Hit followed hit, and after fewer than fifteen minutes of this, the carrier was a gutted wreck on fire from bow to stern and

The destroyer *Vampire* was hit just as hard and followed the *Hermes* soon after. The dive bombers took as alternative targets those other ships still afloat, and these were also rapidly dispatched within minutes. So many hits did Egusa and his pilots score that they were unable to count them all.

Events in the Indian Ocean caused the Admiralty to withdraw Somerville's fleet from the chance of any further confrontation with an enemy so powerful as the Nagumo Force, but the Japanese had never meant their foray to be anything more than a sharp reminder that the Royal Navy—without dive bombers of its own— no longer ruled the waves, and they soon withdrew after inflicting these humiliating defeats on the baffled and bewildered British admiral. The next Japanese drives were north against the Aleutians, south to take Port Moresby in New Guinea, southeast along the Solomon Islands to isolate Australia, and out eastward across the central Pacific to Midway Island to extend their defensive perimeter and draw out the American carriers and destroy them in combat. In enlarging their already considerable commitments, they badly overextended themselves and were checked at each pause with heavy losses. The tide of war in the Pacific began to turn in 1942. In all the resulting major actions, it was the dive bomber that played the overwhelmingly decisive role for both the Americans and the Japanese.

A Japanese invasion convoy bound for Port Moresby was escorted by the light carrier *Shoho* and given distant cover by the *Shōkaku* and *Zuikaku*, each of which had twenty-one D3A1 Vals embarked, under Vice Admiral Takeo Takagi. They were intercepted by an American task force commanded by Rear Admiral Frank Fletcher with the carriers *Lexington* and *Yorktown*. The resulting Battle of the Coral Sea, in May 1942, was the first to be fought by opposing carrier air groups without the combat warships sighting each other at all. It was, as a result, a highly confusing battle.

At 0610 hours on May 7, the Japanese got in the first blow, flying off a strike force against the American carriers which included thirty-six Vals, but these aircraft instead located and attacked an oiling group, completely overwhelming the destroyer *Sims* and the tanker *Neosho* and sending both to the bottom. Meanwhile, a heavy force of U.S. aircraft from their carriers also came into action at 1100 hours when they found the *Shoho*. In all, there were twenty-eight SBDs from *Lexington* and twenty-five from *Yorktown* as dive bombers, and these, along with torpedo bombers and fighters, all concentrated their attentions on this one small carrier. Not surprisingly, she was smothered in hits and near-misses and sank at 1135, the first Japanese carrier to be destroyed. Lieutenant Commander Bob Dixon's excited radio signal to *Lexington* heralded a new era in sea warfare: "Scratch one flattop. Dixon to carrier. Scratch one flattop!"

The coming of darkness aborted a second Japanese strike but hostilities recommenced at dawn, the two opposing striking forces passing each other en route to their respective targets. In both cases, it was the main carriers that were engaged this time instead of the secondary targets of May 7. Thirty-three Vals dive bombed the two American carriers, scoring a hit on *Yorktown* that penetrated four decks and killed sixty-six of her crew, but although badly damaged, she was still capable of operating aircraft. The *Lexington* was hit by two torpedoes and sank later, taking fourteen of her SBDs to the bottom with her.

The American strike included twenty-two Dauntless dive bombers from *Lexington* (with three stray SBDs from *Yorktown*) and twenty-four more from *Yorktown* herself. The units involved were VBS, VSS, VB2, and VS2. They arrived over the Japanese ships at 1050 hours, but the *Zuikaku* evaded attack by steaming into a rain squall, and the bulk of the dive bombers struck at *Shōkaku*. The *Yorktown* strike was intercepted by Zero fighters, and VBS scored only one hit. They were followed down by Lieutenant John Powers in the last plane, and he held his attack dive, even though he had been hit by AA fire time and time again, and finally dropped his bomb at 300 feet before smashing into the sea alongside his target. His bomb carved through the carrier's wooden deck, inflicting heavy damage. *Lexington*'s VB2 under Commander William B. Ault made the final attack and scored a third direct hit. However, like *Yorktown*, the *Shōkaku*, although heavily damaged, did not sink and lived to fight another day.

The loss of one large U.S. carrier and damage to a second were matched by the loss of one small Japanese carrier, damage to a larger one, but the sinking of the tanker and destroyer made Coral Sea tactically a Japanese victory. The invasion fleet, however, turned back unnecessarily, enabling the U.S. to claim a strategic victory.

The most famous carrier-to-carrier battle in history was the Battle of Midway, which followed in June 1942. Although the actual occupation of this tiny atoll was desirable to the Japanese, their main plan all along was to lure the remaining U.S. carriers out in its defense and overwhelm them with superior numbers. However, faulty dispositions of their powerful fleets left the Japanese ships dispersed instead of concentrated and therefore unable to support each other at the vital time. Of the eight Japanese carriers included, four were wasted on secondary tasks, and the outcome of the battle was therefore decided by four Japanese ships—*Akagi*, *Kaga*, *Hiryū*, and *Soryū*—against three American—*Enterprise*, *Hornet*, and the patched-up *Yorktown*, plus the "unsinkable" Midway airstrip. The influence of the nine Japanese battleships, which should have been decisive, was thrown away by Yamamoto because he kept them too far astern of the carriers to be able to intervene.

The initial air strike was launched by Nagumo against Midway Island itself on June 4 and included thirty-six D3A1s led by Lieutenant Takehia Aihaya of *Akagi* and Lieutenant Masaharu Ogawa of *Kaga*. Each Japanese carrier had twenty-one D3A1s embarked, but this battle also marked the operational debut of the D4Y Judy, too, for a pair were embarked in *Soryū*, but only as reconnaissance planes since the aircraft were still not passed as suitable for dive bombing. This strike hit Midway at 0620 hours, but all the U.S. aircraft based there had been scrambled away, and little lasting damage was done.

Return strikes from the island base included sixteen Dauntlesses of VMSB241 led by Major Lofton R. Henderson and eleven

SB2U-3 Vindicators led by Major Benjamin W. Norris. Henderson was a veteran dive bomber pilot who had served in Nicaragua. These two formations attacked at 0755 hours and suffered heavy losses from flak and fighters. In all, eight SBDs and two Vindicators were lost without achieving much in reply. One pilot who made it back counted 259 hits on his aircraft.

Further attacks by shore-based level bombers, torpedo bombers, and heavy bombers also failed to score any hits, despite ludicrous claims by the U.S. Army Air Force to the contrary. The real climax of the battle came at 1027 hours. Nagumo had hesitated in sending off his second strike at Midway, and when word came in of U.S. carriers, he had to re-arm his bombers. This had just been completed when the first U.S. dive bombers arrived overhead unmolested and commenced their dives on the four Japanese carriers. Most of his strike aircraft were still in their hangars while most of his fighters were at sea-level finishing off the American torpedo-bombers. This gave the SBD pilots their chance, and they took it.

Thirty-six SBDs of VB-6 and VS-6, led by Lieutenant Richard H. Best and Lieutenant Wilmer Earl Gallaher, were launched from *Enterprise*, with thirty-five SBDs of VB-8 and VS-8 under Commander Stanhope C. Ring from *Hornet*, but they missed their target and landed later at Midway without sighting the enemy. Lieutenant Commander C. W. McClusky from *Enterprise* fared better than these. Because of the need to recover scouting aircraft sent out by *Yorktown*, seventeen SBDs of VB-3 commanded by Lieutenant Commander Maxwell F. Leslie took a more direct route to catch up and were able to join the *Enterprise* dive bombers in their assault. The Japanese were taken by surprise and suffered heavily.

Kaga was struck by at least four direct hits, which turned her hull into an inferno. She finally sank some nine hours later. Lieutenant Best led the *Enterprise* planes down on *Akagi* with similar results to Leslie's, two hits plunging through her decks into her packed hangars. Racked by a series of internal explosions, she was abandoned and drifted throughout the night before being dispatched by Japanese destroyers the following morning. The third victim of this classic dive bombing attack was the *Soryū*, attacked by Gallaher's section. They hit her three times, igniting her packed aircraft, and she was swept by fires and further explosions, finally sinking at 1913 hours. With the three Japanese carriers went their entire air groups and scores of highly trained navy dive bomber crews.

Only the *Hiryū* remained to launch a counterblow against the three remaining U.S. carriers. This she did at 1100 hours, but eighteen Vals commanded by Lieutenant Michio Kobayashi, with six Zeros, was all they could send in the first wave. Only four fighters were left to guard them against the hordes of Wildcat fighters that pounced on them when they reached the *Yorktown* later, and ten Japanese dive bombers were destroyed before they could commence their runs. The others attacked, two more being shot out of the sky by escorting cruisers. Another Val, shot through, scored a direct hit on the starboard side of the flight deck before crashing into the sea alongside, leaving one wing aboard the carrier. Another bomb penetrated the port side of the *Yorktown*'s flight deck and exploded in her funnel uptakes, while a third hit her to starboard, penetrating four decks and starting fires close to the ship's magazines. Only five Vals returned, having survived this gallant attack against all odds, and landed back on *Hiryū*. But despite her damage, the *Yorktown* stayed afloat at this time although she and an escorting destroyer were sunk by submarine attack later.

At 1331 hours, the *Hiryū* got off a second strike, this time of ten torpedo bombers, and they scored two direct hits. This was the end of the *Yorktown*—or almost—but it was also the last gasp of the *Hiryū*, for at 1703 hours, twenty-four SBDs from *Enterprise* and sixteen from *Hornet* found her and attacked out of the setting sun. Four devastating hits punched into the Japanese ship, enormous fires broke out, and she was abandoned, finally being sunk at 0510 next morning.

The destruction of these four carriers was the greatest victory scored by the Dauntless. The Japanese called off their invasion plans and retired. Even so, they took further casualties. A heavy cruiser squadron had been sent ahead to bombard Midway's defences, but before it could do so it was recalled. A collision took place during the night turn damaging two of these ships and slowing them down. They were still well within striking range of the island next day and were also subjected to prolonged dive bombing attacks from the U.S. carriers.

At 0805 hours, six Vindicators and six Dauntless from Midway made the first strike. The Vindicator of Captain Fleming was heavily hit and crashed astern of the *Mikuma*, but the oft-related story that it hit one of the after turrets is totally untrue. *Enterprise* and *Hornet* launched strong dive bomber attacks on the main Japanese fleet that same afternoon, but they found nothing except a solitary Japanese destroyer, the *Tanikaze*, and she survived the attentions of thirty-eight SBDs.

On June 6, the same two carriers launched attacks on the crippled Japanese cruisers: at 0800 with twenty-six SBDs from *Hornet*; at 1045 with thirty-one SBDs from *Enterprise*; and then two dozen more SBDs from *Hornet* once more. The cruiser *Mogami* was hit several times and wrecked, but she managed to crawl to safety. The *Mikuma* was also struck by many bombs and finally sank in flames with few survivors. Although the *Yorktown* was later sunk, along with an escorting destroyer, by a Japanese submarine, the results of the Battle of Midway were as decisive as any naval battle could be.

A minor part of the Midway operation called for the invasion of some of the Aleutian Islands in the far north of the Pacific. Vals from the carriers *Junyō* and *Ryūhō* participated, making an abortive raid on June 3 when twelve D3A1s from the former ship were weathered out and on the fourth when eleven from *Ryūjō* dive bombed Dutch Harbor. In the absence of ships or aircraft targets, Lieutenant Yoshio Shiga attacked the radio station and oil tanks at 0407 hours. Subsequently, an attack launched against reported American destroyers was also weathered out.

The final stage of the Japanese thrusts for 1942—the drive down the Solomon Islands chain—was halted and then reversed when the U.S. marines landed at Tulagi on August 7 and also Guadalcanal Island across the "Slot," quickly occupying the almost complete Japanese airstrip, which they duly dubbed Henderson Field. The Japanese reacted strongly, and for the next five months, a series of violent sea, air, and land battled raged around the island to gain or hold this one airfield.

A total of 103 SBDs were embarked in the carriers *Enterprise*, *Saratoga*, and *Wasp*, which covered the initial landings, but after limited operations, Fletcher withdrew on August 9. The Marines therefore flew in Marine Air Group (MAG) 23 to operate from Henderson Field, and for a while, the SBDs of VMSB-231 and VMSB-232, with the Mark 3 Dauntless, held the ring under Lieutenant Colonel Richard C. Mangrum. VMSB-232 flew in off the escort carrier *Long Island* on August 20.

Opposing them was the Japanese land-based air fleet at Rabaul some 550 nautical miles away in New Britain, just beyond the operational range of the Val. One Japanese historian later wrote how "Our Val dive bombers, however, were dispatched on missions in whom their crews despaired of survival. Simply stated, the aircraft could not carry sufficient fuel to make the round-trip flight from Rabaul to Guadalcanal and return. Within two days of the American invasion we lost eighteen Val bombers but not one fell to the enemy's guns. Their fuel ran out as they struggled to reach Rabaul, and all these bombers crashed."

An interim air strip was constructed at Buin, which eased this problem. In an attack on August 7, Vals dive bombed and dam-

Dauntless SBDs operating from Henderson Field on Guadalcanal. In 1942, U.S. Navy and Marine Corps SBDs from this small jungle airstrip sank a large number of Japanese ships and helped turn the tide of the Pacific War.

aged the destroyer *Mugford* with sixteen aircraft, while, during a later strike by Vals, one D2A1 was hit by AA fire and crashed into the transport *George F. Elliott* (8,375 tons), which burnt out and later sank.

The Japanese Combined Fleet sortied out to cover a troop convoy attempting to land 1,500 soldiers on Guadalcanal on August 23. Nagumo had the carriers *Shōkaku* and *Zuikaku* on hand with the light carrier *Ryujo* stationed some distance ahead as a lure. The American Task Force 61 under Fletcher had the carriers *Enterprise, Saratoga,* and *Wasp.* On location off the convoy, *Saratoga* flew off a strike force, which included thirty-one SBDs, but they lost their target in a squall and had to land at Henderson Field.

On August 24, the *Ryūhō* group was located, and at 1030 hours, *Enterprise* flew off a strike, which included fifteen SBDs. Meanwhile, Commander Don Felt had landed back aboard the *Saratoga* with his group, and after refueling, his twenty-eight SBDs were launched at 1435 hours. The *Enterprise* planes attacked the *Ryūhō* at 1500 hours, dive bombing from 11,000 feet out of the sun but scoring only near-misses. Two others from the same ship made a surprise attack on the *Shōkaku* at 1545, claiming to have damaged her, but she continued operating.

The *Saratoga* group hit *Ryūhō* at 1620 hours, bracketing her with near-misses before Felt himself scored a direct hit on her flight deck, "slight port and aft of dead center." Seven SBDs from VB-3 followed him down from 15,000 feet and blasted the little carrier to the seabed with three more hits and four near-misses.

In the interim, the two Japanese carriers had got their own air strikes away. Some thirty-three Vals were included in the first wave at 1505 hours. This was followed by eighteen more in the second wave launched an hour later. While the latter failed to find their target at all, the first group sighted *Enterprise* at 1625 and commenced their attack dives. Astern of their target was the new battleship *North Carolina,* her myriad of long-range 5-inch and close-range automatic cannon winking and flaming, putting up a huge barrage over the carrier in front. Val after Val was shot out of the sky by this new battleship, but a few survivors scored three direct hits. The first of these struck the *Enterprise* on the after lift and penetrated three decks before exploding, causing a 20-degree list and heavy casualties. The second hit close by, within 15 feet of the first, destroying all the AA guns on the starboard quarter and killing thirty-nine of their crews as the ammunition exploded. The last bomb hit the flight deck just behind the island and blew a hole in the deck. It was faulty and caused little other damage, so the stricken *Enterprise* remained afloat despite this pounding.

In another counterstrike, two *Saratoga* Dauntless aircraft attacked and hit the old seaplane tender *Chitose*, destroying her port engine room with a hit that tore her side open. With a 30-degree list, she trailed back to Truk. This ended the operation as the Japanese again withdrew from the field of battle.

At Henderson Field, the Marine SBDs were joined by the Dauntless orphans from the damaged U.S. carrier on the August 24— eight from VS-5 and three from VB-6. These were commended by Lieutenant Turner F. Caldwell, and for the next few weeks, this group, Flight 300, became an integral part of the Dauntless team that inflicted heavy casualties on the transports and destroyers of the "Tokyo Express" that were endeavoring to land Japanese troop reinforcements on the island.

These shore-based dive bombers survived bombardments by Japanese battleships, heavy cruisers, and destroyers as well as numerous air attacks. Their achievements were so many that we can only summarize them. They were finally reinforced on August 30 by the twelve SBDs of VMSB-231 under Major Leo Smith.

On August 25, they attacked and sank the destroyer *Mutsuki* and the transport *Kinryu Maru*; they also damaged the light cruiser *Jintsu* with a direct hit between her two forward gun turrets. On the twenty-eighth, they sank the destroyer *Asagiri* and damaged the destroyers *Shirakumo* and *Yugiri* badly and the *Amagiri* slightly. On September 24, the destroyers *Kawakaze* and *Umikaze* were damaged by dive bombing, and on October 5, they also hit the destroyers *Minegumo* and *Murasame*.

On October 15, Dauntless attacks so damaged the transports *Azumasan Maru*, *Kyushu Maru*, and *Sasago Maru* that they had to beach themselves and were destroyed, while the destroyer *Samidare* was also hit. In return blows, the dive bombing Vals from the carrier *Zuikaku* sank the American destroyer *Meredith* and the tug

Vireo the same day. But on October 19, the Japanese destroyer *Ayanami* was damaged by the SBDs.

The last carrier-to-carrier duel in this period took place on October 26, 1942, when Nagumo returned to the fray with the *Shōkaku, Zuihō,* and *Zuikaku* and his full battleship strength. The light carrier *Junyō* was with Admiral Kondo's advance force. Facing this array was the *Enterprise* with TF16 and the *Hornet* with TF17, along with the new battleships *South Dakota* and *Washington.* The resulting battle was known as the Battle of Santa Cruz.

On October 26, the Japanese sighted the American fleet and launched strong air attacks, which included twenty-two Vals in the first wave and twenty in the second. At 0655 hours, the first wave, led by Lieutenant Commander Mamoru Seki, found the American ships and attacked on their own. Their target was the *Hornet,* and the battleships escorting her put up a terrific wall of fire. Nonetheless, the Vals attacked and plunged into it, led by Seki. Although very heavily damaged, his dive bomber continued its plunge straight into the heart of the carrier's hull, its exploding bomb load wrecking the ship's boilers. Three more direct hits were made—one aft to starboard, another on the flight deck—while a fourth gouged its way down to the fourth deck of the carrier before detonation. The *Hornet* slewed round and came to a halt, listing and disabled, and it was then hit by two torpedoes as the Japanese torpedo bombers joined in the assault.

The second wave of Vals, led by Lieutenant Sadomu Takahashi, was waylaid by U.S. carrier fighters and decimated. Takahashi himself had to ditch along with others, but enough got through to plant two direct hits and two near-misses around the *Enterprise* while other Vals dashed themselves against the defenses of the battleship *South Dakota,* flanked as she was by the antiaircraft cruiser *San Juan* and the light cruiser *Portland.* Against this huge array of antiaircraft firepower, all their attacks broke with heavy losses among the dive bombers involved. One Val hit the battleship with a heavy bomb on "A" turret, but failed to inflict damage to such a heavily armored target. Another Val scored a direct hit on *San Juan,* and her flimsy decks offered little resistance, the bomb penetrating almost through to the ship's keel before exploding deep inside and jamming her rudder. A torpedo bomber crashed into the destroyer *Smith*, wiping out her bridge, but she stayed afloat.

The return strike from the American ships found the Japanese carriers at 0840 hours. Two SBDs made a surprise dive and hit *Zuihō* aft with two bombs; these planes were piloted by Lieutenant Birney Strong and Ensign Charles Irvine of *Enterprise*'s VS-10. In the meantime, *Hornet* had launched fifteen SBDs at the same time as *Enterprise* got away another three from VB-10. *Hornet* followed up with a further Dauntless contribution of nine aircraft at 0920 hours. Fifteen dive bombers found their targets and dived down; four were lost to defending fighters on the way down. The remaining eleven scored at least three direct hits on the *Shōkaku*. The *Enterprise* group attacked a heavy cruiser, the *Chikuma*, demolishing her bridge with two bombs while a third penetrated her vitals badly damaging her. In all, a total of twenty SBDs were lost in this battle, but the D3A-1s were almost all wiped out. The crippled *Hornet* was again attacked by the *Junyō's* last six Vals led by the senior surviving dive bomber pilot, Sub-lieutenant Shunko Kato, and they hit *Hornet* yet again. Having taken an enormous amount of punishment, including more torpedo hits, *Hornet* was finally abandoned and sent to the bottom by a Japanese destroyer at 0135 hours on the twenty-seventh.

Despite getting marginally the better of these two set-piece battles, the Japanese carriers withdrew, as did the Americans. The surface ships then took over the struggle, and a series of titanic pitch battles involving warships were fought in the Slot—from battleships blasting each other at point-blank range, down to destroyers and torpedo boats fighting high speed duels in the inky blackness. But most of these great clashes took place by night. In the morning, it was left to the dive bombers from Henderson Field to mop up the cripples and hunt for survivors of the previous night's actions.

On November 7, the destroyers *Naganami* and *Takanami* of the Tokyo Express were hit by SBDs and damaged. Vals from the light carrier *Hiyō* returned the compliment by attacking an American troop convoy on November 11 and damaging the transport *Zeilin* badly, as well as hitting two others, but losing nine out of twelve of their number in doing so. On November 13, Dauntless strikes assisted those from *Enterprise* in pounding the drifting hulk of the Japanese battleship *Hiei*, which had been wrecked in action the night before. The two groups cooperated again on the fourteenth when SBDs from both units attacked a convoy and its escorting cruiser force that was withdrawing after another nighttime encounter. The heavy cruiser *Kinugasa* was sunk while the cruisers *Chōkai*, *Isūzu*, and *Maya* and the destroyer *Michishio* were all dive bombed and severely hit. From the convoy, Dauntless attacks sank the transport *Canberra Maru* and *Nagara Maru*, while the *Sado Maru* was damaged. Additional SBD strikes the same day sank the *Brisbane Maru*, *Arizona Maru*, and *Nako Maru*, drowning some 400 soldiers.

On the twenty-fourth, the SBDs sank the destroyer *Hayashio*, and on December 8, the *Nowake* was hit and abandoned. Finally, on the last day of 1942, the Japanese decided to admit defeat, and Guadalcanal was secured by the Americans, due in no small measure to the efforts of the Dauntless dive bomber.

CHAPTER 20

Full Circle

New Developments and the Return of the Fighter Dive Bomber

While the various factions in Britain argued and debated, a war was being conducted in the Pacific that centered almost entirely on the dive bomber. Throughout 1942, the Dauntless and the Val had fought this war on their own, although both were regarded as obsolete designs. But at the end of 1943, at long last, their replacements began to appear on the battlefield in increasing numbers. The change-over from a peacetime footing to war production had not only affected the production of the Bermuda and Vengeance, but had not helped the Helldiver either. In Japan, the development of the Judy matched the long delays of its American counterpart, but finally, both appeared at the front.

The problem of wing-flutter was not finally solved in the D4Y1 Suisei (Comet), code-named Judy, until the spring of 1943, when it was overcome by strengthening. With this problem solved, the aircraft could thus, in theory, be fully used in its proper role and not just for reconnaissance as hitherto. Full-scale production was got underway by the Aichi Company, almost 600 being turned out in the first year. In combat the Comet did not live up to expectations and the Atsuta in line engine was therefore replaced by a large radial, the 1,560-horsepower Mitsubishi MK80 Kinsei 62. This involved structural alterations forward to fit it to the existing airframe and this version became the Model 33, the D4Y3. A 3a variant was fitted with a 13-millimeter rear gun. The more powerful radial engine increased the maximum speed of this modification to 357 mph.

Meanwhile, as a stop-gap measure, the Val had been improved by re-engining with the 1,300-horsepower Kinsei 54, and extra fuel bunkerage was added. The cockpit was streamlined and a propeller spinner fitted to become the Model 22—1,016 of which were produced by the Aichi and Showa plants to the end of the war, compared with a total of 470 Model 11s.

Gone were the days when numerous models could be tried and tested; the need was for combat-fit aircraft in the maximum numbers. Thus, one navy-designed dive bomber that fell by the wayside was the Nakajima D3N1, a small carrier-based aircraft featuring a retractable landing gear.

One very late development in the dive bomber field was initiated by the army, however. This was the "experimental attacker" aircraft, the Kawasaki Ki119. It was a radial-engined version of the Tony fighter, but larger in size because of the fitting of the 2,000-horsepower Ha104 engine. It had a combat radius of 375 miles, which special drop tanks could increase to 750 miles. It had a wingspan of 45 feet, 9 inches; a length of 38 feet, 10 inches; and a height of 14 feet, 9 inches. Its total weight was 8,766 pounds.

To give island bases protection, the Japanese needed floatplanes. One answer was the Aichi E16A Zuiun, code-named Paul by the Allies. The AM-22 prototype first flew in May 1942.

It was the Japanese who came up with the most novel form of dive bomber—nothing less than a floatplane dive bomber. This was the Aichi E16A Zuiun, designed by Matsuo and Ozawa, the first model of which was completed in May 1942. It was designed to operate over the wastes of the Pacific from remote island bases and was built from the outset with dive bomber capability. It thus featured hydraulically-operated dive brakes mounted on the front leg of the N-struts, but the original design caused severe buffeting and had to be modified. With fully perforated dive brakes the aircraft went into service in late 1943 as the E16A2 Navy Reconnaissance Seaplane.

It was a single-engined twin-float seaplane of all-metal construction with stressed-skin covering, wooden wingtips which folded and control surfaces which were fabric covered. It was a two seater powered by the Mitsubishi MK8D Kinsei 54 radial engine of 1,560-horsepower, which gave it a top speed of 273 mph at 18,045 feet. It was armed with two 7.7-millimeter type 97 machine guns in the wings and a flexible type 92 of similar caliber in the rear cockpit. It had a span of 42 feet and a length of 35 feet, 6½ inches. Some 256 were built and served with the 301st, 634th, and Yokosuka Kokutais. Known to the Allies as the Paul, it was severely mauled during the Philippines campaign of 1944, where it was completely out of its element. In common with most other types of Japanese aircraft, the survivors ended their days in flames off the Okinawa beachhead as Kamikazes.

The Army Ki119 did not even get that far. Although emphasis was laid on both the ease of maintenance, avoiding as far as possible the inclusion of wrought-metal plates of which there was a bottleneck, production was slow. It was designed to attack American task forces far out from Japan's shoreline in the face of overwhelming fighter defences, itself with fighter-like maneuverability. Plans were made to mass produce the Ki119 in underground workshops, but it all came far too late. Work did not commence until March 1945, and full-scale production was hoped for by September 1945.

In the United States, the non-appearance of a replacement led to further improvements to the basic type as an interim measure. For the U.S. Navy, this involved the fitting of the SBD Dauntless with the improved R-1820-60 engine of 1,200 horsepower and increasing the range by extra tankage to 370 gallons. The resulting SBD5 began production in February 1943 and proved by far the largest mark, no less than 2,900 being built before production ceased in April 1944. Comparison with the Val production figures show just how wide the gap was in the respective capacity of the U.S. and Japanese war plants and just how hopeless the conflict had now become for the Japanese as early as 1943.

The U.S. Army's indecision was reflected in its own Dauntless version, the A24. Although the plane was a failure in combat to date, they nonetheless ordered 170 A24A-D/Es (the equivalent of the SBD4) and 615 A24B-DTs (equivalent to the SBD5), which were to be constructed at a new Douglas plant set up at Tulsa. However, in the interim, another change of heart had taken place, and of all these aircraft, only a handful ever saw service. This time, there was some little-known success, with the 531st Fighter-Bomber Squadron operating dive bombing missions with the A24B from airstrips in the Makin Islands during December 1943.

The Curtiss SB2C1 actually joined the fleet comparatively early, despite the many problems surrounding it, embarking with VS9 in the new carrier *Essex* in December 1942, but, once afloat it became clear that its problems were only just beginning! Numerous faults were discovered in this period including tail wheel and hook failures that led to them being relegated to VB17 aboard the escort carrier *Santee* and ashore with test units. Consequently, the initial batch of 200 Helldivers had to be modified again before they could be passed fit for combat.

In a similar manner, those thus modified, when embarked with VB4 and VB6 aboard the new *Yorktown* in May 1943, also fell down badly—so much so that the ship's commander, Captain J.J. Clark, recommended the entire Helldiver program be scrapped. His squadrons were re-equipped with the faithful Dauntless and went off to war. The SB2Cs were dumped ashore and there underwent yet a third modification, involving considerable strengthening, fitting of self-sealing fuel tanks and non-retractable tail wheels, a .30-inch machine-gun mounting replaced by a .05-inch at the same time.

They tried again, VB-17 embarking in the *Bunker Hill* in July 1943 for more sea trials, and when the third modification was completed, she took these Helldivers, some thirty-six in all, out to battle.

Meanwhile, the fitting of the 20-millimeter cannon in wings and hydraulic flaps to production line models resulted in the SB2C-1C in August. The second fleet carrier to embark the modified Helldiver in a fit state to use was the *Intrepid*.

In the meantime, the army experienced similar problems with its own versions, the A25A. Under the same expansion scheme that they adopted with the A24, the U.S. Army Air Force placed orders to obtain 100 SB2Cs from the navy quota in 1940, and confirmed this on the last day of that year. After Pearl Harbor, this modest start was supplemented by orders totaling an additional 3,000 dive bombers of this type, which was beyond the capacity of the parent company to produce on top of its navy orders. Therefore, a plant was set up at St. Louis to subcontract the army specification, this version being named the Curtiss S84 Shrike.

The first Shrike took to the air on September 29, 1942, and still had navy-type folding wings, but so many modifications were required to fit army requirements that it soon became a different airplane. Only ten were built by March 1943, before the folding wing was dropped, different radio sets fitted, and larger wheels adopted, and the contract was transferred to the army as attempts at standardization were merely delaying production of both models.

All this took place during another shift in U.S. Army Air Force policy, which finally rejected the whole dive bomber concept anyway, and the completed aircraft—again redesignated as the RA-25A Helldiver—were employed on target-towing duties, a seemingly inevitable fate for unwanted dive bombers around the world.

A further twist in the complicated story was the allocation of 150 of these A25As to Australia, only ten of which were finally delivered due to delays. In the final event, these—and 270 surplus army machines—were to be modified and transferred to the Marines as land-based dive bombers after production stopped when 900 army types had been completed. All this required additional alterations, and by the time they arrived at the end of 1944, they were of no value to the U.S. Marines either and served in a secondary role as trainers.

In Europe in 1943, the development of the fighter dive bomber was gradually taking hold, and this spread to the Pacific, as we shall see. There gradually emerged a blending of the concepts of the dive bomber and the fighter-bomber, even in those Allied air forces most opposed to specialized dive bombers, the Royal Air Force and the U.S. Army Air Force. Even they could not remain blind to the advantages of dive bombing, and although they stead-fastly refused to admit they had been wrong in public, more and more dive bombing was conducted by them as time went by. Happily, the lifting power of the new generation of fighters enabled them to carry equivalent bomb loads to the old type dive bombers, and with the final acceptance of dive bombing when carried out by such machines, the operational use expanded. But it was a very gradual process in the RAF, and the traditional dive bomber soldiered on in all air arms except the British as 1942 gave way to 1943 and 1944.

The high tide of Axis success in North Africa was reached in September 1942, when Rommel swept across the Egyptian frontier and for a time looked like taking Cairo and the Suez Canal. There was widespread panic behind the British lines at headquarters, but the Germans were at the end of their tether, lacking the necessary supplies and reinforcements for this final push. Rommel had always been heavily outnumbered by the British, despite his successes, and now with the crisis in Russia leaving him unsupported, the scales tilted still further against him.

Operating from airfields at Daba and Fuka, Ju87s of the 3rd Stuka Wing were heavily committed and began again to take some losses from RAF fighters now operating freely in large numbers from the prewar airfields of Egypt. In one such encounter on July 3, 1942, two squadrons of British fighters caught fifteen Stukas over El Alamein and claimed to have shot down thirteen of them. A great victory was announced, and tales were spread of Stukas crashing all over the desert, but despite this, the Ju87s continued to be heavily engaged in the subsequent land fighting to the discomfiture of the British troops, although their numbers dwindled as the crisis after Stalingrad drew increasing numbers of them to more important areas. Attacks by RAF bombers concentrated on Stuka airfields on July 5—which gives an indication of how the RAF really felt about them—and nine were destroyed on the ground. Despite these desperate British attempts to preempt the Stukas, the Ju87s were again prominent in the German attacks of

August 31 and September 1, 1942. Formations of up to forty of these dive bombers spearheaded German armor thrusts. But the Afrika Korps was held by extensive minefields, and the offensive ground to a halt.

Throughout October, heavy rain made the forward airstrips unserviceable, and the bulk of the Stuka forces were pulled back to Sidi Haneish, and with the opening of the British offensive, they were in short supply and unable to contain the overwhelming advance of the 8th Army, which was operating under an enormous fighter umbrella. On November 11, fifteen Stukas of the 1st Group of the 3rd Stuka Wing, operating from Gambut under Colonel Martin Mossdorf, were intercepted by strong fighter forces, which brushed aside their slender screen and destroyed eleven of them in continuous attacks. By November 1942, the 3rd Stuka Wing had pulled back all the way to Tunisia and began transferring units to airfields in the Balkans.

Nonetheless, the Ju87 was again much in evidence in the battles of March 1943, which saw the Americans badly mauled by Rommel; the British attacks were blunted and brought to a standstill for a time. In fact, the position of the previous October was reversed, with the Stukas able to operate extensively from the runways of the Vichy bases, while the airstrips of the Allies were washed out. Never exceeding a total strength of fifty to sixty Ju87s, the Stukas, based in both Tunisia and Sardinia, gave the allies several bloody noses before Tunis finally fell in May 1943. This unexpected reemergence of the Stuka yet again—after the RAF had written it off in the press so many times before—again caused some unrest in Parliament.

In Germany, the Ju87's replacement was having no more luck than similar aircraft in America and Japan. This aircraft was the Me210. The original specification dated back to 1938, which at that time called for an improved twin-engined fighter destroyer to replace the Me110. The second and fourth prototypes (V2 and V4) had, however, been fitted with dive brakes, and in 1940, dive bombing trials were held before they were removed. Despite this, dive bombing testing with the Me210 continued with the V12, and the early production models, Me210-A0s, were built with dive bombing as one of their main functions. Two 1,100-pound bombs were the maximum bomb load carried in this profile. But the Germans did not take the idea much further. The Me210 was used as a dive bomber in combat, but by the Hungarians, who used license-built Me210Cs with their 102 Group as dive bombers in 1944.

Meanwhile, the first American-built dive bombers had entered squadron service with the RAF and, to their embarrassment, proved highly successful. No. 45 Squadron was the first RAF Vengeance unit to see combat. The first mission took place on November 27, 1942, in support of the Arakan offensive. During a brief period of operations, the Vengeance carried out five offensive dive bombing operations. On four of these missions, the targets attacked were enemy-occupied villages, and the fifth was an enemy-defended position with the target indicated by smoke. On each mission, six Vengeance aircraft took part flying in a box of two Vics of three.

With the monsoon season, operations were curtailed, and an intensive period of training was undertaken as the Vengeance allocation enabled the RAF and Indian Air Forces to build up to full wing strength in preparation for the next big push. In India in 1942, there was no doubt at all about the efficiency of the dive bomber and every confidence in its future.

As allocations of Vengeance aircraft suffered the delays mentioned earlier, the Royal Australian Air Force had to make use of anything available in New Guinea, and among the first dive bomber operations they carried out were those conducted by No. 4 Army Co-Operation Squadron in late 1942. This unit was equipped with the Commonwealth Wirraway, a two-seater, low-wing monoplane designed for close-support and aerial reconnaissance. Equipped with two 250-pound bombs on underwing racks, they operated in the winter of 1942-43 in the Papuan campaign. The first Vengeance squadron was formed in Australia in the spring of 1943 and made attacks on Timor with some success, being joined by a second squadron in September.

During 1942–43, the development of the fighter dive bomber was steadily increasing in favor on the Eastern Front, in the Mediterranean, and later in the Pacific, with the British, Germans, Americans, and Italians all producing viable ideas on this same theme. But before the Junkers Ju87 vanished from the daytime skies over the

Eastern Mediterranean sea—its role as a dive bomber being eclipsed by this full-circle return to its origins—the Stuka was to score one last spectacular victory over its old adversary, the Royal Navy.

We have seen how their earlier unhappy experiences with the A24 had put off the development of the dive bomber proper in the U.S. Army Air Force, despite massive, unfulfilled orders for their own adaptations of various U.S. Navy and RAF types being built in America. Failure of these adaptations to arrive in squadron service in time because of production difficulties further worsened the situation when the army variants of the Helldiver and the Buccaneer failed to materialize, in particular the XA32. Then, the Vengeance (A35A) also failed to show up on time, and so it went on. This led the U.S. Army Air Force to adapt the versatile and long-range fighter, the North American Mustang, to a combined Anglo-American design, and include for it a new dive bombing role to fill the gap. Surprisingly, it was at once successful in this role, and it followed the German Fw190 as a dive bomber adapted from a front-line fighter.

In fact, the U.S. Army Air Force development could be said to have preceded the German, for it was in August 1942 that the dive bombing version of the Mustang, the A36A, was ordered, and deliveries followed off the production line almost at once. No

Among the earliest Allied fighter aircraft adapted for dive bombing was the North American Mustang. It could carry two 500-pound bombs.

fewer than six squadrons were so equipped by early 1943. These conversions from the normal P-51 were fitted with dive brakes and could carry a handy bomb load of two 500-pound bombs, one under each wing, in special racks. Powered by a 1,325-horsepower Allison V-1710-87 engine, the A36A could attain a top speed of 356 mph, which made it ideal, when coupled with its high endurance.

By early 1943, the first of these units were moving into the Mediterranean theater, and their first combat sorties took place on June 6, 1943, over Sicily, prior to the Allied invasion of that island (Operation Husky) with the 27th Fighter-Bomber Group. They also dive bombed the island of Pantelleria in July, just before the main assault on Sicily itself. For both operations, the 27th and 86th Groups were employed as dive bombers. Although proving very effective, the A36A took some losses from the superior German flak defenses; both groups lost twenty aircraft between them. But they proved the effectiveness of dive bombing against armor by stopping enemy formations at Salerno during German counterattacks on the Allied beachhead there in September 1943, and they later gave invaluable assistance during the drive on Rome itself.

However, production was limited, while losses and wear-and-tear steadily reduced the numbers of A36As operating towards the end of that year. All such aircraft were therefore concentrated in the 27th Group when the 33rd switched to India, and finally, in 1944, even these were replaced by the P-47 Thunderbolt.

Specialized dive bomber research work in the U.S. Army Air Force had been finally dropped at this time. The final attempt to produce a viable product for that service was the abortive Vultee XA41. This was a very large aircraft, which could carry up to 7,000 pounds of bombs and was armed with four 37-millimeter cannon plus four .5-inch Browning machine guns. Its total weight was a colossal 23,000 pounds, and it was powered by a single 3,000-horsepower engine. However, by the time it was put forward, all army interest in such highly specialized dive bombers was dead, and it was never ordered.

Before the final collapse in North Africa, the Italians had already withdrawn their Stuka units. The 102nd Group was located at Lonate Pozzolo in northern Italy at this time. Their worn-out Ju87B2s and R2s were then replaced by new batches of Doras, and a new formation, the 103rd Group, was set up on February 1, 1943. This unit transferred to Siena Ampugnano in central Italy in March, with command of the 237th being taken over by Captain Leo Vacellio. In May, it was switched to airfields in Sardinia in preparation for operations in the western Mediterranean, but in heavy attacks by U.S. Army Air Force bombers on their bases, it was almost wiped out on the ground before seeing combat.

During the defense of Sicily, a few Italian Ju87Ds operated from Boccadifalco airfield near Palermo and carried out an attack on Allied shipping at Licatabia on July 11, 1943, in which they claimed to have scored some hits. Only four Stukas, led by Captain Cesare Zanazzo took part, all returning to Sardinia with damage. Meanwhile, another Stuka unit, the 121st Group, had been hastily formed with the few remaining Rs. When the attack on Sicily developed, these were rushed into Gioia del Colle airfield in the south of Italy, with the 237th Squadron on July 11, and on the same day, seven of these Stukas, with an escort of Macchi 202s, attacked shipping off the beachheads, claiming two hits. They were intercepted by Spitfires and lost two of their number. The same story continued throughout the brief campaign, and by the end of it, the Italian Stuka formations were again at a very low ebb and took very little part in any subsequent fighting in the mainland campaigns.

Meanwhile, the development of the fighter dive bomber had also taken place in the Italian Air Force. Several types were under development at this time, as follows. The Avia LM02 was a special glider dive bomber, developed especially to attack Allied shipping

FINAL ITALIAN STUKA UNITS OPERATIONAL, 1942–43

Group	Commander	No. of Aircraft	Squadron	Commander
103rd	Lt. Col. Savarino	25 Ju87Ds	207th	Capt. C. Zanazzo
				Capt. V. Marcoccia
121st	Maj. L. Orlandini	12 Ju87Rs	206th	Capt. Zucca
			216th	Capt. Pergoli

This Ju87D-3 of the Italian 121st Independent Dive Bombing Group
is seen taxiing along the runway of Capua airport near Naples in
August 1943.

at Gibraltar, a somewhat ambitious project. It was all-wooden construction and fitted with Junkers dive brakes. The idea was that
this aircraft, fitted with a pair of 1,800-pound bombs, should be
towed across the Mediterranean by a SM79 bomber to about
twenty to thirty miles of the Rock, whereupon it would be released,
carry out its dive bombing attack at about 330 mph, and then
make a water landing off Algeciras with the pilot being picked up
by submarines. This whole concept was the brainchild of Pieraldo
Mortara, an engineer, and backed by E. Lombardi, owner of the
AVIA Company.

It was to have been a glider of great strength. The dive brakes
were to be held by elastic ribbon and, in the dive, when the speed
had built up to about 280 mph holes in the wings would force the
air through, thus extending the brakes. Tested by Nello Raimondo
at Vercelli at the end of 1942, the further development was retarded at this time, for the use of radar made the value of its silent
approach to a heavily defended target useless anyway. Although
AVIA built parts of this strange dive bomber concept for structural
tests and began to assemble a second prototype, all work stopped
in 1943, and it became merely another curiosity of the war.

More realistic and worthwhile was the adaptation of the Reggiane Re2002 fighter, with a Piaggio PIXIX RC45 engine of 1,185 horsepower. It could be used for bombing at angles of 45 degrees with light bombs of 220 or 550 pounds under the wings and was thus tested and allocated to the 101st and 102nd Squadrons based at Lonate Pozzolo in December 1942.

After some teething troubles, these two groups moved to Tarquinia. On July 10, 1943, with twenty and twelve aircraft, respectively, they moved into Crotonone-Isola Capo Rizzuto, making their first dive bombing attacks on ships off Reggio and Augusta. Four Re2002s were lost in this attack including flight leader Guido Nobili. By September 24, these units had only two dozen serviceable aircraft left between them—thirty-two being destroyed—and among the casualties were Gino Pricolo (on July 19) and Major Cenni (on September 4), the two most outstanding Italian dive bomber pilots of the war.

The successes they claimed was a hit on the battleship *Nelson* (not confirmed by British records) and the sinking of the troopships *Talamba* on July 11, *Fort Pelly* on July 20, and *Fishpool* on July 26, which caused numerous casualties. Training in dive bombing continued at Lonate Pozzolo, where the 50th Flight had ten Re2002s on hand until September 8, when all such operations ceased on the Italian surrender. Some captured Re2002s were reputedly used by the Luftwaffe later in France, while the 50th Flight used its dive bombers against their former ally in Greece, Yugoslavia, and Albania until the end of hostilities.

During this period, the ninety IMAM Ro57bis aircraft ordered in 1942 joined squadron service with 97th Group. On July 9, 1943, this unit, led by Raoul Zucconi, had just fifteen aircraft fit for operations, but ten of these were destroyed in Allied air attacks on the thirteenth. The 97th Group moved the few remaining Ro57s to Tarquinia, but they never saw extensive combat.

Back in Britain ordinary fighter-bomber exploits with Kittyhawks and Hurribombers had wrongly been reported by the press as being dive bombing. When the U.S. Army Air Force Mustangs carried out actual true dive bombings, *without* their dive brakes wired shut incidentally, the whole question of why the RAF was still the only major service out of step was raised. The continued delay of the re-introduction of the dive bomber into the FAA was reported to Churchill. The reason for the delay to the Barracuda, it was said, was due to the replacement of its power plant by a less efficient one. As for the American-built dive bombers, although the Vengeance was entering service in India, it received little or no publicity as that would negate the then current propaganda which scorned the dive bomber in press and Parliament. So the Vengeance successes in the Arakan were hushed up. What of the Bermuda situation? In truth, there was little to cheer about here either. The air minister wrote a memorandum to Hugh Molson, a member of parliament, that "it is quite true, as Geoffrey Mander told you, that the long delay in the delivery of these dive bombers is due to failures in production in America. So inefficient indeed was one of the companies concerned that the United States government had to take over the plant."

Nor were things any better six months later. Stafford Cripps at the Ministry of Aircraft Production wrote to Sinclair:

> We have been doing all we can to get ahead with this but it is the most appalling production! We hope to get the first one to Boscombe Down this week. It had been awaiting flying weather only. If everything went perfectly and there we re no accidents or unexpected difficulties (which is most unlikely) we might get the modifications finished and on the first plane in six weeks time and thereafter go ahead with the others. It is, however, far more likely that you will not get any of them under three months from now, and even that date may be postponed.

In the meantime, the dive bomber refused to lie down as an opponent, as well as a self-inflicted headache. With the Italian surrender in September 1943, a vacuum was left in the Balkans and Aegean areas which the Germans quickly filled, disarming the Italians there and moving in strong air and ground forces of their own to protect the southeast flank of Europe. Included in these reinforcements were the Ju87s of the 3rd and 151st Stuka Wings, as well as the long-range Ju88 dive bombers, all of which came from the Eastern Front. At the same time that the Germans were thus increasing their grip on this vital area, the Allies were involved in a dispute over the need to beat them to it. The Americans refused to become involved, and the British lacked the forces to do so effectively. Churchill insisted on sending troops into the islands, with little or no air cover, and then sent the Royal Navy in to support them. The result was a repeat of the Crete fiasco of two years earlier. The British leader had apparently learned nothing about the power of dive bombers.

With the Balkans in the balance, the stakes were high, but the Germans were the quickest to react. The Stukas, based initially on Croatian and Greek airfields, struck hard. On September 21, 1943, they subjected the island fortress of Cephallonia in the Gulf of Corinth to heavy dive bombing attacks, and when this key position quickly fell, they switched their assault to Corfu on September 24, crushing all resistance quickly. The following day, the dive bombers directed their attentions to Split in Yugoslavia, and by the end of the week, all these three vital places were firmly in German hands. Its flank thus safe, the 3rd Stuka Wing was shuttled via Crete to Rhodes and turned on the small British garrisons on Leros, Cos, and Samos to the north of them, and also started to operate against the British and Greek warships, which were these troops' only links with Middle East Command in Egypt.

Continuous attacks by Ju88s resulted in the elimination of the only Spitfire squadrons available for local defense at Cos Island, and the sinking by the 1st Training and Demonstration Wing of the destroyer *Queen Olga* (Greek) and *Intrepid* Leros on September 26 was but a portent of what was to come. The only opposition the Ju87s now faced in the air was from long-range Beaufighters operating from Cyprus and, for a short period until they were withdrawn on orders from Eisenhower, U.S. Army Air Force Lightnings from North African bases.

Rhodes had been secured by the Germans from the numerically superior Italian forces on September 12, and the whole of the 3rd Bomber Wing, with about sixty Ju87Ds, was quickly established there. On October 3 and 4, the Germans invaded and took Cos. More than half the Luftwaffe sorties flown in support of this invasion were by the Stukas, which yet again proved the decisive factor in breaking all resistance.

The 3rd Ground Attack Wing now concentrated on the Royal Navy ships attempting to supply and reinforce the surviving garrisons. On October 7, Ju87s scored direct hits on the cruiser

Penelope, and although one of the 1,100-pound SAP bombs failed to explode correctly, the others damaged her very severely. Two days later, the Ju87s again penetrated a gap in the fighter cover and hit the cruiser *Carlisle* with a heavy bomb aft. Although she struggled back to Alexandria, she was a write-off. In the same attack, the destroyer *Panther* took a heavy bomb amidships, broke in half, and sank with heavy casualties. When the U.S. Army Air Force Lightnings finally arrived, they chased the smaller dive bombers back to Rhodes and subsequently claimed to have destroyed no fewer than fifteen of them, with another three claimed shot down by ship gunfire. These figures are still repeated in books today, but German records clearly show at the time that only half that number failed to return. These losses also failed to prevent the 3rd Ground Attack Wing meting out similar punishment to subsequent naval squadrons that believed such figures.

On October 17, for example, the cruiser *Sirius* was hit by a heavy bomb in an attack by the Ju88s of the 1st Training and Demonstration Wing and limped back to port. The Ju87s sank the motor launches *ML563* and *ML835* in Leros harbor on October 17 and the supply ship *Taganrog* at Samos on the twenty-fourth. On October 28, they caught the landing ship *LCT115* carrying guns and troops off Castelrosso and sank her, while the same Stukas dive bombed the cruiser *Aurora* on the last day of October and put a heavy bomb into her, which killed forty-six of her crew, wounded twenty more, and wrecked her antiaircraft guns, directors, and radars. They also scored a hit on the destroyer *Belvoir* that badly damaged her. The Stukas were equally the key to the swift German invasion and conquest of Leros island itself, which soon followed.

Preparations were then made to take the last remaining Allied-held island, Samos. But before the Germans landed, the bulk of the British garrison was evacuated through "neutral" Turkey, and after a heavy dive bombing attack by the 2nd Group, 3rd Bomber Wing, on Tigani on November 22, Samos fell, leaving the whole of the Balkans firmly in German hands.

TABLE 37: BaSIC DETAILS OF THE SIX MAIN DIVE BOMBERS IN COMBAT SERVICE, 1942–45

Aircraft	SB2C-1	D4Y	Vengeance II	Ju87D	Pe2	Barracuda
Country	USA	Japan	USA	Germany	USSR	Britain
Engine (hp)	1×1,700	1×1,010	1×1,700	1×1,415	2×1,100	1×1,640
Span (ft)	49'8.75"	37'8.75'	48'	49'2"	56'3"	49'2"
Length (ft)	36'7"	33'6.375"	40'	37'8"	40'10"	39'9"
Height (ft)	14'9"	12'3.25"	15'	12'9"	13'1"	15'1"
Max Speed (mph)	285	343	279	255	361	228
Weight (lb)	10,114	5,379	12,480	8,600	13,119	9,350
Ceiling (ft)	23,000	32,480	24,300	24,200	29,500	16,600
Range (mi)	695	978	700	500	1,100	686
No. of Bombs	1	1	4	1	4	1
Bomb Load (lb)	1,000	1,100	2,000	3,960	2,205	1,800
Crew	2	2	2	2	3	3
Designed Base	Carrier	Carrier	Land	Land	Land	Carrier

CHAPTER 21

The Secret Success

The Far East: Allied Operations and Vengeance Missions, 1942–44

At the end of 1942, dive bombers again dominated the scene in all areas of the Far East. U.S. Army Air Force A24s dive bombed Japanese Navy airfields in the Lae and Salamaua area during April 1942, aided by Kittyhawks. In July, they were withdrawn following the heavy losses of April 29. But American P-40s from Darwin were flown into airstrips in New Guinea and began dive bombing with two 300-pound bombs under either wing. They attacked targets in the Buna area and were joined by Royal Australian Air Force Wirraways using two 250-pound bombs for dive bombing, from September onward. A third Australian Vengeance squadron was formed by the end of 1943, and based in New Guinea, it undertook missions in the Nadzab area, operating in strengths of up to thirty-six aircraft and using standard RAF Vengeance tactics as perfected in Burma. Over the six-week campaign, they proved accurate and economical.

The small Royal New Zealand Air Force underwent considerable expansion in 1942–43, but the first dive bomber unit was not established until July 1943, when eighteen SBDs were transferred to No. 25 Squadron at Seagrove. This unit was brought up to full strength from its SBD3s by the purchase of twenty-seven SBD4s later in the same year, and training commenced in their usage at Santo airstrip in the New Hebrides. In March 1944, No. 25 Squadron was modernized by the arrival of twenty-three SBDs, and it then embarked for Bougainville and combat service. The airstrip was under continual shellfire from the Japanese attack when the

301

leading elements flew in, and no sooner had the SBDs landed than they were thrown into action against artillery and other targets.

Later, they also operated against targets in New Britain with Australian Boomerang fighters, also equipped as light dive bombers with 500-pound and 1,000-pound bombs, with great success against isolated Japanese garrisons, before finally disbanding in May 1944.

In the RAF, following the initial operations by the Vengeance aircraft of 168 Wing in November 1942 and the Arakan operations of March–July 1943, the lessons absorbed and the consideration of operating in even larger formations in the future led to the issuing of a tactical memorandum on future employment. It was a valuable document in which to find details of the tactics adopted by the RAF's only dive bombers for the late 1943 offensive, the Japanese counterblow, and the extensive dive bomber operations that continued in Burma up to June 1944.

Trainee pilots from Laverton RAAF base practice the "peel off" for dive bombing attacks in their Wirraways, February 1943.

Based on earlier operations, plus considerable training programs and trials, it was anticipated that the four Vengeance squadrons being employed would have to conduct two types of operations: predetermined operations against known targets and direct support operations with the army, with the squadrons on call through air support control (ASC) organization.

In the first type, the operation assumed the form of any normal bomber sortie with the takeoff time well known in advance, but in the second, the squadrons—or parts of squadrons—adopted various states of readiness after the manner of fighter units. As usual, the main factor in such jungle versions of the "cab rank" system was the rapid takeoff times achieved after the receipt of the call through the ASC. It was anticipated that, in the earliest state, the aircraft could be airborne after a briefing in fifteen to twenty minutes. Naturally, this time varied according to the local conditions, liaison with fighter cover, and other factors; about thirty minutes from the receipt of call was the time estimated.

Another factor vital to the efficiency of the direct support given was the turn-around factor between sorties, which limited the actual number of sorties per aircraft. About forty-five minutes was the estimated turn-around time for the Vengeance to refuel, re-arm, and turn around six aircraft; two hours was estimated for twelve.

For army support operations of this nature, the stand-by crews were briefed by the intelligence officer and the army liaison officer as the information on his battle zone allocated target came through, so that they were up-to-date on the general situation before a specific mission request came in from the front line, which saved considerable time at the main briefing. Meanwhile their aircraft were standing bombed-up and ready to go near the downwind end of the airstrip. In the forward areas, the aircraft were kept at readiness throughout the hours of daylight, so that they could scramble away in the event of hostile bombing attacks.

There were three types of basic attack: (1) high dive, (2) shallow dive, and (3) low level. Although it was stated that the Vengeance could obtain considerable accuracy by shallow diving, it was also made quite clear that better results could be obtained from traditional high dive bombing. Shallow dive bombing was more of a useful alternative should weather conditions over the target consist of low cloud. Low level was also rejected as a suitable Vengeance tactic because "in level flight, the forward visibility is extremely poor owing to the high nose of the aircraft."

It was necessary to approach the target from a turn off from a shallow dive. This left the Vengeance as an extremely vulnerable target to forward enemy flak positions, to which it could not reply. "This type of attack can be better carried out by a more suitable type of aircraft, i.e. a Hurribomber," as it was not true dive bombing.

Method 1 was therefore adopted as the principal Vengeance tactic, as the American, and earlier British reports, had already stated over the years that it should be. "A high degree of accuracy can be obtained in this type of bombing and this is the aircraft's primary role," the memo was forced to emphasize.

The bomb load continued to be as earlier: two 500-pound bombs or four 250-pound bombs carried in her capacious internal bomb-bay. This load could be released in salvo or sticks, but the main bomb load was carried internally. With dive bombing, the bombs were released in salvo, so that they fell in a very concentrated cluster. Thus, again, actual combat experience proved that theory and prewar practice and claims were false. A reasonable stick could be achieved by releasing in the pull-out from a high diving attack if required, the spacing of the bombs being dependent on the rate of pull-out: "From a normal pilot, a stick of four bombs will cover about 150 yards."

The RAF equipped itself with the Vultee A-31 in late 1942 and used it in combat in Burma with great success. Named the Vengeance AN889, it is seen here over England.

The final verdict was that "the Vengeance should be used against small and precise targets where accuracy is essential—while stick and spread bombing for area targets should be undertaken by level bombing aircraft." Quite so.

The Vengeance took over all such duties and operated with fighter cover save when there was sufficient cloud. Takeoff and forming-up procedure was that each dive bomber took off singly at 500-yard intervals when using a good runway. The leader flew straight after taking off for about forty-five seconds and then started a gentle left-hand turn, as the others joined.

When he was satisfied that he had all his formation together, he steepened his turn and set course straight away for the target zone. The time from first takeoff to setting the course by the formation was about seven minutes. Meanwhile, the fighter escort took off after the bombers under their own arrangements and it was left to the flghter leader to locate and take station on the bombers, which was easy enough when operating from the same airfield as indicated in the diagram. Rendezvous over a particular landmark was affected otherwise.

The Vengeance leader climbed at 140 mph to between 6,000 and 7,000 feet, and then climbed at 135mph to 10,000 feet or up to a normal ceiling of 15,000ft. For the flight to the target, the cruising speed was 155–160 mph. The formation that was adopted depended, as always, on the number of aircraft employed, but the "box in line astern" was the most favored. For six aircraft, two Vics in "line astern stepped down" were used. For eight aircraft, the formation was two boxes of four, and for nine aircraft, it was three Vics in "line astern stepped down." With increasing numbers of dive bombers being deployed for the new offensive, even larger formations were considered, but these were thought unwieldy.

Instead, it was deemed advantageous to split the formation up into two sub-formations. With twelve aircraft, two boxes of six were used, the second flying in echelon to the first and stepped down. Trials were conducted with more spread out formations, such as squadron Vic, but it was rejected since little supporting fire could be given and it was thought that "the concentration of fire power provided in the box type of formation is considered more desirable."

In the recommended schemes for operations against naval targets (which in the event did not materialize), navigation duties were

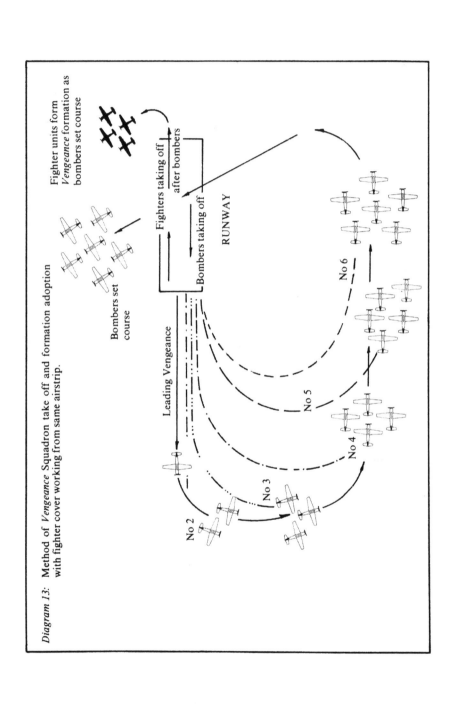

Diagram 13: Method of *Vengeance* Squadron take off and formation adoption with fighter cover working from same airstrip.

Fighter units form *Vengeance* formation as bombers set course

Bombers set course

Fighters taking off after bombers

Bombers taking off

Fighters taking off

Leading Vengeance

RUNWAY

No 2

No 3

No 4

No 5

No 6

laid down in some detail. The navigator was to fly in the leader's air-craft, and it was recommended that he should also be trained in fire control—if not, a separate fire controller was to be carried in the deputy leader's aircraft in the second Vic or four of the leading sub-formation.

For land operations the same principle applied, but it was felt at that time that the introduction of VHF and the limited range of the Vengeance meant that such sorties would only involve pilot navigation and that therefore squadrons would use a gunnery lead-er, flying the leading aircraft as fire controller. Some squadrons preferred this method anyway, and it was duly noted that "this is considered a domestic problem and is left to the individual tastes of each squadron with Wing standing aside."

It was freely admitted that evasive action was not easily affected against determined fighter attack. The usual methods of evasion, turning, undulation, and corkscrewing were to be employed, and so was the old Stuka tactic.

Shallow diving had been found to be effective against Hurri-canes in tests. When diving at an angle of 25 degrees, indicated air speeds of about 260 mph could be held. At this speed, the Hurri-cane has a relatively higher speed of only about 20 mph over the Vengeance formation. This enables the bomber to make good ground towards the target and may well enable them to carry out their attack before being engaged by fighters. The approach to the target is made at a height considerably above the bombing height (10,000 feet), to enable this form of evasion to be used. Ample warning of an impending attack is desirable for the success of this manoeuvred.

This, of course, was just whistling on the wind, for the sort of opposition a hotted up Zero and Tojo fighter could offer was hardly to be compared with a Hurricane, and it is left to the imagination as to what degree of early warning the obliging Japanese fighter pilots would give. It was just as well perhaps that this was never put to the test. Indeed, it was readily admitted that:

> In the event of the formation being seriously jumped and
> it is found necessary to abandon the operation, the forma-
> tion should dive to ground level, if necessary jettisoning

bombs, relying for evasion on their low altitude and concentration of fire power. Little is to be gained by opening
dive brakes as large formations cannot dive steeply and it is
almost impossible for aircraft in formation to extend
brakes in unison.

However, it was further noted that *individual* aircraft diving
away from an enemy interceptor could employ their dive brakes in
the old Stuka manner to cause their pursuer to overshoot. A note
of warning was added, for this was an old trick now: "It is however
the opinion of fighter pilots who have experienced these tactics,
that the wary pursuer will anticipate this action and will rather wait
to catch the Vengeance after he had pulled out of the dive."

When the formation approached the target zone, it lost height
down to around 10,000 feet at the point of the attack. About a
minute (or less) before the dive position was reached, the leader
gave a pre-arranged signal, usually by opening the bomb doors.
The pilot's procedure was then to open bomb doors, fuse and
select bombs, put all petrol switches on, engage low blower, enrich
mixture, and put rudder trim in neutral.

Sections then took up echelon formation in line astern, open
formation. In order to keep position within the optimum diving
cone, it was laid down that not more than four aircraft were to be
in echelon. The rear sub-formation followed in line astern of the
leader, who approached the target in a wide sweep to one target
and then turned in towards it. This maneuver enabled each pilot
to keep the objective in view to one side of the aircraft's nose and,
incidentally, give a little throw-off to the flak predictors.

The leader allowed the target to disappear under the leading
edge of the wing and, after about ten seconds, did a wing-over and
dived "at an angle of 80 degrees *or more steeply*," and opened his
dive brakes as he commenced the dive. The others followed him
down at intervals of about 500 feet in succession. No strafing was
done on the way down, as "front guns are not effective in the dive
and are dangerous to the aircraft in front."

The bombs were released at about 3,000 feet, and pullout took
place below 1,000 feet. While the Vengeance aircraft were carrying
out the actual bombing, their own fighter cover maintained visual

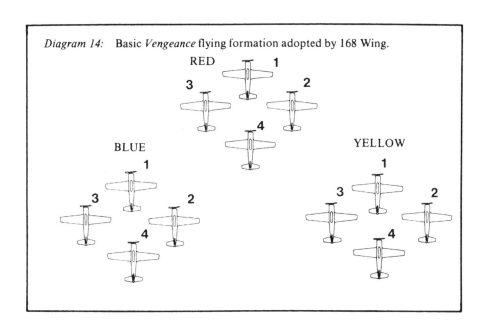

Diagram 14:   Basic *Vengeance* flying formation adopted by 168 Wing.

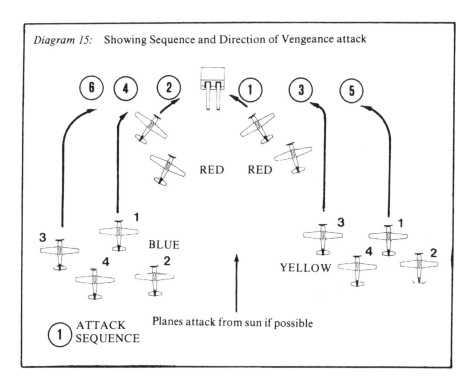

Diagram 15:   Showing Sequence and Direction of Vengeance attack

contact. For the getaway and to form up for the return flight, the Vengeance depended on its speed and turning to avoid the worst areas of AA fire. In order to reform quickly, the following aircraft had to close their dive brakes earlier in the last part of the dive than did the leader, so that he did not have to throttle back for them to catch up, thereby exposing his own aircraft to unnecessary damage. As each aircraft came out of its dive in a different direction, a distant rendezvous spot was selected, in the same general area well away from the target, and in the case of the Vengeance, this had to be predetermined.

Once assembled, the Vengeance aircraft formed up in Vics of three (or boxes of four if there were only eight aircraft) to enable them to concentrate their defences in the recognized way, and at low level. This return was taken at 190 mph with the nose well down, giving a good vantage point in which to take stock of the land contours to give natural cover, as per the textbook.

For shallow dive bombing attacks, if needed, the formation took advantage of the cloud cover to the target area and the attack was carried out from the cloud base to 1,500 feet or lower. With light defenses working against them, this type of attack could be well pressed down to bomb fragmentation height. On sighting, the target the leader would put the whole formation into echelon and approach the target well to one side, as in high bombing. A turn of 45 degrees would be made to the target, and the dive commenced at up to 60 degrees, with getaway at ground level.

Much of the outstanding success achieved by 168 Wing in 1942–44 was because of the enthusiasm and completeness with which the new tactics were worked out in the period before the campaign opened. Despite the fact that they were a unique formation in the RAF's line of battle—and an embarrassment to their senior leaders because of their success on a front the press always ignored or perhaps because of these handicaps—168 made every effort to produce plans, almost from scratch, that covered every aspect of their operations. In the event, these worked out in combat with only slight modifications and with zero losses. This was such a contrast to the gloomy forecasts of the preceding twenty years that they are worthy of examination before they are completely forgotten.

No. 110 Squadron was the main workhorse for these trials and tests, which translated theory into trial, and trial into combat results in the space of six months. By the end of that period the six most experienced pilots were attaining an average error of about 40 yards (sometimes from single dives and sometimes from Vic dives), after an average flying time in the Vengeance aircraft of fifty hours.

It was found that the ideal dive was from approximately 10,000 feet to around 4,000 feet, since this allowed the pilot to go into a sufficiently steep dive, and to remain in it for a long enough time to get an accurate sight, release his bombs and pull out with a reasonable margin of safety. It was thought that this could be extended down to 2,000 feet in some cases, but if the pullout was left later than this, the crew were likely to experience "rather a high 'G'."

The terminal velocity with the dive brakes extended, and one-third throttle was approximately 320 mph at 90 degrees and 290 mph at 75 degrees. As the mainplanes on the Vengeance had no incidence, the angle between the datum line of the aircraft and the actual line of flight was nil at 90 degrees and negligible at 75 degrees. Pilots, as always, had to judge the trial angle of the bomb, which varied with the steepness of the dive, as explained earlier.

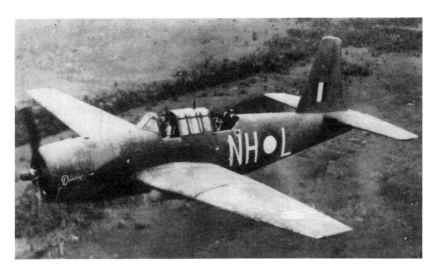

"Dianne," a Vengeance of No. 12 Squadron, RAAF, piloted by Flight Lieutenant C. J. McPherson over Merauke, Dutch New Guinea, on December 23, 1943.

The suggestion that the German method of painting lines on the cockpit cover to represent the angles was rejected without trial. The reason given for this was that "the pilot must concentrate on looking at the target and the nose of the aircraft, and when his head is in a correct position for this, lines of 60 degrees and 75 degrees on the cockpit are outside his vision. To raise the head to look at them during the dive would interfere with the sighting and would also be physically difficult. The angle of 45 degrees is not sufficiently steep and would merely confuse the pilot."

It was found that heights of bomb release could be read from altimeters as the instrument lag was negligible compared with the speed of descent, or in other words, "pilots do not worry about 100 feet or so when approaching the ground at more than 400 feet per second."

The report ended uncompromisingly: "With regard to the Memorandum of the Role of the Vengeance, this is an attempt to establish the policy that the use of this aircraft should be confined as far as possible to the role for which it was designed, and in which it is effective, viz: dive bombing, *and not frittered away on odd jobs for which it is unsuitable.*"

It is doubtful whether this had any effect on Whitehall, however, still bedazzled as they were by the "thousand bomber" raids against civilian targets, for precision was not an argument to win over such men. It is significant that the words used by the young RAF dive bomber pilots in 1943 were almost exactly the same as the epitaph written for the navy's Blackburn Skua three years earlier—another fine dive bomber that had been "frittered away" pretending to be a fighter.

CHAPTER 22

Triumph of the Leathernecks

The Pacific War: American, Allied, and Japanese Operations, 1943–45

The Solomon Islands were still the hot-bed of the Pacific War at the beginning of 1943, for although the Japanese had pulled out of Guadalcanal in defeat, they had no intentions of giving up the whole area, and from their base at Rabaul, they continued to sustain other island garrisons in the face of increasing American pressure. Again, it was Val and Dauntless aircraft that were used. The gradual introduction in the Marine wings of the fighter dive bombers followed developments elsewhere, especially in regard to the powerful Chance-Vought Corsair. Japanese dive bombers found it increasingly impossible to infiltrate the huge AA screens surrounding the American task forces and, more and more, were reduced to suicide attacks. The final battles saw the Helldiver come into its own, and the remnants of the Japanese fleet were destroyed in a whole series of battles and attacks. Finally, the Royal Navy made a brief reappearance in Far Eastern waters, but still without a satisfactory dive bomber of its own, it was forced to use an American torpedo bomber in the dive bombing role, and it later used fighter adaptations.

The destroyers of the Tokyo Express (what the Allies nicknamed the Japanese ships that ferried troops and supplies to New Guinea and the Solomons) continued to suffer at the hands of the SBDs in early 1943 in the Solomons. On January 2, Marine Dauntless dive bombers damaged the *Suzukaze* in the Slot, and on the fifteenth, fifteen SBDs were destroyed in return by the Japanese destroyers *Arashi*, *Hamakaze*, *Tanikaze*, and *Urakaze*, which escaped unscathed.

On January 23, *Saratoga* launched twenty-four SBDs in an attack on Vila airstrip on Kolombangara Island. Twenty Japanese destroyers conducted an evacuation run to Guadalcanal. They were attacked by seventeen Marine SBDs at 1820 hours on February 1, which damaged the *Makinami*. A return strike by Vals from Rabaul damaged the American destroyers *De Haven* and *Nicholas*. A night attack by the Henderson Field Dauntless team failed to score any further hits, nor did another attack the day after.

On April 7, 1943, Yamamato launched Operation I-Go, a series of heavy attacks against U.S. airfields in the region in an attempt to preempt further attacks. Many Vals were employed, including many that were landed from carriers or were operational from land strips. Despite the size of the effort, the Japanese lost twice as many aircraft as they themselves destroyed, and many precious D3A1s and their highly trained crews were thrown away. The empty carriers had to withdraw to replenish with new aircraft and fresh aircrews, and the Val almost vanished from the southwest Pacific for a time.

In the New Georgia campaign, Marine air groups developed close support techniques to a high degree, with air liaison parties under Major Wilfred Stiles. On August 1, 1943, and again on August 25, heavy dive bombing attacks by SBDs and Avengers swung

These SBDs have deposited their bombs on Japanese positions near Rabaul and are homeward bound, April 13, 1944.

the battle against the Japanese. When fresh waves of Vals were again sent in from the ships of Admiral Koga's fleet in November against Bougainville, they suffered a bloody nose; some 75 percent being destroyed, and they again had to be pulled out for further replenishment.

By December, Marine Air Wing Four was operating from Tarawa in the Gilbert Islands, and in March 1944, it moved on to Kwajalein. Their targets were Japanese positions and guns in place on the islands of Jaluit, Manoelap, Mili, and Wotje, as well as airfields. The units employed included VMSB151, VMSB241, VMSB331, and VMSB341, and these were joined by the famous "Ace of Spades" squadron, VMSB231, which was commanded by a real dive bomber ace, U.S. Marine Corps pilot Elmer Glidden. They were all equipped with SBDs, but during 1944, many changed over to the Corsair, which proved itself a formidable dive bomber.

It was first used in this role on March 18, 1944, by VMF111, which dive bombed AA guns on Mille with 1,000-pound bombs. Earlier, VF17, a U.S. Navy unit, had experimented with the same aircraft, with both navy and marine pilots using improvised bomb racks. Subsequent experiments revealed that the Chance Vought F4U Corsair could be safely and efficiently employed as a dive bomber in dives of up to 85 degrees. The plane's six .5-caliber guns were used for strafing in the latter stages of the dive. In fact, the incredible Corsair could eventually be employed to lift *twice* the bomb load of the specially designed Dauntless.

At sea, the carrier-based dive bombers were still roaming across the Pacific. On November 5, 1943, the SBDs from *Saratoga* and *Princeton* decimated a Japanese cruiser squadron at anchor at Rabaul. Twenty-two SBDs were included in that strike mission, and several were lost, but the carnage they inflicted was enormous. The heavy cruiser *Maya* was hit in the engine room, the *Mogami* was seriously damaged, and *Atago* was near-missed by bombs, as was *Takao*, which was taking water. The light cruisers *Agano* and *Noshiro* were both hit by bombs, and the destroyer *Wakatsuki* also badly damaged. The crippled squadron limped back to Truk in the Caroline Islands to repair, and when the new Helldivers of VB 17 made their debut over Rabaul on November 11, they found few targets. The

SB2Cs of VB17 were led by Lieutenant Commander J. E. "Moe" Vose, who had flown SBDs at Midway and Santa Cruz. Now he led the first strike of its replacement. Twenty-three Helldivers took part in this raid from the carrier *Bunker Hill*, along with those from the light carrier *Independence* and SBDs of VB9 from the *Essex*. They sank the destroyer *Suzunami*.

If the Japanese ships had gone, their aircraft had not, for on the airfields were some 270 aircraft, 100 of which had been flown in from the fleet's carriers. With these, the Japanese launched counterattacks against the American task force and caught them with their decks full. Twenty-seven Vals were included in this formation, but they were annihilated by fighters and AA fire, and not a single hit was scored by the Japanese dive bombers on this target. Again battered and depleted, the Vals withdrew.

On December 25, VB17 attacked the Japanese base at Kavieng in New Ireland, sinking a freighter and two minesweepers, and on January 1, 1944, the same unit dive bombed a Japanese cruiser squadron in the same area, damaging the *Oyodo*, *Noshiro*, and the destroyer *Yamagumo*. Aircraft from the carrier *Monterey* also participated in this action.

The next major action was a heavy dive bomber strike on the main Japanese base of Truk in the Carolines, which took place on February 17 and 18, 1944. Dauntless dive bombers flew from the *Essex* and *Yorktown* in this raid, but they were now in a minority, and Helldivers operated from the *Enterprise*, *Intrepid*, *Belleau Wood*, *Cabot*, *Bunker Hill*, *Cowpens*, and *Monterey*. In the two-day period, U.S. Navy aircraft from the nine carriers flew a total of 1,250 sorties, and the Japanese lost the cruiser *Naka*, destroyers *Fumitsuka* and *Oite*, four auxiliaries, six tankers, and seventeen freighters, as well as 250 aircraft, mainly fighters.

Among the few Japanese dive bombers operational against this mighty array were some Suiseis that were making their operational debut as dive bombers, but they could achieve nothing. On March 30, twelve SBDs from *Enterprise* dive bombed the old destroyer *Wakatake* at Palau, sinking her with two direct hits, at the cost of two aircraft. *Saratoga*'s SBDs helped patrol the Marshall Islands but saw no action.

A graphic account of one of the Helldiver attacks on Truk was given by Robert Olds in his book *Helldiver Squadron*, written with typical American style:

> Just west of Uman Island, the formation broke up. Hell-divers, their wing guns flaming, dive on the merchant ship anchorage. Jeff picked out an 8,000-ton cargo ship. Three others followed. Jeff or Cliff made the hit, which went through the forward deck and exploded below. A few miles further north Gus DeVoe and Tee-Square Thomas picked out a merchant ship of 4,000 tons. Their high explosives touched off a rumbling explosion. Fire broke out all over the AK. A large 500-foot merchantman of about 10,000 tons rode at anchor south-west of the island. The *Gedunker* brought his section screaming down as a fan of Avengers approached across the water. When his Helldiver reached 800 feet, Bob squeezed the bomb release and pulled out of his dive. Uman Island was dead ahead. Bob felt the dull "crump" that followed a hit. "Bullseye!" sang out Gene O'Brien. "It burst on the bridge, Mister Friesz."

The Battle of the Philippine Sea in June 1944 was the largest carrier-to-carrier duel in history. Rebuilding their shattered air arm,

The Yokosuka D4Y Judy arrived too late and never fulfilled its expectations.

the Japanese assembled a fleet under Admiral Jizaburo Ozawa with no less than nine aircraft carriers, six of which had dive bombers embarked: *Shokaku, Taiho,* and *Zuikaku,* which had a total of eighty-one Judys plus nine of the reconnaissance version, and *Hiyo, Junyo,* and *Ryuho,* which had a total of twenty-seven Vals aboard plus nine Judy reconnaissance aircraft. The remaining three Japanese carriers did not have dive bombers among their aircraft complements because of the high losses sustained earlier.

They were opposed by Admiral Marc Mitscher, who had no fewer than fifteen fleet and light fleet carriers. Of these, all but two units were equipped with the faithful old SBD. VB10 aboard *Enterprise* and VB16 aboard the new *Lexington* had totals of twenty-three and thirty-four aircraft, respectively. Helldivers now predominated, equipping the dive bomber units of the new *Hornet, Yorktown, Wasp, Essex,* and *Bunker Hill.*

Four waves of attackers were sent off the Japanese carriers at 0830 hours on June 20, out of range of the Americans. Included in the total of 372 planes were most of the dive bombers. They were intercepted far from the American fleet by no less than 450 American fighters and completely wiped out. Only a few aircraft managed to break through this mass of interceptors to make attacks on the task forces, and here an enormous AA barrage—larger than for the whole of the United Kingdom—awaited them. Only one hit was made, while the battleship *Indiana* and the carrier *Bunker Hill* were both near-missed. At a cost of only twenty-nine fighters, the Americans destroyed 242 of the Japanese aircraft, and this carnage was given the appropriate title of "The Great Marianas Turkey Shoot."

On the evening of the twentieth, the return American strike was sent off at extreme range in the gathering darkness. They caught the Japanese fleet refueling and with only twenty-five fighters and twenty bombers left on their decks. American aircraft attacked. Twenty were shot down. *Lexington* launched fifteen SBDs and *Enterprise* twelve, led by Lieutenant Commander Ralph Weymouth and Commander James D. Ramage. Despite being almost unopposed, the only Japanese ships sunk were the carrier *Hiyo* and two refueling tankers, although the carriers *Zuikaku* and *Chiyoda,* the battleship *Haruna,* and the heavy cruiser *Maya* took bomb hits and were damaged. U.S. submarines sank other ships.

This battle marked the end of the dive bombing era at sea for the Japanese, for almost all their aircraft of this type were wiped out, and they reappeared only in small numbers as true dive bombers as distinct from kamikazes. On the American side, the last SBDs were phased out after this action, although the Marine Corps flyers were still using them with good effect in the coming campaigns ashore. More and more, though, at sea in the Pacific as well as ashore in Africa, the merging of the fighter-bomber type and the true dive bomber was coming about. Conversely, the dive bombing technique itself was becoming even more accepted and widespread in its application.

In the Fleet Air Arm, the Grumman TBF torpedo bomber had made considerable impact, its spacious weapons bay being capable of lifting internally a 1,000-pound bomb with no difficulty. As suitable torpedo bomber targets dwindled in numbers, it was employed increasingly as a shallow dive bomber—not only by the U.S. Marines in the Pacific, but more unfortunately by the Royal Navy in the latter stages of the Pacific War.

More than 1,000 of these were taken over by the Royal Navy. The first joined No. 832 Squadron on January 1, 1943. By the war's end, some fifteen FAA squadrons were flying Avengers. The most outstanding of its operations were the attacks made by the British Pacific Fleet carriers *Illustrious, Indefatigable, Indomitable,* and *Victorious* against the oil refineries of Pladjoe and Songei Gerong near Palembang in Sumatra on January 24 and 29, 1945. For the loss of four Avengers, the plants were heavily hit. The planes dive bombed through a balloon barrage and in the face of strong fighter opposition, inflicting grave damage on both plants.

After the Japanese Naval Air Arm had been decimated in the Battle of the Philippine Sea in June 1944, the next American target was the Philippines themselves. The Japanese were prepared to throw in all their remaining fleet to stop this objective being taken, as they would be cut off from their oil supplies. But this meant that their own carriers, with no planes to embark, had only one role, that of an elaborate decoy force to draw away the American carriers and battleships and thus allow the Japanese battleships to slip through and annihilate the American invasion convoy, and the thousands of troops on the beachhead.

Loading drop tanks on SB2C Helldivers aboard the USS *Lexington* before a search mission during the Battle of Leyte Gulf, October 25, 1944.

Accordingly, the plan was put into effect, and while three separate, but powerful, surface fleets made their way to the attack, Vice Admiral Ozawa sortied with the carriers *Chitōse, Chiyōda, Zuihtō,* and *Zuikaku,* as well as the hybrid battleship/carriers *Hyūga* and *Ise* and light forces. On October 24, these ships launched a pitiful air striking force of twenty-three bombers and thirty fighters, followed later by a second, smaller force, from *Zuikaku* only, and waited for the Americans to take the bait.

The fate of the aircraft from these decoy carriers was predictable, for they failed to penetrate the enormous fighter and AA defenses of the three American task forces off Leyte, which consisted of twelve carriers, six battleships, nine cruisers, and forty-three destroyers. So the carrier strikes and the land-based Japanese air attacks which coordinated their efforts caused little or no damage. Only twenty-five Japanese aircraft survived from the seventy-six launched from the carriers, and these, which included only eight D4Y Judy dive bombers, landed on Luzon afterwards.

Meanwhile, the American carriers had been launching massive air strikes at the oncoming Japanese battleship forces. The first wave, which included twelve Helldivers, scored one bomb and one torpedo hit on the giant battleship *Musashi*, in the Sibuyan Sea on the twenty-fourth. These Helldivers came from *Intrepid* and *Cabot*, who were closest to the enemy, and a second force was sent off from the same two ships, which again included twelve Helldivers, and they scored four more bombs and torpedo hits on the same ship. A third wave, from the *Essex* and *Lexington*, with twenty SB2Cs, scored a further four bomb hits on *Musashi* and two on *Yamato*, as well as further torpedo hits on the former. An additional thirty-three Helldivers from *Enterprise, Cabot, Franklin,* and *Intrepid* hit the *Musashi* again and again until she finally rolled over and sank, taking six torpedoes and ten bombs.

Despite the great surface battle that night, when six old U.S. battleships pulverized two of the other Japanese forces, this main Japanese fleet—mistakenly thought to have been turned back after the loss of *Musashi*—had in fact pressed on without further hindrance

Covering the Philippines invasion, a SB2C Helldiver is launched from the USS *Hancock* on November 25, 1944, for a strike on Manila Bay.

and at dawn fell in with a small escort carrier force that had been supporting the troops ashore. Fortunately for the Americans of this group, the Japanese admiral, Kurita, mistook at long range the little "jeep" carriers for fleet carriers. He attacked only half-heartedly before calling off the operation and withdrawing, even though he was almost in gun range of his main objective, the helpless armada of transports and landing ships, which he could easily have annihilated. He thus missed a great chance of a smashing victory.

Meanwhile, the main American fleet had fallen for Ozawa's decoy trap and had sped off to the north to engage. Heavy air strikes were sent in against Ozawa's empty carriers off Cape Engano on October 25. A total of 326 Helldiver and Avenger sorties were made, escorted by 201 Hellcat fighter sorties in six massive waves. They hit and sank all four carriers and a destroyer, the two battleships and the other escorts having done their job of sacrifice escaped. But it was all in vain and the American conquest of the Philippines continued.

The small force of Judy and Val dive bombers on hand to the Japanese in the Philippines when the Americans invaded in October 1944 were soon annihilated on the ground or in the air in near-suicidal missions. One of the most notable Japanese dive bomber sorties was by thirteen Judys from Nichols Field, led by Rear Admiral Masafumi Arima of the 26th Air Flotilla. They attacked the huge American task force on October 15 and were set upon and destroyed by the CAP of Hellcats before they could reach the ships. Arima, seeing the useless sacrifice of all his young dive bomber pilots, decided to sell his own life more dearly. He put his machine into a screaming dive against the aircraft carrier *Franklin*, appearing suddenly out of thick cloud. The heavy AA fire from the target, and the massed escorts caught him in a cone of fire on the way down, hitting him hard enough to deflect his aircraft off course. The dive bomber plunged into the sea hard alongside the carrier, one wing landing on the ship's flight deck. From then on, true dive bomber missions became more rare, and the kamikaze attack took over, utilizing not just dive bomber types but any kind of aircraft that could fly and carry high explosives to the U.S. warships on one-way missions.

Once the American troops were firmly established ashore, the U.S. Marine Corps air groups quickly followed into the newly liberated airfields to provide close support, many still flying the faithful SBD. With their ground-attack methods perfected from their many previous campaigns, these units gave the army invaluable assistance in the protracted period of surface fighting in the islands and the mopping-up operations that continued until the very end of the war.

The reason that the marines were called upon to support the army in this manner was that, despite all the experiments and combat experience, the U.S. Army Air Force was still not fully convinced of the value of tactical air support. Typical of their attitude to the subject was this judgment, given in July 1943: "In the zone of contact, missions against hostile units are most difficult to control, are most expensive, and are, in general, least effective. Targets are small, well dispersed and difficult to locate. In addition, there is always a considerable chance of striking friendly forces."

The marines, however, had worked hard at overcoming these problems, and thus, when on October 10, 1944, Colonel H. Meyer, informed MAG24 that they had been given the job of army support in the Philippines, the marine flyers, then at Bougainville, quickly and enthusiastically organized an intensive course under the direction of Lieutenant Colonel Keith B. McCutcheon, their operations officer. All the doctrines and procedures of this type of operation were assembled and closely studied. A course of forty lectures was given, after being researched, printed, and organized in three days. With MAG32 joining MAG42 for this operation, some 500 officers and gunners of the dive bomber squadrons were put through this detailed course.

The basic guidelines for the subsequent operations were laid out by Lieutenant Colonel McCritcheon in his personal monograph, which laid down that it was always to be a system to be used at the discretion of the ground commander "against targets that cannot be reached by his weapons or in conjunction with the ground weapons in a coordinated attack. Close support should be immediately available and should be carried out deliberately, accurately and in co-ordination with other assigned units." This monograph, *Close Support Aviation*, was to become their textbook in the subsequent perfection of that technique.

During the Lingayen landings in January 1945, the marine SBD squadrons cut their teeth flying 255 sorties and dropping 104 tons of bombs for the loss of just one Dauntless and earning themselves an accolade from Major General Verne D. Mudge. During the capture of San Jose, north of Manila, the 1st Infantry had been badly smashed up by strafing from "friendly" U.S. Army Air Force fighters and took casualties, which made them very reluctant to call on such "help" again. But on February 28, they asked the marine dive bombers to help in a particular tricky operation. The nine Dauntless aircraft made accurate attacks, the most inaccurate of the twenty-seven bombs dropped being only 30 yards from the target spot. This impressed the soldiers so much that from then on nine flights of nine SBDs each were always on standby at the request of the regiment for operations. The Marine dive bombers had made their point.

While the SBD was thus flying its last highly successful missions of the war, the Helldivers with the fleet moved into the South China Sea and conducted a series of heavy strikes against targets at Saigon and Formosa, which wiped out the bulk of the Japanese aircraft based there as well as vital installations. During the dive bombing of Saigon on January 12, 1945, Helldivers from eleven U.S. carriers sank four cargo ships, two oilers, and the Vichy cruiser *Lamotte-Picquet*, as well as destroying the oil storage tanks of the Caltex and Shell depots along the river front. The 300 tons of bombs used by the Helldivers to wipe out these targets in precision attacks contrasted well with the 3,000 tons dropped by B-24s and B-29s of the U.S. Army Air Force which followed. These hit a hospital and the British consulate and killed hundreds of civilians—a butcher's bill common enough to the heavy bomber in World War II, but one that did not subsequently endear the Americans to the French in the postwar period in that part of the world.

The landings on Okinawa that followed provoked the Japanese Navy into launching one last surface ship sortie in a gigantic suicide operation against the American beachhead. The giant battleship *Yamato* (78,000 tons) with her nine 18.1-inch guns was dispatched, with her fuel tanks holding only enough oil to make a one-way trip, together with the light cruiser *Yahagi* and eight screening destroyers.

This force sailed from the Inland Sea on April 6, 1945, and the next day, it was located and set upon by waves of carrier aircraft from the American fleet. Some 386 sorties were flown, with ten aircraft lost. The Helldivers involved in the last great dive bombing battle at sea came from Bombing Squadrons 9, 10, 83, and 84.

VB83 approached the target from 6,000 feet and circled the Japanese force at a range of 6 to 10 miles, periodically under fire from the battleship's main armament. VB83 finally attacked the battleship at 1250 hours in conjunction with Avenger torpedo bombers from *Essex* and scored four hits.

VB84 attacked a destroyer of the screen and scored several hits, leaving their target dead in the water. Explosions followed, which were witnessed by circling planes, and shortly afterwards, the destroyer *Hamakaze* sank by the stern.

VB9 took the light cruiser *Yahagi* as their target, and Lieutenant Wolsey was shot down. The remaining Helldivers scored numerous hits, and the cruiser blew up and sank at 1425 hours.

The final dive bomber attacks were made by VB10, and again, the battleship was the allotted target. They approached her from the east and although four aircraft were hit by AA fire. Most of their bombs were direct hits or near-misses on the already crippled vessel. In total, the *Yamato* was hit by four bombs in the first attack.

TABLE 39: U.S. MARINE SBD COMMUNICATION NETS IN THE PHILIPPINES

No.	Title	Abbreviation	Description
1	Support Aircraft Direction	SAD	A channel linking ALP with the support aircraft commander (SAC) and the airborne air coordinator
2	Support Aircraft Control	SAC	A channel linking the SAC, air coordinator, and supporting aircraft by two-way channel
3	Support Aircraft Direction Emergency	SADE	An emergency channel linking ALPs with the supporting aircraft
4	Support Aircraft Observation	SAO	A two-way channel linking SAO with the air borne observeres

The first two hit amidships on the starboard side, blowing two holes about twenty feet in diameter in the weather deck and destroying a heavy AA turret and several small AA mountings. Two other bombs hit aft of the secondary armament rear mounting, wiping it out with its entire crew, wrecking the directors and penetrating the upper armour deck. A fire was started that was never subsequently brought under control.

No bombs were admitted from the last attack, but there must have been many despite this for she was a sitting duck. Nonetheless, only torpedo hits are credited in Japanese reports. The great ship took eleven and possibly thirteen of these—a tally no ship could withstand—and she finally sank.

The battle resulted in the destruction of the *Yamato*, *Yahagi*, and destroyers *Hamakaze*, *Isokaze*, *Asashimo*, and *Kasumi*, leaving only four destroyers, three of them badly damaged, to return to Japan. It had

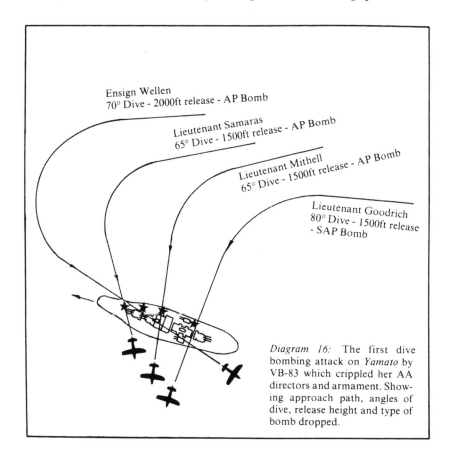

Ensign Wellen
70° Dive - 2000ft release - AP Bomb

Lieutenant Samaras
65° Dive - 1500ft release - AP Bomb

Lieutenant Mithell
65° Dive - 1500ft release - AP Bomb

Lieutenant Goodrich
80° Dive - 1500ft release - SAP Bomb

Diagram 16: The first dive bombing attack on *Yamato* by VB-83 which crippled her AA directors and armament. Showing approach path, angles of dive, release height and type of bomb dropped.

Diagram 17: VB-9's attack on the light cruiser *Yahagi* showing the flight path for all the stages of the attacks made

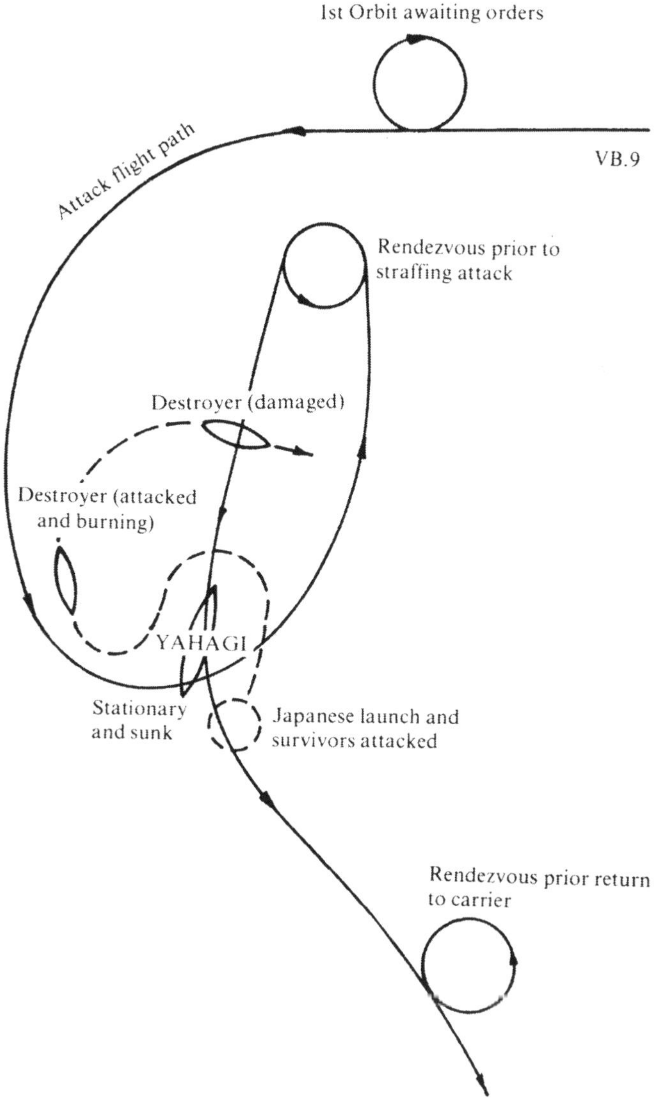

1st Orbit awaiting orders

Attack flight path

VB.9

Rendezvous prior to straffing attack

Destroyer (damaged)

Destroyer (attacked and burning)

YAHAGI

Stationary and sunk

Japanese launch and survivors attacked

Rendezvous prior return to carrier

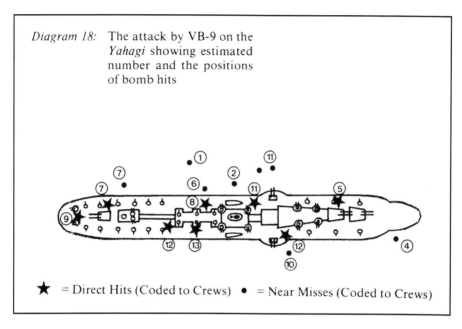

Diagram 18: The attack by VB-9 on the
                Yahagi showing estimated
                number and the positions
                of bomb hits

★ = Direct Hits (Coded to Crews) • = Near Misses (Coded to Crews)

Code to pilots: 1. Lt. H. W. Worley; 2. Ens. J. J. Bell; 3. Ens. W. W. Bowers;
4. Lt. T. F. Schneider; 5. Lt. R. S. Ploss; 6. Lt. J. W. Shreffier; 7. Lt. L. Frewin;
8. Lt. R. L. Verrall; 9. Ens. J. Greenwell; 10. Lt. J. H. Durio; 11. Ens. W. H.
Hanawalt; 12. Lt. Martin; 13. Ens. W. H. Sigman.

cost the Japanese Navy 3,665 officers and men and the Americans
only ten aircraft. Never again did the Japanese fleet venture out of
its harbors—not that it had fuel enough to do so anyway.

The tasks remaining for the vast dive bomber forces of the
American fleet, as well as those Avengers of the British Pacific Fleet
(BPF) that joined forces with them during the closing months, was
the pounding of Japanese air bases, destruction of all merchant
shipping at large, and the wiping out of what remained of the Imperial Fleet as it lay at anchor. In all this activity, the dive bomber
played a major role.

The carrier task forces roamed at will in Japanese home waters,
and the dive bombers and fighter-bombers ranged up and down the
coast in search of targets. Only a small handful of the once-powerful
Japanese fleet remained afloat at the end of this period. Meanwhile,
the BPF had been blooded in its own actions against shore targets.
The Avengers of the BPF earned further laurels during the Okinawa

campaign when they pounded Japanese airfields and installations on the Sakishimi Gunto group of islands to prevent the Japanese flying in aerial reinforcements from Formosa.

Through the months of March and April 1945, the Avengers continued to crater runways and bomb antiaircraft positions—wearisome work with little reward. In June, Avengers from *Implacable* dive bombed Truk in the Carolines, but there was little left of value as targets; the tide of war had long since passed this fortress by. In July, the British bombers took their place alongside U.S. Task Force 38 off mainland Japan, and here more worthwhile targets were plentiful. Hellcats and Corsairs joined in the dive bombing with 500-pound bombs. On July 24, the four British carriers mounted 416 sorties over the Inland Sea. Twelve Avengers each from both *Formidable* and *Implacable* were the first British bombers

SB2C Helldivers from Task Force 38 make low-level bombing runs against a Japanese ship off Nokkaido, July 25, 1945.

to hit Japan proper in World War II, when they attacked Yokushima airfield. Meanwhile, No. 849 Squadron attacked the Japanese escort carrier *Kaiyo* and left her burning and with a broken back— fitting revenge for the *Hermes* three years earlier.

Avengers flew the last combat missions of British forces in the war with strikes against Honshu and Shikoku on July 28, and the following day, they hit Nagoya Bay and Maizuri, sinking a freighter and the destroyer *Okinawa*. On August 9, Avengers dive bombed and sank two auxiliaries in Onega harbor, while Lieutenant R. H. Gray dive bombed another Japanese destroyer and earned a posthumous Victoria Cross in his Corsair. On August 10, targets were found on the Sendai plain.

The last Avenger mission of the war was flown by *Indefatigable*'s bombers on August 15, 1945, against targets around Tokyo itself. Just about the last Japanese dive bomber attack was made against this same ship later that morning. A Judy was detected at 1120 hours over the fleet and immediately went into a vertical dive against *Indefatigable*. It dropped two bombs, which were near-misses, before being shot down by the fleet's AA fire.

Thus, the Japanese dive bombers ended the war as they had begun it—in spectacular fashion.

CHAPTER 23

On to Berlin!

The Final European Campaigns
West and East, 1944–45

By the last quarter of 1943 in Italy, the Axis fighter defenses were on the wane and soon became almost nonexistent. The German Army, however, soon proved itself more than a match for the Allies—even without this support—and the Allies were soon using their air strength more and more as a ground-support system. The favored method was the use of the fighter-bomber with fighter cover overhead in the traditional manner. But once the fighting on land moved up the coast and stabilized, with the Germans well dug in with strongly entrenched positions, the innumerable targets in these regions offered themselves as ideal for dive bombing proper for the area was mountainous, and top cover was found unnecessary. And so, gradually, the Spitfire pilots were converted to ground support operations using the well-known "cab rank" system as before. But gradually, the pure dive bombing side of these missions developed special systems of their own.

Typical of the units involved in this thankless work was No. 43 Squadron flying Spitfires in 324 Wing Desert Air Force and operating from a strip on the beach near the Italian town of Riccione during the winter of 1943–44. Their targets were railways, strongpoints, and even, later in the war, lone snipers. The most common were the rail-cut missions, and the efficient German flak organization proved a tough opponent.

At first the Spitfires carried 250-pound bombs, but these soon proved inadequate and inaccurate in use, and they switched to carrying a single 500-pound bomb under the fuselage on a medium-service bomb rack with two adjustable arms and electrical release. No special bombsight was employed; the graduated lines on the windscreen were tried and rejected by the pilots. Instead, a small dot was marked on the hood to give the correct angle to the horizon.

The most common formation adopted was known as the "fluid four"—four Spitfires flying in box formation 200 yards apart with the two leading aircraft flying straight and true at a height of 18,000 to 20,000 feet, while the rear two weaved on their flanks and varied their height.

An alternative formation was the six-plane box with the front three and mid-after plane flying straight and level, with the two rear flankers weaving. Once the leader had found the target, the whole box circumnavigated the target, retaining its formation to assess it and weigh up the flak position and weaknesses. Once a decision had been reached, they would adopt a line ahead formation ready for the attack dive. When parallel to the target, the leader would bank hard to port and go in out of the sun if possible, at an angle of around 80 degrees, using the propeller-boss to

A Mk9 Spitfire with a 500-pound bomb in place and its pilot, Ginger Hollis. Despite not being stressed for dive bombing, the Spitfire performed notably in that role during the closing stages of the war in Europe.

line up the target. Once the target vanished under the nose, the bomb was released from a height normally between 2,000 and 4,000 feet. At intervals of a few seconds, the rest would follow the leader in at slightly varying converging angles.

At such angles, speed could build up rapidly, going off the clock to around 600 mph, and a certain amount of wing root stress was encountered. Buckling was quite common in No. 43's Mk VIII Spitfires at such speeds during dive bombing, and the aircraft were not given any special bracing in their new role. This was a far cry from the desert for these Spitfire dive bomber pilots—and a far cry, too, from the first dive bomber missions carried out by aircraft of that famous force. This had been conducted in December 1940 by the ancient Gloster Gauntlet aircraft of No. 3 Squadron of the Royal Australian Air Force, armed with 40-pound bombs. They operated as the Allies' only answer to the Stuka in North Africa for a month without loss, and so the Spitfires of 1944 were heirs to a dive bomber tradition—had they known it.

Also heirs to a dive bomber tradition of more potency was the Fleet Air Arm, but after the destruction and retiring of the Skuas in mid-1941, almost two years of war were to pass before they again embarked aircraft capable of dive bombing. This strange period was one of the most intense periods of dive bomber activity of all time, and the Royal Navy missed it. When it did resume operations of this nature, it was once again saddled with a strange hybrid, the Fairey Barracuda.

The TBF Avenger proved suitable for dive bombing later in the war, and the Barracuda was designed and built with dive bombing as one of its major roles, although it was classified for the main part as a torpedo bomber. But its most famous exploits were those associated with dive bombing. It was a three-seat, high-wing monoplane of typical British construction, ungainly and bulky, heir to several changes of specification, unworkmanlike, and unpopular. It was soon replaced aboard the fleet's carriers, but during the brief period it served afloat, it conducted one of the most famous and precise dive bombing attacks of all.

The design dated back to 1937 as a replacement for the Albacore, which itself had carried out dive bombing in the Western Desert in 1941–42 with some success. The first two prototypes had

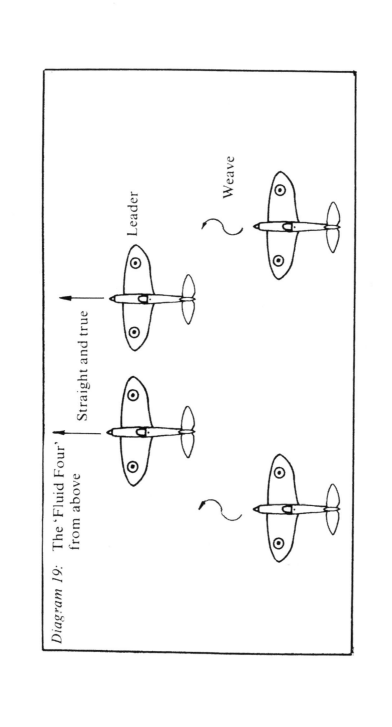

Diagram 19: The 'Fluid Four' from above

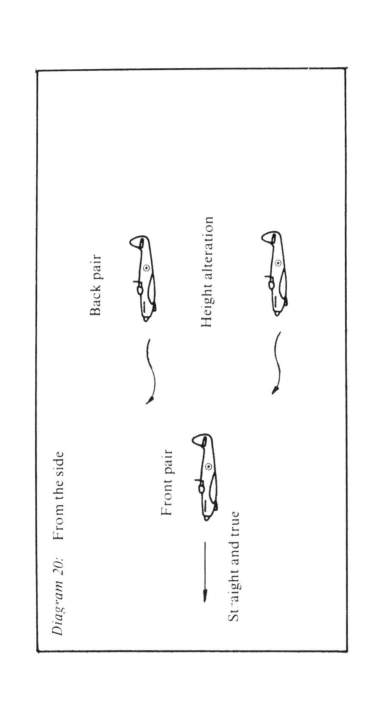

Diagram 20: From the side

Back pair

Height alteration

Front pair

Straight and true

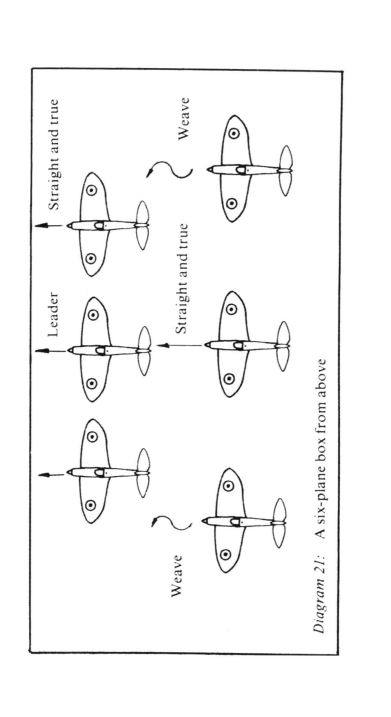

Diagram 21: A six-plane box from above

flown in 1940. Its original power plant was the Rolls Royce Exe, but this was dropped and the Merlin adopted. This was needed for fighters during the aftermath of the Battle of Britain, which further delayed the Barracuda. It was not until 1942 that the first production model flew. Twenty-five Mk1 Barracudas were built before being replaced by the Mk2, which featured the more powerful Merlin 23 engine and a four-bladed instead of a three-bladed airscrew. This version first flew on August 17, 1942, and entered squadron service with No. 827 Squadron in January 1943.

By January 1944, it had equipped twelve squadrons; then it was phased out quickly in favor of the more modern and efficient Avenger. The Barracuda had a top speed of 228 mph and a ceiling of 16,600 feet and could be dived at 280 mph with a load of four 500-pound bombs. Its range was a modest 524 miles. One of its most noticeable features was the Fairey-Youngman diving flaps, which were mounted underneath the trailing edge of both wings. They could be inclined to 30 degrees to act as dive brakes and were very effective.

On April 3, Barracudas from four Squadrons—Nos. 827, 829, 830, and 831—were embarked on carriers *Furious* and *Victorious* of the Home Fleet, ready to conduct a mass dive bombing attack on the huge German battleship *Tirpitz*, which was anchored in Kaa Fjord in northern Norway, where it exercised enormous influence over the convoys to Russia. Torpedo bombing was impossible because of the ship's position and the nets that surrounded her, but dive bombing over the mountains was possible, in much the same manner as the attack on *Scharnhorst* many years before. Again, although the dive bomber force to be employed was much greater, so was the target, and there was obviously no question of sinking her, but it was hoped to immobilize her for a long period by demolishing her upperworks.

Two waves of Barracudas were sent in. The first carried 500-pound Mk2 bombs with instantaneous fuses and with .07-second intervals on the distributor, with the aim of obtaining air bursts from the second and third bombs of the stick which would devastate the ship's upperworks and neutralize her antiaircraft armament. The second wave carried 500-pound SAP MkV bombs with 14-second delay fuses, which would be dropped en masse to ensure

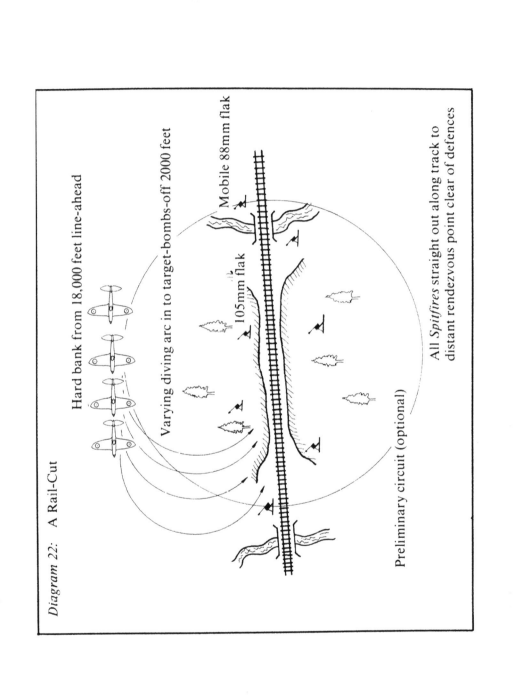

Diagram 22: A Rail-Cut

many hits and the smashing up of her upper decks above her main
armor decks. Others carried 600-pound A/S Mk1 bombs, which
were hydrostatic and, as with the SAP, had a stick spacing of 65 feet
and were designed to burst alongside the ship's hull and open her
up underwater. Finally, the third wave carried the 1,600-pound AP
Mk 1 bomb, which had a .05-second delay. It was hoped that this
weapon, if released from above 3,500 feet, would penetrate the
deck armor.

Intensive preliminary work had been done, utilizing a mock-
up target at Loch Eriboll in which live bombs were employed. The
aircraft were flown off starting at 0405 hours, and escorted by Corsairs, Wildcats, and Hellcats from accompanying escort carriers,
the whole force had departed by 0438 hours. It crossed the coast
at 7,000 feet. The approach was made at 8,500 feet, and a synchro-
nized wing attack was made.

Twenty-one Barracuda formed the first wave and completed
their bombing runs on the *Tirpitz* within the space of one minute.
The first bombs were dropped at 0529 hours from 1,200 feet after
50- to 60-degree dives. The second wave struck half an hour later,
diving from 10,000 feet at angles of 45 to 55 degrees and releasing
higher with their heavier bombs. By this time, the *Tirpitz* was utilizing smoke to hide her, but nonetheless, good practice was made. It
was estimated that no fewer than five armor-piercing (AP) and
four high-explosive (HE) bombs hit the *Tirpitz* in the first wave,
and she took five more hits in the second wave, for the loss of one
Barracuda.

The battleship suffered considerable damaged to her exposed
upperworks, and many compartments above her main armour
were also smashed open. Some 122 of her crew were killed and 316
wounded and she was out of action for three months. It was a
remarkable attack, both in terms of surprise and accuracy. Only the
size of their bomb loads prevented the dive bombers from achieving more than they did. Unfortunately follow-up raids conducted
on 15 May, 14 July, 22 August and 24 August 1944 were not carried
out in such force and achieved much less, as only one further
bomb hit was achieved.

The Barracuda went out to the East Indies with No. 810 and No.
847 Squadrons aboard the *Illustrious*, and they made dive bombing

Heavy formations of Barracuda dive bombers from Home Fleet carriers wing their way across the Norwegian coast to deliver their stunning attack on the German battleship *Tirpitz.* They scored a record
number of hits.

attacks on the oil storage depots and refineries at Sabang between
April 16 and 21, 1944, in conjunction with SBDs from the American
carrier *Saratoga.* Similar raids were made by Barracudas of No. 815
and No. 817 Squadrons from *Indomitable* and No. 822 and No. 831
Squadrons from *Victorious* before these ungainly and little-loved aircraft were dumped ashore and replaced by the Grumman Avengers
as related earlier. These took the Royal Navy's dive bombing teams
to Japan as we have seen.

     Back in Europe in 1944, the Allies were preparing finally to
implement their own version of close support by bomb-dropping
and rocket-firing fighter bombers, and the Tactical Air Force was set
up in November 1943. Hurricanes and Typhoons—and later Spitfire Vs and Xs—were employed by the RAF, as were Mustang IIIs.
From March 1944, these aircraft trained in their role in preparation
for the invasion of France, but they suffered heavy casualties, as
forecast, from German flak. Dive bombing still formed but a minor
part of these operations, which explains their vulnerability. They
were still using the same basic approach as the old Battles of 1940 at
low level and had to relearn the same lessons.

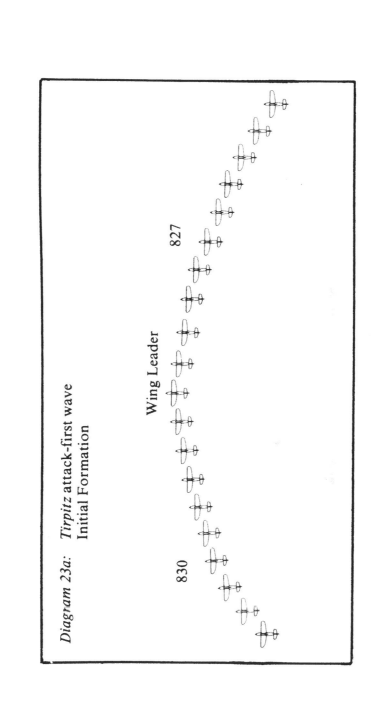

Diagram 23a: *Tirpitz attack-first wave*
Initial Formation

Wing Leader

827

830

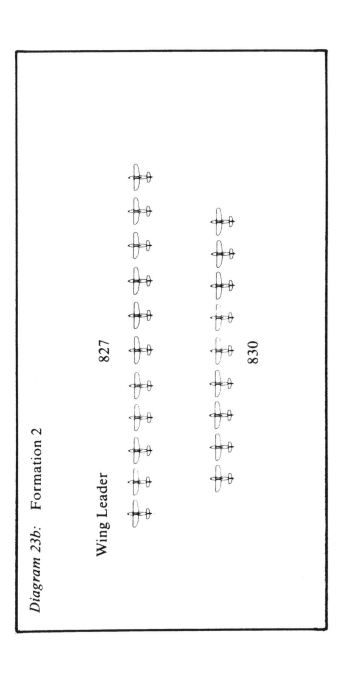

Diagram 23b: Formation 2

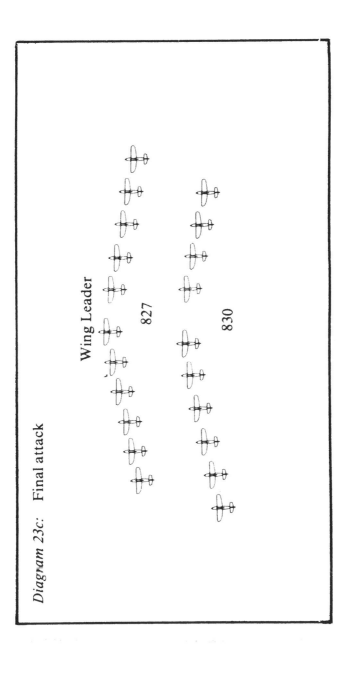

Diagram 23c: Final attack

Wing Leader

827

830

HITS OBTAINED ON TIRPITZ IN ATTACK BY F.A.A. AIRCRAFT
OPERATION 'TUNGSTEN' 3RD APRIL 1944

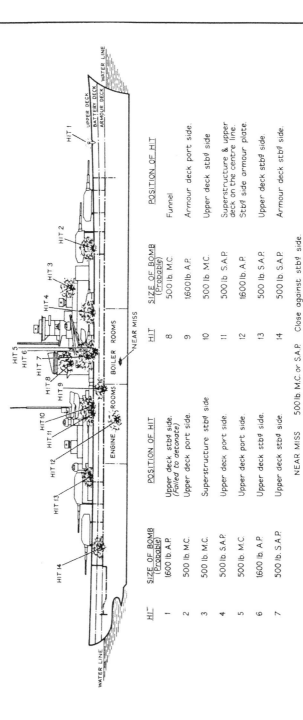

HIT	SIZE OF BOMB (Probable)	POSITION OF HIT
1	1600 lb. A.P.	Upper deck stbd side. (Failed to detonate)
2	500 lb. M.C.	Upper deck port side.
3	500 lb. M.C.	Superstructure stbd side
4	500 lb. S.A.P.	Upper deck port side.
5	500 lb. M.C	Upper deck port side.
6	1600 lb. A.P	Upper deck stbd side.
7	500 lb. S.A.P.	Upper deck stbd side.

HIT	SIZE OF BOMB (Probable)	POSITION OF HIT
8	500 lb. M.C	Funnel
9	1600 lb A.P.	Armour deck port side.
10	500 lb. M.C	Upper deck stbd side
11	500 lb. S.A.P.	Superstructure & upper deck on the centre line.
12	1600 lb A.P.	Stbd side armour plate.
13	500 lb. S.A.P.	Upper deck stbd side.
14	500 lb. S.A.P.	Armour deck stbd side.

NEAR MISS   500 lb. M.C. or S.A.P.   Close against stbd. side.

A.P. = Armour Piercing   S.A.P. = Semi - Armour Piercing   M.C. = Medium Case

The American equivalent, the 9th Air Force, employed their aircraft in a similar manner, using P-51 Mustangs and P-47 Thunderbolts. Their first operational missions, however, showed that they were more willing to take advantage of the dive bombing approach to decrease losses, perhaps adopting it more readily because their aircraft were more robust in construction; only the Typhoon matched them on the British side. On March 5, 1944, for example, Thunderbolts of the 366th Fighter Group carried out a dive bombing attack on the airfield at St. Valery, but with a bomb load consisting only of 250-pound bombs. Similarly, small bombs were also used by the early Mustang dive bombing missions over France, but gradually, their pay load was increased—first to 500 pounds and then to 1,000 pounds.

Although the rocket attack gained the greater publicity during the battles in Normandy after the invasion of June 1944, the Royal Air Force and U.S. Army Air Force fighter-bombers frequently carried out dive bombing missions similar in nature to those described by the DAF in Italy. Spitfires dive bombed gun emplacements in the Calais area and also used this method against pinpoint targets like the V-2 launching sites throughout 1944. American Thunderbolts were usefully employed as dive bombers against vital rail links, bridges, troop concentrations, and strongpoints. The fighter-bombers were joined in this period by traditional dive bomber forces with the reformation of the French Air Force. Thus, the SBD Dauntless finally made its combat debut over Western Europe.

In November 1944, two flotillas (3B and 4B) were formed at Agadir, Morocco, by the Free French with thirty-nine SBD5s supplied by the Americans. After a brief period of training, thirty-two of these aircraft, forming the GAN2 group, flew to Cognac and gave dive bombing support to Free French ground forces engaged in mopping-up operations against the German-held Atlantic ports, seeing action at Rajan, Le Verden, La Coubre, Grave, and the Ile d'Oleron. They flew a total of 1,500 sorties between December 1944 and May 1945 and dropped 500 tons of bombs for the loss of only five aircraft.

The A24B was also taken by the French at this period, some forty-five being handed over. The French formed two dive bomber groups with these, the GBI/17 Picardie and the GCBI/18 Vendee. The formed was based at Rayack in Syria for the re-pacification of

A French Navy SBD of the *Vendée* squadron with sixteen mission mark-
ers painted on. In addition to being used in the Pacific by the U.S.
Navy and Marine Corps, the Dauntless was also used in Europe by the
French.

that area after Vichy rule, but Vendee was based at Toulouse from
September 1944 and attacked German forces in south France. It
then transferred to Brittany and was based at Vannes with a strength
of sixteen A24Bs. From here, it conducted dive bombing missions
until the war's end against German troops in the L'Orient and St.
Nazaire areas, during which time they lost only four aircraft. This
proved an effective reply to the RAF's 1942 warning that the SBD
could not operate in Europe.

But by far the biggest operator of traditional dive bombers and
dive bombing methods during the period 1943–45 continued to be
the Soviet Union. After the Kursk debacle and with the Luftwaffe
heavily tied down in the Balkans in late 1943, the Soviet Air Force
dominated the Eastern Front. The effectiveness of the Pe2 was
increased as its numbers grew and expertise improved. A new
engine, the VK-lOSRF, was fitted in 1943 and some modifications to
the fuselage helped increase its top speed yet further. More important was the improvement of technique.

Colonel A. G. Fedorov carried out tests of the "dipping wheel"
method in combat conditions at Roslav to develop the idea fur-

ther. From this came the use of sections, each one of three aircraft, which broke away from the Vertushka to dive at 60 degrees on flak positions, while the others circled continually. After one attack by one section, another section would break from another angle and so on, continually confusing the gunners and leaving the armored columns exposed

While this became the standard Pe2 technique, selected pilots who were considered to be very proficient at dive bombing were used in specialized attacks on pinpoint targets. Known as snipers, they saw action throughout the summer of 1944 when retreating German forces in the Bobruisk Cauldron sought to break out across the Beresina River in June. Repeated attacks by Pe2 snipers succeeded in destroying the solitary bridge, which trapped the bulk of the German forces.

On the Ukraine front in July 1944, a massive Soviet offensive was spearheaded by the Il2s and Pe2s of the 2nd Air Army, and contributed vastly to breaking up the dangerous German counterattack on July 15. One feature unique to the Soviet Union was the front-line employment of female pilots; at Borisov in June 1944, the

Loading a Pe-2 at a forward air base during the great Soviet offensives of 1944. The Russian dive bombers played a major role in this grand operation.

125th Guards Bomber units under Colonel V. V. Markov included several such resolute females, surely the only women dive bomber pilots to ever see action, although the Germans had several female test pilots who had tested the Junkers Ju87 before the war.

As the Soviet colossus crashed through Eastern Europe in 1944, the allies of Germany hastily made plans to change sides as the tide of war altered. This led to the situation in these battle areas where the Ju87 was actually used against German forces, who for so long had looked to it for succor when hard pressed. On August 23, 1944, the Romanians capitulated, and on the following day, they opened hostilities against Germany. This led them to hastily re-mark their Ju87 Doras with the prewar red, yellow, and blue roundels, and all operational Stukas were formed into the 74th Squadron. In a similar manner, the small batches of Doras belonging to the Bulgarian Air Force and engaged in anti-partisan operations on the Eastern Front switched allegiance in September 1944.

More loyal to the Axis were the Stuka crews of 102/1 *Zuhanóbombázó Század* of the Hungarian Air Force, which were also heavily engaged on the Eastern Front. In steadily decreasing numbers they fought on to the end. Another ally, the Croatian Air Force Legion, was established with a few Doras as the tide of war crept towards the Balkans in 1944. Again they were mainly employed in anti-partisan operations in Yugoslavia, in conjunction with those Italian dive bomber forces that had remained loyal to Mussolini.

By the start of 1945, the Soviets were ready to launch the final offensive against the borders of Germany. Their dive bomber forces suffered a heavy loss on February 15, 1945, when Major General Ivan Polbin was killed, but within a month, the Russians had reached the banks of the Oder River, within forty miles of Berlin itself, and soon they threw strong bridgeheads across it. Heavy Pe2 attacks were mounted against the fortress of Kustrin in March 1945 by the 24th Bomber Air Regiment, which helped contribute to its fall, and on April 16, the final all-out drive on the German capital commenced.

On the German side, the steady replacement of the Junkers Ju87 in the ground-attack units by the Fw190F8 was almost complete by June 1944. A few Stukas remained, mainly with Rudel's famed Immelmann squadron in the east, and a few others in the Balkans.

But the Ju87 had not completely passed from the scene. As they left the ground-attack units they were refurbished as night attack bombers. Some 300 D3 and D5s were thus fitted with flame-dampened exhausts which led back over the wing-root. Seven night bomber wings were then equipped, each with between forty to sixty aircraft and used operationally on the Eastern Front, in north Italy, over France, Belgium, and Holland, and in the final German offensive in the Ardennes in December 1944.

With the Allied advance to the Rhine, repeated attacks were made by the night bomber Stukas on vital bridges, but with little result and heavy losses from both the night fighters of the allies and the normal hazards of such missions. Perhaps their most famous action on the Western Front was the attack on the Remagen Bridge mounted on the night of March 19–20, 1945, by just five Stukas, the remnants of the 1st Group, 2nd Night Bombing Wing, led by Major Rohn.

In April 1945, the 1st Group, 9th Night Bombing Wing, was still conducting operations over Bologna from Villafranca di Verona airfield and later from Ghedi and Thiene. In the east, the handful of Ju87s still operational tried to hold back the Soviet tide along the Oder with some isolated success, but they were eventually overwhelmed by the general collapse in April and May. A large number of the remaining night bombing units were destroyed on the ground in these final days by Allied fighter and bomber sweeps which ranged unchecked over the last scraps of German air space between the two fronts.

In the final days, the Soviet Pe2s were flung into the Battle of Berlin en masse, and regardless of losses with complete air mastery assured, they attacked houses and blocks with maps in hand as the Germans had done at Stalingrad. But on May 8, the last Stukas took off from their base in the east and headed toward the American lines in a final defiant gesture. With three Ju87s and four Fw190s, they flew to the airfield at Kitzingen and crashed their aircraft in front of the astonished Americans. The Stuka was finally dead, five years after the RAF had bragged it was finished.

The final actions for the Soviet Pe2 dive bomber forces lay thousands of miles from this scene, for on the fall of Berlin, many units were hastily shipped eastward to take part in the new war

In May 1945, Soviet armies, spearheaded by Pe-2 dive bombers,
crashed into the final defenses of Berlin.

against Japan that Stalin had finally seen fit to declare. However,
most of the fighting was over before more than a handful of the
Pe2s could contribute, although they were employed to good effect
during the July offensive in Manchuria.

These were, with the previously discussed Helldiver and
Avenger missions over Japan, the last dive bomber operations of
World War II.

CHAPTER 24

The Final Vindication

Postwar Developments and Combat in Indochina, Korea, and Vietnam

With the end of World War II and the advent of the atomic bomb and jet propulsion, it seemed that the era of the dive bomber had passed away. With such developments, the need for accuracy and precision was overshadowed with the new idols of ever increasing speed and mass destruction. It was already forgotten that there was little point in an aircraft going 200 mph faster to the target if, when it got there, its payload missed, or that with weapons like the A-bomb, the destruction would be so great as to make the great powers think carefully before using them and so allow conventional warfare to wage unabated throughout the Cold War. The Communist plan of world subversion depended in large part on the undermining of nations from within, either politically as in Western Europe or by guerrilla warfare as in Asia, Africa, and South America. The policy had met with continued success after 1945, with more and more nations passing under Soviet domination, but initially, before their own will was eroded, the western nations tried to stand up to the threat. Thus, conventional or guerrilla wars were fought against Communist armies in Indochina by the French and in Malaya by the British, and open full-scale Communist invasion was combated by the United Nations—with only the western powers providing the hardware and main manpower—in Korea. All these battlefields gave scope for precision bombing. Later, the United States attempted to save the small nations of the former French Indochina region from Communist takeover, but her allies turned their backs. She also found that there was still, in the 1960s and 1970s, a need for an aircraft that could deliver precision bomb loads into small targets and linger to provide support. Jet aircraft of the day could not do the latter, nor, until the development of the "smart" bomb, could they do the former. And so, against all predictions, the dive bomber soldiered on until the late 1970s.

Let us first examine some of the ideas in the planning or prototype stage, which developed very little once peace arrived in 1945.

COMMONWEALTH WOOMERA

This aircraft was under development in Australia at the end of the war and was another attempt to combine the functions of dive and torpedo bombers with those of light attack bombers. With a length of 39 feet, 7 inches; a span of 59 feet, $\frac{1}{2}$ inch; and a gross weight of 22,287 pounds, the Woomera was powered by two 1,200-horsepower Pratt & Whitney Wasp engines, which gave it a maximum speed of 282 mph. The crew of three and armament of two 20-millimeter cannon and five .303-caliber machine guns were coupled with a ceiling of 23,500 feet and a range of 2,225 miles. The maximum bomb

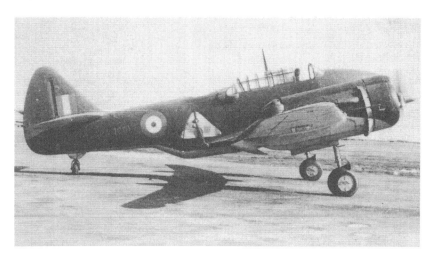

Among the advanced designs under development near the end of the war was the Commonwealth CA-11 Woomera, a twin-engined aircraft of great potential. As the war's conclusion approached, developed ceased after the prototype stage.

load was 3,000 pounds. Although not outstanding, this aircraft featured a novel remote control and a barbette behind each of the engine nacelles. It arrived far too late for the war and never went into service.

FAIREY SPEARFISH

This British aircraft was also designed as a combination of dive bomber and torpedo bomber under specification 0.5/43 as a replacement for the Barracuda, but with a very much improved appearance and performance. It was, of course, too late to see combat in World War II, and the only production order, which was for forty Spearfish to be built at Stockport, was subsequently cancelled when the new government slashed defense spending in the usual manner in 1946.

The Spearfish was a single-engined, mid-wing monoplane powered by a 2,320-horsepower Bristol Centaurus 58, 59, or 60 engines and had a maximum speed of 292 mph at 14,000 feet, with a range of 1,036 miles. It had a length of 44 feet, 7 inches, and a span of 60 feet, 3 inches. Only the second and third prototypes (RA360 and RA363), along with a solitary production model (RN241), ever flew, although one was serving with the Carrier Trials Unit at Lee-on-Solent and Ford as late as 1952.

BLACKBURN FIREBRAND

Originally designed as a fleet fighter to replace the Fulmar, this powerful aircraft had its specification changed several times between 1940 and its eventual appearance in September 1945. The first prototype flew in February 1942, while a second, with 20-millimeter cannon, followed in July of the same year. The adoption of the Seafire meant that fighter coverage was adequate, and the Firebrand was further developed as a torpedo bomber/strike aircraft, as the Firebrand II. The original power plant was the Napier Sabre II engine, but production shortages meant that the Centaurus radial was adopted, and this became the Firebrand III, which first flew in December 1943.

The two dozen production models of this aircraft had followed by the next year, but they suffered from inadequate direction control at takeoff. This fault was rectified by the adoption of a larger fin and rudder, and this became the Firebrand IV. Some 140 of this version were built, the first flying in May 1945.

The Firebrand IV had a length of 38 feet, 11 inches, a span of 51 feet, 3½ inches and a height of 14 feet, 11 inches. It was a single-seater, and its maximum speed was 350 mph. Although dive bombing was not a main feature of this aircraft, it was fitted with dive brakes on the wings and could carry a bomb load of two 1,000-pound bombs. The first squadron was formed in September 1945 (No. 813 at Ford), and further modifications in design resulted in the MkV and MkVa between then and the end of 1947, when about 150 had been built and production ceased.

SAAB-17

In Sweden, development of dive bombers continued during the war, and the final result was the SAAB-17, a low-wing monoplane, powered by the Bristol/SFA MkXXIV engine, but of Swedish manufacture. Bearing a strong resemblance to the ill-fated Brewster Bermuda in appearance, this dive bomber had a 980-horsepower air-cooled radial engine with a top speed of 270 mph, and it had improved ceiling and range. The B17 formed the mainstay of the Swedish dive bomber units during the war years, but in 1945-46, with the introduction of the SAAB twin-engined B18B, this type performed both functions—light bomber and dive bomber—and the specialized types were phased out.

The B18 was not strictly a dive bomber, being a high-wing monoplane with twin tail fins, but bearing some resemblance to the Junkers Ju88 or Dornier Do217 in cockpit layout with all the crew concentrated forward. Two SFA/DB engines, DB605s, gave it a maximum speed of 355 mph and a range of 1,370 miles. It had a bomb load of 2,650 pounds.

ILYUSHIN IL20

In the Soviet Union, the main dive bomber development toward the end of the war was in improvements to the already well-proven Tupolev Tu2. Development continued after the war on the Tu2D series, which featured an increased wing span and redesigned nose, coupled with increased range. The D series had a top speed of 321 mph and a bomb load of 2,204 pounds over 1,864 miles. The Petlyakov Pe2 continued to be the most favored aircraft of this type. In all, some 11,427 Peshkas were built, in particular the Pe21, which was produced from 1943 onward. This aircraft featured the 1,650-horsepower VK 107A direct fuel-injection engines, solid nose, and deeper fuselage. It could carry a payload of 2,204 pounds and had a top speed of 408 mph at 18,800 feet. The first prototype flew in 1944, but this aircraft crashed the following year, and with the end of the war, further development was stopped.

The Ilyushin Il20 was not a dive bomber, but an attack plane designed to act in an anti-shipping as well as ground attack role and was a development of the Shturmovik type. Nicknamed the Hunchback because of its appearance—the object of which was to give the diving pilot the maximum view—the pilot was seated above the 2,700-horsepower engine. The gunner operated a barbette containing two NS23 cannon, while more cannon and rockets could be carried, as well as a maximum bomb load of 2,204 pounds. The whole aircraft was armored in the ground-attack tradition. It had a span of 45 feet, 11 inches; a length of 37 feet, 5¼ inches; and a maximum speed of 320 mph, with a range of 1,044 miles. Although a diving attack must have been essential to attain the accuracy to attack ships, little is known of any special features to facilitate this. In the event the end of the war brought about the cessation of further experimentation on this unique model.

DOUGLAS SB2D1 DESTROYER

The Douglas team under Ed Heinemann had plans ready in 1942 for a similar monster dive bomber to replace the SBD. This was the XS2D-1, a two-seater dive bomber double the weight of the Dauntless. It featured an internal bomb bay and a range of 1,490 miles, and it mounted two 20-millimeter wing cannon and a remote-controlled rear turret carrying twin .5-inch machine guns. It had a tricycle landing gear and was powered by the Wright R3350 15 engine rated at 2,300 horsepower for takeoff. It had a total weight of no less than 19,000 pounds.

The Douglas Destroyer, as it then stood, would have been one of the most powerful navy attack planes built, but the U.S. Navy was already seeking to combine the functions of dive and torpedo bombers, as in the Royal Navy, and the design of the Destroyer was therefore modified to suit this requirement. The result was the single-seater XBTD. By dropping the second crew member and the rear turret the bomb bay was increased in capacity to 3,200 pounds. Dive flaps were fitted operating from the fuselage sides. Top speed was 340 mph in this configuration, and some 358 BTD1s were ordered in April 1942. By 1944, all had been cancelled.

TBM aircraft of VA9A, commanded by Lieutenant Commander Lawrence G. Traynor, on exercises from the USS *Philippine Sea*, June 14, 1948.

MARTIN AM-1 MAULER

This formidable aircraft was Martin's last venture into the dive bomber field, and they went as far as they could in producing a powerful all-round aircraft capable of lifting a very heavy payload with maximum effect. The result was the XTBM, a low-engined monoplane that could carry 7 tons of weaponry into battle. But by the time it appeared, the U.S. Navy was turning away from this concept. Some 750 Maulers were ordered in January 1945, but final production after severe postwar cuts in budgets reduced this to only 149 actually built. These were delivered to the fleet between 1947 and 1949.

Although fitted with slotted dive flaps and capable of employment in torpedo bomber or rocket-firing roles as well as dive bombing, the Mauler was just *too* big for the carriers then available. It had a top speed of 367 mph and a range of 1,300 miles, and it was fitted with 20-millimeter cannon and could land, despite its great bulk, at 88 mph. It was a perfect vehicle for the three new *Midway*-class carriers then entering service, but too late for its time.

As well as the last generation of true dive bombers, most powers continued to operate fighters in this role, continuing the tradition of the U.S. Corsair, the RAF Spitfire, the U.S. Army Air Force Mustang, and the German Fw190. It was mainly the air arms of the two premier navies that adopted this method however. In the U.S. Navy, light dive bombing was done by Grumman Bearcat, a powerful and versatile fighter-bomber, a descendant of the same company's Hellcat. In the Royal Navy, two types predominated, the Fairey Firefly MkV and the Hawker Sea Fury, the latter being particularly suitable and effective in the dive bombing role.

The postwar French Navy was a hodge-podge of types, a mixture of the best of the few surviving French ships, most of which had been destroyed in Vichy service, as well as ex-British and ex-American warships purchased from their overlarge peacetime fleets and even ex-German war prizes. The two carriers *Arromanches* and *Dixmude* reflected this; they had formerly been the

Royal Navy's *Colossus* and *Biter*, respectively. The aircraft they carried after the war were a similar mixture, and the dive bombers were old friends.

At first, they were the SBDs, the bulk of which formed 3F and 4F, respectively, after the war. Against the Soviet-backed Viet Minh in Indochina, they went out in the carriers and conducted numerous missions. During the years 1946-48, the value of such piston-engined precision attacks against elusive targets was proven, and the SBDs were not retired until 1949.

The A24Bs were incorporated into the French Air Force and were mainly employed on training duties from bases at Meknes in Morocco and Cazaux in France at this time, although they were from time to time utilized on survey and patrol duties in North Africa. These "old faithfuls" were finally grounded in 1953.

As late as 1950, the French Navy took delivery of Helldivers from the United States and two fresh flotillas were created, 3F and

The Hawker Sea Fury was a piston-engined fighter of high performance that was used with great success as a dive bomber by the Royal Navy in Korea. Here a light fleet carrier off the coast prepares for a mass strike.

9F, with these aircraft. Forty-eight Helldivers were taken over in the initial batch; two dozen went to 3F in 1951, and a similar number went to 9F later. All these similarly went to Indochina, where once more they were very valuable in containing the growing communist armies. 9F left France aboard *Arromanches* at the end of 1952, and it carried out a total of 824 war missions. Their duties included true dive bombing, strafing, and rocket attacks. Their targets were AA guns, troop concentrations, bridges, and the endless supply convoys wending their way down from China. 9F returned to France in 1953 and converted to Avenger aircraft. After 1954, the remaining Helldivers in French service were utilized as trainers.

When communist North Korea invaded South Korean territory in a blatant act of aggression, the United Nations—for the first and almost the last time in its history until Iraq invaded Kuwait—stood up to the naked aggression. Both U.S. and Royal Navy carriers were used in the four years of combat to provide the troops ashore with close support of the precision types, which meant dive bombing. The British used the Firefly and the Sea Fury with great success. Many of the pilots were veterans of the final stages of the Pacific War and improvised tactics based on those methods.

Targets, more often than not, proved to be bridges, and the communist forces were adept at using slave labor to rebuild these time and time again. They also employed heavy antiaircraft batteries to defend these vital targets, and the continued smashing of them proved a wearying and endless task—and also a thankless one. In two periods, for example, the air group working from HMS *Glory* in 1951–52 flew almost 5,000 sorties and lost twenty-seven aircraft and nine crews.

While the FAA used fighters to dive bomb, the U.S. Navy was more fortunately placed since it had a brand-new dive bomber with which to pound the enemy—brand new, that is, to combat, but, in reality, it was already an elderly warrior, an aircraft that was to soldier on for longer than any other combat plane in the front line, an aircraft that was to become a legend: the Skyraider.

With the aborting of the Destroyer concept, Heinemann and his crew set to work with a will, and after some time, they introduced radical design changes to the XBT2D and came up with a real champion. A bubble canopy replaced the original flared cock-

The Fairey Firefly saw war service in 1944–45 with the British Pacific Fleet in the final drive on Japan as a fighter-bomber making rocket attacks. During the Korean War, later models were used for shallow dive bombing missions.

The Helldiver was phased out of the U.S. Navy in 1949, but the famous dive bomber had not finished combat duties even then. In 1950, the French Navy took delivery of four dozen, which were embarked on the carrier *Arromanches* (seen here) and left for the Far East in 1952.

pit, and the original faired tailplane was smoothed into a gentle curve into the fuselage. The inverted gull-wing of the Destroyer became instead a graceful mid-wing straight design. This provided the extra lift to get the Dauntless II, as it was termed, off the carriers' decks. It weighed about one ton less than the Destroyer, which made it more acceptable in the fleet.

At the same time as this reduction in weight was achieved, its bomb load was increased to a remarkable 5,000 pounds, and its top speed went up to 375 mph. After the initial trial flight in March 1945, the U.S. Navy placed a contract for 548, but with the end of hostilities, this was reduced to only 277. Given the designation AD and subsequently named Skyraider and designated A-1, the new aircraft found itself unique in a very short period. Only four squadrons had been equipped with the Mauler, while the Kaiser Fleetwing project, the XBTK, had been aborted. The Skyraider soon became the only heavy hauler in the fleet, and it expanded through numerous variants between 1946 and 1948, to the AD2 and AD3, and by the early 1950s, continued production had resulted in the AD4 and AD5 types. With the outbreak of the Korean War, the planned termination of the design was hastily shelved.

With the U.S. 7th Fleet in position off the Korean coast, Skyraiders were soon in action. VA55 from the carrier *Valley Forge*, led by Lieutenant Commander D. E. English, was the first into battle with a strike on the aircraft at Pyongyang on July 1950. From then on, ADs were rarely out of the headlines, and new orders for the old "Able Dogs" began to pour in as their merits were seen to be numerous in the new jet age. Just how vast was their contribution to this conflict can be seen by the fact that no fewer than twenty-two different squadrons utilized this aircraft between 1950 and 1953.

Not only did the frontline and reserve navy aircrew enshrine the name of this dive bomber in the Korean skies, ashore the U.S. Marines resumed their close-support mantle with the same aircraft.

The unforgettable SBD Dauntless.

In October 1951, VMA121 equipped with AD3s moved into Korea. Nicknamed the Heavy Hauler and led by Lieutenant Colonel P. B. May, they soon won fresh acclaim, taking heavier and heavier loads into combat and dropping them precisely on target against the swarming enemy hordes.

Much like the aftermath of World War II, a period of run-down followed the ceasefire in Korea, and then, with the renewal of communist aggression against another Asian country, the United States—on her own this time—had to go to its aid. Again, the Skyraider remained the only aircraft able to both deliver and "linger" in the target area to give the sort of cover the troops on the ground really needed, the sort provided by the Ju87 to the Germans and SBD to the U.S. Army in the Philippines during World War II. And so, as the bitter Vietnam War dragged on its ever more weary course, it was the old Douglas A1H that continued to be the mainstay of the rescue and support missions.

Thus passed the last of the dive bombers and with them a whole era of air warfare in which the individual skill of the pilot counted for more than all the technology in the world. Right up to the end, it proved far more adept at doing what all bombers were supposed to do—hit the target.

Bibliography

**PUBLISHED BOOKS ON DIVE BOMBING, AIRCRAFT,
AND RELATED TOPICS**

Berry, W. H. *Aircraft in War and Commerce.* New York: George H. Doran, 1918.

Bishop, Edward. *The Battle of Britain.* London: Allen and Unwin, 1960.

Borelli, G., et al. *Junkers Ju87 Stuka.* Modena, Italy: S.T.E.M., 1975.

Borgiotti, A., and C. Gori. *Gli Stuka Della Regia Aeronautica, 1940–45.* Modena, Italy: S.T.E.M., 1977.

Bridgman, Leonard. *The Clouds Remember.* Aldershot, England: Gale & Polden, 1938.

Brutting, Georg. *Das waren die Deutschen Stuka-Asse, 1939–45.* Stuttgart, Germany: Motorbuch, 1976.

Cabell, Craig, and Graham A. Thomas. *Operation Big Ben: The Anti-V2 Spitfire Dive Bombing Missions, 1944–45.* Staplehurst, England: Spellmont, 2004.

Casey, Louis J. *Naval Aircraft, 1938–45.* London: Hamlyn, 1975.

Cathcart-Jones, Lt. Owen. *Aviation Memoirs.* London: Hutchinson, 1934.

Douglas, Sholto. *Years of Command.* London: Collins, 1963.

Gould Lee, Arthur. *No Parachute.* London: Jarrolds, 1968.

Green, William. *Warplanes of the Third Reich.* London: Macdonald, 1970.

Herlin, Hans. *Udet: A Man's Life.* London: Macdonald, 1960.

Higham, Robin. *Air Power: A Concise History.* New York: St. Martin's, 1972.

Hinkle, Stacy C. *Wings over the Border.* El Paso: Texas Western Press, 1970.

King, H. F. *Armament of British Aircraft, 1909–39.* London: Putnam, 1965.

Lawrence, T. E., *Revolt in the Desert.* New York: George H. Doran, 1927.

Levine, Isaac D. *Mitchell: Pioneer of Air Power.* New York: Duell, Sloan and Pearce, 1943.

Macleod, Col. Roderick. *The Ironside Diaries, 1937–40.* London: Constable, 1962.

Masatake, Okumiya, and Jiro Horikoshi. *Zero! The Story of the Japanese Navy Air Force, 1937–45.* London: Cassell, 1957.

Melhorn, Charles M. *Two Block Fox: The Rise of the Aircraft Carrier, 1911–29.* Annapolis: Naval Institute Press, 1074.

Mizrahi, J. V. *Dive- and Torpedo-Bombers: U.S. Navy.* New York: Sentry, 1967.

Olds, Robert. *Helldiver Squadron.* Washington, D.C.: Zenger, 1980.

Parson, Lee M. *Dive Bombers: The Pre-War Years.* Washington, D.C.: n.p., 1949.

Popham, Hugh. *Into Wind.* London: Hamilton, 1969.

Price, Alfred. *The Bomber in World War II.* London: Macdonald and Jane's, 1976.

Roskill, Stephen. *Naval Policy between the Wars.* London: Collins, 1968–76.

Schliephake, Hanfried. *The Birth of the Luftwaffe.* London: Allan, 1971.

Sherrod, Robert. *History of Marine Corps Aviation in World War II*. Washington, D.C.: Combat Forces Press, 1952.

Simmonds, Ralph. *All About Aircraft*. London: Cassell, 1915.

Sims, Edward H. *Fighter Tactics and Strategy, 1914–79*. London: Cassell, 1972.

Shores, Christopher. *Ground Attack Aircraft*. London: Macdonald and Jane's, 1977.

Slessor, Wing Commander J. C. *Air Power and Armies*. London: Oxford University Press, 1936.

Stewart, Maj. Oliver. *The Strategy and Tactics of Air Fighting*. London: Longmans, 1925.

Smith, Peter C. *Aichi D3A1.2 Val*. Ramsbury, England: Crowood Press, 1999.

———. *Curtiss SB2C Helldiver*. Ramsbury, England: Crowood Press, 1997.

———. *Douglas SBD Dauntless*. Ramsbury, England: Crowood Press, 1998.

———. *Fist from the Sky: Japan's Dive-Bomber Ace of World War II*. Stackpole Books, Mechanicsburg, 2006.

———. *Impact! The Dive Bomber Pilots Speak*. London: W. Kimber, 1981

———. *Luftwaffe Colors: Ju87 Dive-Bomber*. Vols. 1 and 2. London: Classic, 2006.

———. *Petlyakov Pe-2 Peshka*. Ramsbury, England: Crowood Press, 2003.

———. *Skua! The Royal Navy's Dive-Bomber*. Barnsley, England: Pen & Sword, 2006.

———. *Vengeance! The Vultee Vengeance Dive Bomber*. Washington, D.C.: Smithsonian, 1987.

Turnbill, Capt. A. D., and Lt. Cmdr. C. L. Lord. *The History of United States Naval Aviation*. New Haven, Conn.: Yale University Press, 1949.

Winston, Robert Alexander. *Dive Bomber: Learning to Fly the Navy's Attack Planes*. New York: Holiday House, 1939.

Wilkenson, Erik A. *Dive Bombing: A Theoretical Study*. Aktiebolag, 1947.

ORIGINAL DOCUMENTS AND PAMPHLETS

Air Ministry. *Notes on Dive Bombing for the Information of Designers of Aeroplanes for the RAF*. London, 1936.

Air Ministry. *The Theory of Dive Bombing*. London, 1938.

Air Ministry. *Dive Bombing*. London, 1940.

Air Ministry. *Notes on Dive Bombing and the German Ju88 Bombing Aircraft*. London, 1940.

Bellinger, Cmdr. P. L. *Aviation*. Naval War College Lecture, 1 August 1924.

Jones, Maj. Ernest L. *Information Pertaining to the Development of Dive Bombing, 1910–30*. United States Air Force, Historical Division, Research Studies Institute, Maxwell AFB, Alabama, May 1956.

Jones, Maj Ernest L. *Bomb Dropping with Carranza*. "Aeronautics," London, 1 December 1915.

Larkins, William T. *The Evolution of Naval Dive Bombing*. "Flight," London, 1943.

Leighton, Lt. Cmdr. B. G. *The relation between Air and Surface Activities in the Navy*. Lecture to Naval War College, 23 March 1928.

McGee, Capt. Vernon E. *Dive Bombing*. Washington, 1937

Overfield, Lt David B., *Dive Bombing Compared with Bombing from Level Flight*. Washington, 1939.

Royal Aircraft Establishment, Farnborough, *Dive Bombing as Practiced by the German Air Force and a Comparison with Proposed British System*. London, 1940.

Wilson, Eugene E., *The Navy's First Carrier Task Force*. United States Naval Institute Proceedings, February 1930.

SPECIFIC SOURCES

Action Reports and War Diaries and Report on Sinking of Yamato, Microfilm NRS.1971–7.

"Again we missed the dive bomber," Maj. O. Stewart, *Sunday Express,* 28 June 1942.

Air-Ground Support Training Programmed, MAG-24, 8 December 1944.

Air Intelligence Report, 31 October 1936. AIR5/137/04811.

Army Requirements of the RAF for Direct Support in Battle, 30 November 1942. AIR20/4249.

Aviation, Paris, 14 August 1972 (No. 591).

Aviation and Aircraft Journal, Vol. II, No. 14, dated 25 July 1921.

Betwixt Sea and Sky, Gen. Cumbat. Personal Account of August 1942 convoy action.

Board to Consider Naval Aeronautic Policy, 3 May 1927.

Bomb and Bomb Fuses-Investigation of in Connection with Dive-bombing, 18 July 1930.

Bomb Displacing Gear, 12 February 1931.

Bomb Displacing Gear for 1,000-lb Bomb, 15 January1932.

"Bomb dropping from Aircraft," *Aeronautics,* London, October 1914.

"Bomb dropping from Aeroplanes," *Flight,* December 1914.

Bombing, Dangerous Incident to and Methods of Minimizing, 5 December 1929.

Bombing Developments, 11 May 1933. AIR 116 3473.

Bombing from Sopwith Camel using Aldis Sight, 27 May 1918, AIR 1/1200/04632.

"Can we check Rommel without the dive bomber?" Maj. O. Stewart, *Sunday Express,* 31 May 1942.

China Incident—Naval Air Operations (July–November 1937). Japanese Monograph No. 66, U.S. Navy Archives, Washington, D.C.

Command and Employment of Air Power, U.S. War Department, July 1943.

Comparison of British and U.S. Naval Air Services, ADM116 3473.

Confidential Report of Interview with Master of SS Aeneas, 5 July 1940. AIR2/4221.

Contract Nos. 27648 Schedule 900-S8S4 XF1201, Airplane, Conversion to Scout Airplane Change 311, December 1933.

Contract 17648 Navy Contractors Proposals (in view of crash of XSBC-1), 6 July 1934.

Contract 7648-Model XSBC-2 Airplane, 26 June 1935.

Defence, Tobruk, IG Report No. 712. AIR20/970.

"The Dive Bomber Does It Again," by Ronald Walker, *News Chronicle,* 11 April 1942.

Dive-bombers in Close-support of the Army, 6 May 1941. AIR20/2970.

"Dive Bombers, the Army and Navy View," *Daily Sketch,* 3 March 1942.

"Dive Bombers—Why This Awful Delay?" by Gen. Sir R. Gordon-Finlayson, *Daily Sketch,* 2 April 1942.

"Dive Bombing," Maj. C. S. Pearson, *The Aeroplane,* 1942.*Dive-Bombing—A Review of Policy,* 9 May 1940, AIR2/3176/54583.

Dive Bombing Technique with High-speed Aircraft of Clean Aerodynamic Design, 2 April 1936. AIR2/1655/5/36709.

Dive Flaps on SB2U-1 Airplane, 30 January 1939

Diving Tests on Martin MM Airplane, 3 April 1930, William H. McAvoy.

"The Elements of Bomb Dropping," *Flying,* October 1917.

Experimental Dive-bomber Airplane (Class VB), 14 August 1931.

Experimental Funds 1935, 24 July 1934.

Experimental Light Bombing Practice, 27 May 1927.

Experiments and Production Aircraft Procurement for Fiscal Years, 1934, 1935 and 1936, 19 January 1934.

1st Meeting Bombing Policy Sub-Committee, 22 March 1938. AIR2/1787/04811.

Flying the Vought SB2U, Boone T. Guyton.
Hart K-2466 Diving Bombing Trials, February 1934. AIR2/655/831592.
Hart K-2967 Diving Bombing Trials, March 1934. AIR2/655/831592.
"The Heritage of Flight,"*Aerospace Historian* 16, No. 2, summer 1969.
Interview by Maj. Gen. Ross Erastus Rowell, U.S. Marine Corps, Aviation History Unit, 24 October 1916.
Isle of Ely and Wisbech Advertiser, 28 September 1932.
Japanese Navy Air Force—Air Ministry Intelligence Memorandum. AIR/1021647/04811.
Letter from from Maj. Alan E. Marsh, *Globe & Laurel* LXXXIII, No. 6, December 1974.
Low Height Bombing from Scouts, 18 May 1918, AIR 1/1200/04632.
Maritime Aeronautics, 1 January 1923.
Meeting to Consider Dive-bombing, 19 September 1938. AIR2/1787/04811.
Milwaukee Journal, Lt. Louis Olszyk, 23 September 1944.
Minutes of 9th Meeting of the Bombing Committee, 27 April 1936. AIR14/288/IIH/241/4/104.
Model BT-1 and SBD-l Airplanes—Improvements in Stalling Characteristics, Devices for, 22 January 1940.
Model SB2U-1 and SB2U-2 airplanes—Conversion to Permit Dive-bombing Ops, 16 November 1939.
Naval Air Division Forms by Surviving Crews, 23 November 1939 (729/39) ADM 199 478/X/04326.
Note on Dive-bombing for Information of Designers, March 1936, Air Ministry Confidential Scientific and Technical memoranda.
Notes by Director of Naval Air Division on Report, 25 April 1940. ADM199 478/X/04326.
Notes on Air Tactics, Air Ministry Memorandum 1941. AIR23/5287.
Notes on Hawker Hart Bought and Imported from Britain for Sweden, Flygvapnet, 1977.
Notes on Tactical Qualities of the Dive-bomber, 9 September 1943. AIR20/4249.
Operational Order No. 1, 9 April 1940. ADM 199 478/X/04326.
"Our New Dive Bombers," *Daily Sketch,* 20 February 1942.
Outline of Naval Armament and Preparations for War, Part 1 (1922–34), Japanese Study Monograph No. 145, U.S. Navy Historical Center, Washington, D.C.
Outline of the History of Dive-bombing in Sweden, Col. Nils Kindberg, *Flygvapnet,* 1978.
Policy of Procurement of Experimental Dive-bombers, 25 August 1931.
Report of Acceptance Trials of Model BM-1 Airplane, 21 September 1931.
Report of Air Attacks on HMS Illustrious on 10 January 1941, Operation MC4, 26 January 1941.
Report of Board to Consider and Recommend upon Present Aeronautical Policy, 11 May 1927.
Report of CO HMS Glorious, Dive-bombing Tests, 1939. AIR2/3176/04811.
Report of HMS Wessex, 19 June 1940. AIR2/4221/04811.
Report of No. 5 Group—High Diving Bombing Trials, 27 March 1941. AIR14/672/IIH/41/3/38.
Report of No. 100 (T.B.) Squadron, Dive-bombing Tests, 8 October 1938. AIR2/1787/04811.
Report of Production Inspection Trials on XBF2C1 No. 9269 and BF2C 1 (Experimental and Production Models), 29 May 1933.
Report on Operation "Tungsten", 5-10 April, ADM199 941.
Report on the German Air Force, 1936. AIR5/137004811.

Report on U.S. Dive Bomber Supply Situation. AIR20/1763.

Reports on Armstrong-Whitworth Fighter Dive Bomber, 10 April 1936. AIR2/607/359533/34.

The Rise and Fall of the German Air Force, Air Ministry, Pamphlet 248, 1948.

Scientific American, supplement No. 2103, April 1916.

Secret Report on Damage in Action to HMS Boadicea and Bulldog, 12 June 1940. AIR2/4221.

"Skua'd Prisoners for Breakfast," *Globe & Laurel* LXXXIII, No. 5, October 1974.

Specification No. 0.27/34—Dive Bomber Fighter, 12 December 1934. AIR2/607/359533/34.

Statement by Maj. Norbert Carolin to Major Jones, AC/AS Intel, 1943.

"Still Kicking against the Dive Bomber," Maj. O. Stewart, *Sunday Express,* 5 July 1942.

Summary of Air Intelligence Report No 302. AIR22/9/04811.

Svenskt Flyg och dess Mdn, KSAK, Stockholm, 1940.

Tactical Trials on Vengeance Dive-bomber and *Dive Bombing in Vengeance,* 4 October 1943, AIR 19/233.

12th Meeting of Advisory Committee on Aircraft for Fleet Air Arm, 15 November 1934. AIR2/607/359533/34.

USAS Bulletin, No. 304,16 November 1918.

Use of Aldis Sight when Carrying Out Dive-bombing, 26 February 1937. AIR14/2904362.

VB Airplanes-Request for Informal Quotations, 15 March 1934.

Vengeance Operations in Arakan, Tactical Memo No. 35, AHQ India. AIR23/3288.

Vengeance Operations in Burma, AIR23/5288/06726.

VF Squadron Two-Individual Battle Practice (light bombs)—Report of scores, 28 December 1926.

VSB Airplanes-Request for Informal Quotations, 19 March 1934.

VSB and VB Airplanes—Proposals, 25 April 1934.

"Would Sealion have succeeded?" by Alfred Price. Contained in *The Battle of Britain,* London: New English Library, 1977.

XTSM-1, Dive Test of, Memo of Conference Plans Division, 16 October 1929.

GENERAL WORLD WAR II BOOKS

Bryant, Arthur. *The Turn of the Tide, 1939–43.* London: Collins, 1957.

Churchill, Winston S. *The Second World War.* Vols. 1–4. London: Cassell, 1948.

Crimp, R. L. *Diary of a Desert Rat.* London: Cooper, 1971.

Cynk, Jerzy B. *The History of the Polish Air Force, 1918–68.* London: Osprey, 1972.

d'Aatier de la Vigerie, Gen. Francois. *Le Ciel n'etait pas vide.* Paris: Julliard, 1957.

Goutard, Col. Adolphe. *The Battle of France.* New York: I. Washburn, 1959.

Guderian, Gen. Heinz. *Panzer Leader.* London: M. Joseph, 1952.

Horsley, T. *Find, Fix and Strike.* London: Eyre and Spottiswoode, 1943.

Irving, David. *Hitler's War.* London: Hodder & Stoughton, 1977.

Jackson, B. R. *Douglas Skyraider.* Fallbrook, Calif.: Aero Publishers, 1969.

McKee, Alexander. *The Coal-Scuttle Brigade.* London: Souvenir Press, 1957.

Maugham, Barton. *Tobruk and El Alamein.* Canberra: Australian War Memorial, 1956.

Marder, Arthur J. *Operation Menace.* London: Oxford, 1976.

Neave, Airey. *The Flames of Calais. A Soldier's Battle.* London: Hodder & Stoughton, 1972.

O'Ballance, Edgar. *The Indo-China War, 1945–1954.* London: Faber and Faber, 1966.

Roskill, Capt. S. W. *The War at Sea.* 4 Vols. London: Her Majesty's Stationery Office, 1954–1966.

Ruby, Gen. Edmond. *Sedan: terre d'epreuve.* Paris: Flammarion, 1948.

Rudel, Hans-Ulrich. *Stuka Pilot.* New York: Ballantine Books, 1958.

Schmidt, Capt. H. W. *With Rommel in the Desert.* London: Harrap, 1951.

Smith, Peter C. *Task Force 57.* Manchester, England: Crecy, 2001.

Smith, Peter C. *Midway: Dauntless Victory.* Barnsley, England: Pen & Sword, 2007.

Taylor, A. J. P. *Beaverbrook.* London: Hamilton, 1972.

Taylor, Telford. *The Breaking Wave.* London, Weidenfeld & Nicolson, 1967.

Tedder, Lord Arthur. *With Prejudice.* London: Cassell, 1966.

Tomlinson, Michael. *The Most Dangerous Moment.* London: Kimber, 1976

Index

Page numbers in italics indicate tables or illustrations

Adams, C. D., 90, 95
Aichi company, 55–56
Aihaya, Takehia, 272
aircraft
AD4, 361
AD5, 361
Aichi Am-17, 134
Aichi B7A Ryusei, 178–79
Aichi D1A, *56*
Aichi D3A Type 99 Val, 134, 135,
   137, 137–38, 178, *265*, 322
Aichi D3A1 Val, 161, 263
Aichi E16A Zuiun, *284*, 285
Arado Ar81, *120*, 121, 125
Arado Ar81 V2, 121
Archangelsky Ar-2, 252–53, *253*
Avenger, 319, 322, 329, 330
Avia LM02, 293–95
B17, *244*
BE2c, *9, 10*
Bermuda, 283
Blackburn Firebrand, 353–54
Blackburn Firebrand III, 353–54
Blackburn Firebrand IV, 354
Blackburn Skua, 107, 161–64
Blackburn Skua II, *239*
Blackburn Skua K5178, *105*
Blohm and Voss Ha137, 121, 122,
   125
Blohm and Voss Ha137B, 122
Boeing F4B4, 60
Boeing FB, 34
Breda Ba88, 156
Breda Ca65, *154*
Breda 65, 153
Breda, 201, 154
Breguet 690, 144
Breguet 691AB2, 144

Breguet 698, 144
Brewster SB2A Buccaneer, 175–78
Brewster SB2C-1, 177
Brewster XSB2C-1, 177
Brewster XSBA-1, *65*, 65–66, 176
Brewster XSBC2–1, 176
CANSA Fc12, 154–55
Caproni Bergamasca API, 222–23
Caproni Ca310, 155–56
Caproni Ca335 Tuffo, 154
Chance Vought, *177, 211*
Chance Vought F4U Corsair, 315
Chance Vought SB2U Vindicator,
   146
Chance Vought SB2U-1 Vindicator,
   68, 69
Chance Vought SB2U-2 Vindicator,
   69, 70
Chance Vought SB2U-3 Vindicator,
   70
Chance Vought SBU, 59
Chance Vought SBU-1, 60, *61*
Chance Vought V156, 146–49
Chance Vought V156F Vindicator,
   147–49, *209*
Commonwealth CA-11 Woomera,
   352, 352–53
Consolidated XB2Y-1, 44
Curtiss A24 Banshee, 173–75
Curtiss A24A-D/E Helldiver, 286
Curtiss A24B Helldiver, 291, 345,
   358–59, *360*
Curtiss A24B-DT Helldiver, 286
Curtiss A25A Helldiver, 287
Curtiss A36A Helldiver, 291–92
Curtiss BF11C-3, 45
Curtiss BF2C-1 Hawk, 45
Curtiss BFC-1 Hawk, 45

Stackpole Military History Series

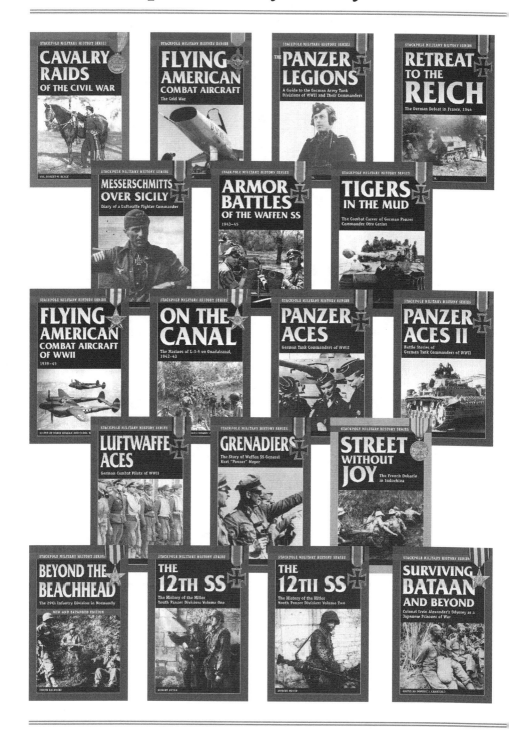

Real battles. Real soldiers. Real stories.

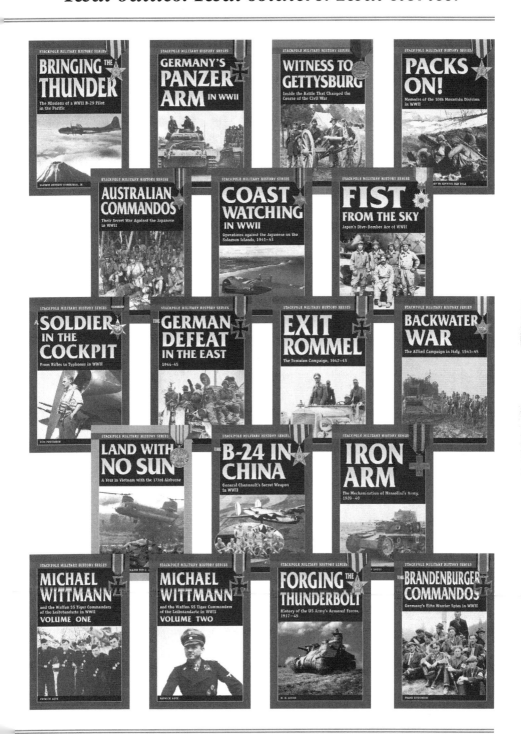

Stackpole Military History Series

Real battles. Real soldiers. Real stories.

Stackpole Military History Series

FLYING AMERICAN COMBAT AIRCRAFT

THE COLD WAR

Edited by Robin Higham

During the Cold War, American aircraft came into their own as sleek, vigilant, legendary machines that defined an era. Equipped with cutting-edge technologies, including the jet engine, these high-powered warplanes fought in Korea, Vietnam, and smaller-scale conflicts around the globe. In these exciting firsthand accounts, expert pilots remember the drama and adventure of being at the controls of classic planes like the F-15 Eagle, B-52 Stratofortress, F-84 Thunderjet, C-141 Starlifter, F-100 Super Sabre, and many others.

$19.95 • Paperback • 6 x 9 • 448 pages • 143 b/w photos

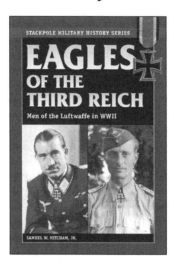

Stackpole Military History Series

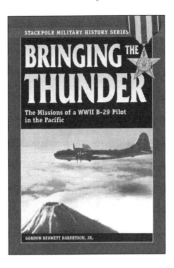

BRINGING THE THUNDER
THE MISSIONS OF A WWII B-29 PILOT IN THE PACIFIC
Gordon Bennett Robertson, Jr.

By March 1945, when Ben Robertson took to the skies above Japan in his B-29 Superfortress, the end of World War II in the Pacific seemed imminent. But although American forces were closing in on its home islands, Japan refused to surrender, and American B-29s were tasked with hammering Japan to its knees with devastating bomb runs. That meant flying low-altitude, nighttime incendiary raids under threat of flak, enemy fighters, mechanical malfunction, and fatigue. It may have been the beginning of the end, but just how soon the end would come—and whether Robertson and his crew would make it home—was far from certain.

$19.95 • Paperback • 6 x 9 • 304 pages • 36 b/w photos, 1 map

WWW.STACKPOLEBOOKS.COM
1-800-732-3669

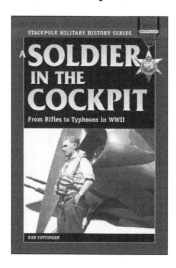